EDWARD YOUNG

Highmore's portrait of Edward Young, 1754.
*Reproduced by kind permission of the Warden
and Fellows of All Souls College, Oxford*

EDWARD YOUNG

The poet of the Night Thoughts

1683–1765

by

HAROLD FORSTER

THE ERSKINE PRESS

1986

First published in 1986 by the
Erskine Press, Alburgh Harleston Norfolk

British Library Cataloguing in Publication Data

Forster, Harold
    Edward Young : poet of the Night thoughts,
    1683–1765.
    1. Young, Edward, *1683–1765* – Biography
    2. Poets, English – 18th century – Biography
    I. Title
    821'.4   PR3783

ISBN 0–948285–08–7

Printed and bound in Great Britain by
Antony Rowe Limited
Chippenham

DEDICATION

To my darling daughter Penny,
who shared Harold's sense of humour and who
for hours on end accompanied us as we drove
the length and breadth of England on research.

C.F.

PUBLISHER'S PREFACE

Harold Bagley Forster was born in 1913 and educated at Winchester and King's College, Cambridge where he obtained a first class degree in Classics.

After a distinguished career, serving mainly with the British Council overseas, he devoted himself to the life and works of Edward Young, writing numerous books about this almost forgotten genius. Sadly he did not live to see this, the first ever biography of the poet of the *Night Thoughts*, for he died on 16th June 1985. He was unable therefore to read his copy in proof. His typescript was immaculate: we have followed this in composition, even in cases where modern setting practice might, arguably, conflict, because we believe that this is what he would have wished.

He has been described as a 'gentle scholar whose wit and humour, tolerance and resilience made him a delightful companion and friend'.

The last word must be with Professor Henry Pettit, Emeritus Professor of English in the University of Colorado, 'we have lost the one scholar who knew the most of anybody about Young'.

CONTENTS

INTRODUCTION

'A very good heart', said Pope; 'a mind in which the higher human sympathies were inactive', declared George Eliot. 'For intrigue and cabal he is utterly unacquainted', wrote Mrs Montagu; 'he hunted preferment as a pig hunts truffles', assert the compilers of *The Stuffed Owl*. 'A man of genius and a poet', was the verdict of Dr Johnson; 'the *Night Thoughts* is one of the dullest and falsest poems that ever achieved fame', pronounces Dr Havens of Harvard. The startling divergence between the picture of Edward Young drawn by those who actually knew him and the generally accepted modern image of the poet, exemplified by these quotations, led me to study his life and works in greater depth in the hope of solving the puzzle of this extraordinary contradiction.

There is nothing unusual, of course, in posterity disagreeing with the contemporary estimate of a writer and in such cases posterity has the last word. But on the question of his character it is surely his contemporaries who must be believed, and in the case of Young our estimate of his character vitally affects our estimate of his poetry. For Young was essentially a *moral* poet, and if we feel his morality was insincere and hollow, the whole value of his work is undermined. George Eliot confessed that her denunciation of the *Night Thoughts* was entirely opposed to her 'youthful predilections and enthusiasm' and arose from comparison of his poems with the 'well-attested facts of his life'. Hannah More adored his work until she found he had solicited the help of the King's mistress for his advancement in the Church. The charge of hypocrisy is deadly; and ever since George Eliot's philippic against Young's character under the title of 'Worldliness and Otherworldliness' the *Night Thoughts*, once acclaimed as a world masterpiece and translated into every tongue of Europe (including Magyar and Turkish) has – to use the words of Sir Robert Birley – 'sunk without trace'.

A biography thus seems peculiarly necessary in the case of this poet since our view of his conduct colours our appreciation of

his poetry. Was he the 'polite hermit and witty saint' of Mrs
Montagu, or the author who, according to Dr Havens, 'spent the
best part of his life seeking those tinsel trappings which his poem
belittles'? Were his *Night Thoughts* the outpourings of genuine
grief or the sour 'Complaint' of disappointed ambition?
Nowadays Young's work is not judged on its intrinsic merits but
seen through a fog of moral disapproval that distorts our view
and discourages our approach. 'Clear your mind of cant,' said
Doctor Johnson; and if a new picture then emerges – neither
saint nor hypocrite – we can perhaps look again at his poetry
with eyes unclouded by personal prejudice. It is the main
purpose and hope of this study of his life to achieve a clearer
view of the man, and hence of his work.

Though many short lives of Young, from 'Johnson' to the
D.N.B., have been published, only one attempt at a full-scale
biography has hitherto appeared in English, H. C. Shelley's *The
Life and Letters of Edward Young*, Pitman, 1914, which was based
on the discovery of the Portland correspondence at Longleat,
published by the Historical Manuscripts Commission in 1904.
Even at the time, however, this work was unsatisfactory, since
the author was apparently unaware not only of the valuable
researches of the French scholar, Walter Thomas, in his very
thorough thesis, *Le Poète Edward Young, Etude sur sa vie et ses
œuvres*, Paris, 1901, but even of the extensive Richardson
correspondence printed in the *Monthly Magazine* nearly a
hundred years before. Nor did Shelley take the trouble to
examine the originals of the Portland letters, of which no less
than seventy-eight had been left unpublished by the Historical
Manuscripts Commission.

Since then, two more important series of Young's letters have
been printed, the Tickell correspondence in 1931 and the
Reynolds series in 1938. These are covered in a short critical
biography by Isabel St John Bliss in Twayne's English Authors
series, New York, 1969, intended as 'an introduction to the
writing of Edward Young'. But the publication of Henry Pettit's
exhaustive collection of *The Correspondence of Edward Young*,
Oxford, 1971, showed how much other material, both in letters
and records, was available for the biographer of the poet. As an
aspirant for that task, I have had the privilege of collaborating
with Professor Pettit in his researches for some twenty years and

the present work contains a good deal of fresh material that fell outside the scope of even the most generous footnotes to the letters.

Notes and references

In the text there is a double system of notation, *letters* for footnotes, *numbers* for references. The footnotes, giving explanatory or supplementary information, are printed at the foot of the page; the references, simply citing the sources, are listed at the end of the book, chapter by chapter.

References are given for all quotations and dates (except well-known historical ones) and are shown in abbreviated form. A summary of the abbreviations, divided into manuscripts, printed books and newspapers or periodicals, will be found at the head of the reference list. Where the abbreviation is not listed, e.g. for a rare work quoted only once, the details of the source will be found in the text.

Though all possible references have been checked with the original sources, I have preferred to cite the latest or most easily available text, e.g. a footnote in Pettit rather than a local parish register; Young's *Complete Works* rather than the individual first editions, wherever possible and appropriate. In a few cases, where I disagree with an editor's placing of an undated letter or document, I have noted the fact with the words 'N.B. dating' against the reference; but I have not attempted to set out the argument, which would far exceed the limitations of a note.

Spelling and punctuation have been modernized, for ease of reading and sometimes of understanding; and foreign quotations have been translated.

Index

The index covers the names of all the *persons* mentioned in the text or notes, apart from classical figures, modern editors and critics, and a few contemporaries of the poet referred to merely in passing, e.g. in quotations or as recipients of letters.

The names are indexed under the form in which they occur in connection with Young, e.g. the Duchess of Portland under *Portland* rather than her maiden name of Cavendish-Harley or her husband's surname of Bentinck. Where the same person is mentioned by more than one name (Lords, Bishops, married ladies, etc.), the entry will be found under the most familiar form, with cross-references to the others; e.g. George Dodington, formerly Bubb, finally Lord Melcombe, is indexed under *Dodington*; Mary Granville, first Mrs Pendarves, then Mrs Delany, under *Delany*.

Acknowledgments

First and foremost I owe an incalculable debt to my three friends and colleagues of the 'Youngsters', Henry Pettit of Colorado, Branch Johnson of Welwyn and Edward Collins of Reading, who generously shared with me all their discoveries and spent so much time answering the queries which, owing to my posting abroad, I could not investigate for myself. Among other workers in the field of Young studies special mention must be made of Charles Frank of Illinois, Trevor Mills of Oxford, Wolfgang Butzkamm of Münster, the late Professor Mutschmann of Marburg, and Graeme Roberts of Aberdeen.

The roll of those from whom I have received valuable assistance and information is so long that it is impossible to name and thank them all individually. I can only give general thanks for their invariable courtesy and helpfulness to the archivists, librarians and officials of All Souls College, Oxford; Balliol College, Oxford; Barclay's Bank (Gosling's Branch), Fleet Street; the Bodleian Library; the British Library; the Brotherton Library, Leeds; Cambridge University Library; Chiddingfold parish, Surrey; Corpus Christi College, Oxford; Dr Williams' Library, Gordon Square, London; the Guildhall Library, London; Hampshire County Record Office; Hertfordshire County Record Office; the History of Parliament Trust; the Honnold Library, California; the Huntington Library, California; Longleat, Wiltshire; New College, Oxford; Oxfordshire County Record Office; the Public Record Office; Salisbury Diocesan Record Office; Somerset House; Surrey County Council; Upham parish, Hampshire; the Victoria and Albert Museum; Welwyn parish, Hertfordshire; Westminster Public Library; Winchester College; Winchester Diocesan Registry; Windsor Castle; and Worcester College, Oxford.

But I should not omit to recall the advice, encouragement and help, on a more personal basis, of Nicolas Barker of *The Book Collector*; Sir Robert Birley; J. M. G. Blakiston of Winchester

College; T. C. Duncan Eaves of Arkansas; Catharine Firmin of the Oxford Collection of the Honnold Library; David Fleeman of Pembroke College, Oxford; David Foxon the bibliographer; Harlan Hamilton of Case Western Reserve; John Harvey of Winchester College; Philip Hobsbaum of Glasgow; Theodore Hofmann of Messrs Hofmann and Freeman; Ben Kimpel of Arkansas; the late 'Tim' Munby of King's College, Cambridge; the late Allardyce Nicoll; Norman Philbrick of the Philbrick Library, California; Dr G. R. Rolston of Haslemere; Lord Rothschild; John Sparrow, Warden of All Souls; and the late Sir Harold Williams.

CHAPTER 1

A Nest of Singing Birds

1683–1702

Edward Young was a poet born in the wrong age. Nature equipped him for an earlier or later period, Elizabethan or Romantic; fate placed him squarely among the Augustans. Born in 1683, he was younger than Swift and Addison and Steele, older than Pope and Gay. Though constantly searching for originality, though recognized by his contemporaries as distinctive, he might well have ended as a mere satellite amid that brilliant galaxy. His collected works, published when he was fifty-eight, consisted of the usual ingredients of the time – epigrammatic satires and flattering epistles in heroic couplets, bombastic tragedies in blank ·verse and deplorable odes in Pindarics – and their superior wit and force would hardly have preserved his celebrity in the eyes of posterity. But age and bereavement broke the chains of classic restraint, and at that very time he was embarking on his second and greater poetical career. Longevity gave him the chance denied him by his birth.

He was baptized on 3 July, 1683[1] at Upham near Winchester, a parish of which his father was Rector. The Rectory was his home for the first twenty years of his life and the family seem to have been happy there, for they continued to reside at Upham even after the father's elevation to the Deanery of Salisbury in 1702. The family, as Young knew it, consisted of his parents and two sisters, one two years older called Judith after her mother, the other, Anne, a year and a half younger. There had also been an elder sister, Jane, but she had been buried five months before Edward's birth; and in June, 1690 Judith followed her to the grave. Thus the statement of Herbert Croft (who wrote the biography of Young for Johnson's *Lives of the Poets*) that Anne was the only daughter of the family, though inaccurate, was in effect true as far as Edward was concerned. He was not quite seven when Judith died; and so for practical purposes his family circle was confined to his father, his mother and Anne.

The dominant influence in that circle was clearly his father.

Of his mother we know nothing except her Christian name, Judith, and her age – she was thirty-six or thirty-seven at the time of her son's birth. His father, also named Edward, and aged about forty in 1683, was sufficiently distinguished as a writer of sermons to figure in Wood's *Athenae Oxonienses*, in which it is stated that he was the son of 'Jo. Young of Woodhay in Berkshire, gent.'[2] The family has now been traced back three more generations to Thomas Young of Bristol, grocer, who died in 1533.[3] Two years before, at the Heralds' Visitation of Bristol in 1531, the family's coat of arms was registered – the same arms that figure on the tombs of the poet and his sister Anne.[a] The descendants of Thomas prospered and multiplied, and Mr Collins's researches have revealed their wide ramifications among the landed gentry of the West Country and the leading citizens of Bristol and London. Thomas's son William married the daughter of the Mayor of Bristol and bought the manor of Ogbourne St George, Wiltshire; the second of his six children, also William, moved to Woodhay, and the eldest of this William's fourteen children was John Young of Woodhay, mentioned by Wood. As the Youngs spread their connections over Wiltshire, Somerset, Berkshire and Hampshire, they married into the local squirearchy and among their alliances are to be found baronets, knights, sheriffs[b] and all the 'county'. Some of the daughters married clergymen, but the learned tradition was not strong in the family – one of John's uncles studied law, one brother went to Oxford – and the younger sons were generally sent into business. Thus two of John's sons (uncles to the poet) were John Young of Cornhill, citizen and draper (mentioned in Pepys's diary),[c] and Henry Young of the Worshipful Company of Clockmakers. It was an exception when their brother Edward went into the Church.

Though John Young came from Woodhay, his son Edward was born, according to Wood, at Brampton in Yorkshire, and this is confirmed by the record of his admission to Winchester

[a] The Young arms date from at least 1455, when they were recorded in the College of Arms for John Yonge, Sheriff of London, later Sir John, Lord Mayor (d. 1481).

[b] On 26 February, 1695 the elder Young preached before James Hunt of Popham, Sheriff of the County of Southampton, who was his nephew.

[c] He was the 'flagmaker', from whose house Pepys watched the Coronation procession, 23 April, 1661.

College.[4] John seems to have spent at least four years there, from 1638 to 1642,[5] during which the poet's father was born. But this unexplained migration to the north was only temporary and he was back again in Berkshire in 1650 to prove his mother's will.[6] In 1657 he secured his son's admission to one of the places on the foundation at Winchester, which duly led to a Fellowship at the sister foundation of New College, Oxford, where the poet's father matriculated on 11 September, 1661 at the age of 19.[7]

The future Dean may not at first have intended to enter the Church, since the first degree he took in 1668 was that of Bachelor of Civil Law. But two years later he was ordained priest by Seth Ward, Bishop of Salisbury.[8] Soon he began to make a name as a preacher and on 17 February, 1678 he delivered a sermon before the Lord Mayor of London.[9] About July he was appointed one of the chaplains to the gallant Earl of Ossory, who commanded the English forces in the Netherlands, probably through the good offices of the Earl's new secretary, John Ellis, his contemporary at Oxford. But he was not keen to accompany his patron on his campaign in Flanders and on 'Act Sunday' (7 July, 1678) he wrote to Ellis:

> If I can have a fair excuse with a salvo of my credit with my Lord, I should choose to decline. For my College requires indispensably my attendance at the Michaelmas Audit . . . but I would not insist on the quitting of my College if the concern only reached myself. I am obliged to a care that I have not power to lay down . . . I have a wife and child, whom my absence will necessarily expose to misery and any farther miscarriage to beggary.[10]

These arguments were a little specious; if he was married and for long enough to have a child, he should have resigned his Fellowship already, and one can only suppose he had concealed his marriage. Anyway they did not convince the Earl and the chaplain duly followed him to Flanders – without losing his Fellowship.

It was not an easy assignment, as is shown by a report, dated 12 September, from his schoolfellow Francis Turner (later Bishop of Ely) at The Hague to the Archbishop of Canterbury. The Earl 'found at his first coming a bold and busy faction of

Popish officers that bore down all, and would have made it uneasy for any clergyman or indeed Protestant layman to live among them. But this noble lord set up as zealously for his own religion as they for theirs. He brought over a discreet, learned and devout man as his chaplain (his name is Young, a Fellow of New Coll: in Oxford). He set up daily prayers in the field, and it was a brave sight to see the Duke of Ormond's eldest son kneeling with his blue garter in the dirt.'[11]

The chaplain's reward came after Ossory's return to England at the end of the year. On 18 December his College appointed him to their living of Newnton Longville[12] in Buckinghamshire; but he still did not resign his Fellowship, which the statutes allowed him to retain for another twelve months. On 29 December[13] he preached before King Charles himself at Whitehall and his sermon was published by His Majesty's special command. But now Ossory was directed by his father, the great Duke of Ormonde, Viceroy of Ireland, to cut down his expenses and he began to try to find Young another place. On 18 February, 1679 he wrote to his father:

> I wish you had Mr Young, my chaplain, in your family, for he is eminent both for preaching and good living, and not being troublesome. Besides, he is an Oxford man.[14]

The Duke did not respond to the suggestion; but his son wrote again on 6 October, recommending his protégé for the Bishopric of Kilkenny; and again on 6 January, 1680:

> I wish Dr Young that was in Flanders with me were preferred in Ireland. He is an extraordinary pious man and an excellent preacher. He is an Oxford man and very well reputed in the University.[15]

Alas, like his son after him, the Rev. Mr Young found that the favour of the great was a chancy thing and the death of Ossory on 30 July, 1680 put an end to his hopes of quick promotion in Ireland, that happy hunting-ground of ambitious clerics.

Meanwhile, however, he had taken more effective steps to ensure his future by exchanging his Fellowship of New College on 16 August, 1679[16] for one at Winchester, where owing to the rise in land values the Fellowships had now become more profitable than those of the senior sister at Oxford. As residence was not necessary and marriage was allowed, these highly desirable appointments were generally reserved for a tight little ring of county families. Finally on 15 November, 1680,[17] after his patron's death, he exchanged his benefice of Newnton Longville for the more convenient living of Upham and quickly moved in, his signature appearing in the parish register as early as 12 December. Here he settled down for more than twenty years and raised his family.

As a preacher he was in constant demand, frequently called away to give sermons to important people on important occasions. On 17 February, 1681, summoned by the Archbishop of Canterbury to preach a course of sermons in Lent, he pleaded a violent cold caught on a journey with his 'little family (for with such luggage[d] I was now travelling)'.[18] In September, 1682[19] he was appointed by Bishop Ward to the Sarum prebend of Gillingham Minor; in February, 1683[20] he preached to the Lord Mayor at Guildhall; and on 25 January, 1685[21] he delivered the address at the consecration at Lambeth of a brother-Fellow of Winchester, Thomas Ken, as Bishop of Bath and Wells. Clearly he was well regarded by the authorities of Church and City, and even royal favour is alleged by Giles Jacob in his *Poetical Register* (1720), where it is stated that Princess Anne 'honoured him with standing Godmother to this our Poet'.[22] A cryptic reference to an 'obligation . . . received from your royal indulgence'[23] in the dedication to Queen Anne of Young's first poem may perhaps refer to this otherwise unsupported story.

On 12 July, 1686[24] the Prebendary was chosen to preach at Salisbury at the visitation of the Metropolitan Commission of Inquiry into the quarrel between the aged Bishop Ward and the Dean and Chapter. The sermon was in Latin and the scholarly eloquence of his plea for reconciliation so struck Bishop Sprat that he expressed regret to the Chapter that the preacher had one of the poorest prebends, and the Commission recommended to the Archbishop of Canterbury not only the publication of the sermon but the promotion of its author.[25] The sermon was duly printed in 1686, and two years later a verse translation, entitled *The Idea of Christian Love*, was

---

[d] The 'luggage' at that time consisted of his wife and daughter Jane. Judith was not born till five months later.

published by one William Atwood at the suggestion of the poet
Edmund Waller. At the end of the volume Atwood added 'some
copies of verses from that Excellent Poetess Mrs Wharton with
others to her'[26] – an exchange of pious poems between Mrs
Wharton, Waller and himself. The poetess was Anne, daughter
of Sir Henry Lee of Ditchley, Oxfordshire, and first wife of
Thomas Wharton, the Whig party organizer. Apparently on the
strength of their appearance together on the title-page of
Atwood's book Croft asserts that the elder Young and Mrs
Wharton were 'well acquainted' and even that 'Wharton, after
he became ennobled, did not drop the son of his old friend'.[27] It
may be so – certainly Wharton's son (by another wife) was a
patron of Young's son, while a Lee cousin actually married him.
But the acquaintance cannot have been connected with the
sermon, since Anne Wharton died on 24 October, 1685, before
it was ever preached. A more probable consequence was the
preferment of the preacher on 14 January, 1688[28] to the richer
Prebend of Combe and Hernham.[c]

By 1688 the struggle between the Church of England and
King James had become acute and such a popular preacher
as Young could hardly avoid becoming involved. He showed
himself a firm supporter of the Anglican cause, boldly
addressing the Judges of the Western Circuit in 1686[29] – soon
after Jeffreys's 'Bloody Assize' – on the theme of 'humane
judicature' and striving to persuade the Dissenters to join forces
with their fellow Protestants. The explosion came in May, 1688,
when the King ordered the clergy to read his Declaration of
Indulgence suspending all the penal laws against both Roman
Catholics and Dissenters. On 18 May the famous seven Bishops,
led by Archbishop Sancroft and including two of Young's
Wykehamist friends, Ken of Wells and Turner of Ely, petitioned
against the order; and two days later Young preached at Bow
Church 'exhorting to union in religion', followed by a 'friendly
call to our Dissenting brethren' before the Lord Mayor.[30] On 8
June the Bishops were committed to the Tower, but their trial
and acquittal at the end of the month sounded the knell of
James's attempts at autocratic rule and led to the Revolution of

[c] The costs of the Visitation were paid proportionately to the value of the
prebend (Chapter Act Book, 21 August, 1686). Gillingham Minor was rated at
£8 p.a., Combe & Hernham at £35.10s.

November, 1688. In the crisis of conscience that followed Young
was obviously a supporter of the new dispensation. He may have
known the new King, William of Orange, when he was serving with
his forces in Flanders, and he was a close friend of Tillotson, who
took over the Archbishopric of Canterbury from the 'non-juring'
Sancroft, and of Gilbert Burnet, the historian, who landed with
William at Torbay and was appointed to Salisbury in March 1689
on the death of Bishop Ward. It is not surprising, therefore, that by
1693 we find him as Chaplain in Ordinary to Their Majesties, as is
shown by an Easter sermon published that year by the Queen's
command.[31] Queen Mary evidently appreciated his eloquence, for
she also commanded the publication of two more sermons
preached at Whitehall in April, 1694[32] under the title of *The Great
Advertisement, that a Religious Life is the best way to present Happiness* – a
doctrine echoed again and again in his son's *Night Thoughts*.

The death of the Queen on 28 December, 1694 did not affect his
position at court and he continued as chaplain to the King. In May
1695[33] a new 'friend at court' appeared in the person of his old
colleague John Ellis, who was appointed Under-Secretary of State
and held on to the post for ten years under four different
Ministers. Young kept up a warm correspondence with him, and
Ellis was always ready to oblige. On 18 March, 1699 the Rector
wrote from Upham:

> They say the King intends for Newmarket Tuesday in
> Easter week . . . but for a Chaplain to go to Newmarket and
> have all ask what he makes there (for according to my last
> year's experience there is no use either of prayer or grace, and
> the preaching is seized by Cambridge as their privilege) is a
> pleasure I would willingly escape, and I fancy you may
> contrive it for me with as much ease as ask what's o'clock.[34]

Ellis fixed things for him, getting his colleague Mr Stanley to
nominate the Vicar of Newmarket as Young's substitute, and the
chaplain duly delivered his two sermons at Whitehall without
having to follow the King down to the races afterwards. Next year,
1700,[35] a similar arrangement was made, again through the
intervention of Stanley, now Sir John[f] – and this may have been

---

[f] John Stanley (1659–1744) of Grange Gorman, Ireland, was created Baronet on
14 April, 1699. He married Anne Granville, whose brother, Lord Lansdowne, and
niece, Mrs Delany, both played a part in the story of the poet.

the start of a family friendship for forty years later we find Sir
John Stanley mentioned as an old friend in the poet's letters.[36]
The court sermons of that year on *The Wisdom of Believing* were
duly published,[37] but the royal commendation did not save the
Chaplain from attack by the Deists and a minor religious
controversy of the kind so popular at the time broke out with
some 'remarks' on these discourses in a pamphlet called *The
Excellency of Reason Demonstrated* and 'a censure of the remarks'
entitled *The Excellency of Reason no Argument against the Wisdom of
Believing*.[38] As this reply was printed with the preacher's
collected sermons, it is probable that he wrote it himself. At any
rate it is echoed by his son throughout the *Night Thoughts*, where
the poet strove to convince the infidels with their own weapons
of reason. There is no doubt of the father's influence on the
thinking of the poet.

Meanwhile the son had reached a sufficient age to leave traces
of his independent existence. On the Election Roll of
Winchester College in 1694 he figures eleventh out of sixteen
names with his age given as ten.[39] This confusing statement was
due to the system whereby, though the election was held
between 7 July and Michaelmas – by which time young Edward
was certainly eleven – the ages given were those of the
candidates at Michaelmas last past, i.e. 29 September, 1693. Thus
when he was actually admitted to the school on 15 January,
1695,[40] he was in fact eleven and a half. Election to these
coveted places was mainly through influence and as Edward's
father was one of the Fellows we can draw no conclusions as to
his scholastic merit. His school career indeed, as we follow it
from year to year in the annual Long Rolls[41] (school lists),
indicates no special distinction and some of his younger
classmates outstripped him in the race for the corresponding
places at New College. Starting in the bottom class, the Second
Division of 'Fourth Book', he progressed regularly but slowly:
fourteenth in Fourth Book, 1696, behind a younger poet-to-be,
Edward Holdsworth; tenth in 1697, with Holdsworth fifth and a
new boy of his own age, another future poet called Cobden, at
the top; twenty-ninth and last in Fifth Book, 1698, behind
Holdsworth, Cobden and yet another poet-to-be, William
Harrison, aged fourteen. On 20 October, 1698[42] he was one of
those who took the Scholar's Oath, having reached their

fifteenth year; and in the following years he moved slowly up Fifth Book behind Harrison, Cobden and Holdsworth, reaching the top form, Sixth Book, in 1701. The only hint we have as to his conduct suggests that even then he was absent-minded in little things; in 1699[43] his name figured in a list of those reported to the Headmaster for not having their 'scholastic equipment' in readiness. In July, 1701 he reached the age of eighteen, the normal time for leaving the school; but his 'notional' age for examination purposes was still seventeen and he duly sat for the New College election that year, gaining nineteenth place on the roll.[44] This was nowhere near good enough to secure a vacancy, but it was vital in giving him another chance, as those already on the roll were allowed to stay on for their nineteenth year.

The year 1702 was thus a critical one – and it was critical for the father as well as the son. Not only was the Rector concerned with his boy's chances of succession to a place at New College but also with his own chances of preferment in the Church. On 16 February he wrote to the invaluable Ellis from Winchester:

> Upon the late disposal of the Deaneries of Exeter and Lincoln a friend was pleased to ask some of the Commissioners why they never thought fit to remember me; it was answered by the Archbishop that they did remember me effectually and had resolved that if I survived the vacancy of Wells, that should be mine. Salisbury is now void before it, and because I have been reproached ·by some of themselves for not making application, I beg you to visit my Lord Bradford and let him know I presume to desire his Lordship to drop a word in my behalf to the Archbishop and the Bishop of Sarum for that Deanery.[45]

The Earl of Bradford was the Treasurer of the Household and had been so, except for a brief period under James II, for the last thirty years. A pious old gentleman of eighty-three, he was an admirer of Young's preaching and readily took the step suggested. The strings worked smoothly and on 25 February[46] the Rector's name was recommended by King William for the Deanery of Salisbury. On 5 March a warrant was duly drawn up for despatch to the Chapter. But then came a nasty hitch. On 8 March, before he could sign the warrant, the King was killed by a fall from his horse. The delay, however, was short; on 14 March[47] the new Queen Anne renewed the warrant, Young was elected Dean on the 16th and ceremonially installed on the 27th.[48] On 17 April he was re-appointed Chaplain to the Queen[49] and also Clerk of the Closet.[50] The operation was rounded off with the publication later that year of the new Dean's *Sermons on Several Occasions*[g] in two volumes, gratefully dedicated to the Earl of Bradford.

So far, so good. But the Dean had other urgent business and spent April in some very active lobbying in London in his character of Fellow of Winchester. The story is told in the diary kept by Richard Traffles, the new Warden of New College, on his visit to London, 9 April to 15 May, 1702,[51] about the matter of 'reversing the King's letters'. By this he meant the royal privilege of nominating by letter one of the candidates for election to New College, a privilege shared by the Bishop of Winchester. As the two top places on the roll were already reserved by the Founder's directions for any Founder's Kin who might be of a suitable age, these two additional nominations seriously reduced the chances of ordinary candidates to succeed on merit. The examination for New College was no mere formality like that for entry to Winchester. About twenty-five senior boys underwent a real test of learning before an 'Election Chamber' representing both Colleges and the order of the candidates in the final roll *ad Oxon* by no means tallied with that of the school lists. Traffles therefore objected to the system of letters of recommendation, which worked to the detriment of merit, and his object was to persuade the Queen to give up her nomination.

Several Fellows of Winchester and New College came up to London to help the Warden and he noted on 14 April that 'Mr Young, Dean of Sarum, then was very active in this affair and undertook to engage the Bishop of London in it; taking with him all my papers which stated this business.'[52] At a meeting on 20 April at the Archbishop's lodgings the Bishop of Winchester 'declared freely his desire to have the Queen's letters got off and

[g] Dean Young's sermons went into a 2nd edition, 1706, and 3rd, 1720. They were praised by John Wesley and recommended in 1780 in 'Letters from a Tutor to his Pupils' (*GM*, LXI, 982). Southey read them in 1836 and copied several extracts in his Common-place Books.

that he gave over his own privilege of sending a letter to the
Election in order to show his most hearty approbation of it.'[53]
But the Archbishop revealed that there was opposition from the
Secretaries of State on political grounds: the late King had
already granted a letter for the ensuing election to a cousin of
the Earl of Bridgwater, William Egerton by name, and naturally
they did not want to offend this important nobleman.[h] In the
end a compromise agreement was worked out by which they
would accept Egerton's nomination as long as it was the last
one, though Traffles protested that there were ten or twelve
candidates that deserved preference over him. The Archbishop
and the Dean of Sarum 'seemed to allow of' this plan and at the
Primate's request the Dean drew up a summary of their case,
which was sent with the petition to the Queen. The Coronation
on 23 April held things up a little, but on 15 May Traffles
received word that the Queen 'had granted a stop of letters for
her time'[54] and he hurried round to the Secretary's office, where
the helpful Mr Ellis promised to take care of the official order.

On the Warden's return to Oxford he was greeted with a
letter from Upham, dated 23 May, which ended:

> Your next care must be not to let conscience grow too
> fast, it will quite hinder business; it was the other day no
> bigger than a man's hand and now it covers the sky. I am
> afraid you will find none to act for Egerton, though that be
> the price of future freedom.[55]

A rough draft of Traffles's reply, scribbled on the back of this
letter, shows that it was the Dean's task to persuade the Warden
of Winchester to accept the compromise. Traffles himself
promised to do 'as much as he should' for succession to the
places at New College, though he was against 'marketing in
resigners' and for the 'banishment of affection from the Election
Chamber'.[56] Obviously he was hinting at the candidature of the
Dean's own son. Perhaps the Dean was hoping that in return for
his support of the disappointing compromise, which would get
rid of only one nomination in 1702, the Warden would show
special favour to his son in the election or allow his Fellows to
trade their resignations to create more vacancies. But in any case

---

[h] Scroop Egerton, 4th Earl of Bridgwater, succeeded his father, who had been
First Lord of the Admiralty, in 1701. He was later made a Duke (1720).

the boy would have to work extra hard to get within striking distance of a place. He passed his nineteenth birthday in July but was allowed to sit for election and, either through his own efforts or the electors' indulgence, he secured eighth place on the roll.[57] Above him were two Founder's Kin, Egerton, and four genuine candidates, of whom one, Harrison, was a year younger and could wait for next year; below him, for once, were Cobden and Holdsworth. Then, being nineteen, he was superannuated and, hoping against hope for enough vacancies to occur before the next election, he left the school.

Despite his comparatively undistinguished record[i] his eight years at Winchester had by no means been wasted and he had imbibed a lifelong love of the Greek and Latin classics. In later years another Wykehamist, Joseph Spence of the *Anecdotes*, noted down the poet's comparisons of the *Iliad* and the *Odyssey*,[j] Cicero and Demosthenes, Horace and Juvenal;[58] while one of his curates (Wykehamist again) described in a satirical novel 'the joy it gave him to quote a bit of Latin' and ended the tale with the moral, 'Latin is not to be talked at *all* times.'[59] At the school, though, talking Latin was just what the boys were meant to do and they became so fluent that Young was able later to coach a noble pupil by doing 'nothing but read Tully and talk Latin for six weeks'.[60] Tully (Cicero) was studied from Fourth Book upward, but otherwise the scholars' diet was exclusively poetical, from Ovid and Terence in the junior classes to Homer, Virgil, Martial, Hesiod and Musaeus in the Sixth. There was continual practice of grammar, rhetoric, declamation and composition, particularly of Latin verses, including the exercise known as 'varying', where the boys had to produce extempore verses on a set theme. Years later Young could still remember some examples and quoted to Spence a couplet by his friend Harrison, who 'had a sweetness of versification in these even

---

[i] Dr Johnson, according to Mrs Thrale (Hill-Powell, V, 269, n3), despised Young as a scholar because he was 'totally ignorant of what are called *rhopalic* verses', i.e. verses in which each word contains one syllable more than the word immediately preceding it.

[j] E.g. 'In the *Iliad* you are always fully engaged in the part you are reading; in the *Odyssey* you are always wishing for the event. The latter is masterly in raising that appetite which is particular to romance; the other is full in each part. One always affords the pleasure of expectation, the other of fruition.' (Osborn.)

beyond that of Ovid . . . Holdsworth[k] had a great fluency and would repeat twenty or thirty verses at a heat; but they were not remembered generally, as Harrison's used to be.'[61]

Not only was the curriculum severe and strenuous, but the scholars' life was Spartan in the extreme. Roused at 5 a.m., they made their beds, swept their chamber and went to chapel at 5.30. From 6 to 9 o'clock they were in school and only after that did they get breakfast. After study in their chambers and another hour in school they dined at noon, then went back to school till 5 p.m. Supper and further study in chambers followed till evening chapel at 8; and so to bed, where the prefect read a chapter of the Bible before lights out. In winter they might be allowed a 'half-faggot' for their chamber fires, but the dining hall and schoolroom were unheated, even though a grand new school hall had been built in 1687, the old 'School' chamber being too small to hold all the pupils, now that the fame of Winchester's education had attracted nearly eighty rich or aristocratic 'Commoners' to attach themselves to the College. Warden Nicholas had nobly contributed over half the cost of the new hall, but his munificence was made possible by hogging most of the College's income,[l] with the result that the scholars' rations in Young's day were very poor.[62]

Yet in spite of the hardships there is no doubt that the little victims regarded their *alma mater* with lifelong affection and pride and considered the public school the best system of education. Writing forty-five years later to the Duchess of Portland, Young told the anxious mother:

> Your Grace has sent Lord Titchfield to Westminster; no doubt it gave your Grace some care and concern, and so will everything in life that is valuable and worth our wishes. It is

[k] The name is given by Spence as 'Oldisworth', whom Osborn takes to be William Oldisworth (1680–1734), the miscellaneous writer. There was a Commoner of that surname at the school from 1695 to 1698 (Holgate, *Long Rolls*) but 'Oldisworth jun.', listed among the Scholars in 1695, is a mistake for Holdsworth and it seems probable that Spence made the same mistake. Edward Holdsworth, afterwards famed for his Latin poem *Muscipula*, sat in the same class as Young and Harrison for several years, whereas Oldisworth was in a different class.

[l] The Fellows gave £10 or £20 each towards the total cost of £2600 (Mr Young, £10); the Warden made up the deficiency of subscriptions, £1477. But then his stipend and allowances came to £495 p.a., the Fellows £41 each.

greatly for my Lord's advantage, and therefore will be
greatly for your Grace's happiness. Whatever advantages a
private education may have, two very great ones it certainly
wants, emulation and early experience in the tempers and
talents of others; the first is the greatest spur to diligence
and the last an absolutely necessary qualification for making
any figure in public life.[63]

It was the discipline of communal living, of a society where they
learnt both to compete and co-operate, that seemed so valuable
to the poet.

The Headmaster, the Usher and their schoolfellows were the
most important influences in the scholars' impressionable teens,
for they hardly saw their homes. One month at Whitsun was the
only regular holiday at home; some lucky boys might get *exeats* to
'go into the country' during the Christmas vacation, but the Easter
vacation was spent by all at school. Young himself doubtless saw
more of his parents than most boys, for his home was not far from
Winchester and his father was a Fellow. But though the rhetorical
style of his verse may have derived from his eloquent father, his
love of poetry and particularly his admiration for Milton can be
directly attributed to his years in the 'nest of singing birds'[m] that
Winchester had become under the Headmastership of William
Harris. Although no official provision was made in the
curriculum for English studies, the scholars were in fact required
to write English verse translations of the classics; 'they turn Virgil
into English verses and Hesiod into Latin',[64] reported a visitor
about 1670. By the time Young entered the school Harris had
been Headmaster for sixteen years and was at the height of his
powers, although he actually died in 1700 during the poet's time
at school. It was then that the school produced such a flock of
'singing birds'. William Somervile, who was to write *The Chace*, left
in the year that Young arrived; John Philips, author of *The
Splendid Shilling*, overlapped him for three years; of his classmates
Harrison's *Woodstock* was praised by Addison, Holdsworth's Latin
mock-heroic *Muscipula* or *Mouse-Trap* was so popular that no less
than six translations were published, and Cobden was a prolific
occasional versifier. Add to these Young himself and it makes a
record of which any teacher might justly be proud.

[m] Dr Johnson's description of Pembroke College, Oxford, in his day.

But more interesting than the mere number of poets is the number that wrote their major works in blank verse. Since the death of Milton blank verse had fallen into disuse among versifiers, who were obsessed with the heroic couplet, and though *Paradise Lost* never ceased to have its admirers, it was not until 1701 that the revival of the Miltonic style began – with a burlesque. This was *The Splendid Shilling* of John Philips, who went on to serious excursions in blank verse with *Blenheim* in 1705 and *Cyder* in 1708. Though by that time a few others had ventured into the Miltonic field,[n] Philips's lead was recognized by the Augustans and Thomson apostrophized him thus in *Autumn*:

> Philips! Pomona's bard, the second thou
> Who nobly durst in rhyme-unfettered verse
> With British freedom sing the British song![65]

Philips's taste for Milton was developed at Winchester, according to the *Biographia Britannica*, which says he seldom joined in play with the other boys, but 'generally retired then to his chamber where he procured a person to attend him and comb his hair, of which he had a very handsome flow. In this very singular recreation he felt an exquisite delight . . . It was in these intervals chiefly that he read Milton; however, this was not before he was well acquainted with both Virgil and Homer, and the frequent imitations he found of these authors in *Paradise Lost*, falling in exactly with his own turn, hence he conceived an ardent passion for the English poet, and some small pieces which he composed at this time showed that he had imbibed a good share of Milton's style and manner before he left Winchester.'[66] No doubt the eccentricities of Philips made a deep impression on his school-fellows, and it is reasonable to suppose that his example influenced his contemporaries[o] and that Young's lifelong devotion to Milton was born at school.

[n] R. D. Havens, *The Influence of Milton on English Poetry*, Harvard, 1922, in his exhaustive bibliographies lists only five poems 'influenced by *Paradise Lost*' before *The Splendid Shilling*. Of these three were not in blank verse and one, though written in 1698, was apparently not published. This leaves only 27 lines of Miltonic imitation in the second edition of Roscommon's *Essay on Translated Verse* (1685) predating Philips. Havens gives ten more items (not all in blank) before *Blenheim*. Dramatic blank was regarded as a quite different matter.

[o] Somervile in *Hobbinol*, Canto III, calls Philips 'that great bard' who 'first taught my grov'ling Muse to mount aerial'.

Another consequence of his schooling at Winchester was the striking number of his friends that turn out to be Wykehamists – not only those who were actually at school with him, like Harrison the 'partner of his soul',[67] Harris who married his sister, Cobden who wrote verses to him, Egerton[P] and Cary with whom he often stayed, but many of a later vintage, like Christopher Pitt, the poet whom he called his 'son',[68] and Joseph Spence who pumped him for anecdotes, and Joseph Warton who dedicated to him the revolutionary *Essay on Pope*. And there were the Commoners as well, like his patrons Bubb Dodington and Speaker Onslow and the Duke of Chandos, or his only known pupil Lord Burghley. Of course he made plenty of other friends at Oxford and after; but the frequency with which Wykehamists occur at every stage of his story shows that the old school feeling was well developed even in those days[q] – and, as today, it was no disadvantage to him.

When Edward Young left Winchester in 1702, he had not indeed achieved the goal of a Fellowship at New College, but he had gained a thorough knowledge of the classics, a taste for Milton, and a host of friends.

[P] Egerton became Rector of Penshurst, 1720–38, and his grandson, Sir Egerton Brydges, reported in the *Gentleman's Magazine* (LXI, 982) that he had 'often heard with delight' of Young's visits to his grandfather at Penshurst.

[q] In 1759, for instance, Dodington was Steward of the Wykehamist Dinner. (*The Wykehamist*, no. 243, p. 346.)

CHAPTER 2

Nine Oxford Poets

1702–1714

The Warden of New College had recommended the 'banish-ment of affection from the Election Chamber', but that did not mean that he would not do for affection whatever was legitimate under the statutes. When his old friend's son was superannuated, he admitted him as a Gentleman Commoner of the College and took him in as a lodger in his own quarters to save him the consequent expense. Thus Edward Young matriculated at Oxford on 3 October, 1702[1] and began his long career at the University – which covered twenty-eight years and three Colleges – among his fellow-Wykehamists.

Meanwhile the Dean travelled busily between Salisbury, Winchester and Upham, where he kept the living till his death. He seems indeed to have spent more time at his Rectory than his Deanery; the Chapter records show him presiding at only one meeting in 1702 and none at all in 1703![2] On the other hand his letters show that he was at Upham or Winchester in May, 1702,[3] March, 1703[4] and October, 1703,[5] while his daughter's marriage at Upham in June, 1704[6] suggests that it had remained the family home. The travelling perhaps was bad for him and his letter of 13 March, 1703 to Ellis was once more to beg off Newmarket duty on the excuse that 'my infirmities forbid me to attempt the journey'.[7] From this time on we find several references to his declining health and he was evidently eager to settle the future of his children as soon as possible.

Unfortunately the unexpected death of Traffles on 30 June, 1703[8] and the final extinction of his son's hopes of a Fellowship in September made it necessary to seek new accommodation for Edward. An offer of similar hospitality from Thomas Turner, the President of Corpus Christi College, who was brother of Bishop Turner, was gratefully accepted and in October the poet transferred to that College, again as a Commoner.[a] On the 13th of that month Dean Young wrote to Turner from Upham:

> My son should not have come alone, I would have accompanied him into the hands of your government but that my crazy temper will not permit me to adventure so long a journey. I have always permitted him to his choice, and his first choice was to be bred a scholar, and he has now made a second to proceed to divinity; nor am I displeased at it, hoping that his manners and garb and acquaintances and study will be so formed as to comport with his design. I should be glad if he meet with a tutor of a free informing conversation; for one that will converse with him at a leisure minute will do him more good than the gravest systematical lectures. But this and all his conduct I humbly commit to your direction, desiring you sometimes to admonish him that his education is his fortune, his father having no other to leave.[9]

These words show that the father understood his son's ideas of scholarship were not those of pedantry and was somewhat concerned at his unconventional behaviour. It appears that the young man, travelling by himself, must have lingered by the way, for there is no trace of him in the Corpus Buttery Books up to 21 October, 1703.[10] Unluckily there is a year's gap in the records after that and, as Commoners did not figure in the Admissions Book nor sign out in the Absence Book, it is not till the opening of the 1704–5 Buttery Book on 27 October[11] that we find Young's name among the six junior members of the College. From these kitchen accounts we can at least tell when he stayed in College and when he was absent, and no doubt the varying amount of his weekly bills (usually 4 to 5 shillings, but once up to £1.9s.6d.) could yield a fuller picture if the notes of his expenses were more legible.

At the same time the Dean was busy settling the future of his other surviving child, Anne. The opportunity came with the death on 21 September, 1703[12] of the Rev. John Layfield, Rector of Chiddingfold, a living in the gift of the Dean of

---

[a] The *Biographia Britannica* supplement, 1766, quotes 'Dr Eyre of Grays Inn, who was his schoolfellow at Winchester': 'This gown was put on out of regard to his birth, to say nothing of the less expense attending it at that College than at any other.'

Sarum. A pamphlet dated January, 1705 and entitled *An Account of Mr H——s's Election at Winchester College* gives a hostile version of the Dean's conduct in the matter. The target of this attack was John Harris, third son of Sir Richard Harris, Recorder of Winchester, and grandson of a former Warden; born in 1680, he entered the school two years before Young and left in 1699 for New College.[13] According to the *Account*, the Dean decided that the Rectory of Chiddingfold should go to whoever he chose as his son-in-law and the choice fell on Harris, who 'being well related and capable of making a suitable settlement, was thought to deserve more than the living of Chiddingfold with the Dean's daughter.'[14] It was therefore agreed to add a Fellowship of Winchester to her dowry, the only difficulty being that Harris was still too young for priest's orders and had not yet completed even his Bachelor's degree. While he was qualifying himself, the living was left vacant and the Dean approached the other Fellows about his own replacement at Winchester. But unfortunately the Society objected to the candidate's lack of years and seriousness and 'it was conceived that it was a thing without precedent that a Fellowship should pass with a daughter and be made part of a marriage settlement.'[15] The Dean, however, thought his proposal very reasonable and considered himself ill-used by his colleagues.

At this point, in April 1704,[16] the Dean's health broke down and in May he resorted to Bristol hot wells, leaving his resignation with Warden Nicholas to be offered at a convenient opportunity. The warden acted a week or two later, choosing a moment when only four Fellows were in residence to call a meeting at one day's notice. He then declared the Dean's place void and proposed the name of Harris to fill the vacancy. Two of the Fellows indignantly protested at the prejudice of the rights of the absent Fellows and the corrupt practice of 'succession' or resignation in favour of a nominee, and after much learned argument they walked out. The Warden and the two remaining Fellows then voted Harris into the vacancy and admitted him forthwith. In this manner on 26 May, 1704[17] Dean Young resigned his Fellowship of Winchester and John Harris succeeded to it. Two days later Harris was instituted as Rector of Chiddingfold[18] and one month after that, on 29 June, he married Anne Young at Upham.[19] The *coup* was thus successfully carried off; but the pamphlet indicates that the matter was still at issue in January, 1705, as the malcontent Fellows were appealing to the Visitor, the Bishop of Winchester, to declare the election void. The Dean's luck held, however, as the great age of the Bishop was such as to 'forbid any troublesome solicitation'[20] and by the time he eventually died in 1707 it was too late. The Reverend John Harris continued to hold his Fellowship undisturbed till 1748,[21] when he in his turn handed it on to his son – the Dean's grandson.

The dispute, however, must have been a continuing source of anxiety to the Dean; and now his son added again to his worries. First it had been superannuation; then the death of Traffles; and now actual misbehaviour. A long letter to the President of Corpus, undated but assignable to the autumn of 1704,[b] gives the story:

> Believe me, I am one that love not singularities, that hate all gaps in public discipline, and therefore as I never understood (till your letter) that my son ever aimed at an exemption from lectures and disputations, so I never gave countenance to any such exemption either in word or desire. I knew my son had a fastidious whimsical fancy which was like to lead him to the love of such studies only as were apt to gratify and nurse up his infirmity and make the drier part of philosophy fall into contempt with him as an insipid thing. I therefore sent him to your College with this charge, 'Son, remember to pay all possible respect to your Tutor, for thereby you may possibly gain him to permit your access to him now and then for a private conversation, wherein your notions of what you have read may be adjusted and fixed upon your mind and made ready for your use, and without this all that is read may possibly be found to pass through you like a sieve.' Coming to Salisbury this summer, I asked him how matters went; he told me his tutor was, as a man of great worth, so of great business, which kept his pupils at an awful distance from him, so that no such familiarity could be expected there. I said no more,

[b] The letter shows that Edward was back at Oxford after a summer visit to Salisbury, during which he complained of his tutor. In 1703 he did not go up to Corpus till October, and in 1705 the Dean died on 9 August, before Edward returned to College.

but conceived in my thoughts the design of desiring you to befriend him in an assistant as I did in my last – but of this boldness in my son to absent himself from exercise, and this contumacy to persist when under censure, I never suspected to hear. Indeed, my suspicion when awakened has carried me on to look into other matters, where he appears very blameable; for I find that since Easter last he has privately taken up ten pounds and never brought it to account, which is a dishonest act and a worse indication. Good Mr President, help as you can to make this vain youth wiser; and (through you) I desire Mr Perkes to do the same. For if you do not help him, I cannot; because all that he may expect of fortunes from me depends entirely on his good manners.[22]

Whether by the phrase 'fastidious whimsical fancy' the Dean meant his son's taste for poetry we cannot be sure, but evidently his request for a tutor of a 'free informing conversation' had been ignored and the young man was reacting rebelliously against the dry aloofness of Mr Edmund Perkes. Though still under thirty, Perkes was far too busily engaged in theological controversies to spare time for his pupils.[c] His factious and intolerant pamphleteering was not the kind of religious thinking to appeal to Edward's soaring fancy, and perhaps it was this that caused him to give up his intention of studying divinity. At any rate he began to absent himself from the College more and more often, a week in March, 1705, another in May, two weeks in June, and then after only three days in College for nearly two months from 1 July to 27 August.[23]

This last and longest absence may have been due to the failing health of his father. In May of the previous year the Dean had been so seriously ill that his life was in danger; his letter to Turner of autumn 1704 began 'I have been of late very ill';[24] and his earlier reference to his 'crazy temper' suggests that these recurrent illnesses were sudden and unpredictable, in fact, heart attacks. His end was sudden. On Monday, 6 August, 1705[25] he presided over a Chapter meeting at Salisbury; on Thursday the

---

[c] Hearne, who described Perkes as 'a person noted in his College and the University for his probity, honesty, useful learning and willingness to assist and encourage all bookish men', records him as author of pamphlets against Dodwell, Barclay the Quaker and the Protestant Dissenters. (Hearne, I, 266.)

9th[26] he was dead.[d] The following Sunday Bishop Burnet began his sermon with the words:

> Death has .been of late walking round us and making breach upon breach upon us and has now carried away the head of this body with a stroke; so that he, whom you saw a week ago distributing the holy mysteries, is now laid in the dust. But he still lives in the many excellent directions he left us, both how to live and how to die.[27]

The Dean was buried in the south transept of his Cathedral under a plaque with a Latin inscription which stresses his erudition, integrity and faithful service to the Church of England. This public tribute is said by Nichols[28] to have been written by his son; but the son's private feelings were expressed in a moving letter to a College friend, Samuel Reynolds.[e] It is perhaps appropriate that this, the first specimen of the poet's writing that we have, should be about death:

> Yesterday morning I lost (pardon if grief and confusion want address) the best of fathers. My affliction is so great I know not yet how to wrestle with it. My greatest relief is making my complaint to my friends and pleasing myself with the thought that they will condole with me if they really are so. I would but can no more.'[29]

Although the Dean was in his sixty-third year and had so often been ill, he appears to have been unprepared for death, for he left no will. On 27 August[30] letters of administration were granted to his widow Judith,[f] and on the 28th[31] we find his son back at Oxford, having no doubt helped his mother to clear up her husband's affairs. He then remained quietly in College with occasional short absences till 13 June, 1706, when he left for a

---

[d] There is a slight confusion about the exact dates. The Chapter Act Books report the meeting as on *Tuesday* 6 August. The Diary of Thomas Naish, the Dean's surrogate, says the Dean 'dyed this morning' under *8* August. But the 9th is the date given on his tomb.

[e] Samuel Reynolds (1681–1746) was at Corpus from 1698 to 1705, when he became a Fellow of Balliol. He was the father of Sir Joshua Reynolds.

[f] A second 'admin.' was granted to his son on 26 July 1718, possibly in connection with a property at Thatcham, Berks, left to the Dean by his brother Henry, the clockmaker.

longer spell. He reappeared for one night on 25 June, having
perhaps heard of the sudden death of his tutor, Mr Perkes, that
morning from apoplexy,[32] and on three odd days afterwards,
possibly for the funeral, before vanishing for almost four
months. From this time on his attendance at College was very
sporadic – only six days between July, 1706 and August, 1707,
then fourteen weeks at Oxford, followed by nearly eleven
months absence from mid-November, 1707 to mid-October,
1708.[33] It was during one of these long absences that the young
man wrote to President Turner from Chiddingfold,[g] apologizing for 'having been absent much longer than usual' and
requesting leave for 'continuance of the same' as 'my
circumstances make it more convenient for me to be in the
country'.[34] It is dated simply 'June 9th' with no year, but the
phrase 'much longer than usual' indicates that it was his first
prolonged absence, i.e. 1707. By 9 June he had been away for
seven months and an apology was certainly called for. But why
was it 'more convenient' for him to be in the country? Was it for
the sake of poetry, or economy? On later occasions we know that
he retired to Chiddingfold to work on his poems, but there is no
positive evidence of his practising poetry till 1710.[h] The real
reason for his staying away from Oxford may have been the
expense of a Gentleman Commoner's life, now that he no longer
had a father earning a decanal salary.[i]

At the end of 1708 came an important turn in his fortunes,
which seems attributable only to the devotion of his father's
friends. In spite of his neglect of his formal studies and his
prolonged absences from the University he was nominated a
Scholar of All Souls College on 27 November by the Archbishop
of Canterbury, Thomas Tenison, on a devolution.[35] With the
nomination impending he hurriedly resumed residence at
Oxford on 19 October[36] for a last few weeks in Corpus before
transferring to All Souls, where his name appears in the Buttery
Books in the week starting 27 November,[37] the date of his

[g] A postscript, 'My mother gives her most humble service', shows that Mrs
Young had gone to live with her daughter and son-in-law.

[h] Young is not mentioned among the Oxonian poets listed by Thomas Tickell,
one of his closest friends, in his poem *Oxford*, 1707.

[i] The Deanery of Sarum was valued at £900 p.a. and with it went the prebend
of Heytesbury, worth £40 a year. (B. Williams, *The Whig Supremacy*, 1962, map 1.)

appointment. But he was no longer studying divinity; the vacancy for which he was named by the College Visitor was one of two Law Fellowships that the Warden and Fellows had failed to fill within the statutory time. Since he was neither a Scholar nor a graduate but described simply as 'e Collegio Corporis Christi', he must be reckoned very lucky to have been given such a plum. From now on, provided he did not grossly misbehave, his future was assured; he had adequate emoluments and comfortable rooms at the College, and a Fellowship that was a sinecure would follow automatically.

At first his residence at All Souls was pretty regular – a week absent in June, 1709, two weeks in October and about a month over Christmas, after he had safely completed his first year and been duly elected a Law Fellow on 2 December.[38] But though now described as a student of civil law, he continued to be deeply interested in religion, as is shown not only by his first works but also by the story that Dr Johnson was so insistent on having included in the *Life of Young*.[j] This concerned his common-room disputations with another Fellow, Matthew Tindal the 'atheist', who complained: 'The other boys I can always answer because I always know whence they have their arguments, which I have read a hundred times; but that fellow Young is continually pestering me with something of his own.'[39] In a College where half the Fellows were theologians this was a real tribute to the sincerity as well as the originality of Young's religious ideas.

And now at last we come upon definite evidence that Young was writing poems and had already won a certain reputation among his friends for strength of thought and expression. In 1710 a slim folio, entitled *The Laurel and the Olive*, by George Stubbes, Fellow of Exeter College, was dedicated to a nineteen-year-old undergraduate of the College named George Bubb, and Bubb returned the compliment in some flattering verses to the author that included the following lines:

> Unrivalled charms bloom in your matchless song,
> Sweet as smooth G——h and bold as nervous Y——.[40]

---

[j] Croft added a footnote in the 1790 edition of the *Life of Young* recalling that Johnson never suffered him to depart without some such farewell as this: 'Don't forget that rascal Tindal, Sir. Be sure to hang up the atheist.'

This is doubly interesting, not only as the first mention of Young's poetry but the first record of his lifelong friendship with Bubb. Though they did not quite overlap at Winchester, where Bubb was a Commoner from 1704 to 1707,[41] he came up to Oxford at sixteen and, unlike Young, lost no time in presenting himself before the public. In 1708 he contributed a Latin poem to the Oxford Exequies on the death of the Queen's consort, and by 1710, it seems, he was a patron of letters. Able and ambitious, he had the advantage, despite his plebeian name, of being the destined heir of a rich and influential maternal uncle, George Dodington,[k] whose name in due course he adopted.

What the bold and nervous verses of Young must have been is shown by the publication early in the following year of an extract from his poem *The Last Day*. These, his first published verses, appeared in the *Tatler* of 22 March, 1711 – but this was not the *Tatler* of Steele and Addison. It was a continuation, on the Tory side this time, produced at the instigation of St John and Swift and edited by none other than Young's school-friend William Harrison. The extract was introduced by a letter from New College, signed T.L.,[l] in these words:

> I am making a collection of the best verses that are stirring for your service. Mr Y——g tells me he has left his poem entitled *The Last Day* in your hands, to make what use of it you should think proper. There is in that excellent work a nobleness of thought, as well as strength of expression, which I have not met with in any of our modern writers.[42]

The editor's response was to print the first hundred lines of the poem, with the promise of more in later numbers of the paper. But in fact no more appeared, although the periodical ran for another twenty-five numbers. T.L. added:

[k] His father, Jeremiah Bubb, rumoured to be an Irish adventurer or Weymouth apothecary, actually came of a respectable northern family; his grandfather was a Colonel, his father a J.P. (Carswell, *The Old Cause*, 1954, 138). Dodington was a West Country magnate, who controlled six parliamentary boroughs and was a Commissioner of the Admiralty.

[l] Possibly Thomas Lee, Fellow of New College, 1703–20, who had been at Winchester with Young from 1693.

The same gentleman, I hear, designed a tragedy for the
stage this winter, which was entirely approved by five or
six of the best judges in the kingdom; but Mr Cibber
happening to dissent from them, the town was disappointed of that entertainment.[43]

It is clear that, although another two years passed before the
publication of his poem and another eight before the
performance of his first tragedy, Young was by now an active
and recognized author. Yet 1711, when he was absent from All
Souls for nearly the whole year, saw no production and neither
did 1712, which he spent almost all at Oxford – and then
suddenly in 1713 began a positive spate of publication.

Young's first published poem was not *The Last Day*. On 10
March, 1713[44] Bernard Lintott published Young's *Epistle to the
Right Honourable George Lord Lansdowne*, whereas *The Last Day* did
not receive its *imprimatur* at Oxford until 19 May.[45] But the
Epistle was certainly written later, for Lansdowne had only
received his title on 1 January, 1712,[46] while the last lines refer
to an event that took place less than a month before the poem's
publication, the death of Harrison on 14 February, 1713.[47]
George Granville, Lord Lansdowne, was a most suitable choice
as patron for a would-be poet and playwright, as he was not only
a rising figure in the new Harley administration but himself a
practitioner of verse and drama. The fact that the Minister was a
Tory and the poet a Whig is neither here nor there. The parties
were by no means exclusive or inimical on a personal or literary
plane, for all their pamphlet warfare.[m] Addison wrote an
epilogue for Lansdowne's *British Enchanters* and Pope dedicated
Windsor Forest to him. Now that he was in power, 'Granville the
polite' was an obvious target for literary addresses, and Young,
as we shall see, claimed a personal connection as well.

The *Epistle to Lansdowne* was a poem with a strictly practical
purpose, to obtain protection for the poet's dramatic aspirations
and, therefore, like all his occasional verse, it was omitted from
his own collected works in 1757. Indeed he seems to have had a
particularly modest opinion of this piece, for when Curll was

[m] Harrison, a Whig, was recommended to Swift and Addison. Swift told Stella
on 30 June, 1711, 'I have now had almost all the Whig poets my solicitors.'
(Williams, *Stella*, 304.)

preparing an earlier collection Young wrote, 'Nor have I the
Epistle to Lord Lansdowne: but if you will take my advice, I would
have you omit *that*.'[48] Yet for the biographer it is full of
revealing lights upon his character and ideas. The first 185 lines
are devoted to the praise of Lansdowne as a member of the Tory
government that was negotiating the peace treaty at Utrecht.
There was no insincerity here; the nation was weary of the war
that dragged on despite the splendid victories of Marlborough,
and the peace was generally popular. Tickell, whom Swift called
'Whiggissimus',[49] wrote an *Ode on the Prospect of Peace* that
quickly passed through six editions. No such success awaited
Young's first public appearance. Yet a comparison of the empty
clichés of Tickell with the awkward but feeling words of Young
makes one realize the difference in calibre between these two
friends. Where Tickell drew a conventionally heroic picture –

> The hardy veteran, proud of many a scar,
> The manly charms and honours of the war;[50]

Young was shocked by the sight of the real veterans:

> On gain or pleasure bent, we shall not meet
> Sad melancholy numbers in each street
> (Owners of bones dispersed on Flandria's plain
> Or wasting in the bottom of the main);
> To turn us back from joy, in tender fear
> Lest it an insult of their woes appear,
> And make us grudge ourselves that wealth, their blood
> Perhaps preserved, who starve or beg for food.[51]

The poet then turned to his hero's literary triumphs, extolling
historical tragedy as the inspiration of generous and noble
feelings and asserting the superiority of the native British drama
over the classic school of France:

> The French are delicate and nicely lead
> Of close intrigue the labyrinthian thread;
> Our genius more affects the grand than fine,
> Our strength can make the great plain action shine:
> They raise a great curiosity indeed
> From his dark maze to see the hero freed;
> We rouse th' affections and that hero show
> Gasping beneath some formidable blow:
> They sigh, we weep; the Gallic doubt and care

> We heighten into terror and despair,
> Strike home, the strongest passions boldly touch
> Nor fear our audience should be pleased too much.
> What's great in nature we can greatly draw,
> Nor thank for beauties the dramatic law.[52]

This was no mere patriotic boasting; it was a proclamation of romantic allegiance in defiance of the ruling taste. And as a budding dramatist Young turned back to Shakespeare as his ideal:

> To claim attention and the heart invade
> Shakespeare but wrote the play th' Almighty made.
> Our neighbour's stage-art too bare-faced betrays,
> 'Tis great Corneille at every scene we praise;
> On nature's surer aid Britannia calls,
> None think of Shakespeare till the curtain falls;
> Then with a sigh returns our audience home
> From Venice, Egypt, Persia, Greece or Rome.[53]

After this Young got down, as it were, to business – to call his patron's attention to his own theatrical efforts. If Lansdowne, as the poetic descendant of Shakespeare,[n] and the Duke of Shrewsbury, as the descendant of a Shakespearian hero,[o] should smile –

> E'en I, by far the meanest of your age,
> Shall not repent my passion for the stage.[54]

The effect of this broad hint was rather spoiled by the Duke's resigning the office of Lord Chamberlain (who licensed all the plays) before the poem's publication. But another one hundred and thirty lines of panegyric on Lansdowne were perhaps not wasted, and they were followed by the praises of his 'darling friend' –

> That lovely youth, my lord, whom you must blame
> That I grow thus familiar with your name.[55]

This claim to a personal link through his patron's favourite was

---

[n] His tragedy *Heroic Love*, 1698, extravagantly praised by Dryden, was revived at Drury Lane on 19 March, 1712. In 1701 he produced a comedy, *The Jew of Venice*, adapted from Shakespeare.

[o] The Duke was descended from John Talbot, 1st Earl of Shrewsbury, the English General in *Henry VI, Part I*.

explained by Curll[p] as referring to 'his lordship's nephew, who took orders.'[56] But the nephew in question, Bevil Granville, was only about ten years old when this poem was written.[q] Was Young perhaps tutoring the boy during his long absence from All Souls in 1711? Or was Curll's footnote, nearly thirty years later, mistaken?

On this note Young probably intended to conclude. But in a kind of postscript, awkwardly tacked on as a contrast to his patron's happiness, the poet 'bewails that most ingenious gentleman, Mr William Harrison, Fellow of New College, Oxon.':

> Alas! with me the joys of friendship end;
> O Harrison! I must, I will complain;
> Tears soothe the soul's distress, tho' shed in vain.[57]

The sudden and pathetic end of his best friend, just as he was preparing his first poem for publication, was a shock that Young felt he must express, even though it was hardly appropriate to his theme. Poor Harrison, whom he described as 'a little brisk man, quick and passionate; . . . foppish; . . . a pretty look and a quick eye',[58] had been a general favourite. Addison recommended him to Swift, who called him 'a young fellow here in town we are all fond of, . . . with a great deal of wit, good sense and good nature.'[59] Though his Tory *Tatler* had not been a great success, he was sent to Holland in April 1711 as Queen's Secretary in the Utrecht negotiations, and in January, 1713 he was chosen to bring over to England the Barrier Treaty. 'He went to court very richly dressed,' Young told Spence, 'on a birthnight within the month after his return; caught a violent cold there, which turned to a fever that carried him off.'[60] On 14 February Swift wrote to Stella:

> I took Parnell this morning and we walked to see poor Harrison . . . I told Parnell I was afraid to knock at the door; my mind misgave me. I knocked, and his man in tears told me his master was dead an hour before . . . No loss ever grieved me so much.[61]

[p] In a footnote to his edition of Young's *Works*, 1741. There is no footnote in the original edition.

[q] Bevil, younger brother of Mary Granville (later Mrs Delany), left Westminster School in 1721/22. Lord Lansdowne wrote to Bevil's father on 15 Feb, 1723 about the boy's 'resolution of devoting himself to the Church'. (Llanover, I, 76.) After various disappointments (including a rejected play in 1729) Bevil emigrated to Carolina, where he set up as a preacher in 1733. He died in Jamaica in 1736.

Young, as an intimate friend from childhood, was even more affected. He was at Oxford up to 13 February[62] and must have learnt of Harrison's illness that day, for he wrote:

> With aching heart and a foreboding mind
> I night to day in painful journey joined,
> When first informed of his approaching fate;
> But reached the partner of my soul too late.
> 'Twas past, his cheek was cold; that tuneful tongue,
> Which Isis charmed with its melodious song,
> Now languished, wanted strength to speak his pain,
> Scarce raised a feeble groan, and sunk again . . .
> His spirit now just ready to resign,
> No longer now his own, no longer mine,
> He grasps my hand, his swimming eyeballs roll,
> My hand he grasps and enters in my soul;
> Then with a groan – Support me, O! beware
> Of holding worth, however great, too dear![63]

The future poet of the *Night Thoughts* had described his first deathbed.

On 6 April, 1713 Thomas Hearne, the crusty Oxford antiquary, noted in his diary 'the following verses written in the Boghouse of Mother Gordon's at Headington':

> Alma novem claros peperit Rhedicina poetas,
> Trapp, Young, Bubb, Stubb, Crabb, Fog, Cary, Tickell, Evans.[64]

And he added, 'All bad poets'. They were not perhaps a very distinguished group, the 'nine celebrated Oxford poets', led by the Professor of Poetry, Joseph Trapp. But this satirical couplet shows at least that Young was now a leading figure in the University's poetic circles. Three of the nine have already been mentioned – Bubb, Stubbes and Tickell, and the first and the last were among his closest friends. So was Walter Cary of New College, an old schoolmate, who was satirized by Pope as 'Umbra', the poets' paradise;[r] 'our friend Evans', as Young calls

---

[r] Cary just overlapped with Young at Winchester and followed him to Oxford in 1704, aged eighteen. Pope in his verses on *The Three Gentle Shepherds* (c. 1713) coupled him with Ambrose Philips and Eustace Budgell as a pastoral poet, though none of his verses have been traced. The Character of 'Umbra', who flits from poet to poet at Button's and finally, left by all, 'sits down and writes to honest Tickell', belongs to the same period, though not published till 1727 in the last volume of the *Miscellanies*. He was identified as Walter Cary in the *Characters of the Times*, 1728.

him in a letter to Tickell,[65] was a witty cleric;[s] and John Crabb, late of Exeter College, was patronized by Bubb.[t] Only Fog remains unidentified.[u] But Young could disregard the pinpricks of the University wits, for he was already accepted in a literary circle of far greater distinction, that of the leaders of Augustan letters, Addison and Steele,[v] though, being based on Oxford, he never became identified with the Button's clique.

On 9 May, 1713 the *Guardian* printed an essay on sacred poetry, which it considered 'should be our most especial delight', and the writer quoted three examples of such verse 'taken out of a manuscript poem on the Last Day, which will shortly appear in public'.[66] This time the puff was well-timed, for *A Poem on the Last Day* received its *imprimatur* from the Vice-Chancellor of Oxford University ten days later and finally achieved publication on 14 July,[67] over two years after the first extracts in the *Tatler*. It was a long poem, just over 1000 lines of heroic couplets, divided into three books; and the subject was the Last Judgment, which was described in such naively apocalyptic terms as often to make it exquisitely bathetic to modern ears, earning it a place in that hilarious anthology of bad verse, *The Stuffed Owl*. Here, for instance, is the scene of the Resurrection after the Last Trump:

> Now charnels rattle; scattered limbs and all
> The various bones, obsequious to the call,
> Self-moved advance; the neck perhaps to meet
> The distant head, the distant legs the feet.[68]

But that is not the whole story. Young falls harder from flying higher, and there are times that he rises to considerable heights. But he was always the most unequal of poets, seemingly devoid of critical sense, so that although he is said to have polished his

[s] Abel Evans published *The Apparition*, a satire on Tindal, in 1710.
[t] Crabb had written a *Poem upon the Late Storm* in 1704 and was given the Rectory of Tarrant Hinton, Dorset, near Eastbury. He was still there in 1749, when Dodington's diary mentions him coming to dinner at Eastbury. (*Political Journal*, ed. J. Carswell & L. A. Dralle, 1965, 10.)
[u] Alternative versions give 'Grubb' or 'Cobb' in place of Fog. But Grubb died in 1697 and Cobb was a Cambridge man.
[v] Young's obituary in the *Biographia Britannica* alleged that he was 'one of the writers of the *Spectators*'; his French biographer, Thomas, suggests that he contributed to Steele's *Guardian* under the pseudonym 'John Lizard', as these papers were dated from Oxford and dealt with subjects that interested Young, such as the Book of Job.

verses laboriously, his felicities appear almost accidental, while his tendency to get carried away by the luxuriance of his imagination made it difficult for him to sustain his inspiration over the length of his poems. Dr Johnson summed up the eighteenth-century view:

> His numbers are sometimes smooth and sometimes rugged; his style is sometimes concatenated and sometimes abrupt, sometimes diffusive and sometimes concise. His plan seems to have started in his mind at the present moment and his thoughts appear the effect of chance, sometimes adverse and sometimes lucky, with very little operation of judgment. He was not one of the writers whom experience improves and who, observing their own faults, become gradually correct. His poem on the *Last Day*, his first great performance, has an equability and propriety which he afterwards either never endeavoured or never attained. Many paragraphs are noble and few are mean, yet the whole is languid; the plan is too much extended and a succession of images divides and weakens the general conception.[69]

It is difficult nowadays to see what Johnson meant by 'equability' in a work with such heights and depths, and one is more inclined to agree with the verdict of Edmund Gosse:

> In spite of some coarse imagery and a good deal of needless bombast, it possesses considerable gloomy force. The final book is the best and the address of the lost soul to God, beginning –
> > Father of mercies! why from silent earth
> > Didst thou awake and curse me into birth? –
> if of dubious piety, is not equalled for poetic felicity elsewhere in Young's writings outside *Night Thoughts*.[70]

Young's contemporaries, however, found the poem wholly admirable[w] and duly paid tribute in commendatory verses. Thomas Warton of Magdalen, the future Professor of Poetry,[x] exclaimed at his heavenly gift –

> To think so greatly and describe so well[71] –

---

[w] A second edition was published at Oxford, 1713, and a third, corrected, in London, 1715, by Bettesworth, Curll & Pemberton.

[x] Father of the early Romantics, Joseph and Thomas Warton.

and Thomas Tristram of Pembroke spoke significantly of his 'towering muse' soaring –

> Where only Milton gained renown before.[72]

The poem is full of echoes of *Paradise Lost* and at the same time of foreshadowings of the *Night Thoughts*, written thirty years later. Such lines as –

> Man's is laborious happiness at best[73] –

might well be attributed to the later poem, and from the start he invoked his Muse as a 'melancholy maid',

> . . . whom dismal scenes delight,
> Frequent at tombs and in the realms of night.[74]

Young's love of gloom and churchyards did not begin with the death of his wife or the disappointment of his episcopal ambitions. Long before he was married or in orders he proclaimed his taste for the darker features of Romanticism.

Steele again gave generous and practical support with a review in the *Englishman* of 29 October, 1713, commending Young for choosing such a subject at an age when most poets devote themselves to themes of gallantry and urging the patrons of letters to encourage one whose poem had 'so many noble flights, . . . and those apparently proceeding from a well-disposed heart.' He ended:

> I shall not go on further in this gentleman's eulogium. A man is better discovered by his own sentiments than those of another concerning him. In his Dedication to the Queen he discovers a noble magnanimity in the two following paragraphs, which shall end my this day's business.[75]

It is significant of the rapid change in literary taste that the paragraphs that Steele chose for quotation – the vision of Queen Anne winging her way up to heaven – were the very ones to which later critics, from Croft onwards, have taken grave exception for gross flattery. To his own age Young's compliments seemed noble, and it was only later in the century, when the public replaced the 'great' as patrons of literature, that this convention of flattery went out of fashion. It is true that this dedication was left out of Young's collected *Works*, 1757 – but so were all his other dedications, and all his occasional poems too. To treat such omissions as 'suppression', as Croft does,[76] is to misunderstand the strictly occasional and practical character of Augustan dedications.

The dedication of *The Last Day* must have been written at least two years after the poem itself, for its references to the Queen 'composing the strifes of Europe'[77] point to early 1713. This dating is supported by a privately-printed poem, unrecorded till 1961,[y] entitled *An Epistle to the Lord Viscount Bolingbroke, sent with a Poem on the Last Day.* Though it bears no name, this four-page folio pamphlet is dated at the top 'All Souls Coll. Oxon. March 7' and the text makes it clear that the writer was the author of *The Last Day.* The imprint at the foot of the last page runs 'London, Printed in the Year 1714', but both the sense of the epistle and certain hard facts[z] indicate the date of composition as March 1713 and it was presumably sent to Bolingbroke in manuscript together with the poem. The author's purpose was to approach the Queen through her Minister for permission to dedicate *The Last Day* to Her Majesty. In this poem his 'daring Muse' had –

> . . . sung the world's last scene,
> The greatest subject, to the greatest Queen:
> In both presumptuous . . .[78]

but now he was even bolder:

> Yet would I fain (for all must tempt their fate)
> Approach great Anna, and my crime compleat.
> This you, my Lord, can grant.[79]

As Secretary of State Bolingbroke was certainly in a position to do such a favour; but, as with Lansdowne, Young had another reason, besides political influence, for choosing him as patron:

> Nor think, great Bolingbroke, the Muse so rude
> As wholly unentitled to intrude;
> It is your own I bring; what you inspired

---

[y] At Col Wilkinson's sale at Sotheby's, 27–29 March, 1961. This unique copy is now in the Oxford Collection of the Honnold Library, Claremont Colleges, California, by whose permission I am able to quote from it. (See the article by Mrs Catharine K. Firman, curator of the collection in *Notes & Queries*, June, 1963.)

[z] Bolingbroke did not receive his title till July, 1712; on 7 March, 1714 Young was not at All Souls.

And from a Muse your genius formed, required;
He dropped, I seized a theme so wondrous fair,
Which seeks in its distress your guardian care.[80]

A marginal note explains 'Mr Philips' and confirms the conjecture of earlier biographers that Young took over the idea of *The Last Day* from his schoolfellow John Philips, who was planning a poem on the same subject when he died on 15 February, 1709.[81] Philips had written *Bleinheim*, the Tories' reply to Addison's *Campaign*, at Bolingbroke's country seat at Bucklebury and their friendship was celebrated in his Alcaic *Ode ad Henricum St John*. Apparently Bolingbroke – not yet openly a Deist – had suggested the subject of the Last Judgment which Philips began and Young inherited, and evidently he approved of the latter's version since it is duly dedicated to the Queen.

Even in such a brief and businesslike *Epistle* Young showed himself the same man as the poet of the *Night Thoughts*. It opens with a picture of the poet meditating on the banks of the Isis:

> Shut from the sun, I now delight to rove
> In the still covert of the gloomy grove;
> Now stretched on grassy banks, enjoy his ray;
> Or with the windings of the river stray;
> And thank the trembling osier for a thought,
> Or by the fly or passing breeze am taught . . .
> For nothing springs, or hastens to decay,
> But has its secret lesson to convey.
> Did but the mind awhile on objects rest
> And educate the hints which they suggest,
> In shaken grass Omnipotence might nod
> And creeping insects speak the will of God.[82]

Here is the moralizing on nature, the paradoxical contrasting of extremes, the delight in gloom that became famous thirty years later. And the lines that follow are even more explicit:

> A kind of dreadful pleasure I have found
> In viewing Hell's dark realms and depths profound;
> I gazed astonished and enjoyed the fright,
> Turned pale and trembled with a strange delight;[83]

while his astronomical vision of the descent from 'beyond the limits of the starry pole' –

> To this abode of sorrow, land of night,
> Falling ten thousand thousand fathoms down
> To reach the grovelling stars and humble moon –[81]

at once brings to mind the 'space flights' of *Night IX*.

So after more than two years' frustration Young's *Last Day* was at last successfully launched through the intervention of Bolingbroke – and it is possible that Lord Lansdowne likewise interested himself in the poet's theatrical projects. At any rate Steele in his review of the poem on 29 October went on to advertise a forthcoming play too:

> I am very glad . . . to understand that Mr Young, who writ a poem on the Last Day, has now a tragedy in the theatre. It is to be supposed a man will have an eye to his first appearance in public, in all he builds upon it; and the author of the piece on the Conflagration can never descend to publish what is trivial or vicious.[85]

The phrase 'in the theatre' indicates that Young's tragedy had reached the stage of rehearsal. Yet once again, as in 1710–11, he was disappointed. On 20 November he left Oxford, but within a week he was back again.[86] Was this the crisis? Was it the same play that Cibber had turned down before, and did he again decide against it at the last moment? At all events poor Young had to wait another five years before one of his tragedies reached the stage.

Meanwhile he had shared with seven other poets the honour of having his commendatory verses on Addison's *Cato* prefixed to the seventh edition of the play,[aa] issued on 26 June, 1713[87] – fourteen lines of compliment on the 'pure immortal flame' of Addison's portrayal of his hero. Although the strictly classical style of *Cato* was just what he had criticized in the *Epistle to Lansdowne*, his admiration for the chief part was genuine and years later he told Spence:

> His love part in *Cato* was certainly given to the taste of the times; it is extremely cold and stiff. I believe he was so taken up in his chief character, which he has finished in so masterly a manner, that he neglected the under-parts.[88]

[aa] The other poets were Steele, John Hughes, Eusden, Tickell, Digby Cotes, Ambrose Philips and George Jeffreys.

Young's verses on *Cato* are of no interest in themselves, only as showing his standing as a poet and his continued friendship with the Whig writers in spite of his courting of the Tory ministers. The same may be said of another fourteen-line poem of this time. Steele's *Poetical Miscellanies . . . by the Best Hands*,[bb] published on 29 December, 1713,[89] included some uninspired couplets by Young *On Michael Angelo's Famous Piece of the Crucifixion, who is said to have stabbed a person that he might draw it more naturally* – rather a lengthy title for such a short piece. But though the verses can hardly have increased Young's reputation (he was not at his best in short poems) their appearance in a collection by the 'Best Hands' was good advertisement, especially as Steele printed Thomas Warton's complimentary verses on *The Last Day* immediately before them.

During 1713[90] the poet had been pretty regular in his residence at All Souls – three weeks absent in February at the time of Harrison's death; another three weeks in April, probably in connection with the dedication to the Queen; and one week in November, perhaps for the abortive production of his tragedy. In 1714 the pattern was the same and his only considerable absence, from mid-February to 25 March, may be attributed not only to his seeing a new poem through the press but also, perhaps, to the illness of his sister Anne. After her marriage to John Harris the couple had gone to live at his rectory at Chiddingfold, where their two children were born, Jane in January, 1709 and Richard in September, 1711.[91] Old Mrs Young joined them after the Dean's death and Edward became a regular visitor and a life-long friend of Harris. On 23 March[92] Anne died in her twenty-ninth year;[cc] and two days later her brother returned to All Souls. One month after that, on 23 April,[93] he at last graduated as Bachelor of Laws, four and a half years after his election to a Fellowship of All Souls, five and a half years after entering the College, and eleven and a half years after his matriculation at the University!

The new poem, *The Force of Religion, or Vanquished Love*, advertised as 'in the press' on 23 March,[94] was published in

---

[bb] The imprint is misprinted MDDCXIV, for 1714.

[cc] An eloquent and emotional inscription on Anne's tomb in Winchester Cathedral is probably the work of the grieving husband rather than the poetical brother. The plaque shows the Young arms.

London by Edmund Curll and did not actually appear for another two months, on 25 May, 1714.[95] The subject is Lady Jane Grey, who is pictured as passionately in love with Lord Guildford Dudley, yet preferring to sacrifice his life and her own rather than turn Roman Catholic. One might suppose that, coming out when it did, with the Queen dying and the Pretender waiting in the wings, the poem would have been construed as a warning against the return of a Popish monarch. Yet it seems to have created no stir, either political or literary. It was 'never popular',[96] said Dr Johnson; and though Curll re-issued it with title-pages claiming a second, and even a third, edition (the latter with the added sub-title 'Illustrated in the Story of Lady Jane Grey'), these re-issues were probably due to the publisher's opportunism rather than to public demand. The 'second edition', though dated 1715, was actually brought out on 28 August, 1714,[97] during the period of suspense between the Queen's death and the arrival of her Protestant successor; and the 'third edition' may have been prompted by the success of Nicholas Rowe's tragedy on the same theme,[dd] which ran for ten nights in April, 1715.[98]

The poem seems to have been taken simply as a compliment to 'female virtue', exemplified by the poet's patroness, the young Countess of Salisbury, whom the poet had somehow observed at her prayers:

> There is not in nature a more glorious scene than he enjoys, who by accident oversees a great and young and beautiful lady in her closet of devotion; instead of gaiety and noise and throng, so natural to the qualities just mentioned, all is solemn and silent and private.'[99]

No doubt the poet received the usual pecuniary reward for this dedication – unless the Countess was the 'Ladyship' to whom Young addressed a letter of complaint at her ignoring his offering[ee] – but nothing further is known of any connection

---

[dd] Rowe examined but did not use the materials gathered by the Bohemian poet Edmund Smith, who was at work on a play about Lady Jane when he purged himself to death in 1710. As 'Rag' Smith was a boon companion of John Philips, Young may have taken the hint from him, as he did with *The Last Day* of Philips.

[ee] It was more probably Lady Elizabeth Germain (Pettit, 62).

between him and the Salisbury branch of the Cecils. All that Dr
Johnson could find to say of *The Force of Religion* was, 'It is
written with elegance enough; but Jane is too heroic to be
pitied.'[100] Perhaps the Cecils agreed. Posterity at any rate has
been content to leave it at that.

CHAPTER 3

Mr Secretary Addison

1714–1719

On 1 August, 1714 Queen Anne died and under the Succession
Act of 1701 the crown passed to her nearest Protestant relation,
George Elector of Hanover, instead of her Catholic half-
brother, James the 'Old Pretender'. The situation was critical,
for many Tories still favoured the true Stuart line, while
Bolingbroke was playing both sides. The regency committee,
known as the Lords Justices, proclaimed King George and sent
hastily for the new monarch. The Elector left Hanover on 31
August, decreed Bolingbroke's dismissal at The Hague, and
entered London in triumph on 20 September.

During this seven weeks' interval Young, working with
unusual speed, produced a poem which hailed the Hanoverian
succession in loyally Whiggish couplets. His verses *On the Late
Queen's Death and His Majesty's Accession to the Throne*, came
out on 17 September,[1] the day before the new King landed at
Greenwich, and were addressed to his friend Joseph Addison in
his capacity as Secretary to the Lords Justices. Young declared
he had long wished to show his gratitude and 'please the public
by respect to you' and professed his disinterested motives in the
rather unconvincing lines:

> Know, Sir, the great esteem and honour due
> I chose that moment to profess to you,
> When sadness reigned, when fortune, so severe,
> Had warmed our bosoms to be most sincere.
> And when no motives could have force to raise
> A serious value and provoke my praise
> But such as rise above and far transcend
> Whatever glories with this world shall end.[2]

It is difficult, however, not to suspect that this proclamation of
loyalty to the new government might have been inspired by the
hope of obtaining some employment from Addison, now that
he was back in office; and in one who had recently been

complimenting the Tory ministers it looks suspiciously like time-serving. But Young had always remained on close terms with Addison, even when out of power, and his devotion to the Anglican church, exemplified in *The Force of Religion*, made him a natural supporter of the Protestant succession. He had praised his Tory patrons for their policy of peace and he repeated the same sentiments in his new poem:

> To crown the whole, great joys in greater cease
> And glorious victory is lost in peace.[3]

The late Queen's piety was given credit for Marlborough's victories:

> Argyle and Churchill but the glory share,
> While millions lie subdued by Anna's prayer:[4]

and the 'great stranger', King George, was told:

> That king's a Briton, who can govern well.[5]

Young's admiration for Addison was genuine enough and lasted all his life. Forty years or more later he described him to Spence:

> Addison was not free with superiors, rather a mute. When he began to be company, he was all so himself or he went on in a noble stream of thought and language, and all the company were fixed in hearing him. I like his *Campaign*, though so many speak against it. He was certainly a very good poet; but after all what will carry him down to posterity must be his prose writings.[6]

Steele too was remembered with grateful affection:

> Sir Richard the best-natured creature in the world; even in his worst state of health he seemed to desire nothing but to please and be pleased.[7]

But his memories of Swift were mixed. There is often a touch of prickliness in references of Young to Swift and Swift to Young that suggests that their spirits were not exactly in accord. Young could appreciate Swift's humour, as in this anecdote:

> Ambrose Philips was a neat dresser and very vain. In a conversation between him, Congreve, Swift and others the

subject ran a good while on Julius Caesar . . . Ambrose asked
what sort of a person they supposed Julius Caesar was? 'A
small man and thin-faced.' 'Now for my part,' says Ambrose,
'I should take him to have been of a lean make, pale
complexion, extremely neat in his dress and five feet seven
inches high': exactly describing himself. Swift, who
understood good breeding perfectly well and would not
interrupt anybody while speaking, let him go on and, when
he had quite done, said, 'And I, Mr Philips, should take him
to have been a plump man, just five feet five inches high, not
very neatly dressed, in a black gown with pudding sleeves.'[8]

But he added that Swift 'had a mixture of insolence in
conversation';[9] and he illustrated it with another story:

> 'I'll send you my bill of fare,' said Lord Bolingbroke, when
> trying to persuade Dr Swift to dine with him. 'Send me your
> bill of company' was Swift's answer to him.[10]

Now Swift was out and Addison was in, and one might have
supposed that Young would haunt the court to follow up his
poetical approach. But, surprisingly, he remained quietly at All
Souls and relapsed into a silence that lasted for over four years,
except for a Latin oration. He does not even seem to have left the
College when his mother died at Chiddingfold, where she was
buried on 8 December, 1714.[11] For one who later made so much of
the deaths of his loved ones it seems odd that he should not have
attended the deathbed or at least the funeral of his mother, who at
sixty-eight was the last survivor of his immediate family circle.
Judith Young is a shadowy figure,[a] but there is no reason to doubt
her son's affection. Could it be that he could not face a scene so
unbearably affecting, just as on his own deathbed he could not face
a reunion with his own forgiven son? Or had winter weather
interrupted communications between Chiddingfold and Oxford?
We do not know – indeed we know very little about his life in the
next two years, when he was more continuously in residence at
Oxford than ever before or after, engaged in the routine business
of the College but not in fruitful poetic activity. Although there are
hints that he was busy on various literary schemes, the first spate of
publication in 1713–14 was followed by another long drought.

[a] She is mentioned once in her son's letters, in a postscript of greetings to the
President of Corpus. (See Chap. 2, note g.)

At Oxford Young was remote from the literary politics of Button's Coffee-house, where the tension was rising between the Addisonian establishment and the brilliant young outsider, Alexander Pope. Young's friendship with Pope had begun some time before and a letter from Pope to Gay, dated 4 May, 1714, suggests that they had often listened to him reciting his unacted tragedies, or perhaps that dramatic poem *The Force of Religion* (of which he gave Pope a fine-paper copy, now in the Rothschild collection):

> In a word, Y——g himself has not acquired more tragic majesty in his aspect by reading his own verses than I by Homer's.[12]

Pope had signed a contract with Lintot for a translation of Homer's *Iliad* on 23 March, 1714; but the trouble was that Tickell did the same thing with Tonson two months later, on 31 May. Young thus found himself in the invidious position of being friends with both the rival translators. The crisis came in June, 1715. On the 6th the first volume of Pope's Homer[b] came out, and on the 8th Young wrote to him from Oxford:

> Just now I received the Homers, which with that you design for the public library (of which I will take the care desired) are in number but eleven, whereas the list you sent was of twelve . . . P.S. The mistake was easy, nor would I have you give yourself farther trouble. I will expect mine at leisure.[13]

Pope had entrusted Young with the distribution of the subscribers' copies in Oxford and had apparently forgotten Young's own copy, because of the extra one for the Bodleian Library.[c] In the same week Tickell's version of the *Iliad*, Book I, was published and the two translations roused a learned and furious controversy at Oxford.

To Pope's suspicious mind this confrontation by a satellite of Addison seemed a deliberate and jealous attempt to sabotage his

---

[b] It contained the first four books of the *Iliad*. Addison was among the subscribers, but not Tickell.

[c] An incomplete letter from Young to Lintot lists the twelve copies for distribution, headed by the 'Publick Library', and ends, 'Thus you see the twelve are disposed of and no one remains for myself, though Mr Pope's letter says he ordered one for myself also to be sent.' (Pettit, 4.)

great undertaking, and from there he went on to accuse
Addison himself of being the real author of the Tickell version.
As the principal witness called by him in evidence against
Addison was Young, it is better, perhaps, before we come to
Pope's account of the matter twenty years later, to consider the
contemporary facts. The first is that Tickell in his preface
disclaimed any intention of trying to outdo Pope and declared
he was publishing the one book merely as a specimen:

> I must inform the reader that when I begun this first
> book I had some thoughts of translating the whole *Iliad*,
> but had the pleasure of being diverted from that design
> by finding the work was fallen into a much abler hand. I
> would not therefore be thought to have any other view in
> publishing this small specimen . . . than to bespeak, if
> possible, the favour of the public to a translation of
> Homer's *Odysseis*, wherein I have already made some
> progress.'[14]

The second fact is that Young in a letter to his old friend on 28
June showed no shadow of suspicion that the work might really
not be Tickell's; nor was there any reason for suspicion, as the
Tickell papers show that the translation was indeed his own.
Young's letter is frank but kind, doing his best to console Tickell
for a manifest defeat and to encourage him to go on with his
Odyssey project. If Young had had any idea that the revered
Addison might be the real author, he would hardly have written
so freely:

> To be very plain, the University almost in general gives
> the preference to Pope's translation; they say his is written
> with more spirit, ornament and freedom, and has more
> the air of an original. I inclined some to compare the
> translation with the Greek; which was done and it made
> some small alteration in their opinions, but still Pope was
> their man . . . Upon the whole I affirm the performance has
> gained you much reputation, and when they compare you
> with what they should compare you, with Homer only, you
> are much admired. It has given, I know, many of the best
> judges a desire to see the Odyssey by the same hand . . . Nor
> think my opinion groundlessly swayed by my wishes, for I
> observe, as prejudice cools, you grow in favour and you are
> a better poet now than when your Homer first came down.

I am persuaded fully your design cannot but succeed here,
and it shall be my hearty desire and endeavour that it
may.[15]

There was no question of Young deserting his old friend for
Pope, nor of his betraying Pope in speaking up for Tickell, since
the latter had given up the *Iliad*. He was doing his best for both –
and he remained friends with both.

Some time between 1734 and 1736, however, Pope told
Spence the following story: Addison, when asked to read over
the draft of Pope's translation, had said he would rather be
excused, as Tickell 'had formerly, whilst at Oxford, translated
the first book of the Iliad' and now intended to publish it, so that
to read Pope's version might have an air of double-dealing.
'Soon after it was generally known that Mr Tickell was
publishing the first book of the Iliad, I met Dr Young in the
street and upon our falling into that subject the doctor
expressed a great deal of surprise at Tickell's having had such a
translation so long by him. He said it was inconceivable to him
and there must be some mistake in the matter; that he and
Tickell were so intimately acquainted at Oxford that each used
to communicate to the other whatever verses they wrote, even to
the least things; that Tickell could not have been busied in so
long a work there without his knowing something of the matter,
and that he had never heard a single word of it till on this
occasion.'[16] This surprise of Young's persuaded Pope that
Tickell could not be the author of the translation and he jumped
to the conclusion that Addison himself had written it on purpose
to spoil Pope's chances, using Tickell as his 'front'.

But all that Young had said (if we may believe the evidence of
Pope twenty years after the event) was that Tickell could surely
not have written the translation *at Oxford*, and the allegation that
Tickell had done so was based on Pope's own version of his
conversation with Addison. On this flimsy basis was built up the
case against Addison,[d] which culminated in the deadly satire on
Atticus. Whether Tickell had really commenced the translation

---

[d] Among 'th'expecting croud' in *Mr Pope's Welcome from Greece* (1720) Gay
included not only 'tragick Young' but also –

> Tickell, whose skiff (in partnership they say)
> Set forth for Greece, but foundered in the way.

(Chalmers, X, 474.)

after he ceased to reside in Oxford, and whether Addison pre-dated it in the hope of avoiding the questions of Pope, we can only conjecture. The one thing we can be sure of is that Young had no intention of harming his friends Tickell or Addison by his incautious remarks. Pope on a later occasion commented on Young's 'very good heart' and his lack of common sense, and both these characteristics were only too evident in this story. It was typical of his innocence that he should express such unguarded astonishment to one so quick to suspicion and offence as Pope; himself not prone to such feelings, it did not occur to him that he might cause trouble between his old and new friends.

Apart from the battle of the Homers his life went on tranquilly at Oxford and he played his full part in the somnolent activities of All Souls. He is listed as Bursar of Law in 1715 and Dean of Law at the end of 1716; he signed the minutes of College meetings[e] and witnessed the admission of new Fellows.[17] In June, 1716 he was chosen as one of the orators at the foundation ceremony of the new library bequeathed to the College by Colonel Christopher Codrington, who combined a Fellowship of All Souls with a military career and a rich property in the West Indies. Codrington's body was brought home from Barbados and on 19 June it was solemnly interred in the College Chapel with a Latin panegyric by the Public Orator. Two days later,[18] after the laying of the foundation-stone, another Latin speech was delivered at the celebratory dinner by Edward Young. These events were duly noted by Hearne in his diary, and when the speeches were published on 7 January, 1717, he commented sourly:

> The two speeches . . . are most wretched stuff, being neither Latin nor sense. There is a dedication at the beginning, in English, to the ladies who were present at laying the foundation stone, written by Young. But 'tis very vile and miserable.[19]

We need not take Hearne's criticism too seriously, especially in

[e] On 16 November, 1716, when four dispensations were granted in spite of the Warden's dissent, he characteristically recorded more than was discreet in the minutes and crossed out four lines with the note, 'What is lined over I registered through mistake and blot out on better consideration.'

view of Young's teasing footnote about a 'learned mole' called
Hearnius. But the *Oratio Codringtoniana*, Young's only published
work in Latin, was just a by-product of his College duties and he
himself advised against its inclusion in the booksellers' collection
of his *Works*, 1741.[20] The dedication to the Ladies of the
Codrington Family was written in English, as female education
was not supposed to rise to Latin, and in the vein of rather
kittenish playfulness that was thought suitable to a feminine
audience, a vein that later was so much appreciated in his
correspondence with Duchesses and Blue-stockings:

> When I had once determined to print, my business was to
> hide the slenderness of the performance and send it abroad
> in some importance foreign to its own worth. My art was,
> Ladies, to throw over it something like (with respect be it
> mentioned) a *hoop-petticoat*, to swell it into notice and make
> it strut in the reader's imagination beyond itself. Nothing
> then certainly so proper as a *female patronage*.[21]

While Young was vegetating in academic retirement, his
friends were rising in the world. George Bubb had been duly
elected Member of Parliament for one of his uncle's pocket
boroughs, Winchelsea, in 1715; but it was talent as well as political
pull that brought him the appointment in the same year as envoy
to Spain, where he remained till the end of 1717. Thomas Tickell
was rising as a satellite of Addison, working in his office when
the essayist was appointed Secretary to the Lord-Lieutenant of
Ireland at the end of 1714 and becoming Under-Secretary in
April, 1717 when Addison rose to the office of Secretary of State
for the Southern Department. In this capacity Tickell
corresponded officially with Bubb in Spain and on 20 July, 1717
he took the opportunity to exchange news of old friends:

> As I am in Mr Secretary Addison's office, I have a just
> pretence to offer (my) services . . . The acquaintance I had
> the good fortune and honour to have with you in the
> University makes me hope you will believe that I shall with
> perfect pleasure lay hold of every opportunity to obey your
> commands . . . Mr Cary, who is just returned to town from a
> survey of his lady's jointure in Wales, tells me that Mr
> Young has promised to pass part of the summer with him at
> Sheen . . . I beg you will give my most affectionate services
> to Mr Stubb.[22]

Bubb, Stubb, Cary, Young and Tickell – here are more than half of Hearne's nine Oxford poets associated in the same letter. Stubbes had been taken to Spain as Bubb's chaplain; and Cary had just married a rich widow with strong Parliamentary connections, who quickly launched him on a successful political career.[f]

The opportunity presented by the promotion of his friends Addison and Tickell evidently re-awoke Young's ambitions and in May he went to Chiddingfold, where he spent most of the summer, writing in the peace of the country. His letters, all dated from Haslemere (which was the post office for Chiddingfold)[g] cover a period from late May to late September, though he may have fitted in his visit to Sheen in July or August. In this rural retirement he began a poem in honour of Addison, but soon ran into difficulties owing to the modesty of his patron. On 27 June he wrote to Tickell:

> I am satisfied that the advice you give me does, as you tell me, proceed from perfect friendship . . . Since my first method was not advisable, give me leave to make you my patron . . . and I am pleased it should be a public monument of my gratitude to my two best friends. Besides, suppressing it is witholding from you and Mr Addison an excuse for showing me favour beyond my merit, when occasion offers. As to Mr A——n I have no title to his favour, what he does is of his pure goodness and you know how indulgently some construe attempts of this nature. Besides, I have had no opportunity before of complimenting the government. I flatter myself the thing is capable of receiving your favour and that, with it, it will be no enemy to my reputation in verse . . .
>
> P.S. I would willingly hear soon from you, it being late in the year; besides, an occasional thing will suffer by being

[f] Cary married Elizabeth, daughter of Anthony Sturt, MP and widow of John Jeffreys, MP, of Brecon and Sheen, on 4 January, 1717. Young witnessed her will on 23 August, 1720. She died in 1722. Her husband became Clerk to the Privy Council in 1717; MP, 1722; Master of the Mint, 1725; Lord of Trade, 1727. In 1731 he went to Ireland as Chief Secretary, becoming an Irish MP and Privy Councillor, and in 1738 Clerk of the Green Cloth. He looked after Dodington's interests in Ireland and was attacked by 'that eternal snarl' Swift at a public dinner in 1735. (H.M.C., Various, VI, 63.)

[g] Young's letter of 9 June (1707) to the President of Corpus was addressed 'Chiddingfold by Haslemere in Surrey.' (Pettit, 2.)

tardy and losing the season. As you read I desire you to
mark what you think fit to be altered . . . for on such a
subject I would be as correct as possible. The design of my
papers is to give a sketch of Mr A——n's life. I warm myself
to the undertaking by first touching on some particular
circumstances of it and fall into a professed attempt of the
whole. This is a design in which I cannot despair of your
best assistance, and a design that has carried me beyond my
former abilities. Possibly some particulars of Mr A——n's
life may occur to you which I ought not to have omitted. If
so, pray let me know them, I shall think no time or pains too
much in finishing a piece of such a subject.[23]

But the poem never appeared and it looks as if Tickell
managed to suppress the unwanted tribute in spite of all
Young's eagerness. On 19 September Young wrote that he was
'glad to hear there is anything right in my verse' and he begged
Tickell 'to mark what places Mr Addison would have altered'.[24]
He added that he hoped to find the corrections ready when he
visited London the following month. But in town he must have
met with further and final discouragement, for he was back at
All Souls in the first week of October[25] and no more was heard
of the project. A couplet in his verses on the death of Addison
suggests that the essayist's refusal of incense was due to his
humility:

> Now, and now first, we freely dare commend
> His modest worth, nor shall our praise offend.[26]

But the Secretary of State may have wished to avoid any
obligation to his importunate admirer. Though he asserted in
the *Spectator* that 'men of learning who take to business
discharge it generally with greater honesty than men of the
world'[27] and backed his opinion by appointing the poets Tickell
and Budgell as his secretaries, he may well have felt that Young's
notorious lack of discretion unfitted him for a public post.
Young had just given a typically ill-timed display of this
failing. At the end of May he had been visited at Chiddingfold
by a College friend, Thomas Newcomb, who had been the senior
undergraduate of Corpus when Young entered in 1703.[28]
Newcomb, now a cleric, was a persistent and voluminous
versifier and brought with him the manuscript of an *Ode to the*

Memory of the Countess of Berkeley, daughter of his patron the Duke of Richmond. Young gave his friend a letter of introduction to Edmund Curll, who had published *The Force of Religion* and the London edition of *The Last Day*. In August Curll brought out Newcomb's *Ode*, prefixing an extract from Young's letter as a kind of advertisement, which so upset Young that on 29 August he inserted the following notice in the *Evening Post*:

> Whereas Mr Curll the bookseller has published an Ode as recommended by Mr Young, this is to give notice that Curll was not authorized so to do by Mr Young, and that the letter prefixed to the Ode was not written by him.[29]

Whether, as has been suggested,[h] this strange statement was prompted by panic at the thought of offending Addison, who at that time was opposing the policies of the Earl of Berkeley, or simply by personal annoyance, it was a prime example of the poet's proclivity for rushing in where angels would fear to tread. Curll was thoroughly in his element in a public quarrel and knew how to derive the maximum publicity out of it, to Young's discomfiture. The first shot in his campaign was an open letter to Young in the *Weekly Journal* of 31 August:

> On the 26th of May last you sent me a poem enclosed in a cover . . . and with it two letters, one from the author and another from yourself; yours, which I have now before me, I here transcribe it verbatim: Mr Curll, I have perused the poem of the Reverend Mr Newcomb, which you receive with this, with much pleasure and I believe you will find your advantage considerable in printing it . . . The first charge against me in the advertisement is that I have published this ode as recommended by you. Pray, sir, is it not a recommendation when you acknowledge the great pleasure you received in reading it? Secondly, I was not authorized so to do by you. Nor was I prohibited by you from doing it, and I had the author's consent to what I did.[30]

This was followed up on 3 September with an advertisement for Newcomb's *Ode* in the *Evening Post*, again giving the text of Young's letter with further comments, ending 'I hereby give

[h] By Miss Helen Leek, 'The Edward Young-Curll Quarrel', *Papers of the Biographical Society of America*, lxii (1968), 321–35.

notice that any gentlemen may see the original, and likewise desire no further correspondence with Mr Young, since he is pleased to deny his own hand.'[31] Curll's next attack was made through poor Newcomb, who stated in the *Evening Post* of 7 September that he felt obliged to attest that the letter was '(as far as it had any relation to the poem)' genuine; that he stood amazed at Young's denying it, 'as well as his ungenerous treatment of me without giving me the least intimation of his unkind design'; and he thought he was not to be blamed for trying 'to make my own vindication reach as far as his scandal has done'.[32]

Newcomb was obviously unhappy about being dragged into the fray, but he was not nearly as worried as Young himself under this bombardment. A letter to Tickell on 14 September shows that his main anxiety was that the controversy might harm his reputation with Addison:

> I shall be very anxious till you are so kind to let me hear how clear I stand of the scandal of that villain in your own opinion, and whether I suffer in his, on whose good thoughts my greatest hopes rely.[33]

He announced that his vindication would appear in next Friday's *Evening Post*, said Newcomb had now recanted and begged Tickell to confirm the truth for himself by examining the original in Curll's hands. The vindication was originally sent to Jacob Tonson and the manuscript still exists in the Tonson papers in the British Museum.[i] Tickell evidently tried to dissuade his friend from publication, for on 19 September Young wrote again from Haslemere:

> On second thoughts I'm wholly of your opinion as to Curll, but supposing that the advertisement I sent Mr Tonson lay unprinted because Mr Tonson was out of town, I sent another which I fear it is too late to recall; but I shall go no farther.[34]

It was indeed too late, for it was printed in the *Evening Post* of that same day, 19 September:

---

[i] Professor George Sherburn in 'Edward Young and Book Advertising' (*Review of English Studies*, IV, 414–17) suggests that the whole quarrel was just an advertising gimmick in the manner of Pope and Voltaire. But advertising what? It did not help Young, only Curll, and the poet's letter to Tickell on 14 September shows definitely that he was no accomplice of the bookseller.

Some time in May last the Reverend Mr Newcomb read
to me an Ode on the Death of the Lady Berkeley and
desired me to direct him to a bookseller. I gave him a letter
to Mr Curll . . . My letter ran thus (viz) 'Mr Curll, I have
perused the poem . . . which you receive with this, with
(much) pleasure. (He enquired of me for a bookseller and I
directed him to you.) I believe you will find your advantage
in printing it.' The part enclosed thus ( ) is omitted in the
letter published, which omission makes the letter look like a
recommendation to the public (as Mr C. would have it), not
to the bookseller (as it was designed by me) and therefore
the whole drift of the letter being thus altered by that
omission, I denied it to be mine. If Mr C. had thought the
omission material, he should not have made it; if he
thought it not material, he should at least (when he accused
me of so foul a crime as that of denying my hand, and that
so often and so violently) have owned that there was indeed
a small alteration in the letter published from the original,
but such as he thought of no consequence to the meaning of
the whole.[35]

Curll did not bother to answer this not very convincing or
cogent explanation and there the matter rested. This storm in a
teacup is just another illustration of the poet's lack of common
sense. He should either have made a full statement of his
objections in the first place or not have taken on so unscrupulous
an adversary as Curll at all. Fortunately his friendship with
Newcomb was soon repaired, but the affair caused him much
distress and may well have put paid to his prospects with the
discreet Mr Secretary Addison.

Disappointed over his poem to Addison, Young returned to
Oxford in October, but not for long. On 13 December he left
again and was away till April, 1718.[36] On 2 May[37] he took up the
duties of College Bursar, but in mid-July he vanished once
more. The rest of 1718 is a blank, but he must have been busy
with his writing, for 1719 started with another long poem and, at
last, the performance of his tragedy.

On 10 February, 1719[38] Jacob Tonson published Young's
Paraphrase on Part of the Book of Job. The poet had been at work
on these verses since at least mid-1717, when he sent 'a piece of
Job'[39] for Tickell's criticism, and probably from mid-1716, when
he mentioned the poetry of Job in his Latin oration. Johnson

said, 'When once he had formed a new design, he then laboured it with very patient industry and . . . composed with great labour and frequent revisions.'[40] Yet the end-product seldom shows much benefit from all the revision by himself and corrections by his friends. His strong point was the rush of original ideas and striking images, not correct technique, and when he tried to tame his Pegasus the result was apt to be excessively tame. Such is the *Paraphrase on Job*, which reduces to couplets the 38th chapter of the Biblical book, containing the Almighty's rebuke to Job, which, said Young, 'is by much the finest part of the noblest and most ancient poem in the world'.[41] The dedication to the Lord Chancellor[j] admitted 'uncommon liberties', but claimed that his 'little performance' had been 'very indulgently spoken of by some whose judgment is universally allowed in writings of this nature'[42] – probably a reference to Addison, who was no longer available as a patron, having been obliged by ill health to resign nearly a year before.

Nowadays one is little inclined to agree with those judicious persons that Job has gained anything by this exercise; it is flat, rhetorical and exaggerated. Even Johnson could find no more to say for it than that as a version it was 'not unsuccessful'.[43] But Young himself was always fond of it and in 1739 he told the irrepressible Curll, 'You seem in the collection you propose to have omitted what I think may claim the first place in it, I mean a Translation from Part of Job.'[44] The public agreed and called for a second edition within a month;[45] and by a coincidence there have survived two copies of the second edition with the annotations of two fellow-poets, Isaac Watts and Aaron Hill.[k] The pious hymn-writer was enthusiastic – 'the finest descriptive poem I ever read', he wrote on the title-page. Nevertheless he tried his hand at improving several passages and sent the annotated copy to the author, who noted the emendations with interest and approval. Hill was less favourably impressed and his critical marginalia are by no means complimentary. Three times

[j] Lord Macclesfield, appointed in May, 1718; now chiefly remembered for his impeachment for corruption, but called a Maecenas by Warburton. Young confessed he did not know him, but chose him as 'one distinguished for a refined taste of the polite arts'.

[k] Watts's copy is in Dr Williams's Library among the papers of John Jones, Young's last curate, to whom it was given by the poet's son in 1766. Hill's copy is in the Bodleian.

he noted an anti-climax, three times absurdity, two poor images and a miscellaneous selection of tautology, bombast, nonsense, trifling puns and poor turns. Yet his objections are not the same as we should make now. His 'frightful anti-climax', for instance, is one of Young's favourite contrasts of the mighty and the minute, which is really rather striking and effective:

> What worlds hast thou produced, what creatures framed,
> What insects cherished, that thy God is blamed?[16]

Young in his apocalyptic vein was peculiarly liable to bathos, but to modern taste it is found rather in such passages as this:

> Who in the stupid ostrich has subdued
> A parent's care and fond inquietude?[17]

The *Paraphrase* was another of Young's ambitious failures, like *The Last Day*, that pointed the way to his eventual triumph in the *Night Thoughts*, when he had liberated himself from the inhibitions of the classic manner and couplet.

In the same month as the publication of *Job* Young wrote another short poem, but not for the public ear. It was his habit to send poetical compliments to his friends and patrons and an elegantly written manuscript of eight quatrains in the British Library is headed.*To the Lady Giffard, on the Countess of Portland's being ill of a Fever* and signed 'with the truest respect'[48] by Young. The date, February, 1718/19, has been added in another, contemporary hand. Lady Giffard was Martha,[l] sister and constant companion of the statesman and essayist Sir William Temple, after whose death in 1699 she settled at East Sheen near the estate of her other brother, Sir John Temple, Speaker of the Irish House of Commons. The Countess of Portland was her niece Jane, daughter of Sir John, twice widowed[m] and now governess to the daughters of the Prince of Wales. A clue to the origin of Young's friendship with the Temple family is afforded by a letter of November, 1719[49] to

---

[l] Her husband had died in 1662 after only thirteen days of marriage. Bridget Johnson, mother of Swift's Stella, was her waiting-woman.

[m] Jane Temple married, first, Lord Berkeley of Stratton, who died 1696; second, in 1700, Hans Willem Bentinck, the Dutch General whom William III made Earl of Portland, as his second wife. Her husband died in 1709, and her stepson was raised to *Duke* of Portland in 1716.

Lady Giffard, mentioning Mr Cary as a mutual acquaintance. Walter Cary had invited Young to Sheen in 1717, so we may take it they had met then;" and as one of the Temples was to become a key figure in the *Night Thoughts*, Cary's invitation proved of unexpected literary significance.

Lady Giffard was a formidable old lady who had written a *Character of Sir William Temple* and clashed with Swift over his editing of her brother's *Memoirs*. Though now in her eightieth year, she retained the full vigour of her mind. Years later Young told the Duchess of Portland:

> Lady Giffard, a sister of the famous Sir William Temple and a supposed partner in his works, enjoyed great health into extreme old age. Being well acquainted with her, I asked her by what means she carried such perfect health into such a length of life. She told me that her chief receipt for that great blessing was 'to be always a-doing'; in proof of which she assured me that she began to learn Spanish and made herself mistress of it after threescore.[50]

Young's verses to her made no pretension to being anything but a charming compliment and were never printed till Thomas found them in 1901:

> How does her matchless strength of mind
> Superior triumph over time!
> Whene'er she speaks, we lose her age
> And listening wonder at her prime.
> Like her and like the deathless bays
> May Portland too in winter bloom,
> Advance in years nor feel their weight,
> The Giffard of an age to come.[51]

With another six verses in the same style the poet cemented his friendship with the eldest of the Temples, who in return gave him helpful advice about his theatrical plans, now at long last about to come to fruition.

February, 1719 must, indeed, have been a very busy month for Young, with rehearsals for the first of his plays to reach the

---

" Lady Giffard had once lived at what was now the Carys' house in Sheen, where, as Tickell told Bubb, 'Sir William Temple was our friend's predecessor.' (Pettit, 18, n. 2.) The property, leased by Sir William, was afterwards acquired by John Jeffreys, first husband of Elizabeth Cary.

stage as well as the printing of his first poem for five years. On 7 March[52] his tragedy, *Busiris King of Egypt*, was produced at Drury Lane and after eight years of frustration his 'passion for the stage' was rewarded with extraordinary success. The play ran for nine nights between the opening and 15 April,[53] which meant that he enjoyed three 'author's benefits', bringing in a handsome sum of money. In those days this was a good run and *Busiris* was described as one of the 'four taking plays of this season'.[54] On 8 April it was published by Tonson[o] with a dedication to the young Duke of Newcastle, in which the author acknowledged some 'undeserved and uncommon favour' in an affair 'foreign to the theatre'[56] as well as his indulgence as Lord Chamberlain, which assured the play's success 'in a season of some danger to it'.[p] Letters in the same month from the provinces and Ireland show how far and fast the fame spread of the 'celebrated Busiris'.[57]

Busiris, in fact, was something of a sensation. But it is difficult for a modern reader to see what made it stand out from the ruck of 'heroic tragedies', full of bombastic ranting and exaggerated passions. The construction is clumsy; the ancient Egyptian setting unconvincing; and the characterization utterly one-dimensional. Even in the first flush of its success, however, it was not without its critics. Bishop Rundle of Derry regretted that he could not 'agree with the town in their applause of it';[58] old John Dennis attacked it for including 'the peculiar barbarity of our English stage',[59] a rape; and 'Corinna, a country parson's wife',[q]

[o] Isaac D'Israeli (*Miscellanies*, 238) says Lintot's account-book records a payment of eighty guineas for the copyright of *Busiris*. This is explained by the agreement of Tonson and Lintot on 16 February, 1718 to be 'equally concerned in all plays they should buy, eighteen months following the above date'. (Nichols, *Anecdotes*, VIII, 303.) Perhaps it also explains the story that Young told to Spence: 'Tonson and Lintot were both candidates for printing some work of Dr Young's. He answered both their letters in the same morning and in his hurry misdirected them. When Lintot opened that which came to him, he found it begin, "That Bernard Lintot is so great a scoundrel that &c." It must have been amusing to have seen him in his rage, he was a great sputtering fellow.' (Osborn, 848.)

[p] The Duke of Newcastle was appointed Lord Chamberlain in 1717 at the age of twenty-four. Unfortunately we know nothing of his favours to Young, theatrical or non-theatrical. In after years he was to prove far less helpful to the poet.

[q] Thomas takes her to be Mrs Elizabeth Thomas, 'Curll's Corinna' of the *Dunciad*. But though she used this pseudonym, Mrs Thomas would not have called herself 'a country parson's wife'.

went into a detailed and deadly analysis in her *Critical Remarks on the Four Taking Plays of this Season*. She complained that 'the fable . . . is so confused and incoherent that it is almost impossible to tell the plain story of it'; that 'though the scene is Egypt, the manners are all English' and 'our author, I suppose, has taken the idea of Mandane and love from some French romance, where the customs and manners of nations are never regarded'; that the character of Busiris is 'too whimsically fantastical to merit anything but a laughter . . . He rants, talks loud and bounces, but does nothing at all; and indeed the whole part might be left out of the play, though it gives its name to it'; and that 'we have no notion of opening and shutting of *scenes*, that is, removing of walls and partitions merely to show that the author's ill contrivance can find no other ways to do. Indeed, this gentleman has had so little regard to the Unity of Place that the play in that particular is all one piece of confusion'. And Corinna summed up as follows:

> To conclude, whatever real perfection of tragedy this gentleman falls short of in the fable, manners and sentiments, he has not failed in the diction, which is everywhere masterly.[60]

In her conclusion the critic touched the secret that made Young's play stand out – its language. For in his dramatic verse he freed himself from the shackles of the Heroic couplet and let his imagination go in a riot of blank verse. In this, and in his disregard for the classic unities, he went back to the Elizabethans – or at least to their successors. 'The verse and language', says Gosse, 'have the violence, with some of the tragic glow, of Lee,[r] whom Young seems to have taken for a model.'[61] As usual death and darkness brought out his best manner and the *Night Thoughts* are often foreshadowed:

> So black the night, as if no star e'er shone
> In all the wide expanse; the lightning's flash
> But shows the darkness . . .[62]

while the numerous death-scenes give ample scope for such typical reflections as these:

[r] Horace Walpole remarked of 'theatric genius' that it 'grew stark mad in Lee; whose cloak, a little the worse for wear, fell on Young; yet in both it was still a poet's cloak.'

> Vain man! to be so fond of breathing long
> And spinning out a thread of misery.
> The longer life, the greater choice of evil;
> The happiest man is but a wretched thing
> That steals poor comfort from comparison.[63]

Or:

> How like the dial's tardy-moving shade
> Day after day slides from us unperceived:
> The cunning fugitive is swift by stealth;
> Too subtle is the movement to be seen,
> Yet soon the hour is up – and we are gone.[64]

Busiris, however, after its initial success, was seldom revived in the eighteenth century and the verdict of the age, pronounced by the *Biographia Dramatica*, is unlikely to be reversed. The critic described it as 'written in a glaring, ambitious style, like that which we probably should have met with in the dramas of Statius', and he went on: 'The plot of this play we believe to be of the author's contrivance. The dialogue contains many striking beauties of sentiment and description, but is wanting in that power which not only plays with the imagination but seizes on the heart.'[65] Young's first tragedy is interesting for what it promised rather than what it achieved.[s]

During all this excitement Young was naturally too distracted to concentrate on his academic studies and on 16 March[66] his College kindly granted him a dispensation from taking his doctor's degree for a term. But he was not wholly taken up with his own affairs. He found time to write a sixteen-line commendatory poem for a volume of funeral verse by a Scottish poet, Joseph Mitchell,[t] in memory of his brother. One of the dead man's friends also contributed to *Lugubres Cantus*, which came out in July, 1719, and Young's verses welcomed the rise of a Scottish school of poets:

[s] The *Biographia* commented on Young's tragedies in general: 'The three tragedies concluded by suicides in three pairs . . . That our poet, who never wanted words, was poor in other dramatic stores is evident from this cloying repetition of the most hackneyed incident that occurs in modern tragedy.'

[t] Joseph Mitchell (1684–1738) was one of the first Scottish poets to settle in London after the Union and became known as 'Sir Robert Walpole's poet'. Improvident and churlish, he battened on the kindness of his fellow-poets, including Aaron Hill, who presented him with a drama which was performed, and even published, as his.

> Our hopes and fond endeavours now succeed,
> *Edina*'s bards begin to raise their head,
> Avouch whate'er they please to write and claim
> What we must yield – an equal right to fame.[67]

It cannot be said that this hitherto unnoticed poem of Young's will enhance his poetical reputation, but it does show the generous readiness to help and encourage other poets that was characteristic of him throughout his life. We may blame his lack of judgment, for the *Lugubres Cantus*, despite the advertisement of Young's name and those of Ambrose Philips and Isaac Watts, dropped dead from the press, but we cannot deny his goodness of heart.

Another dispensation, granted on 26 May,[68] proved unnecessary, for the poet returned to Oxford on 5 June and finally graduated LLD on 10 June, 1719,[69] five years after taking his Bachelor's degree. But he only stayed in College till the 18th,[70] when he rushed to the deathbed of Addison, a scene which he vividly described forty years later in his *Conjectures on Original Composition*. He was not actually present himself, for Addison had died on the 17th, but Tickell was there and Young claims that 'that account of it here given he gave to me before his eyes were dry'.[71] In a letter to the Duchess of Portland Young remembered:

> More than once I have heard the famous Mr Addison say
> that it was much his wish – if it so pleased God – to die in the
> summer, because then, walking abroad, he frequently
> contemplated the works of God, which gave such a serious
> turn and awful composure to the mind as best qualified it to
> enter the Divine presence.[72]

Addison did die in summer, and he died in peace. The story is well known: how on his deathbed, 'life now glimmering in the socket', he sent for his stepson, the Earl of Warwick, forcibly grasped his hand and softly said, 'See in what peace a Christian can die.'[u] And this story comes from Young.[73] For the moment, however, he contented himself with a public tribute, the *Letter to Mr Tickell, occasioned by the Death of the Right Hon. Joseph Addison, Esq.*

[u] Horace Walpole commented on Young's story, 16 May, 1759: 'Unluckily he died of brandy – nothing makes a Christian die in peace like being maudlin.' (Lewis, IX, 236.)

Strangely, considering Young's deep reverence for Addison, there is nothing to distinguish this piece from the conventional elegies that poured from the press on such occasions, nothing personal or deeply felt like the lines on Harrison. The *Letter* goes through the customary catalogue of the deceased's career and works, with the customary compliments, as on his essays:

> The various labours of his easy page,
> A chance amusement, polished half an age.[74]

It starts with an address to Tickell, which, though warm, is general, and ends by urging him on to his duties as editor of Addison's works. Such stuff compares badly with the genuine emotion that inspired Tickell's own elegy on his master:

> [He] taught us how to live; and (oh! too high
> The price for knowledge) taught us how to die.[75]

It seems curious that Young, with his devotion to Addison and his addiction to death, should let so little of his feelings come out in his *Letter to Tickell*. His account of Addison's death in prose, published in 1759, is far more vivid and moving than his memorial verses published in 1719. Could the explanation be that these verses were originally written as a tribute to the living Secretary of State and not intended to be elegiac? That in fact, apart from the introductory and concluding lines to Tickell, this was the abortive 'occasional thing' of 1717, which was to be 'a sketch of Mr Addison's life'?[76] It was certainly produced very quickly, being published on 18 July, just one month after Addison's death. The lines on his modesty, already quoted, come from the *Letter* and suggest that this same tribute had been previously refused by the living subject; and the poem, read in this light, seems much more natural and explicable. A change of tense here and there is all that is necessary; put 'sings' instead of 'sung' in the following lines and you have the punch-line of an approach to a patron instead of the climax of a memorial tribute:

> But why so large in the great writer's praise?
> More lofty subjects should my numbers raise;
> In him (illustrious rivalry!) contend
> The statesman, patriot, Christian, and the friend.
> His glory such, it borders on disgrace
> To say he sung the best of human race.[77]

CHAPTER 4

Whartoniana

On 24 March, 1720[1] Philip, Duke of Wharton, granted to Edward Young by deed poll an annuity of £100 for life. The preamble, written in what Croft describes as 'a style princely and commendable, if not legal', begins: 'Considering that the public good is advanced by the encouragement of learning and the polite arts, and being pleased therein with the attempts of Dr Young . . .'[2] Such a generous reward for a few poems would appear excessive even with such an extravagant youth as the Duke, and one suspects some more practical reason – yet the poet's only known service to his patron was six weeks' tutoring in Latin. Croft attributes the Duke's favour to family friendship, citing the alleged connection between Dean Young and the poetic Mrs Wharton; in her husband, later the Marquess of Wharton, 'Young found a patron, and in his dissolute descendant a friend and a companion.'[3] But there is no real evidence of any connection before the coaching job, which can be assigned to the late summer of 1719. Young himself is the authority, telling Spence:

> At that time of his life when the Duke's most vehement ambition was to shine in the House as an orator, he found he had almost forgotten his Latin and that it was necessary, for that view, to recover it. He therefore desired Dr Young to go to Winchendon[a] with him; where they did nothing but read Tully and talk Latin for six weeks. At the end of which the Duke talked Latin like that of Tully. The doctor . . . called him a truly prodigious genius.[4]

Philip Wharton was indeed a brilliant young man, but with the instability that sometimes goes with genius.[b] Born in December,

[a] Winchendon in Buckinghamshire was the Duke's favourite country seat.
[b] Addison, who was Secretary to Thomas Wharton as Lord-Lieutenant of Ireland, suffered from the boy's mischief. Young told Spence: 'Addison was charmed with his son . . . not only as his patron's son but for the uncommon degree of genius that appeared in him, and used to converse and walk often with

1698, he had already demonstrated his oratorical gifts in 1717, though still in his minority, in the Irish House of Lords. But Young could not have been coaching him for the *Irish* House, as he was either at All Souls or Chiddingfold throughout the period between Wharton's return from France in December, 1716 and his departure for Ireland in August, 1717;[5] and he would surely have made the distinction. On 28 January, 1718,[6] immediately after his return, Wharton was raised to a Dukedom at the age of only nineteen;[c] but he still had to wait till he came of age in December, 1719 to enter the English House of Lords. The Tully story must therefore belong to the months between Addison's death and October, 1719, when we find Young taking another tutoring post.

On 14 October Maurice Johnson, steward to the Earl of Exeter, wrote that 'Mr Young, now LLD, who wrote the *Poem on the Last Day* and *Busiris*, is taken into the Earl of Exeter's family as tutor to his Lordship's eldest son, Lord Burghley, and is going to travel with him.'[7] The young man, who had been a Commoner at Winchester, was now going up to Oxford, so that it was possible for Young to combine his tutorial duties with residence at All Souls. From 30 October to mid-May[8] he was based on his College with occasional short absences and a series of three letters to Lady Giffard, dated 22 November, 1719, 17 January and 6 February, 1720, were all sent from Oxford. Though mainly concerned with his latest theatrical plans, the last shows that he was still tutoring his lordling – and that the job was no sinecure:

> I have lately, Madam, been a little alarmed, Lord B——y
> having seen a lady in this place who has given him the

------

him. One day the little lord led him to see some of their fine running horses; there were very high gates to the fields and at the first of them his young friend fumbled in his pockets and seemed vastly concerned that he could not find the key. Addison said 'twas no matter, he could easily climb over it. As he said this, he began mounting the bars, and when he was on the very top of it, my little lord whips out his keys and sets the gate a-swinging and for some time kept that great man . . . in that ridiculous situation.' (Osborn, 835.)

 [c] Wharton was granted a Warrant on 25 July, 1717 for the creation of his Dukedom on coming of age (probably to counteract the Pretender's offer of the shadow Dukedom of Northumberland). On his return from Ireland a Patent was passed for his immediate promotion 'in regard of the good services he has performed and the great genius he has shown in the Parliament of that Kingdom'. (*Weekly Journal*, 25 Jan., 1718.)

palpitations of the heart. I design therefore soon to leave
this place and, if possible, the thoughts of the fair lady
behind us; though his Lordship is at present so true a lover
as to vow wretchedness for life, the wretchedness either of
despair, or possession, for she is much beneath his quality;
but this is a secret. To amuse his Lordship for the last ten
days I have had him about the neighbouring country to see
sights, but I was not able to find any prospect or building
sufficiently beautiful to rival Mrs —— in his thoughts.[9]

Nevertheless indiscretion was evidently warded off, for the
poor boy was still unmarried when he died in 1722, less than
four months after succeeding to the Earldom. Meanwhile the
Exeters were apparently pleased with the tutor's success in
dealing with this awkward situation and anxious to retain his
services.

The remainder of the letter, like the previous ones, was
devoted to his proposed tragedy on the Earl of Essex. Lady
Giffard was helping him with rare books and anecdotes on the
subject; on 22 November he acknowledged receipt of the *Cabala*,
a collection of Elizabethan letters including ten from Essex, and
also her help in 'dressing' his hero, adding, 'I think him the
truest Englishman I ever knew, for he is bold, generous and
indiscreet.'[10] On 17 January he discussed Banks's play on the
same subject, *The Unhappy Favourite*, and thanked his elderly
friend for her corrections,[d] especially about Lady Essex. He had
been 'so hurried of late, as men often are with doing of nothing,
that I have not found time to transcribe the second act; but as
soon as it is fair, it shall wait upon you, for after that present of a
first act all the others are a debt.'[11] On 6 February[12] he had
checked her information and was planning to use it – and that is
all we know of his abortive tragedy of Essex, as unfortunately we
have no more of his letters to Lady Giffard. The old lady did not
die for another three years, on 31 December, 1722, and Young
certainly kept up his friendship with the Temples, with calls on
the head of the family[e] and messages to all her relations. Fifteen

[d] Young had followed Banks in making Essex marry Sir Philip Sidney's
daughter, the Countess of Rutland, instead of his widow. James Ralph in 1731,
Henry Jones in 1753 and Henry Brooke in 1761 made the same mistake in
their plays on Essex.
[e] Henry Temple, son of Sir John, created Viscount Palmerston in 1723.

years later he became a relation himself by the marriage of his stepdaughter to Lady Giffard's grand-nephew.

But for the moment both the Temples and the Exeters faded out before the dazzling Duke of Wharton. To blame the poet for accepting the patronage of a young man of such extraordinary promise, just because we know of his later infamy, is a most unjust piece of hindsight. He had been wild certainly, with his 'Fleet wedding', his Pyrenean bear, his debts and his flirtation with the Jacobites;[f] but since 1717 he seemed to have sobered down. In the Irish Parliament he had won laurels both in debate and committee; he had returned to his wife and an heir was born in 1719; he lived in the seclusion of Winchendon, studying hard for his future duties as a legislator. If the government thought so well of him as to give him a Dukedom at nineteen, it requires no apology that a would-be playwright should be pleased to receive his favour. In March, 1720 he suddenly reappeared on Young's horizon with what looks like a takeover bid. In February Young was still working for the Exeters; but then, as he later told the law-courts, 'at the Duke's special instance and request he quitted the service he was in, in the Earl of Exeter's family, and thereby lost an annuity of £100.'[13] It looks as if the Exeters tried to persuade him to stay with the offer of a £100 annuity and the Duke matched it – without any tiresome tutorial duties. Young was still at Oxford on 1 March[14] and he remained there till the 17th. Then he was away for a fortnight, and during that time the Duke signed his annuity.

The 'takeover' theory would at least explain the rather excessive reward for six weeks' work; the Duke was wilful and prodigal enough to pay anything for his whims. But why was he so keen to obtain the poet's services? Since their sessions at Winchendon Wharton had entered the House of Lords and quickly made a sensation. On 4 February he delivered such a philippic against the Ministry as to cause the Secretary of State, Lord Stanhope, to burst a blood vessel. Stanhope died next day;

---

[f] In 1715, aged sixteen, Philip Wharton married secretly the daughter of an obscure General, hastening his father's death from disappointment. In 1716, sent to study in Geneva, he soon deserted, leaving a half-tamed bear for his Huguenot tutor. At Avignon the Pretender offered him the shadow Dukedom of Northumberland, and at Paris Wharton borrowed £2000 from James II's widow. In December he returned to England and was welcomed back into the Whig fold.

but fate struck back and one month later Wharton's baby heir was buried at Winchendon.[15] Was the Duke seeking consolation or distraction from the poet's company? Strangely, his new pensioner returned to Oxford on 1 April[16] for five weeks before vanishing for four months. Perhaps he had to finish the term with Lord Burghley.

In spite of an income of £14,000 a year the Duke was deep in debt and already looking for ways of raising ready money. In January[17] he persuaded his wife to give up her dowry in return for a settlement, if widowed; on 18 March[18] he mortgaged some of his lands to a wealthy citizen called Stiles,[g] whose name will recur only too often in the story of Young; and in July he went over again to Ireland to sell off the vast estates acquired by his father during his Lord-Lieutenancy. The discovery by Mr Edward Collins of this second visit to Ireland serves to explain a major puzzle in the life of Young. His *Conjectures on Original Composition* (1759) contain a famous story about Swift:

> I remember, as I and others were taking with him an evening's walk, about a mile out of Dublin, he stopped short; we passed on; but perceiving that he did not follow us, I went back and found him fixed as a statue and earnestly gazing upward at a noble elm, which in its uppermost branches was much withered and decayed. Pointing at it, he said, 'I shall be like that tree, I shall die at top.'[19]

When was Young in Dublin? The biographies, following Croft's lead, attribute his visit to the year 1717 in the train of Philip Wharton and cite a letter from Wharton to Swift, dated only 'Monday morning':

> Dear Dean, I shall embark for England tomorrow. It would be necessary for me to take leave of Lord Molesworth on many accounts; and as Young is engaged in town, I must infallibly go alone, unless your charity extends itself to favour me with your company there this morning.[20]

[g] Benjamin Haskin Stiles, brother-in-law of Sir John Eyles, Sub-Governor of the South Sea Company, made an immense fortune in the South Sea Bubble. In August, 1720 he bought Moor Park, Rickmansworth, where his landscaping efforts were satirized in Pope's *Epistle to Burlington*. (Chalmers, XII, 240.) But the Bubble cannot be blamed for Wharton's debts, as the subscription lists were not even opened till April, 1720.

Wharton did indeed leave Ireland on Tuesday, 7 January, 1718. But Swift was not in Dublin at that time and Young, who was in residence at All Souls till 12 December, 1717,[21] would hardly have crossed the Irish Channel in mid-winter for the last three weeks of his patron's stay there. Nor does it seem probable that if Wharton was really his patron at that time, there should be no further trace of his connection with the Duke for over two years.

The revelation of the Duke's second Irish visit solves these problems and fits the sequence of events neatly. On Tuesday, 5 July, 1720, Bishop Downes of Elphin wrote to Bishop Nicolson of Derry:

> Lord Wharton came over on Sunday last and has already sold all his estates in this kingdom.[22]

On Saturday, 30 July the *Weekly Journal* reported that 'on Sunday last the Duke of Wharton landed at Chester from Ireland'.[23] These two statements fix the Duke's stay in Ireland from Sunday, 3 July to Saturday 23rd at the latest; but it may have been even shorter. The newspapers were not always accurate and the Warden of All Souls wrote on 4 August[24] that the Duke had called at his Rectory of Hawarden near Chester, on 'Saturday was sennight', which works out as 23 July. Wharton therefore must have arrived in England by Friday 22nd; it was normal to land at Hoylake and proceed to Chester next day. The crossing might take 24 to 36 hours and embarkation was often held up for several days by contrary winds; so that Wharton's letter to Swift may reasonably be assigned to Monday 18 July, though he cannot actually have sailed till Wednesday or Thursday. Swift *was* in Dublin at that time, while the reference to Young now causes no difficulty or doubt; the poet had entered the Duke's service in the previous March and was absent from All Souls from 10 May till 8 September.[25] Moreover his patron went out of his way, as soon as he set foot in England again, to visit the Warden of Young's College and offer him a princely contribution towards the completion of the Codrington block of buildings. Young's visit to Dublin and Swift's famous prophecy can thus be fixed within a period of just over a fortnight in July, 1720.[h]

---

[h] The *Memoirs of Charles Lee Lewes* (1805) allege that Young congratulated Tom Elrington 'personally on the spot' on his performance of Zanga at the

Warden Gardiner's letter told how the Duke began by promising £600 and ended by signing a contract for £1183,[i] 'given with all the civility and readiness imaginable, and with the kindest expressions of his regard to the University, of whom his Grace intends shortly to receive a Doctor's degree'.[26] Bishop Tanner, at that time chaplain of the College, also reported the unexpected benefaction by 'that young nobleman of excellent parts'.[27] Neither of them mentioned Young's part in the matter, but it is difficult to believe that the Duke's sudden interest in All Souls was not prompted by his favourite Fellow. From the first obituaries the poet was credited with inspiring the benefaction, and indeed he hinted as much himself in his dedication of *The Revenge*. Wharton's motives, of course, were not purely benevolent. On 2 August Edward Harley[j] reported:

> Duke Wharton is again turned Tory, being disgusted at the Ministry for not making him Lord Lieutenant of Bucks. He has promised to be the friend of the Church and the University . . . He has already promised to give £600 to All Souls College and intends to come over to the University to have a Doctor of Laws degree conferred on him.[28]

Unfortunately the promised money was never paid. In spite of the contract the College never saw a penny till after Wharton's death and years of law – and it was the same with poor Young and his deed poll.

The Duke, in fact, was a high-class confidence trickster and the poet in his innocence an ideal victim. In September Young returned to All Souls and resigned the office of Dean of Law,[29] and it seems likely from the dedication of his next work that he spent much of the following seven months with his patron at Winchendon, hard at work together on his new tragedy – quite a different one from the half-finished drama on Essex. The new play was called *The Revenge* and the dedication to Wharton is revealing:

Theatre Royal, Aungier Street, Dublin. But *The Revenge* was not produced till 1721 and the Aungier Street theatre was not opened till 1734. Elrington played Busiris in London and, as he returned to Dublin in 1720, Young might have seen and applauded him in that role.

[i] Downes reported the Duke had sold three estates for £131,000.

[j] Edward Harley (1664–1735) was brother of Robert, Earl of Oxford; MP for Leominster, and Auditor of the Imprest.

Your Grace has been pleased to make yourself accessory to the following scenes, not only by suggesting the most beautiful incident in them, but by making all possible provision for the success of the whole. Your great delicacy of taste in compositions of this kind has so assisted this poem, and the indulgence of your nature has so endeavoured to shorten the great distance between your Grace and its author, that I have been scarce able to consider you in any other light than as one entirely devoted to these amusements and pursuing the same studies with myself.[30]

Clearly the latest enthusiasm of the versatile young genius was the drama[k] and in Young he found a boon companion. After talking of his patron's public fame, 'who made a name in senates in his minority', Young went on:

I, my Lord, whose knowledge of your Grace lies more in private life, can tell them (the world) in return of one who can animate his country retirement with a kind of pleasures sometimes unknown to persons of distinction in that scene; who can divide the longest day into a variety of polite and useful studies, . . . who can carry from his studies such a life into conversation that wine seems only an interruption of wit; who has as many subjects to talk of as proper matter on those subjects, as much wit to adorn that matter and as many languages to produce it so adorned as any of the age in which he lives. And yet so sweet his disposition that no one ever wished his abilities less.[31]

The poet then acknowledged the Duke's generosity both to the author and his College, which 'by the most graceful and engaging manner in conferring it, more than doubled its value', and continued, 'As for my own particular obligations to him . . . I beg leave to refer him to the whole future course of my life

---

[k] 'The last mental exertion', says Croft, 'of the superannuated young man in his quarters at Lerida in Spain was some scenes of a tragedy on the story of Mary Queen of Scots.' In fact it was begun much earlier; the writer of a letter (possibly Young) on 14 August, 1726 spoke of searching in his papers for 'the Act of the Duke of Wharton's tragedy of Mary Queen of Scots' and quoted four lines (printed in Walpole's *Royal and Noble Authors*). Lewis Melville's biography of Wharton assigns the play to 1722, when he was associating with Lady Mary Wortley Montagu, who wrote a prologue for it (printed in Dodsley's *Collection*, vol. I).

for my sense of them. My present fortune is his bounty, and my future his care.'[32]

Poor Young was still dazzled by the brilliance of his patron, fooled by his charm, his talents, his specious munificence and his still more specious patriotism – the Whig poet congratulated him on his enemies because 'they are the most inveterate to your Grace, whom your country pursues with her greatest dislike'.[33] But can Young, in his country retirement, have been entirely unaware of the vicious side of Wharton's character, the depraved tastes that earned him the presidency of the Hell-fire Club?[l] So notorious did the Club's activities become that it was suppressed by royal decree on 28 April, 1721 – just ten days after the first performance of *The Revenge*, while Young's encomiastic dedication was published with the play on the very next day, 29 April.[34] Pope remarked that Young's want of common sense made him pass 'a foolish youth, the sport of peers and poets',[35] and Croft hinted that 'when first Young found himself independent and his own master at All Souls, he was not the ornament to religion and morality which he afterwards became.'[36] But the only story of actual misbehaviour on the poet's part does not involve the Duke, of whom nothing wilder is recorded in his relations with Young than that 'when the doctor was very deeply engaged in writing one of his tragedies, that noblemen . . . procured a human skull[m] and fixed a candle in it and gave it to the doctor as the most proper lamp for him to write tragedy by.'[37]

The worst charges against the poet are to be found, surprisingly, in the *Memoir of the Revd Joshua Parry, Nonconformist Minister of Cirencester*, who cited the authority of Lord Bathurst for these stories:

[l] In the Lords' debate on the Hell-fire Club Wharton denied that he was a patron of blasphemy and quoted texts from his family bible. Young attacked the 'Tartarian Club' in his fourth satire (1725), but his target was 'Gehenno', whom Horace Walpole identified as Sir William Stanhope, brother of Lord Chesterfield, known as 'Hell-fire Stanhope'.

[m] Young himself denied this story; yet Spence retained the anecdote, which has become so firmly established in tradition that it is to be found in several modern reference books – applied to the *Night Thoughts*! Spence's friend, Dr Glocester Ridley, 'remembered a report current at Oxford that, when Young was composing, he would shut up his windows and sit by a lamp even at midday, nay, that skulls, bones and instruments of death were among the ornaments of his study.' (Osborn, 847, note.)

Of Dr Young it is related . . . that he was, in the early part
of his life, a man of very lax morals. The old inhabitants of
Fairford in Gloucestershire formerly did not scruple to say
that Dr Young was more than once seen to run naked about
the streets with some of the Hillsborough family, who were
then proprietors of the great house there and were the
companions of his revels." On another occasion some of his
friends, riding near that place, were alarmed with the cries
of a person in distress within a tilted waggon; they to their
astonishment found the sufferer to be Dr Young, whom
the waggoner was beating and, being asked the reason
of this outrage, replied, 'The scoundrel would kiss my
grandmother.'[38]

If this is true, it suggests high spirits rather than vice, a drunken
frolic perhaps, for Young undoubtedly appreciated the bottle.
In the *Epistle to Lansdowne* he wrote:

> How often have I seen the generous bowl
> With pleasing force unlock a secret soul
> And steal a truth, which every sober hour
> (The prose of life) had kept within her power.[39]

He loved the after-dinner session of sparkling conversation
with such companions as Wharton, where wine seemed 'only an
interruption of wit',[40] or Dodington, when he was

> Charmed with his flowing Burgundy and wit.[41]

If he sometimes got carried away into follies, as at Fairford, his
escapades, though wild, sound harmless enough – the result
perhaps of a bet that he would run naked down the street or kiss
someone's grandmother. This is hardly 'Hell-fire' style, and if
Wharton indulged in any frolics at Winchendon they were
probably no worse than these.

The result, at any rate, of Young's association with Wharton
was the first of his works that really deserves the attention of

---

" Trevor Hill of Hillsborough, Co. Down, created Viscount Hillsborough in
1717, frequently figures, together with Wharton, in the horse-racing items in the
newspapers. Hearne (VIII, 406) wrote of him on 30 July, 1725: 'A very
handsome man, and is one of those wanton immodest gentlemen that a year or
two ago used to ride naked and made strange work with young women and
others, of which we had accounts in the public prints, till at last a carter
happened to whip some of them, as they were thus naked, at a place in
Buckinghamshire, after which we heard no more of their pranks.'

posterity, *The Revenge.*° To his contemporaries he was already
one of 'our most considerable English poets',[42] as listed in Giles
Jacob's *Poetical Register* in 1720; one of the contenders for the
laurel on the death of Rowe in 1719, according to the satirical
verses of the Duke of Buckingham:

> Trapp, Young and Vanbrugh expected reward
> For some things writ well; but Apollo declared
> That one was too flat, the other too rough,
> And the third sure already had places enough.[43]

But none of his works so far would distinguish him today from
the Augustan ruck of Trapps and Tickells. Always a slow starter,
he did not produce a memorable work till he was nearly forty.
On 18 April, 1721[44] his second tragedy was performed at Drury
Lane and, though it only ran for six nights compared to *Busiris's*
nine, it held the stage for over a hundred years.

The Revenge is a play with a strong superficial resemblance to
Othello. It is a drama of jealousy and there is a Moor (Zanga),
though in this case he is the instigator, not the victim, of the fatal
plot. But though Young, with his admiration for Shakespeare,
no doubt had *Othello* in mind, his plot was based on an actual
murder committed in Spain a few years before. The story was
told by John Hughes in the *Guardian* in 1713;[45] all the
circumstances were, as the *Biographia Dramatica* pointed out, 'so
exactly followed by Dr Young as to leave no doubt but that he
was led to the story of this play by the perusal of that
narrative'.[46] In any case his contemporaries found that, even if
he owed something to Shakespeare, he had in some respects
improved on *Othello.* The article in the *Biographia*, attributed to
George Steevens, the editor of Shakespeare, considered Zanga's
motives more justly and nobly founded and Alonzo's jealousy
better grounded and longer resisted than Othello's; and he
assigned to this piece 'a place in the very front rank of our

---

° On the Duke's side the influence of Young may have been responsible for his
ode on *The Fear of Death*, posthumously published in 1739, folio. Addressed to
the 'Sovereign Queen of awful Night', it expresses one of Young's favourite
themes of the *Night Thoughts* in the lines:
> We dread we know not what, we fear we know not why,
> Our cheated fancy shrinks, nor sees to die
> Is but to slumber into immortality.
>   (T. Cibber, *Lives of the Poets*, 1753, IV, 290.)

dramatic writings'.[47] Another editor of Shakespeare, Dr Johnson, also acquitted Young of imitation:

> *The Revenge* approaches much nearer (than *Busiris*) to human practices and manners and therefore keeps possession of the stage; the first design seems suggested by *Othello*; but the reflections, the incidents and the diction are original. The moral observations are so introduced and so expressed as to have all the novelty that can be required.[48]

There is no doubt that *The Revenge* is an excellent example of its genre, far superior to *Busiris* in every way although less successful on its first appearance. The characters are more rounded and convincing and the progress of the action is more natural, with variety and even suspense, while the language is more flowing and consistently eloquent, avoiding his unlucky tendency to bathos. As in *Busiris*, there are several soliloquies on the disappointments of life and the advantages of death that anticipate the *Nights*, such as:

> None here are happy but the very fool
> Or very wise; and I want fool enough
> To smile in vanities and hug a shadow;
> Nor have I wisdom to elaborate
> An artificial happiness from pains;
> E'en joys are pains, because they cannot last . . .
> How many lift the head, look gay and smile
> Against their conscience? And this we know;
> Yet, knowing, disbelieve and try again
> What we have tried and struggle with conviction.
> Each new experience gives the former credit,
> And reverend grey Threescore is but a voucher
> That Thirty told us true . . .[49]

or Alonzo's declamation in the fourth act:

> Day buries day; month, month; and year the year.
> Our life is but a chain of many deaths.
> Can then death's self be feared? Our life much rather.
> Life is the desert, life the solitude;[P]
> Death joins us to the great majority.[50]

In *The Revenge* these speeches fit into the action and carry it

---

[P] Cf. *Night Thoughts*, I, 115:
> This is the desart, this the solitude.

along. Nor is it only in the sententious passages that Young
shines; the dialogue flows easily and avoids excessive declamation. In the scene where Zanga craftily plays on Alonzo's
suspicions, which he has aroused with a forged letter to his
master's bride from her former betrothed, the matter-of-fact
tone of the hypocritical comforter is artfully contrasted with the
agitated heroics of the lover. It is too long to quote, but it is easy
to see how effective it could be in the hands of a skilful actor.
The author for once showed real stage sense and gave the
players big opportunities in the leading parts, especially that of
Zanga, which became a favourite with the stars of the theatre for
more than a century. After its first comparatively cool reception
The Revenge gradually established its place in the theatrical
repertory. In 1744,[51] thanks no doubt to the success of the *Night
Thoughts*, it actually had a longer run than at its first appearance,
twelve nights in all, while in 1752[52] both the patent theatres had
rival productions running at the same time. But its popularity
did not end with the eighteenth century. Byron chose the speech
of Zanga for declamation at Harrow in 1806;[53] in the same year
Washington Irving was 'completely overpowered'[54] by Kemble's
acting of the part; Hazlitt reviewed Kean's Zanga in 1815,
Maywood's in 1817 and Macready's in 1820;[55] while Mitford
remembered in 1833[56] seeing 'more than one of our noble tragic
actors' in the part. Zanga had become a sort of test role for the
stars, like Hamlet today, and though the 'heroic' style is out of
fashion nowadays, perhaps a star could revive it.

When the play was published, the author received only £50
for the copyright[57] – less than for *Busiris*.[q] It is to be hoped that
Wharton rewarded the dedication generously, though perhaps
he had done enough if, as alleged, he took the whole house on
the poet's benefit night. Such a prodigal gesture would be
characteristic of the Duke, who was supposed once to have given
Young £2000 for a poem;[r] certainly he preferred to squander

[q] Joseph Warton commented, 'To drive a bargain was not the talent of this
generous and disinterested man.' (*Essay on Pope*, II, 471.)

[r] The anecdote, told to Spence by Rawlinson, was denied by Young and is, as it
stands, impossible: 'A little after Dr Young had published his *Universal Passion*,
the Duke of Wharton made him a present of £2000 for it. When a friend of the
Duke's . . . cried out on hearing it, "What! Two thousand pounds for a poem?"
the Duke smiled and said 'twas the best bargain he ever made in his life, for 'twas
fairly worth four thousand.' (Osborn, 846.) By 1725, when the *Universal Passion*

his money rather than pay his debts. The poet returned in due course to his College[s] and by November[58] he was again acting as Bursar of Law. But he had not yet lost touch with, or faith in, his patron, as is shown by the odd events of March, 1722.

At the end of 1721 political observers reported that the erratic Duke had made another of his switches of allegiance. On 6 December Dr William Stratford noted that Wharton had 'left the Tories and returned to those from whom he came, and kissed the King's hand yesterday'.[59] His betrayal of the Tories caused an incident in the House of Lords which led to unexpected consequences for Young. The details are again drawn from Parry's reminiscences of Lord Bathurst, who was a firm Tory:

> One day, after a debate of more than usual vivacity, while various peers were waiting for their carriages in the lobby of the House of Lords, it happened that the Duke and Lord Bathurst stood near each other by the fire. The Duke, referring to the past debate, . . . quoted to Lord Bathurst certain lines from Ovid's *Metamorphoses* . . .
>
> 'My dear Duke,' replied Lord Bathurst, 'Your Grace is always quoting lines from the voluptuous Ovid, who seems to be your favourite author. I can refer you to a sentiment perfectly applicable to the present occasion from an author much superior to Ovid!'
>
> He then quoted a couplet from Virgil, which the Duke professed not to understand.
>
> 'Then I will translate them for you,' said Lord Bathurst, taking hold of the Duke's velvet coat:
>
> > 'This wretch deceives his friends, betrays the state,
> > To dress in velvet and to eat on plate.'
>
> 'I wish,' said the Duke with an air of assumed coolness, 'that I was always able to dress in velvet and to eat on plate.'
>
> 'What! does that translation dissatisfy your Grace? Then I will give you another, which may be more applicable:

---

came out, Young had long broken with the Duke – who by then had only £2000 a year left for himself (Master of the Rolls' judgement, 29 August, 1723). Perhaps the 'poem' in question was really *The Revenge*.

[s] The All Souls Buttery Books are missing from the end of 1720 to the start of 1725. The Steward's weekly summaries are less revealing, but indicate absence for most of the period except for the annual 'Gaudy' on All Souls Day.

This wretch deceives his friends, betrays the state,
Yet pawns his velvet coat and sells his plate!'

On receiving this bitter sarcasm from Lord Bathurst the
Duke turned away without reply and immediately quitted
the lobby of the House. He, however, deeply felt the retort
and did not suffer his resentment to sleep. The general
election (of March, 1722) was approaching, and he gave a
thousand pounds to the celebrated Dr Young to go to
Cirencester to oppose the candidate supported by Lord
Bathurst.[60]

Young's excursion into active politics has been known ever
since Croft quoted 'second Atkyns, case 136, Stiles versus the
Attorney-General, 14 March, 1740'. From this it appeared that
the Duke had given Young a bond dated 15 March, 1721 (i.e.
1722) 'conditioned for the payment of £600 in consideration of
his taking several journeys and being at great expenses in order
to be chosen a Member of the House of Commons at the desire
of the said Duke, and in consideration of his giving up two
livings of £200 and £400 per annum value, in the gift of All
Souls College, on the promises made by the said Duke of serving
and advancing him in the world.'[61] The livings can only have
been expectations, as Young had not yet taken orders and the
minutes of All Souls show no important presentations till the
Rectory of Buckland in December, 1723.[62] Two more Rectories,
however, followed within the next year, so that Young might
reasonably have anticipated an early presentation if he took
orders at this time. But he seems to have preferred to remain
a layman, trusting to the Duke, who now put him up for
Parliament. Why? Young's was not a practical mind at all, he had
no head for business and he was utterly unfitted for that hard-
headed assembly. His eccentricities and absence of mind were
common jokes among his friends, who agreed that for all the
brilliance of his wit he was conspicuously lacking in common
sense. The Duke himself pointed this out in a poetical list of
impossibilities called *Wharton's Whens*:

When poet Young for judgment we admire . . .[63]

Yet he not only picked him as his candidate but promised him
financial backing. Still odder, Young stood for Cirencester, a
safe Tory seat where the Duke had no patronage or influence;

and in spite of all his expenses there is no sign of a poll in that constituency in 1722.[1]

The memoirs of Parry provide a plausible explanation. Benjamin Bathurst, the leading Tory candidate at Cirencester, was the brother of the Duke's enemy, which explains the invasion of that constituency. Wharton needed a Whig candidate quickly and picked on Young, possibly because a more experienced politician would never have undertaken to contest such a Tory stronghold. At any rate Young made his several journeys and paid his great expenses in his campaign for election – but then why did he not carry it through to the poll? Parry gives an answer that, if true, is characteristic of Young's unworldliness:

> The electors, conformably to their established custom of reserving their votes for a third man, came forward on his behalf in such numbers as to promise a favourable issue to the contest. Lord Bathurst was alarmed, and being a somewhat better politician than his opponent, invited Dr Young, whom he well knew, to dine at his house with a select party of friends, of whom the candidate supported by Lord Bathurst was one. The unsuspecting poet fell into the snare and accepted the invitation; but in the midst of his conviviality a message was brought to him that his party, convinced by his dining with Lord Bathurst that he had formed a coalition with his opponent, were violently incensed against him and that they had assembled in great numbers around the park gate, threatening to tear him in pieces as soon as he should make his appearance. In reality Lord Bathurst was obliged to provide a large number of his own adherents in order to escort the Doctor to his inn and protect him against his friends. These friends, however, were not so easily appeased. They afterwards broke by violence into the chamber in which Dr Young was in bed and, headed by a cooper armed with his adze, so furiously menaced the apostate that, according to the humorous relation of Lord Bathurst, 'I was obliged,' said Dr Young, 'to kneel in my shirt and use all the rhetoric of which I was master, to save my life. Oh, that cooper!'[64]

[1] W. R. Williams, *Parliamentary History of the County of Gloucester*, states that there was a contested election, followed by a petition; but the History of Parliament Trust informs me that this took place in 1624, not 1724. The newspapers of the day report no poll for Cirencester.

It was at this stage, one supposes, that he applied to the Duke
for the repayment of his expenses, since he had now no hope
of recouping himself in other ways. The Duke's bond for £600
was dated 15 March, 1722,[65] just a week before the election. But
Young may by then have become a little disillusioned about
Wharton's promises, for up to now he had not received a penny
of his annuity. He must have begun to press for payment; but
the Duke always preferred to promise than pay and managed to
cajole the poet into accepting the mirage of greater prospects in
place of the substance of his legal claims. On 10 July, 1722[66] an
indenture was signed between Wharton and Young under
which the Duke acknowledged owing his protégé a total of £350
and compensation for inducing him to give up his post with
the Exeters. In return for Young's releasing him from these
obligations he contracted to grant the poet a second annuity of
£100, making £200 a year in all. Two days later[67] Wharton
charged the lands held in trust by Mr Justice Denton with the
payment, but before the conveyances could be executed, the
Duke's other creditors were suing him – and poor Young was
still fighting for his annuities twenty years later. The suit was
brought on 5 March, 1723[68] by no less than fifteen 'judgment
creditors', who requested that the trust-lands should be sold to
pay for the Duke's debts, and among these creditors is found
'your orator Edward Young by a judgment for £1200', i.e. the
penalty of double the bond for his election expenses in case of
non-payment. The case was known as 'Stiles v. Wharton Dux'
from the major creditor, who was owed no less than £42,000!
Indeed the scale of Wharton's extravagances was almost
incredible, considering his enormous income – his total debts by
the time of his death came to £235,093.3s.4d.! Amid such sums
poor Young's claims did not carry much weight. On 29 August,
1723[69] the Master of the Rolls ordered the sale of the Duke's
trust-estates to pay the creditors in order of priority. But the
process of selling the lands and ascertaining the priority of all
the claims meant that the case dragged on for years with no
tangible benefit to the poet.

It is obvious from Young's suing the Duke that he had realized
the worthlessness of his patronage and only hoped to salvage
something from the wreck of his brilliant dreams. From the time
of the second annuity in July, 1722 we hear no more of his

connection with Wharton except in the legal context, and
though there were still three years to go before the 'scorn and
wonder' of the age finally retired to the Continent and the cause
of the Pretender, it appears that the poet's association with him
ended here. With his high hopes shattered, he turned to an old
friend as his new patron, none other than his fellow-poet of
Oxford days, George Bubb, who had now succeeded to the
name, estates and political power of his uncle Dodington." On
the brink of forty he had to face the fact that his career so far
had been a blind alley. For all his poetical and dramatic repute
he was still a dependent. He began to think seriously about
following in his father's footsteps.

" Bubb's uncle died in 1720. His heir assumed his name and dropped his own,
signing himself from that time simply as 'George Dodington', though he was
generally called Bubb Dodington. He became Lord-Lieutenant of Somerset in
1721 and MP for Bridgewater from 1722 to 1754.

CHAPTER 5

A Fool at Forty

1722–1726

On 30 August, 1722 King George held a great military review on
Salisbury Plain, an occasion which inspired one of the gossipy
verse epistles of a young New College man called Christopher
Pitt, who spent his life as a country parson on the family living of
Pimperne in Dorset, near to the Dodington estate at Eastbury.
There he devoted himself to poetry, his most ambitious efforts
being translations of Vida's *Art of Poetry* and Virgil's *Aeneid*;[a] but
he also composed a number of amiable familiar poems to his
friends. Among these is an *Epistle to Dr Young, at Eastbury, on the
Review at Sarum*, 1722:

> While with your Dodington retired you sit,
> Charmed with his flowing Burgundy and wit,
> By turns relieving with the circling draught
> Each pause of chat and interval of thought,
> Or through the well-glazed tube, from business freed,
> Draw the rich spirit of the Indian weed,
> Or bid your eyes o'er Vanbrugh's models roam
> And trace in miniature the future dome, . . .
> Or, lost in thought, contemplative you rove
> Through opening vistas and the shady grove, . . .
> There if you exercise your tragic rage
> To bring some hero on the British stage, . . .
> From fabled worthies call thy Muse to sing
> Of real wonders and Britannia's King.[1]

Fortunately, perhaps, Young did not respond to his friend's call
to celebrate the 'godlike figure' of George I, although Pitt
declared it to be:

> A theme that asks a Virgil or a Young.[2]

---

[a] Young enlisted his help for Pope's *Odyssey*. Pitt wrote to Spence, 18 July,
1726: 'Mr Pope has used so little of the 23rd *Odyssey* that I gave Dr Young, that
if I put it in among the rest I shall hardly incur any danger of the penalty
concerning the patent.' (Sherburn, II, 382.)

The poem is interesting for its description of the poet at ease in the home of his old friend and new patron, drinking his port and smoking, discussing the plans for the colossal mansion at Eastbury, or wandering through the woods, deep in thought. Richard Cumberland, the playwright, asserted in his *Memoirs*[3] that *The Revenge* was written at Eastbury. But he must have confused it with Young's next tragedy, *The Brothers*, in which we know that Dodington took a keen and critical interest. After the collapse of his expectations from the Duke of Wharton Young was very anxious for a big success with his new play. On 2 May, 1723[b] he wrote to Pope, asking a favour that tradition alleges to have been a prologue – 'that instance of your friendship . . . I'm very sensible I can receive from no one but yourself'.[4] Pope was evidently reluctant, as this was Young's second application; 'I should not urge this thing so much,' he wrote, 'but for very particular reasons; nor can you be at a loss to conceive how a *trifle of this nature* may be of serious moment to me.'[5] If the request was indeed for a prologue, it seems that Pope was too busy with his translation of the *Odyssey* to oblige his friend, for when the play was eventually produced, it was without the advantage of a prologue by Pope. Lady Mary Wortley Montagu[c] on the other hand was almost too helpful, for the author wrote on 'Friday noon':

> Madame, – The more I think of your criticisms, the more I feel the just force of them. I will alter which are alterable; those that are not I beg you to make a secret of and to make an experiment on the sagacity of the town, which I think may possibly overlook what you have observed; for the players and Mr Dodington, neither of whom were backward in finding fault or careless in attention, took no notice of the flaw in Demetrius' honour or Erixene's conduct, and I would fain have their blindness continue till my business is done. The players are fond of it and, as it has been said on a point of a little more importance, *si populus vult decipi, decipiatur.*[6]

[b] The letter does not give the year; but Sherburn (II, 171) assigns it to 1723 because Pope used the back for a draft of his *Odyssey*, Book III.
[c] Lady Mary's son was tutored by the Rev. John Forster, who, according to Nichols (*Anecdotes*, IV, 26), 'was introduced into the family of Mr Montagu by the celebrated Dr Young'.

Though this letter is not dated, it must belong to the autumn of 1723 since the play was already in the hands of the actors, and Young was evidently in a hurry. Lady Mary had suggested an advantageous alteration in the fifth act,[d] and he proposed to wait on her with the revised version in three days, adding, 'I have more depending on the success of this particular piece than your Ladyship imagines.'[7]

On the last day of the year the literary gossip column of the *Universal Journal* reported that despite the cold reception of new plays by the 'ill-judging Vulgar' a new tragedy by Gay was to be produced in a few days, 'after which a new play of Dr Young's ... will immediately be put into rehearsal'.[8] Gay's *Captives* duly appeared at Drury Lane on 15 January, 1724 and ran for seven nights; and Young's *Brothers* was then taken in hand, as we learn from another report in the *Universal Journal*, dated from Button's Coffee-house, 8 February:

> For these two hours past the conversation has been turned upon *The Brothers*, a new tragedy of Dr Young's, now rehearsing. It is impossible to guess at the success of it, so very uncertain is the judgement of the Town; and as for my part, I have very little hopes of it; there's never a ghost, never a flying dragon, nor so much as one poor windmill throughout the whole play. I am surprised the Doctor should be so little acquainted with the prevailing humour of the Town; the poor man confides wholly in strong masculine sense, with which his play abounds, and I believe him as old-fashioned as to think himself writing in good Queen Bess's days, when such a fellow as Shakespeare could be relished ... Horatio did not hesitate to say he thought it (the brothers' trial) as fine a written scene as had appeared on the stage for these many years ... and Mr Young seems to depend very much upon that scene. But doubtless he'll be mistaken, for I am credibly informed the manager of the New House has formed a resolution that it shall be acted to an empty pit and boxes, there being a new entertainment in grotesque characters getting up there, entitled *The Cruel Uncle, or The Children in the Wood*, so very artfully contrived that at the instant Perseus and Demetrius

---

[d] Halsband (II, 35, n. 2) says her most important change was to allow the heroine to descend to the hero's dungeon instead of passively awaiting news of his fate.

are entering upon that scene, ... Harlequin and Scaramouch will be making their appearance at the other house. The consequence of this is easily foreseen; Booth and Cibber will preach to bare walls, whilst Lanyon and Dupre dance before a full audience.[9]

Pantomimes had become the rage and were the speciality of John Rich, who had opened the new theatre at Lincoln's Inn Fields in 1714 as a rival to Drury Lane. Young was thus the victim of the war between the theatres and evidently, in spite of such stars as Booth, Cibber and Mrs Oldfield, Rich's campaign was successful, for later that month the poor poet wrote again to Lady Mary:

> A great cold and a little intemperance has given me such a face as I am ashamed to show, though I much want to talk with your Ladyship. For my theatrical measures are broken; *Mariamne* brought its author above £1500, *The Captives* above £1000, and *Edwin*, now in rehearsal, has already before acting brought its author above £1000.[c] Mine, when acted, will not more than pay for the paper on which it is written ... I am determined to suppress my play for this season at least.[10]

The *Universal Journal* confirms that Young quickly carried out his decision, in its issue of 25 March:

> Mr Young, I am informed, has taken the play from the house and put it off till next winter. Several will doubtless be surprised at a poet's deferring his benefit for near a twelvemonth and some I know blame him for it; but for my particular part I very much applaud his conduct. Who that had any talent for dramatic poetry would venture a good tragedy at a time when nothing but farce and puppet show will go down with the town? ... What I am most surprised at is that the author should talk of venturing his play amongst us next winter, as if we were to recover our senses by that time.[11]

[c] *Mariamne* by Elijah Fenton was revived on 29 January, 1724 after a run of 16 nights in 1723; Gay's *Captives* ran 7 nights from 15 January; *Edwin* by George Jeffreys opened on 24 February at Lincoln's Inn Fields. This letter can therefore be dated mid-February. But the financial success of Jeffreys's 'theatrical measures' is puzzling. *Edwin* only ran for four nights and his dedication to the printed play confessed that 'it happened to be at a conjecture not the most favourable for acting tragedies'.

Perhaps Young did understand that his worldly hopes were now ruined, for it was after this disappointment that he began the first positive moves towards the refuge of the Church. He now turned to his old friend Thomas Tickell, who had crossed to Ireland and was appointed Secretary to the Lords Justices of that kingdom on 4 May, 1724.[12] The new Lord-Lieutenant was Lord Carteret and Young hoped much from his friend's influence with this powerful and cultured nobleman, who now had all the extensive patronage of the Church of Ireland at his disposal. The Protestant establishment there offered the readiest pickings for impatient clerics, with plenty of Bishoprics and Deaneries and no great need to linger too long among their Catholic flock. Young, starting late and taking orders from motives of career rather than vocation, was anxious to ensure a flying start and looked to Ireland for this. Nor were his hopes unreasonable, for Tickell spoke to Carteret's secretary, Thomas Clutterbuck, who wrote to Young on 20 June:

> If your resolution to take orders is fixed and you are determined to do it, I have leave from my Lord Carteret to tell you that he will immediately make you one of his chaplains and provide for you, as soon as he has taken care of three persons who are now upon his hands.[13]

Now it was only a question of time, or timing, for the poet. He still hoped to produce the play in the autumn and complete a projected satire before undertaking the more austere life of a cleric. But armed with Carteret's promise and a friend at court in Tickell, he was too confident and consequently too dilatory in taking the final plunge. Throughout the summer and autumn he was continually protesting his determination to take orders and continually putting it off, until his patron's patience was exhausted. The sorry story is illustrated by the slowly rising flood of letters to Tickell, gradually becoming more frantic as his rosy hopes faded. Once again his lack of judgement spoiled his chances.

The first of these letters was sent from Haslemere in August. Tickell was evidently getting anxious, but his friend was not yet convinced of the urgency of ordination:

> What you take for irresolution in me is only delay. I'm absolutely determined to take orders, but had reasons for

> deferring it to the spring. However, on hearing again from you I shall take orders immediately, if that delay in the least hurts my expectations from my Lord Carteret . . . P.S. What I apprehend is that his Lordship may construe my delay a disrespect to his favour.[14]

It seems highly probable that this was just what His Lordship did feel, and he was not used to being treated in such an offhand manner. Yet a month later, on 20 September, Young was still down at Chiddingfold and immersed in his literary projects, including what was to prove the second of his memorable works, the series of satires on *The Universal Passion*:

> I am particularly unhappy that the sea is between us at this time, for though I hope you will not read the satire I send without a pen in your hand, yet it must have received greater advantage if I was with you too. In this work I think I have more than a common title to your assistance, since the first hint of it came from you. 'Tis my last and I'd have it as blameless as I and my friends can make it . . . If Swift and you converse, I should be glad if he saw the satire too.[15]

By 10 October the poet had got as far on his Surrey round as Sheen, where he was staying for about a month with Walter Cary. By that time the Lord-Lieutenant had left for Ireland and Young had to try and justify his delay:

> There has been yet no ordination since the grant of my Lord's favour to me. I hope therefore my not being yet in orders will not be imputed to me as a neglect . . . I had thoughts of deferring orders till the spring on account of affairs I was to make up with D. Wharton, and a subscription which I thought would run better before I was entered into another way; but I have thought better of it . . . If I can get a private ordination, I will; if not, there is a public one at Xmas which I will not omit.[16]

Ten days later, still from Cary's, he was again importuning Tickell and enclosing a letter for Clutterbuck too. He was now really worried, declaring that he had consulted Clutterbuck before deferring orders and pleading for special indulgence because of the 'very great injury I at present suffer from the Duke'.[17] In his clumsy way he had managed to lose the favour of his new patron before he had been able to reap any benefit from the illusory bounty of his former protector.

Desperately he prepared a statement setting out 'the whole affair in one view', but as in his quarrel with Curll, his full explanation came too late:

> I did not take orders immediately, 1st because I had three before me and so I thought there was no haste; 2ly for the reasons . . . relating to the Duke of Wharton . . . I durst not defer orders without consulting Mr Clutterbuck, who pleased to write that 'In that I could not do amiss, for that he was persuaded my Lord's promise would stand good' . . . If indeed my Lord imagined I set so little and unjust a value on it that I meant it only as a refuge in case I could not succeed elsewhere, 'twas most deservedly withdrawn. But that this was by no means the case I call you to witness . . . Had I other patronages in view I should not probably have spent that very interval of time in forming addresses to my Lord Carteret as I actually did: one in verse as a dedication of a satire I am about to print, which Mr Clutterbuck thought as well let alone, for that my Lord was not fond of poetical compliments; another in prose craving his Lordship's patronage to a piece of divinity which I have finished by me; but Mr Clutterbuck said from my Lord that he was my friend already and that I might make others by that address . . . I omitted but one Ordination and shall omit no more after I have withdrawn my play and taken all other steps suitable to a determined resolution . . . My repentance, I am sure, has been very sincere about it and I beg my Lord's pardon in the most humble manner if my conduct is disapproved of by him.[18]

If all this is true, the advice of Mr Clutterbuck seems to have been singularly inept. The poet had got the worst of both worlds; he had lost favour because of his theatrical hopes and now he had lost his theatrical chances in trying to regain that favour. His play was again withdrawn, he had no patron for his satire or his sermon, and he was not even in orders yet! No wonder he was worried.

The worst of it was that the Lord-Lieutenant had already started dispensing preferment. In the most urgent and agitated letter of all, dated 16 November from 'Mr Dodington's at Chiswick', Young told his friend he had seen in the news that 'two of my Lord's chaplains are already provided for, and what a heartbreaking must it be for me, who have a promise . . . in the fourth place, which is already second, to be in the least doubt of that blessing'.[19] Now he was in such a hurry to qualify himself that he seems to have anticipated, at least on paper, the date of his ordination. On 2 December he announced: 'This day I carried my Testimonium from the College for orders to the Bishop of Winchester, who will ordain me next Sunday sennight which is Ordination Sunday'[20] (i.e. 13 December); while on 14 December he wrote: 'This is to let you know that I am in orders, the want of making which step was, I presume, the reason that hitherto my Lord has not declared his good pleasure concerning me ... I am ready on the very first notice of it to go for Ireland.'[21] Ordination Sunday was in fact a week later, 20 December,[22] and it was on that date that Young was actually ordained by the Bishop of Winchester at his chapel in Chelsea.[f] But the records show that it was only Deacon's orders that he entered at this time – he did not take priest's orders for another four years.

These newly-established facts, the two withdrawals of his play and his two ordinations, clear up the confusion in previous biographies over the tradition that *The Brothers* was withdrawn because of the poet's entry into orders – events attributed to a variety of dates from February, 1724 to April, 1728. The tradition is vindicated; but it was the second withdrawal and the first ordination, both belonging to the end of 1724.

Young was now poised for his ecclesiastical career. But though he had sacrificed his theatrical hopes, he had not given up his interest in the theatre – in the very letter that announced his ordination he also reported the damnation of Cibber's *Caesar in Egypt*.[23] Nor was he prepared to suppress his latest – and, he said, last – verses, even though, being satirical, they were distinctly less suitable to his new profession than some of his earlier works. *The Universal Passion* is indeed the most worldly of his poems; yet the series was published, and partly composed, during his first years in the Church. This does not mean that he was insincere in assuming the role of clergyman. Though he confessed about fifteen months later that 'my prudential motives for taking orders was my expectation from my Lord',[24] he had

---

[f] The Winchester Ordination Register for 1724 is missing; but Young's signature, with three others, appears in the Subscription Book (subscription to the 39 Articles) on 19 December, with a note of their ordination below, signed by the Bishop.

always had a deep and genuine interest in religión, as his poems
and the evidence of Tindal show. But that is not the same thing
as having a vocation for the pastoral life and for forty years
Young avoided following in his father's footsteps. When he did
finally decide to take to the cloth, however, he did so
conscientiously, as Pope told Warburton:

> Young had much of a sublime genius, though without
> common sense; so that his genius, having no guide, was
> perpetually liable to degenerate into bombast. This made
> him pass a foolish youth, the sport of peers and poets;[g] but
> his having a very good heart enabled him to support the
> clerical character when he assumed it, first with decency
> and afterwards with honour.[25]

While he waited optimistically for his summons to Ireland,
Young busied himself with the publication of his satire, or series
of satires as it had now become; and for once he pushed things
forward briskly. In September[26] he sent Tickell the draft for
correction; by October[27] he had prepared a verse dedication to
Lord Carteret and was about to print; and on 16 November,
after that nobleman's refusal of the dedication, he told Tickell of
his revised plans:

> That satire I have now divided into distinct epistles,
> which I propose publishing one after another, directed to
> people of fashion, for one of which I have the offer of Mr
> Walpole's patronage. What I desire to know is if from doing
> so I can possibly hurt myself with my Lord Carteret; if so,
> be sure I shall not do it. For all I can expect from Mr
> Walpole is a larger gratuity, which in this case you know is
> absolutely a trifle.[28]

When therefore he issued the first of the five epistles at the
end of January, 1725,[29] it was addressed to an unexceptionable

---

[g] Pope himself was one of these, according to Ruffhead: 'When he (Young)
determined on the church, he did not address himself to Sherlock, to Atterbury
or to Hare for the best instructions in theology; but to Pope, who in a youthful
frolic advised the diligent perusal of Thomas Aquinas. With this treasure Young
retired from interruption to an obscure place in the suburbs. His poetical guide
to godliness, hearing nothing of him during half a year and apprehending he
might have carried the jest too far, sought after him and found him just in time
to prevent an irretrievable derangement.' (Hill, III, 375.) Though clearly
apocryphal, this story illustrates the general opinion of Young's unworldliness.

Whig magnate, the Duke of Dorset – the bitter rivalry between Walpole and Carteret made it too risky to accept the offer of the Prime Minister as long as he had expectations from the Lord-Lieutenant. An advertisement at the end stated that the second satire was in the press, yet it did not actually appear till 2 April[30] and then without a dedication. The last four lines ran:

> This humble verse, O —— , may it be
> A monument of gratitude to thee,
> Whose early favour I must own with shame,
> So long my patron and so late my theme.[31]

These lines were dropped in the second and all subsequent editions of the satires, except for the unique and puzzling 'sixth' edition of 1763,[h] which not only restored them but filled in the blanks. The half-title bears the words 'To the Right Honourable the Earl of Scarborough'; the two-syllable blank in the verses above is filled with his family name, Lumley; and another blank of three syllables with Scarborough. Still stranger, this 'sixth edition' contains thirty-eight lines never before printed, while otherwise it follows the text of the original folio, not the corrected version of 1728. It looks as though it was reprinted from the original sheets of a suppressed issue of *Satire II* – presumably a piracy, though bearing the imprint of Tonson and published during the poet's life. The delay in issuing the second satire would be explained if a last-minute refusal of the dedication by the Earl necessitated the suppression and revision of the first printing. With no time to find a substitute, Young was obliged to leave blanks; but a compliment to 'art-loving Scarborough' in his last satire confirms their acquaintance and strengthens the plausibility of the dedication – though how the Earl had been 'so long' Young's patron is unexplained.[i]

The other three satires of the first series are straightforward: *Satire III* was addressed to Dodington on 26 April, 1725,[32] *Satire IV* to Speaker Compton on 11 June,[33] and *Satire the Last*, after an agonized pause, to Sir Robert Walpole on 17 January, 1726.[34]

---

[h] First described by Dr C. E. Frank in his unpublished doctoral dissertation on Edward Young's Satires (Princeton, 1939).

[i] Richard Lumley, second Earl of Scarborough from 1721, was Master of the Horse to the Prince of Wales from 1714 to 1727. Did he perhaps recommend Young for a place in the Prince's household, as chaplain to the Princess?

The tribute to Dodington was the most sincerely felt, for this old friend, now a Lord of the Treasury, had looked after Young all through the critical period of his ordination. His letters of 16 November, 2 December and 14 December, 1724 were all written from 'Mr Dodington's, Chiswick', while that of 2 March, 1725 came from his friend's town house at Covent Garden. It was thus no flattery when the poet opened his third satire:

> Long, Dodington, in debt, I long have sought
> To ease the burden of my grateful thought;
> And now a poet's gratitude you see,
> Grant him two favours and he'll ask for three.
> For whose the present glory or the gain?
> You give protection, I a worthless strain.
> You love and feel the poet's sacred flame
> And know the basis of a solid fame;
> Though prone to like, yet cautious to commend,
> You read with all the malice of a friend;
> Nor favour my attempts that way alone,
> But, more to raise my verse, conceal your own.[35]

Dodington deserved the compliment. He had genuine good taste and critical sense; besides Young he patronized Thomson, Fielding and Voltaire, and he tried to help Johnson. He was enough of a poet to figure in the *Oxford Book of English Verse*[j] and such a skilled reader of poetry that once, provoked by Thomson's flat recitation of his own verses, he snatched the copy from the poet and read them for him. The comparative smoothness of the couplets in Young's satires may well owe something to his long stay with Dodington during their composition, while the fact that the idea of dividing up the satire and the offer of Walpole's aid were first reported from Chiswick suggests that Young's host may have proposed the new scheme and probably procured the Prime Minister's patronage.

Though the Augustan Age was full of satirists, the *Universal Passion* made an immediate sensation. When they were collected (with two later satires on women), Young called them 'characteristical satires', and this is an accurate description. They deal with types in the manner of Theophrastus and the imitators

[j] No. 443, the ode 'Shorten Sail' (sent to Young in 1761). Dodington also published an *Epistle to Sir Robert Walpole*, 1726, which is sometimes printed with Young's *Works*.

of his *Characters*, particularly La Bruyère, from whom Young certainly borrowed.[k] Another source was the *Spectator*, from which he seems to have drawn the original idea of his 'universal passion'.[l] In no. 73 Addison had written:

> It is very strange to consider that a creature like man, who is sensible of so many weaknesses and imperfections, should be actuated by a Love of Fame; that vice and ignorance, imperfection and misery should contend for praise and endeavour as much as possible to make themselves objects of admiration.[36]

Young made this theory the basis of his series of satires and in the preface to the collected edition (to which he gave the additional title *Love of Fame*) he claimed 'an unity of design not . . . attempted before'.[37] Though we now know that the first five were conceived as a unit anyway, his basing of the whole on a universal psychological principle gives these satires exceptional continuity and interest. They form a brilliant series of sarcastic vignettes of London society under George I, but the author claimed in his preface that he was 'not conscious of the least malevolence to any particular person through all the characters; though some persons may be so selfish as to engross a general application to themselves'.[38] Curll nevertheless printed a Key, while Horace Walpole annotated his copy with probable identifications.[m] Yet it remains true to say that Young attacked the folly rather than the individual, unlike Dryden before him and Pope after him, and that he preferred to laugh at his butts rather than snarl with hatred. He propounded his theory of satire in the preface:

> Laughing satire bids the fairest for success. The world is too proud to be fond of a serious tutor, and when an author is in a passion, the laugh generally, as in conversation, turns against him. This kind of satire only has any delicacy in it.

[k] Thomas points out the characters of Florio and Fleuriste, Narcissus and Narcisse, etc.

[l] Young told Tickell, 20 September, 1724, that the first hint of the satire came from him. (Pettit, 28.) Did Tickell suggest that his friend should versify Addison's idea.

[m] Curll's Key was printed in Young's *Poetical Works*, 1741, which was not authorized by the poet. Walpole's notes were made many years after, as one refers to the *Gentleman's Magazine* for September, 1785.

Of this delicacy Horace is the best master: he appears in
good humour while he censures, and therefore his censure
has the more weight as supposed to proceed from
judgement, not from passion.[39]

The critics agreed, and even before the series was completed,
the anonymous author was complimented on his civilized
attitude in *The Authors of the Town*, attributed to Richard Savage,
who commented:

You but assume the foe, to act the friend.
Pleasing, yet wounding, you our faults rehearse.
Strong are your thoughts; enchanting rolls your verse,
Deep, clear and sounding; decent, yet sincere;
In praise impartial, without spleen severe.[40]

The same point was made over fifty years later by Joseph
Warton in his *Essay on the Genius and Writings of Pope*, speaking of
the *Universal Passion*, 'a work that abounds in wit, observation on
life, pleasantry, delicacy, urbanity and the most well-bred
raillery, without a single mark of spleen or ill-nature'.[41] Warton,
of course, was comparing Young's satires with Pope's and he
made the valid point that Young's were 'the first characteristical
satires in our language',[42] written five or six years before the
Moral Essays of his friend. Pope, in fact, followed Young's lead,
not only in his characters but in his modified principle of the
'Ruling Passion', which allowed him more latitude and variety of
treatment. But though Pope surpassed and overshadowed his
model in the eyes of posterity, his debt to Young was obvious to
his contemporaries.[n]

Warton's point was that Pope's 'spleen and ill-nature' were not
necessary in a satirist. His bitter personal attacks on Atticus and
Sporus and Sappho may have made Pope's satires more relished
in his own day but do not necessarily give him the same
advantage with a later generation. While we need a battery of

---

[n] e.g. Lady Anne Irwin in 1733, enclosing Pope's *Epistle to Lord Bathurst*: 'The
style of the whole is like Young's *Universal Passions*.' (HMC, Carlisle, 97.) Horace
Walpole noted in his copy 'several passages Pope borrowed from these satires
and improved'. Joseph Warton in his *Essay* (II, 281) remarked about the *Epistle to
Dr Arbuthnot*: 'Before this epistle was published, Dr Young addressed two epistles
to our author in the year 1730 concerning the authors of the age; in which are
many passages that bear a great resemblance to each other, though Pope has
heightened, improved and condensed the hints and sentiments of Young.'

notes to appreciate the deadly subtlety of the allusions to 'ass's milk' and the like, Young's generalized attack on the characteristic failings of humanity is immediately intelligible and, humanity being incorrigible, often applicable to modern types too. We have met the hearty sportsman,

> . . . whose drink is ale,
> Whose erudition is a Christmas tale,
> Whose mistress is saluted with a smack
> And friend received with thumps upon the back;[43]

and the 'jet set':

> In gay fatigues this most undaunted chief,
> Patient of idleness beyond belief,
> Most charitably lends the town his face
> For ornament in every public place;[44]

and the name-dropper:

> To glory some advance a lying claim,
> Thieves of renown and pilferers of fame;
> Their front supplies what their ambition lacks;
> They know a thousand lords – behind their backs![45]

His gallery included ambitious generals:

> One to destroy is murder by the law
> And gibbets keep the lifted hand in awe.
> To murder thousands takes a specious name,
> War's glorious art, and gives immortal fame;[46]

and free-thinking progressives:

> C———, who makes so merry with the creed,
> He almost thinks he disbelieves indeed;
> But only thinks so; to give both their due,
> Satan and he believe, and tremble too;[47]

and millionaire collectors:

> Unlearned men of books assume the care,
> As eunuchs are the guardians of the fair;[48]

and (to end appropriately) pedantic scholars:

> Some for renown on scraps of learning dote
> And think they grow immortal as they quote.[49]

The affected and the frivolous, the flattering and the flattered, the prodigal and the mean, and many more were Young's prey; nor did he forget the venality of his own kind, the 'men of ink'. In these trenchant sketches he was able to give full play to his talent for epigram, so that the work is full of well-known quotations, such as:

> None think the great unhappy but the great;[50]

or:

> Where nature's end of language is declined
> And men talk only to conceal the mind;[51]

or:

> How commentators each dark passage shun
> And hold their farthing candle to the sun.[52]

But sometimes, as in all his works, the rush of his ideas and the aptness of his metaphors carried him away, as in the lines comparing literary critics to fireworks:

> Critics on verse, as squibs on triumphs, wait,
> Proclaim the glory and augment the state;
> Hot, envious, noisy, proud, the scribbling fry
> Burn, hiss and bounce, waste paper, stink, and die.[53]

The last line is really too ingenious – Young never learnt to control his own fireworks.

This sustained display of brilliance brought immediate and lasting celebrity to the poet who denounced the love of fame. They were at once reprinted by the pirates of Edinburgh and Dublin, the former probably including Allan Ramsay, who expressed his admiration with complimentary verses as well as by infringing Young's copyright. The poems hardly needed the energetic puffing of the *Plain Dealer*, a periodical run by the egregious Aaron Hill with the assistance of William Bond and Richard Savage. Savage was a passionate admirer of Young, Bond more critical, and two years earlier they had quarrelled over his poetry. On 3 May, 1723 Hill had addressed a pompous rebuke to Savage for his 'violence in defending Mr Young even where he is not defensible' and attributed it to 'a quick and generous sense of his personal regard of you'. This, however, did not justify a 'positive puffiness ... It's one thing to treat a gentleman ill, and another to speak frankly of his writings. This was Mr Bond's case ... You ought, I assure you, to be a great champion in wit, if you would defend Mr Young's poetry from all the assaults it lies open to ... Mr Young has a thousand things in his writings very finely conceived and expressed with a noble strength of eloquence; and he has as many every way the reverse.'[54] Now the quarrel was forgotten and the *Plain Dealer* wrote on 5 February, 1725 that the first part of a satire, just published under the title of *The Universal Passion*, though anonymous, was 'easily distinguished to be the work of some considerable genius', and quoted some passages showing 'the most shining marks of a spirit that is truly poetical'.[55] *Satire II* was given a more ingenious treatment with a letter on 9 April, supposedly from a lady:

> Many a lady has been charmed into a passion for her future lover upon sight only of his picture; but my fate is the very reverse of this. For before I saw the *picture* of my Florello, I was almost in love with the *original*, whereas now I am fallen absolutely in love with the picture and can scarce bear the sight of that odious lover of mine who sat for it. The picture, you must know, is a kind of paradox, for it is drawn but in black and white and yet glows with the liveliest force and most natural mixture of strong colouring. It is one of a valuable *collection* which was exposed to the public sale last week under title of *The Universal Passion*.[56]

There were, however, those who disapproved, like 'Hesiod Cooke', whose *Battle of the Poets*° pictured Dennis secretly visiting the enemy camp of Pope's followers on the night before the battle:

> On Young he entered, whom he sleeping found
> With all his works in noble splendour round.
> Upon his latest rhymes he drew his arms,
> Enraged at trifles that debase the charms;
> The rest he left untouched, to merit true,
> The beauties many and the faults but few.[57]

° In its first, pre-*Dunciad* version, 1725. Cooke dared to criticize Pope's Greek scholarship with the result that he was pilloried in the *Dunciad*. He then produced a revised version of the *Battle of the Poets*, in which all the references to Young were omitted.

A note identified the censured trifles as his satires, which were evidently thought unworthy of the author of *The Last Day*. Such a mild reaction to Young's satire supports the criticism of Swift that 'the Doctor is not merry enough nor angry enough for the present age to relish as he deserves';[58] and the Dean himself made merry with his friend in his verses *On Reading Dr Young's Satires*, written after the publication of *Satire the Last*, with its compliments to Walpole and the King:

> If there be truth in what you sing,
> Such godlike virtues in the King,
> A Minister so filled with zeal
> And wisdom for the Common-weal;
> If he who in the Chair presides
> So steadily the Senate guides; . . .
> If every peer whom you commend
> To worth and learning is a friend,
> If this be truth, as you attest,
> What land was ever half so blest! . . .
> Or take it in a different view:
> I ask, if what you say be true,
> If you allow the present age
> Deserves your satire's keenest rage,
> If that same *Universal Passion*
> With every vice has filled the nation, . . .
> If these be of all crimes the worst,
> What land was ever half so curst?[59]

Swift's sarcasm on the contrast between Young's satire and his encomia was rather unfair. The satirist praised Walpole for bringing peace and prosperity to Britain –

> Her public wounds bound up, her credit high,
> Her commerce spreading sails in every sky –[60]

in contrast to the 'madness of ambitious men':

> When after battle I the field have seen[P]
> Spread o'er with ghastly shapes, which once were men; . . .
> Are there, said I, who from this sad survey,

[P] Was this mere poetic imagination? Though haunted by the sight of the mutilated veterans of Marlborough's wars, Young never, as far as we know, saw a battlefield. The Parson Young who wandered into the enemy camp, absorbed in a book, and was arrested as a spy, was the Rev. *William* Young (Fielding's Parson Adams).

This human chaos, carry smiles away? . . .
How was I shocked to think the hero's trade
Of such materials, fame and triumph made![61]

He did not agree that the business of satire was only to
denounce; good examples were needed to set against the bad.
His preface declared:

> Some satirical wits and humourists, like their father
> Lucian, laugh at everything indiscriminately; which betrays
> such a poverty of wit as cannot afford to part with anything,
> and such a want of virtue as to postpone it to a jest. Such
> writers encourage vice and folly, which they pretend to
> combat, by setting them on an equal foot with better things;
> and while they labour to bring everything into contempt,
> how can they expect their own parts should escape? . . . It is
> this conduct that justly makes a *wit* a term of reproach.[62]

And he illustrated his view in the character of 'Hilario', who was
identified in some keys as Swift himself:

> By your example would Hilario mend,
> How would it grace the talents of my friend,
> Who, with the charms of his own genius smit,
> Conceives all virtues are comprised in wit!
> But time his fervent petulance may cool;
> For though he is a wit, he is no fool.
> In time he'll learn to use, not waste, his sense,
> Nor make a frailty of an excellence.
> His brisk attack on blockheads we would prize,
> Were not his jest as flippant with the wise.
> He spares nor friend nor foe, but calls to mind,
> Like Doomsday, all the faults of all mankind.[63]

Among the best-known epigrams of the *Universal Passion* was
the line,

A fool at forty is a fool indeed.[64]

Young was just past forty when he was writing these satires and
this was perhaps a rueful reference to his own situation, vainly
seeking his first preferment at that age. Despite the depth and
acuteness shown in these satires, Lord Carteret remained
obstinately unresponsive to the poet's ever more querulous
pleas. The letters to Tickell during 1725 make tiresome reading,

as Young followed at a distance and with increasing agony the distribution of the ecclesiastical prizes of Ireland to his rivals. A stream of inquiries, complaints and reminders from March to December finally provoked Tickell into threatening to give up his efforts and turn him over to his 'powerful solicitors'[65] in London. Young hastily sent an apology, early in January, 1726, pleading that Tickell and Clutterbuck were 'all that I do, or can, rely on'.[66] But Tickell's rebuke may have finally disillusioned him with his prospects of preferment from the Lord-Lieutenant, for it was at this stage that he turned to Carteret's opponent, Walpole, who had offered his patronage over a year before. On 17 January, 1726[67] *Satire the Last*, inscribed to Walpole, was entered at Stationers' Hall.

Young did not entirely abandon the chase, however, and when Lord Carteret returned to England, he took up the cudgels for himself and was able to report to Tickell on 23 May that My Lord had renewed his promise. But meanwhile his new policy had paid off and he was able to add casually that 'the King has been pleased to give me a pension of £200 per annum, which I think it my duty to let you know, who have shewn so kind a concern for my welfare'.[68] This handsome pension was granted on 3 May, 1726, backdated to Lady Day 1725.[69] The warrant cites no reason for the grant and, since Walpole was not in the habit of pensioning literary merit, Young's biographers have assumed that he must have performed some political service to the government. They support this theory with a letter written two months earlier, on 1 March, to Lady Mary Wortley Montagu,[70] which mentioned that he was obliged to go down next day to Wycombe election.[q] This election was the result of a petition by the defeated Opposition candidate, who was again declared the loser; but after yet another petition the government candidate was unseated and the Mayor and Postmaster gaoled for corruption. It is suggested that Young went to Wycombe with Dodington in 'the normal role of a clergyman in the train of a patron'.[71] But it is hard to believe that his presence at the election was so important and influential as to earn a reward of £200 a year for life – especially when the

---

[q] Lady Mary had asked him to bring some 'trifle', presumably literary, but the poet excused himself because of a bad cold and his imminent visit to Wycombe.

final result was a government defeat. It is too much to connect this brief excursion into politics with his pension, which it should be noted was dated back to months before the election.

The pension was, in fact, awarded for poetical, not political, services. The *London Journal* of 16 July, 1726 was quite explicit:

> His Majesty has been pleased to grant to the Rev. Dr Young, Chaplain to her Royal Highness the Princess of Wales and author of the fine satires called *The Universal Passion*, a pension of £200 per annum, as an encouragement to poetry; which that gentleman has handsomely acknowledged in his late poem on the *Instalment*.[72]

No official record of Young's appointment as chaplain to the Princess has been traced. But years later the poet claimed to have served George II both as Prince and King, while the cantankerous Hearne did not demur at the description of Young as Chaplain in Ordinary to the Princess, which he copied from the *Reading Post* on 20 July, adding characteristically, 'N.B. This gentleman, who is Fellow of All Souls College, is a most conceited person of very vile principles and a very poor, mean poet in the opinion of the best judges.'[73] Whatever Hearne's opinion of the poet's work, the reason for the award is confirmed by a contemporary note in the margin of the original warrant issued to Walter Chetwynd, the Paymaster, recording the recipient as 'author of the Universal Passion & several poetical pieces';[74] and even the extremely hostile writer of some *Remarks Critical and Political upon a late poem entitled The Instalment* made no suggestion that Young had done anything but literary service to Walpole with his poetical panegyrics.

The Instalment, published on 5 July,[75] was one of the most fulsome and hastily-produced of Young's occasional poems, being inspired by the installation of the Prime Minister on 26 June as a Knight of the Garter – the first commoner to be so honoured since 1660. It is more of a credit to the author's sense of gratitude than of poetry; at least he publicly acknowledged his debt. Even his friends could not say much for these grateful hyperboles, however much obliged themselves to the author, like the young Scots poet, James Thomson, who had only come down South the previous year in the wake of his friend David Malloch, now anglicized to Mallet. Through Mallet Thomson was introduced to Aaron Hill and the *Plain Dealer* circle, with whom Young was friendly.[r] But this did not inhibit him from commenting on 2 August:

> I have not seen these Reflections on the Dr's *Instalment*, but hear they are as wretched as their subject. The Dr's very buckram has run short on this occasion; his affected sublimity even fails him and down he comes with no small velocity.[76]

The 'Reflections' were presumably the *Remarks Critical and Political upon a late Poem, intitled The Instalment*, that had come out on 22 July,[77] attributed to that crusted Tory, Shippen, who denounced the poet as showing

> the most abject spirit of flattery and prostitution, as well as the grossest indelicacy and want of address, that perhaps ever appeared in any writer, even of the same stamp.[78]

But even Shippen paid Young's reputation a grudging tribute:

> This author has been long famous for the warmth of his imagination and the sublimity of his diction, which may sometimes perhaps swell into forced allusions and hyperbolical expressions. But we ought at least to expect *common sense* and *good English* from a man of his learning and degree, as well as some share of prudence and discretion from one who has so long enjoyed the intimacy of a certain courtier and a state-wit.[79]

Shippen's ironical conclusion was that the poem was so bad that either the author had 'a malicious design of traducing this eminent patriot under a pretence of extolling him; or else that he is a very wrong-headed sycophant and has the worst knack of flattery of any man living'.[80] The last words are perhaps the truest; Young had no knack of flattery and his efforts to oblige were generally clumsy and overdone. But at least in the *Instalment* he was motivated by gratitude, not venality.

The 'courtier and state-wit' must surely refer to Dodington, and his appearance in this context reinforces the idea that he

---

[r] On 15 August, 1726 Savage wrote to Mallet from Twickenham: 'Since my rural retirement I have been visited by Dr Young, who mentions you often with an affectionate and uncommon ardour.' (McKillop, 47.) Pope, in a letter to Hill on 29 October, 1731, mentions that they first met at Dr Young's, probably in mid-1726.

was involved in the poet's tribute to the Premier and the Premier's pension for the poet. Perhaps it was Dodington's idea to backdate the pension to the appearance of the first of the *Universal Passion* series, so that it should appear as a reward for the whole poem, not merely the dedication of *Satire the Last*. But though it was granted in the name of literature, that does not mean that Sir Robert's appreciation of Young's merits was entirely disinterested. Maybe it was worth his while to satisfy the whim of a rising young colleague who controlled no fewer than seven seats in Parliament.

CHAPTER 6

On Women
1726–1728

There is a gap of six months in Young's correspondence with
Tickell from 23 May, 1726,[1] when he announced his pension, to
6 December,[2] when he reported his return to London after
being out of town all the summer. After his visit to Twickenham
in August he evidently went to Dorset to spend the autumn with
Dodington, busy on the continuation of his satires, *On Women*
this time. The first of these, which came out early in 1727, closed
a passage in praise of country life thus:

> There too the muses sport; these numbers free,
> Pierian Eastbury! I owe to thee.[3]

He must also have been occupied with preparing the
subscription edition of his works,[a] which had been hanging fire
since before his ordination. He first mentioned to Tickell 'a
subscription which I thought would run better before I was
entered into another way' on 10 October, 1724,[4] and four
months later on 2 March, 1725 he reported that he had actually
'set a subscription a-foot'.[5] Nothing more was heard of this
project for a year or more, though meanwhile he helped to
gather subscriptions for another collection, the *Miscellanies* of
his scapegrace friend Richard Savage, and arranged for its
dedication to Lady Mary Wortley Montagu, whom he thanked
on 1 March, 1726[6] for the generosity of her present to the
editor.[b] Eventually he produced a sample of his own projected
collection, an issue in quarto on fine paper of the *Paraphrase on*

---

[a] Boswell recorded that when he and Dr Johnson called on Young's son at
Welwyn in 1781, 'Mr Young mentioned an anecdote that his father had received
several thousand pounds of subscription money for his *Universal Passion*, but had
lost it in the South Sea. Dr Johnson thought this must be a mistake; for he had
never seen a subscription book.' (Hill-Powell, IV, 121.) It was certainly a mistake;
the South Sea crash occurred in 1720, long before the satires were written.

[b] Lady Mary probably rewarded Savage's dedication with more than the
customary 20 guineas. (Halsband, II, 61, n. 2.) Among the subscribers were
Young himself, Walter Cary and Bevil Granville.

Job, third edition, as the half-title indicates. The title-page, which bore only the words *A Specimen for Subscribers*, a motto and the imprint 'London: Printed by W. Wilkins, at the Dolphin in Little-Britain, 1726', with a list of 'Proposals' on the verso, has fortunately survived in three copies,[c] though removed from others when the remainder was sold off in 1729.[d] The Proposals begin as follows:

> I. That this Author's Works, in Prose and Verse, the greatest part of which are yet unpublished, shall be printed in three quarto volumes, on the same paper, and on the same letter, with this specimen.
> II. The price to subscribers three guineas; two in hand, and one on delivery of the first volume, which is ready for the press.[7]

Then followed the instructions for payment, at Tonson's, White's Chocolate House and two other addresses, and a reminder to subscribers to take up their receipts and leave their names. This was followed up by a public advertisement in three newspapers for three days (*Daily Journal, Daily Post, Daily Courant*, 18, 20 and 21 February, 1727), announcing that Dr Young's Works were ready for the press, repeating that 'the greatest part, . . . was never yet published', and asking for subscribers' names and first payment to be sent to two addresses that are different from those given in the *Specimen* – Boxe's Coffee-house and the *London Gazette*.[8] And with that, apparently, the dream faded away.

It is strange that, for all the celebrity and popularity of his latest poems, Young's subscription should have failed, for no such edition ever came out.[e] Nor have we any idea what all the unpublished works, stressed in both advertisements, could have

[c] In the Huntingdon Library, San Marino, California, by whose courtesy I have been supplied with a photocopy of the preliminary pages.

[d] On 22 February, 1729, in an advertisement in the *Daily Post* for Young's *Apology for Princes*, the publisher Worrall listed other works of Young to be had at his shop, including the 'Paraphrase on Job, printed on a fine Royal Paper'.

[e] On 16 July, 1726 the *Dublin Weekly Journal* advertised Dr Edward Young's *Poetical Works*, containing, 'I The Force of Religion, II A Paraphrase . . . on Job, III A Poem on the Last Day, IV The Universal Passion in five satires, V An Epistle to Sir Robert Walpole.' (The *Epistle to Walpole* was actually by Dodington.) This was not a subscription edition but a made-up collection of Dublin 12 mo editions, published by Thomas Whitehouse.

been. He could hardly have been referring to his satires *On
Women*, of which the first had been published ten days earlier[f]
on 8 February.[9] These two satires were numbered V and VI and
inserted in the collected editions before that dedicated to
Walpole, which continued to be known as *Satire the Last*. (They
will be considered together after the publication of *Satire VI*,
completing the plan of *The Universal Passion*, in February, 1728.)
Perhaps the poet intended to print *The Brothers* with his *Works*
and (since the advertisement mentioned prose) the 'piece of
divinity' which he had wished to dedicate to Lord Carteret in
1724.[10] But these could hardly be said to form 'the greatest part'
of the collection – had he written more works, which never saw
the light?

Young's letters to Tickell in 1727–8 were less importunate,
now that he had an assured income, and more entertaining for
posterity because, apart from the occasional plaint, he seems to
have changed his tactics, keeping the pot of Tickell's friendship
boiling with news instead of protests, London's latest gossip
instead of Dublin's latest silence. This was the time of the
opening of the war on the dunces and though Young himself
took no part at first, he enjoyed a ringside seat, being an intimate
of Pope's circle and himself one of the stars of that constellation
celebrated in Allan Ramsay's poem of 1728, *The Quadruple
Alliance*:

> Swift, Sandy, Young and Gay
>   Are still my heart's delight;
> I sing their songs by day
>   And read their tales by night . . .

Ramsay then described their different qualities, Young's being
his 'Horatian flame', and the verses ended:

> Swift, Sandy, Young and Gay,
>   Lang may you give delight;
> Let all the dunces bray,
>   You're far above their spite.[11]

Swift too included him in their fraternity in a letter of 1732

---

[f] A presentation copy to George Clarke, Fellow of Worcester College,
formerly of All Souls, is dated '3 Feb 1726' (i.e. 1727).

about 'Mr Pope, Mr Gay the author, Dr Arbuthnot, myself, Dr Young and all the brethren whom we own'.[g] He added, 'Dr Young is the gravest among us, and yet his satires have many mixtures of sharp raillery',[12] and it was perhaps this gravity that made Young comment to Tickell on 21 February, 1727:

> You have Swift with you and all his wit, for I am one of those few who think he left but little behind him in *Gulliver*, at least of that kind which I most like.[13]

The same letter reported on the other members of the 'alliance' as well, Pope who 'does nothing, but lives on his acquired fame, as the bear sucking on his paws', and Gay who was 'about some fables'; and there were plenty of other items of literary news for his exiled friend, including 'Mr Voltaire, a French author', who was 'publishing by an English subscription an epic on Harry the 4th of France', and 'a piece called *Summer* that has a degree of merit in it'.[14]

These last two, the exiled Frenchman and the unknown Scotsman who had written *Summer*, had both been taken up by Dodington. Voltaire had arrived in England the previous June with an introduction from Horace Walpole the elder, the Ambassador at Paris; but Thomson owned his entry into the Dodington circle to Young. The Scots poet had published *Winter*, the first of the *Seasons*, in March, 1726, dedicated – without permission – to Sir Spencer Compton, who took no notice till the *Plain-Dealer* commented sharply on his neglect. The sequel was told to Spence by Mallet:

> Dodington gave his services to him (Thomson) by Dr Young and desired to see him. That was thought hint enough for another dedication to him; and this was his first entrance to that acquaintance.[15]

When *Summer* came out, therefore, in February, 1727, it was

---

[g] Cf. Fielding, *Covent Garden Journal*, no. 23 (21 March, 1752), on the reign of 'King Alexander, named Pope': 'No person durst read anything that was writ without his licence and approbation; and this licence he granted only to four during his reign, namely to the celebrated Dr Swift, to the ingenious Dr Young, Dr Arbuthnot and to one Mr Gay, four of his principal courtiers and favourites.'

dedicated to his new patron in terms that Young certainly never outdid:[h]

> And thou, my youthful Muse's early friend,
> In whom the human graces all unite;
> Pure light of mind and tenderness of heart;
> Genius and wisdom; the gay social sense,
> By decency chastised; goodness and wit,
> In seldom-meeting harmony combined;
> Unblemished honour and an active zeal
> For Britain's glory, Liberty and Man![16]

Thomson was again mentioned in Young's next letter to Tickell, on 20 April, but his 'piece in blank verse on the death of Sir Isaac Newton' was judged 'not very extraordinary'.[17] And then on 5 June came the advance news of Pope's *Miscellanies*:

> Pope, Swift and Arbuthnot are coming abroad in a triple alliance of wit. The work is now in the press ... Swift is under mortification for not receiving the first visit from our great men, which he insists on, and they know their own interest so little as not to comply, so that he is like to return to Ireland for homage or his ambition must starve. Pope in his part abuses Philips very intrepidly, since the sea is between them ... Gay has just given us some fables, fifty in number and about five are tolerable. I wonder Pope can be so dull. I wish he had Aesop's head as well as shoulders.[18]

Young seems to have been in a very disgruntled mood. The *Craftsman*[i] was 'a dull paper' despite Bolingbroke, Pulteney and Chesterfield;[j] 'our Universities are asleep and the Church snores';

---

[h] Fielding went even further in his epistle to Dodington, *Of True Greatness*, written as late as 1741; it included a compliment to Dodington's own verses and his patronage of 'the Muses and their darling Young'. (*Complete Works*, ed. W. E. Henley, 1903.)

[i] Young himself was one of the targets of the *Craftsman* because of his connection with Walpole. On 13 February, 1727 it called him Sir Robert's 'own immortal poet', ironically quoting *The Instalment*; and in *The Progress of Patriotism* it pictured 'our British Horace, famed for wit', dining with the 'Man of Power' and his cronies. (*Craftsman*, 1731, I, 118; V, 329.)

[j] Young knew Chesterfield before he succeeded to his Earldom on 26 January, 1726. He told Spence: 'There was a club at the King's Head in Pall Mall, that arrogantly called themselves "The World". Lord Stanhope, then (now Lord Chesterfield), Lord Herbert, &c, &c, were members. Epigrams were proposed to be writ by each after dinner. Once when Dr Young was invited thither, he would have declined writing because he had no diamond. Lord Chesterfield lent him his, and he wrote immediately:
> Accept a miracle instead of wit;
> See two dull lines with Stanhope's pencil writ.' (Osborn, 852.)

and a glumly moralizing paragraph anticipated the heavier parts
of the *Night Thoughts* and *The Centaur not Fabulous*:

> I never knew so warm, so universal and so expensive a
> pursuit of pleasure as at present among us; and yet I find
> not more happy men than formerly; which confirms me in
> an opinion which I have long held, I mean that pleasure
> chiefly consists in well knowing what is *not* to be found, as
> true riches consist in knowing what we do not want, and a
> great part of wisdom is knowing what we need not know.[19]

The unusually sour and cynical tone of this letter might perhaps
be explained by disappointment over the failure of his
subscription edition. Or was he feeling generally dissatisfied and
out-of-tune with the whole spirit of Augustan literature – in spite
of the success of his own classic-style satires? An anonymous
experiment in rampant romanticism, which appeared just at this
time, suggests that the poet was seeking something different.

Cynthio, a funeral poem, though advertised in the newspapers
at the beginning of June,[20] went unnoticed and unknown to
Young's earlier editors and the author might never have been
identified if H. F. Cary, preparing his edition of *Milton, Thomson
and Young* (1841), had not noticed a presentation copy in the
British Library with the signed inscription 'To Mr Victor in
Grays' and the date 'June 9th 1727'. A manuscript note under
the title confirms Young's authorship and indicates the occasion
as the death of the Marquess of Carnarvon,[k] heir to the Duke of
Chandos, whose grief for a 'pious son' was commiserated at the
end by the poet, who claimed to share his sorrow in the loss of a
'faithful friend'.[21] The contrast between the magnificent Duke,
to whom the poem was addressed, and the obscure hack, to
whom this copy was presented, affords an amusing illustration
of the wide spectrum of Young's friendships. Benjamin Victor
claimed, fifty years later,[l] to have been introduced to the poet in
1724 by Richard Savage: 'a friendship ensued, which subsisted
without interruption above thirteen years. I loved Dr Young – I

[k] Lord Carnarvon was up at Balliol College, Oxford, 1719–21, and
contributed £200 to the new buildings of All Souls. He died on 8 April, 1727 at
the age of twenty-four. Was he another of Young's pupils?
[l] In his *Original Letters*, 1776. The letter quoted is dated 1756; but as it refers
to Young as both alive and dead and mentions George III, it is clearly a pastiche
and cannot be relied on for accuracy.

had reason for it; he loved me and did me many services'.[22] On the Duke's side the acquaintance may have dated from 1721, since he possessed a richly bound manuscript of *The Revenge*, and certainly from 1726,[m] when Young sent him a copy of *Satire the Last* with a ten-line presentation inscription, beginning:

> Accept, my Lord, the satire which I send;
> For who to satire is so fit a friend?

and ending:

> From other great ones I can tribute raise
> Of vice or folly to enrich my lays;
> But Chandos, an unprofitable thing,
> Can nought on earth but his protection bring.[23]

The contrast between *Cynthio* and the satires on which the poet was still engaged is extraordinary. In the *Universal Passion* Young rose to his height as a classic poet, handling the Heroic couplet with Augustan skill; in *Cynthio* his octosyllables are almost startling in their bold use of the full romantic apparatus:

> Yes, welcome Darkness, welcome Night!
> Thrice welcome every dread delight
> Beneath the moon's malignant beam,
> The lonely grot, the sullen stream,
> The nodding brow of ruins high,
> The birds obscene that o'er them fly,
> Or rivers old that with a roar
> Their darkened waves beneath them pour
> Through moss-green arches' mouldering stone
> And to the mournful fancy groan;
> The meteor's blaze, the clouds that roll
> And blot the daylight from the Pole:
> The dreary heath where, tales report,

[m] The MS of *The Revenge*, now in the Bodleian, has a covering letter from the Duke's chaplain, Daniel Perkins, to Rawlinson, 10 September, 1747, which says he had heard the Duke express himself with great esteem of Dr Young; 'and from a copy of verses in MS, sealed to the blank leaf opposite to the title-page of his last Satire, dedicated to Sir Robert Walpole, I am pretty sure the Dr had an equal esteem for his Grace.' (MS Rawl., Poet. 229.) *Satire the Last* was published in January 1726. Pettit dates the verses 1728 on the strength of a later letter, 6 December, 1786, from the Provost of Queen's College, Oxford, forwarding the MS to the Duke's successor and alleging it was 'intended as a general dedication of his satires', first collected in March 1728. (Pettit, 60.)

> Old Hecate keeps her baleful court,
> And thieves the murdered wretch have thrown;
> The blasted oak that stands alone;
> In pathless woods the deepest gloom,
> And evening visits to the tomb;
> When midnight seals the common eye,
> The funeral torch slow-gliding by, . . .
> The solemn aisle, where dead men crowd,
> The vault, the sexton and the shroud,
> The final office (awful sound!),
> The *Dust to dust*, the closing ground, . . .
> I hear, I feel yon dismal knell,
> I see the churchyard's bosom swell,
> Too full of man, with death o'ercharged,
> Methinks the spectres stalk enlarged![24]

This is not so much the stuff of the *Night Thoughts* as of the height of the Gothic movement.

Immediately after this, on 11 June, 1727, King George I died at Hanover, and Walpole's position became very precarious. But Queen Caroline's influence, backed by a handsome rise in the Civil List, saved the Prime Minister; his rivals were disappointed and Lord Carteret retired to Ireland again as Lord-Lieutenant. Young's prospects therefore remained as before, except that he might hope for some favour from the new Queen, as her chaplain when Princess. He hastened to draw her attention with a sermon preached at St George's, Hanover Square, 'soon after the late King's death', which was published under the title of *A Vindication of Providence, or a True Estimate of Human Life* with a dedication to the Queen as the 'greatest encourager of arts'.[25] Though dated 1728, it came out on 17 November, 1727,[26] and on that day Young sent a copy to Tickell, with others for Lord Carteret and Mr Clutterbuck.[27] The title-page announced this work as 'Discourse I' and a note promised the second discourse soon. But no second part ever appeared, although the *True Estimate* was popular enough to go into three editions by 1729. Croft tells a story that the second part was indeed written, but that before any copy could be made it was torn in pieces by a lady's monkey.[28] The trouble was that the first part was designed to show the worst side of life, which the second was to correct; and the result was that this sermon presented a very one-sided

picture of human life, defeating the intention expressed in his
dedication:

> The design is of great consequence and, I think, new: it is
> to remove a prevailing and inveterate mistake, ... that
> false opinion, that reflection on Providence, that this world
> is in its own nature, that is, by God's appointment, a world
> of sorrow, a scene of misery, a vale of tears ... Whereas this
> treatise shall endeavour to make it manifest ... that God
> does not only permit but enable us, and not only enable but
> enjoin us, to be happy; happy to a much greater degree
> than we are, that is, than we choose to be.[29]

In the event the *True Estimate* had just the opposite effect and
gave Young a reputation for gloom that was summed up by the
learned Miss Elizabeth Carter in 1744:

> Indeed this melancholy turn of thought runs through all
> Doctor Young's writings, but in nowhere so much as in what
> he calls his 'True Estimate of Human Life', one of the most
> sombre pieces surely that ever a splenetic imagination
> drew.[30]

It has even been suggested that when Young came to try to write
of the happier side, he found it impossible;[31] but this
underestimates both the ingenuity and the cheerfulness of the
writer. However splenetic the ideas, the style of the sermon was
full of liveliness and wit, which might account for its popularity.
It is the first example (unless we count the dedication to the
Codrington ladies) of his prose style, that bore its finest fruit in
his *Conjectures on Original Composition*, and one wonders if this
discourse, 'in which the passions are considered in a new light',
was really the 'piece of divinity' of 1724,[32] since it takes up no
fewer than sixty-four pages in quarto – surely rather lengthy
even for those days of marathon preaching!

Lord Carteret still took no notice of this proof of his client's
clerical merit – or perhaps Tickell failed to pass the copies on, as
Young sent him another in February, 1728.[33] Carteret was really
behaving rather badly and Young complained on 17 November
that 'My Lord, when I waited on him, spoke not in such a
manner as I wished and indeed expected ... My Lord seems to
disown that he has ever made any promise to patronise me,
which is severe.'[34] But though he had wasted over three years in

pursuing the will-o'-the-wisp of the Lord-Lieutenant's favour, he could always turn to Dodington, with whom he spent the autumn at Eastbury in a literary house-party:

> Mr Thomson, a Scot, is writing on the Seasons in blank verse, though no imitator of Milton; what I have lately seen in manuscript on the Spring has an undoubted taste and merit in it . . . We have had no attempts of any note but Mr Voltaire's epic, which is thought to have considerable merit. The author I know well; he is a gentleman, and of great vivacity and industry, and has a good deal of knowledge out of the poetical way.[35]

From the fact that Young now, in November, 1727, knew Voltaire well, whereas in February he had only been 'Mr Voltaire, a French author', we may safely conclude that it was during 1727 that the two met and matched their wits at Eastbury. In his *Dedication to Mr Voltaire* of the *Sea-Piece*, nearly thirty years later, Young wrote:

> 'Tell me,' say'st thou, 'who courts my smile?
> What stranger strayed from yonder isle?'
> No stranger, sir, though born in foreign climes.
> On Dorset downs, when Milton's page
> With Sin and Death provoked thy rage,
> Thy rage provoked *who* soothed with gentle rhymes?
>
> *Who* kindly couched thy censure's eye
> And gave thee clearly to descry
> Sound judgment giving law to fancy strong?
> *Who* half inclined thee to confess –
> Nor could thy modesty do less –
> That Milton's blindness lay not in his song?[36]

This refers to Voltaire's objections in his *Essay on Epic Poetry* to the allegory of Sin and Death in *Paradise Lost*, which provoked one of Young's best-known extempore epigrams,[n] when he replied:

[n] Mrs Pendarves (later Delany) reported the epigram in February 1728, but attributed it to Lord Hervey. (Llanover, I, 160.) There are several versions, the one quoted being from Croft. Goldsmith commented in his *Memoirs of M. de Voltaire*: 'The wretchedness of the epigram will readily convince those who have any pretensions to taste that Dr Young could never have been the author.' (*Collected Works*, III, 253.)

> You are so witty, profligate and thin,
> At once we think thee Milton, Death and Sin.[37]

Joseph Warton reported the host's own verdict on the 'wit-combats' at his most famous house-party:

> Nobody ever said more brilliant things (than Young) in conversation. The late Lord Melcombe (Dodington) informed me that when he and Voltaire were on a visit to his Lordship at Eastbury, the English poet was far superior to the French in the variety and the novelty of his *bon mots* and repartees; and Lord Melcombe was himself a good judge of wit and humour, of which he himself had a great portion.[38]

It is only fair to remember that Voltaire was presumably talking in English, which he confessed in the preface to his *Essay* 'he cannot pronounce at all and he hardly understands in conversation'.[39] But that did not diminish his Gallic self-confidence, as another of Young's reminiscences shows:

> Voltaire, like the French in general, showed the greatest complaisance outwardly and the greatest contempt for us inwardly. He consulted Dr Young about his essays in English[o] and begged him to correct any gross faults in it. The Doctor set very honestly to work, marked the passages most liable to censure, and when he went to explain himself about them, Voltaire could not help bursting out laughing in his face.[40]

Down in the country Young had been busy, as usual, composing and when he returned to town in November, he set about the publication of his final satire on women. It came out on 24 February, 1728[41] and completed the plan of *The Universal Passion*, though numbered the 'Sixth' out of seven. *Satire VI* was dedicated to Lady Elizabeth Germain, though the poet confessed he did not know her – surprisingly, for the 'incomparable Lady Betty' was a close friend of Swift, a lady of

---

[o] In the winter of 1727 Voltaire published in English his *Essay upon the Civil Wars of France . . . And also upon the Epick Poetry of the European Nations from Homer down to Milton*, as a trailer for the *Henriade*, published in March, 1728. In his twenty pages on Milton he said, 'The fiction of Sin and Death seems to have in it some great beauties and many gross defects'; but he concluded that 'there are perfections enough in Milton to atone for all his defects'.

wit, spirit and great wealth.[P] The previous satire bore no inscription, but like *Satire II* there was the hint of an anonymous patron:

> A theme, fair ————! doubly kind to me,
> Since satirising those is praising thee,
> Who wouldst not bear, too modestly refined,
> A panegyric of a grosser kind.[42]

Dr Frank notes that a second such blank was identified by Horace Walpole as Henrietta Howard, the Queen's bedchamber woman – and the King's mistress.[q] He suggests that the first blank is probably the same and that Mrs Howard, like Lord Scarborough, declined to be named in the poet's dedication. This seems a plausible theory, since she and Young had been colleagues in the service of the Princess of Wales and she was the favourite of all the wits, who used regularly to congregate in her rooms at St James's Palace. Young had already complimented her in passing in his fourth satire ('And Henrietta like a Muse inspires')[43] and now – if Walpole is right – he paid her a longer tribute:

> She strikes each point with native force of mind,
> While puzzled learning blunders far behind.
> Graceful to sight and elegant to thought,
> The great are vanquished and the wise are taught.
> Her breeding finished and her temper sweet;
> When serious, easy; and when gay, discreet;
> In glittering scenes o'er her own heart sincere;
> In crowds collected and in courts severe;
> Sincere and warm, with zeal well understood,
> She takes a noble pride in doing good.
> Yet not superior to her sex's cares,
> The mode she fixes by the gown she wears;
> Of silks and china she's the last appeal,
> In these great points she leads the commonweal;
> And if disputes of empire rise between

[P] Pettit (pp. 62–3) prints a letter from Young to an unnamed 'Ladyship', complaining that she had ignored his recent address to her and sending another 'trifle' as a reminder. The editor plausibly suggests that the addressee was Lady Elizabeth Germain.

[q] Walpole often conversed with Mrs Howard (by then the Countess of Suffolk) after she settled at Strawberry Hill in 1759, so she may herself have been the source of his identifications.

Mechlin, the queen of lace, and Colberteen,
'Tis doubt, 'tis darkness! till suspended fate
Assumes her nod to close the grand debate.[44]

The poet's close association with Mrs Howard and his high
regard for her are considerations that must be borne in mind.
when we come to a later and more controversial approach to
her.

The two satires *On Women* were twice as long as the preceding
ones. The poet 'thanked their faults for such a fruitful theme'[45]
and exposed, without bitterness or coarseness, a comprehensive
gallery of feminine types. But one wonders where he acquired
such a wide understanding of feminine character, since women
had apparently played little part in his forty years and there are
none of those stories of romantic attachments or sentimental
sufferings usually associated with poetical biography. The only
anecdote that shows Young as a ladies' man does so only
incidentally and cannot be claimed as reliable evidence:

> He was once on a party of pleasure with a few ladies,
> going up the water to Vauxhall; and he amused them with a
> tune on the German flute. Behind him several officers were
> also in a boat rowing for the same place and soon came
> alongside of the boat where the Doctor and the ladies were.
> The Doctor, who was not very conceited of playing, put up
> his flute on their approach. One of them instantly asked
> why he ceased playing or put up the flute in his pocket. 'For
> the same reason,' said he, 'that I took it out, to please
> myself.' The son of Mars very peremptorily rejoined that if
> he did not immediately take out his flute and continue the
> music, he would instantly throw him into the Thames. The
> Doctor, in order to allay the fears of the ladies, pocketed the
> insult with the best grace he could and continued his tune
> all the way up the river.

The story continues with the poet tracking down the officer in a
lonely walk at Vauxhall, challenging him to a private duel and
insisting on swords. 'The duellists met the next morning at the
hour and place appointed. But the moment the officer took his
ground, the Doctor presented to his head a large horse pistol.
"What," said the officer, "do you intend to assassinate me?"
"No," said the Doctor, "but you shall this instant put up your

sword and dance a minuet, otherwise you are a dead man."
Some short altercation ensued, but the Doctor appeared so
serious and determined that the officer could not help
complying. "Now, sir," said the Doctor, "you forced me to play
yesterday against my will, and I have obliged you to dance this
day against yours; we are again on an equal footing, and
whatever other satisfaction you demand I am ready to grant."
The officer forthwith embraced the Doctor, acknowledged his
impertinence and begged that for the future they might live on
terms of the sincerest friendship, which they did ever after.'[46]

Young's letters are hardly more revealing about his feelings
for women. Once, on 23 May, 1726,[47] congratulating Tickell on
his marriage, he expressed the wish that he could follow his
friend's example; and on 20 April, 1727[48] he at least showed an
eye for a pretty girl, reporting 'a great show of ladies and
butterflies' in Kensington Gardens, where 'to the dishonour of
Christianity a Jewish lady carried away all the adoration of the
place'. But the only names we know of ladies in the poet's life
were his patronesses like old Lady Giffard, Lady Mary Wortley
Montagu, Mrs Howard and, about this time, the 'young' Duchess
of Marlborough. A richly bound manuscript of *The Brothers*, now
in the Rothschild Library,[r] contains an extraordinary 'private
dedication' to the Duchess in Young's autograph, but without a
date. The wording suggests a relationship of more than usual
warmth between poet and patroness:

> I beg leave to dedicate the following play to your Grace's
> *private* amusement. I publish it to what I most esteem in the
> world when I publish it to your Grace; and more is
> superfluous. Nor do I less gratify my ambition than my
> gratitude in what I now do. I address myself to the
> daughter of the Duke of Marlborough, and to the mother
> of Lady Mary . . . The picture I have drawn in the following
> scenes of a parent's affection had been much more perfect,
> had I had the honour of sooner knowing the charms of
> such a daughter and your Grace's delicate sensibility of
> heart. Your Grace's exquisite relish for Shakespeare is a
> demonstration of your superior taste in this kind of writing;

[r] I am indebted to Lord Rothschild for permission to examine this manuscript
from his collection. There are considerable textual differences from the printed
version, both additions and omissions.

nor do I know any exception to your Grace's refined taste of
real merit in every way, but your partiality shown to me. Yet
this is not without its excuse if the profoundest veneration
and most peculiar attachment of heart may be allowed, with
generous minds, to hide a multitude of faults.

Madam, a *private dedication* is perhaps without precedent,
and I am glad of it. For a person possessed of so peculiar a
manner of obliging should, if possible, meet with as
peculiar a manner of gratitude for it. I am for ever, with a
devotion you only could occasion and you only can
understand, Madam, your Grace's most dutiful and most
obedient humble servant.[49]

The only other evidence of Young's friendship with the Duchess
is one of the anecdotes recorded by Spence, that 'the Duchess
showed me a diamond necklace . . . that cost seven thousand
pounds' and was purchased with the money Congreve left
her'.[50] This suggests that Congreve may have been the link
between them, especially in view of the compliments to Lady
Mary, that belated baby whose paternity was assigned by rumour
to the playwright.[t] If so, the acquaintance would date from
before January, 1729, when Congreve died; and the story shows
that it continued after his death. The strange thing about the
manuscript is that the flyleaf bears the inscription, 'Presented by
Dr Young to Sir William Bunbury, 1748',[51] which can only mean
that the poet never presented it to the Duchess after all. Did his
heart fail him at the boldness of his dedication? Or did the
Duchess forestall him with her death in October, 1733?

Whatever the poet's experience of women, these satires were
the most successful of the *Universal Passion*, as the subject was
suitable for the delicate, 'laughing' style of Young – though one
must take leave to doubt the effectiveness of such treatment,
since so many of the feminine foibles exposed by Young are as
prevalent as ever in our own day. We have all met the hostess
who thinks it her duty to keep up the conversation at all costs:

---

[s] Young's comment was, 'How much better would it have been given to poor
Mrs Bracegirdle' (the actress with whom Congreve was intimate till he met the
Duchess). (Osborn, 798.)
[t] Lady Mary Godolphin was born to Henrietta, Duchess of Marlborough, in
1723 – six years after the marriage of her elder sister to the Duke of Newcastle.
Her mother had married in 1698 at the age of seventeen.

> Nor far beneath her in renown is she
> Who through good breeding is ill company;
> Whose manners will not let her 'larum cease;
> Who thinks you are unhappy when at peace . . .
> A dearth of words a woman need not fear,
> But 'tis a task indeed to learn – to hear.[52]

Or there is the cocktail-party devotee:

> Such Fulvia's passion for the town, fresh air
> (An odd effect!) gives vapours to the fair.
> Green fields and shady groves and crystal springs
> And larks and nightingales are odious things;
> But smoke and dust and noise and crowds delight
> And to be pressed to death transports her quite.[53]

The frank outspoken girl was known to the eighteenth century:

> Thalestris triumphs in a manly mien;
> Loud is her accent and her phrase obscene.
> In fair and open dealing where's the shame?
> What nature dares to give, she dares to name.[54]

And so was her revolutionary sister, all protest and permissiveness:

> Amasia hates a prude and scorns restraint;
> Whate'er she is, she'll not appear a saint.
> Her soul superior flies formality;
> So gay her air, her conduct is so free,
> Some might suspect the nymph not over good –
> Nor would they be mistaken, if they should.[55]

Warton thought the characters of women 'incomparably the best'[u] of Young's series and pointed out that they were published eight years before Pope's essay on the same theme. Dr Johnson recited two extracts from memory in the wilds of Skye, the characters of Brunetta and Stella. Here is Brunetta:

> Brunetta's wise in actions great and rare,
> But scorns on trifles to bestow her care.
> Thus every hour Brunetta is to blame,
> Because the occasion is beneath her aim.[56]

---

[u] The Bluestockings did not agree. Mrs Chapone wrote to Miss Carter in 1750: 'I think the first four satires equal to any of Pope's. Those upon women are, in my opinion, much inferior to the others, which I hope may be accounted for to the credit of the sex.' (Chapone, *Posthumous Works*, 1807, 43.)

Stella on the other hand was one of Young's complimentary portraits:

> O no, see Stella – her eyes shine as bright
> As if her tongue was never in the right.
> And yet what real learning, judgment, fire!
> She seems inspired and can herself inspire.
> How then (if malice ruled not all the fair)
> Could Daphne publish, and could she forbear?
> We grant that beauty is no bar to sense,
> Nor is't a sanction for impertinence.[57]

Daphne, Stella's opposite, was the pretty pseudo-intellectual who is listened to for her looks:

> O'er the belle-lettre lovely Daphne reigns;
> Again the god Apollo wears her chains.
> With legs tossed high on her sophee she sits,
> Vouchsafing audience to contending wits.
> Of each performance she's the final test;
> One act read o'er, she prophesies the rest,
> And then, pronouncing with decisive air,
> Fully convinces all the town – she's fair.[58]

The biographer of Lady Mary Wortley Montagu accuses Young of satirizing his patroness as Daphne; but might she not be Stella? Walpole plumped for Tullia, the lady who earned the proverbial lines:

> With skill she vibrates her eternal tongue,
> For ever most divinely in the wrong.[59]

Famous quotations like the last line, or this –

> Nor take her tea without a stratagem,[60]

are scattered up and down the length of the *Universal Passion.* Yet how many of those who repeat them nowadays have any idea of their source?

The publication of *Satire VI* was followed a month later, on 18 March, 1728,[61] by the issue of a collected edition in octavo of the seven satires with a new general title, *Love of Fame,* and the preface which has already been quoted. It was called the 'second edition, corrected and altered', and the revision was thorough, with about a third of the lines showing changes, omissions and additions.[v] With this Young wound up his satirical efforts for the present, just at the time that his friend Pope was embarking on *The Dunciad*, as a letter of 5 February reported to Tickell:

> Mr Pope is finishing a burlesque Heroic on writers and the modern diversions of the town; it alludes to Homer and Virgil throughout. The fifth book of Virgil is burlesqued into games in which booksellers run for authors and p—ss for authoresses, &c, as is likewise part of the sixth by a vision of heroes in dullness, &c; 'tis near done and what is done is very correct.[62]

He also mentioned Gay, whose '*Beggar's Opera* has a run, which is well for him – he might run if his play did not', and 'poor Steele . . . laughing under a mountain in Wales',[w] and other poetical friends. But it is strange that he said nothing about Richard Savage, who at that moment was the centre of a sensational scandal. Already notorious for his claim to be the bastard son of Earl Rivers and the Countess of Macclesfield, he was now lying in Newgate, awaiting execution for killing a man in a tavern brawl on 27 November, 1727. But his friends stood by him and Young, not content with sending him a 'letter most passionately kind',[63] visited him in prison[64] and on one occasion brought him five guineas from Pope.[65] Eventually Savage was pardoned and released in March, 1728, and he expressed his gratitude in *The Wanderer*, giving first place among the 'instructive volumes of the wise and good' to:

> What Young satiric and sublime has writ,
> Whose life is virtue and whose muse is wit.[66]

That March the third volume of the *Miscellanies* of Pope and Swift came out with its *Treatise of the Bathos, or Art of Sinking in Poetry*. The poetasters whose works were quoted as examples of the Bathos were naturally infuriated, and on 14 April Young reported to Tickell that he had 'no manner of news but that the offended wits are entered into a club to take revenge on Swift

---

[v] Young's preoccupation with his revised version perhaps explains why the folio edition of *Satire VI* was full of errata, whereas the other folios were almost flawless.

[w] In 1724, by agreement with his creditors, Steele had retired to Carmarthen, where he died on 1 September, 1729.

and Pope for their late attack, and that hitherto they have justified all that can be said against them'.[67] But the poor dunces were always one move behind their tormentor. As we have seen, Pope had already prepared his next assault and the counter-attacks of his victims only gave him the excuse to launch *The Dunciad* in May. Unfortunately we cannot follow the campaign, as seen by Young, any further, for with his letter of 14 April, 1728 his correspondence with Tickell ceased. It ceased, moreover, on its old note of complaint, for the news of the dunces was only a postscript, while the body of the letter was given up to renewed protests at Lord Carteret's treatment of him:

> I see some church preferment has been lately disposed of. I know not what to say on that head; no promise could have been more express than that my Lord Lieutenant gave me.[68]

So ended Young's four-year siege of the Lord-Lieutenant, who returned to England soon after. Carteret really does seem to have behaved rather shabbily, giving the poet two express promises and keeping neither. One can hardly blame his client for the dig in *Satire V*:

> Wealth is a cheat; believe not what it says.
> Like any Lord it promises – and pays.[69]

We should not, however, make the mistake of supposing that the cessation of Young's letters to Tickell was due to despair or disgust at his friend's ineffectiveness. The reason was simply that Tickell himself came over to England with his wife that summer, a prospect that Young welcomed in a letter of March.[70] With the return of both Carteret and Tickell from Dublin in 1728 the poet finally abandoned his vain pursuit of preferment in Ireland.

CHAPTER 7

Fit for Pindar

1728–1730

Though the mirage of an Irish mitre had now faded away, Young still had high hopes of the new Queen. He had been her chaplain; he had dedicated his sermon to her; and he had ended his last satire *On Women* with an elegant compliment to the paragon of Queens:

> Midst empire's charms how Carolina's heart
> Glows with the love of virtue and of art!
> Her favour is diffused to that degree,
> Excess of goodness! it has dawned on me.
> When in my page, to balance numerous faults,
> Or godlike deeds were shown or generous thoughts,
> She smiled, industrious to be pleased, nor knew
> From whom my pen the borrowed lustre drew.[1]

He also attended court assiduously and described to Tickell the celebration of her birthday on 1 March, 1728:

> The birthday was very splendid and full; the riot and throng of it was uncommon. But I hear of no mischief occasioned by it but the death of one gentleman, who dropped down with his glass in his hand, and the publication of two or three panegyrics . . . The Archbishop of Canterbury, who has been ill, sent his compliments to the Queen on her birthday by Dr Mead and let her know he was much better. But his Grace desired Dr Mead not to mention it to any of his brethren of the clergy, because it was a day of rejoicing. You see there are jokes upon the bench, and that is all. Tillotson is quite dead. Those among us who pretend to copy him are like those in poesy who pretend to copy Dryden. They have a little of the form but none of the power.[2]

Young's courting of Caroline paid off and on 30 April, 1728[3] he was appointed Chaplain in Ordinary to the King. But this was an honorary appointment, carrying no salary and involving only one or two sermons a year, since there were four chaplains in waiting each month, Young's month being June. It has naturally been assumed hitherto that he must have been ordained a priest by this time; but in trying to establish the date of his ordination Mr W. Branch Johnson, the historian of Welwyn (where Young lived from 1730 till his death), unearthed some surprising facts. In the *Liber Cleri* of Lincoln, in which diocese Welwyn fell, a note was taken of the orders exhibited by the clergy at the Bishop's first visitation, and against Young's name appear the words 'P. 9th June 1728 by R. Winton'.[4] A similar note on the dorse of the deed presenting him to Welwyn confirmed the date and place, and a further examination of the Winchester Subscription Books revealed the signature 'Edw. Young' on 9 June, 1728,[5] this time 'ad Sacrum Presbyteratus Ordinem admittendus'. As this date was a Sunday, his ordination as a priest must have taken place on the same day and, as his name occurs alone, it was presumably a private ordination. Paradoxical as it may seem, Young managed to get appointed Chaplain to the King before he was a fully-qualified priest – and as his duty month was June, he can only just have achieved priesthood in time.

Ready as ever to express his gratitude, the poet produced a new work with a dedicatory *Ode to the King* prefixed, to coincide with his first royal sermon. *Ocean, an Ode*, the first of his unlucky excursions into the lyric field, came out on 8 June,[6] 'occasioned by His Majesty's royal encouragement of the sea service'[7] in a recent speech on naval affairs.[a] It was prefaced by a critical discourse on lyric poetry which demonstrates in acute form the gulf between the poet's ideas and practice in his classic period. The Augustan Age was not, of course, an auspicious era for lyric verse; the classic mind recognized that the ode was a form of poetry where its characteristic virtues of reason and restraint were not applicable, but it still preferred to turn for guidance to Greek or Latin models rather than rely on native feeling. Of the ancient lyric poets the most obviously unrestrained, and therefore inspired, was Pindar, and so the would-be writers of odes attempted to be 'Pindaric'. As Young put in in his preface:

[a] On 27 January, 1728 the new King called for less violent methods of recruitment for the Navy than the press-gang and for further endowment of Greenwich Hospital for worn-out sailors.

> The ode, as it is the eldest kind of poetry, so it is more
> spiritous and more remote from prose than any other in
> sense, sound, expression and conduct . . . its conduct
> should be rapturous, somewhat abrupt, and immethodical
> to a vulgar eye. That apparent order and connexion, which
> gives form and life to *some* compositions, takes away the
> very soul of *this*. Fire, elevation and select thought are
> indispensable; an humble, tame and vulgar ode is the most
> pitiful error a pen can commit . . . And as its subjects are
> sublime, its writer's genius should be so too; otherwise it
> becomes the meanest thing in writing, viz. an involuntary
> burlesque . . . Thus Pindar, who has as much logic at the
> bottom as Aristotle and Euclid, to some critics has appeared
> as mad, and must appear so to all who enjoy no portion of his
> own divine spirit. Dwarf understandings, measuring others
> by their own standard, are apt to think they see a monster
> when they see a man.[8]

Alas, the metre that Young chose was methodical to excess,
without even the calculated abruptness that gave variety, if not
rapture, to other Pindaric efforts.[b] With his patriotic belief in the
right of modern writers, like Shakespeare and Milton, to be
ranked with the ancient masters, he was bold enough, after the
conventional homage to Pindar, Anacreon, Sappho and Horace,
to add:

> But, after all, to the honour of our own country I must add
> that I think Mr Dryden's *Ode on St Cecilia's Day* inferior to no
> composition of this kind. Its chief beauty consists in adapting
> the numbers most happily to the variety of the occasion.
> Those which he has chosen to express majesty, viz.
>
> > Assumes the God,
> > Affects to nod,
> > And seems to shake the spheres,
>
> are chosen in the following ode, because the subject of it is
> great.[9]

---

[b] Isaac Watts summarized and exemplified the 'Pindaric' theory in one of his
own odes:
> Such is the Muse: lo, she disdains
> > The links and chains,
> > Measures and rules of vulgar strains,
> And o'er the rules of harmony a sovereign queen she reigns.
> > > (Chalmers, XIII, 41.)

Young therefore repeated this metre without variation throughout his seventy-three stanzas and the jingle of the short lines, combined with the bombastic diction and inflated sentiments of Pindaric sublimity, makes it irresistibly comic. His ode sank into what he most condemned, an 'involuntary burlesque', as in this description of a stormy sea:

> And storms deface
> The fluid glass
> In which ere while Britannia fair
> Looked down with pride
> Like Ocean's bride,
> Adjusting her majestic air![10]

No one, even in his own day, commended Young's odes and therefore, perhaps, they took no notice of the preface to *Ocean*. In it the poet made a plea for originality which, when repeated thirty years later in his *Conjectures on Original Composition*, was to have a profound influence on the European Romantic movement. But in 1728 he was a voice crying in the wilderness and such heretical doctrines as these went unremarked:

> Above all in this, as in every work of genius, somewhat of an original spirit should at least be attempted; otherwise the poet, whose character disclaims mediocrity, makes a secondary praise his ultimate ambition; which has something of a contradiction in it. Originals only have true life and differ as much from the best imitations as men from the most animated pictures of them. Nor is what I say at all inconsistent with a due deference for the great standards of antiquity; nay, that very deference is an argument for it, for doubtless their example is on my side in this matter. And we should rather imitate their example in the general motives and fundamental methods of their working than in their works themselves. This is a distinction, I think, not hitherto made, and a distinction of consequence. For the first may make us their equals; the second must pronounce us their inferiors even in our utmost success. But the first of these prizes is not so readily taken by the moderns, as valuables too massy for easy carriage are not so liable to the thief.[11]

In *Ocean* Young claimed originality for his subject, 'in its own nature, noble; most proper for an Englishman; . . . and (what is strange) hitherto unsung.'[12] But his choice was cerebral, not spontaneous; it did not arise from personal experience, since he only crossed the sea twice in his life – once to Ireland in 1720 and the other time long after *Ocean*. This may help to explain the singular depths to which he sank in his series of 'naval lyrics'. There was nothing truly observed in them; the images were purely literary and even the humanity that was shocked by the sight of the maimed veterans of Marlborough's wars was lost in his unreal visions of gloriously battling fleets. His patriotic sea-pieces reflected the rising spirit of confident imperialism that inspired Thomson's *Rule, Britannia*.

At the end of *Ocean*, however, the poet suddenly changed his mood. The storms of the sea recalled the storms of life and his desire for peace from the struggles and pretences of town and court. 'In landscapes green true bliss is seen,' he declared, ending with a wish:

> O may I steal
> Along the vale
> Of humble life, secure from foes.
> My friend sincere,
> My judgment clear,
> And gentle business my repose . . .
>
> When temper leans
> To gayer scenes
> And serious life void moments spares,
> The sylvan chase
> My sinews brace;
> Or song unbend my mind from cares.
>
> Nor shun, my soul,
> The genial bowl,
> Where mirth, good nature, spirit flow.
> Ingredients these,
> Above, to please
> The laughing gods, the wise below.
>
> Though rich the vine,
> More wit than wine,
> More sense than wit, goodwill than art
> May I provide;
> Fair truth my pride,
> My joy the converse of the heart.[13]

Here in the description of his quiet country pleasures – hunting,
poetry, wine, talk and friendship – he knew what he was talking
about and the verses, personal and unpretentious, have a certain
charm; and he ended on a note of philosophic resignation,
casting away his 'golden dreams':

> My hours my own,
> My faults unknown,
> My chief revenue in content.
> Then leave one beam
> Of honest fame,
> And scorn the laboured monument.[14]

Young's wish for quiet retirement was not yet to be fulfilled,
but there is a great dearth of information about his activities for
the next year or two owing to the ending of his correspondence
with Tickell. The next definite date is 30 January, 1729,[15] when
he was invited to preach to the House of Commons at St
Margaret's, Westminster, on the anniversary of the martyrdom
of King Charles I. The following day the House passed a vote of
thanks for his sermon, adding 'that he be desired to print the
same, and that Mr Dodington, Mr Cary and Mr Gibson do
acquaint him therewith.'[16] Evidently the Oxford poets were still
sticking together – Walter Cary was now MP for Dartmouth and
a Lord of Trade. The sermon was duly published, with a
dedication to the members of the Commons, on 27 February,[17]
under the title of *An Apology for Princes, or the Reverence due to
Government*. It consisted mainly of abstract considerations on the
duties of kings and the difficulties of government, with little
reference to the circumstances of King Charles's death. As
Mitford put it, 'There is always ingenuity of thought and fertility
of allusion, but . . . it reads like a translation glittering with the
pithy apophthegms and pointed sentences of Seneca.'[18] In the
first edition the text runs to forty-seven pages – less indeed than
the *True Estimate* but still too much, one would think, for the
patience of his Parliamentary audience. With the sermon-
reading public it did not prove as popular as his previous
discourse, which reached its third edition this year; and though
Croft asserts that Young 'became a very popular preacher and
was much followed for the grace and animation of his
delivery',[19] he only published one more sermon, and that thirty

years later. Perhaps he was discouraged by the reception accorded to his best efforts by the court of George II, if the following story is to be believed:

> One Sunday, preaching in his turn at St James's, he found that though he strove to make his audience attentive, yet he could not prevail, upon which his pity for their folly got the better of all decorums, he sat back in the pulpit and burst into a flood of tears.[20]

For nearly a year Young seems to have given up poetry, though not his interest in poets. In October 1728[21] Benjamin Victor published a poem *On the Arrival of H.R.H. Prince Frederick* with a dedication to Walpole's son-in-law, Lord Malpas, to whom Young had introduced him; and on 1 April, 1729 Young wrote a letter of introduction for Thomson,[22] who was gathering subscriptions for a collected edition of *The Seasons*,[c] to Joseph Spence, the new Professor of Poetry at Oxford. Spence was a Wykehamist of a younger generation, the friend and contemporary of Christopher Pitt, and had been elected Professor the previous July on the first day that he became eligible. By his temperate and appreciative essay on Pope's *Odyssey* he had won that poet's favour, and he was beginning to keep those notes of the conversation of his literary friends that furnish us with so many lively and authentic stories of Young. The first of the anecdotes derived from Young date from the period 1728–30 and concern Addison, and the last ones from thirty years later.

During April Pope produced his new Variorum edition of the *Dunciad* with its elaborate mock-scholarly apparatus of prolegomena, footnotes and the rest. The references to Young were, of course, friendly;[d] the prolegomena cited the 'witty and moral

---

[c] Young himself was among the 450 subscribers to the handsome quarto that came out in 1730 and included the first publication of *Autumn* with its recollections of Dodington's hospitality at Eastbury, 'the Muses' seat',
>   Where in the secret bower and winding walk
>   For virtuous Young and thee they twine the bay.   (Chalmers, XII, 440.)

[d] Pope could not, however, resist a dig at his friend's more extravagant flights with a parody in Book III of 'two sublime lines' from the *Epistle to Lansdowne*, 467–8:
>   Who the sun's height can raise at pleasure higher,
>   His lamp illumine, set his flames on fire.

Imitated in *Dunciad*, III, 259–60:
>   Yon stars, yon suns, he rears at pleasure higher,
>   Illumes their light and sets their flames on fire.
>   (Chalmers, XII, 334)

satirist's'[23] invocation to Pope at the beginning of the *Universal Passion*, and the text linked him with Swift and his old friend Abel Evans as victims of Curll:

> To seize his papers, Curll, was thy next care;
> His papers light fly diverse, tossed in air;
> Songs, sonnets, epigrams, the winds uplift
> And whisk 'em back to Evans,[e] Young and Swift.[24]

Now, as the War of the Dunces raged ever fiercer, Young at last decided to take an active part with *Two Epistles to Mr Pope concerning the Authors of the Age*, which came out on 26 January, 1730[25] and naturally supported his friend's line. But, as in the *Universal Passion*, the targets were generalized and the attacks without personal malice, so that these satires take their place rather as a continuation of his previous series than as a genuine intervention in the *Dunciad* campaign. He had already touched briefly on the 'men of ink' in his fourth satire and now he took up the theme *in extenso*. The first Epistle attacked the general rage for writing, specially those who prostituted their pens with venal praise. The second, from Oxford, was more of a moral essay on the art of writing. The style sparkles as ever with epigrams, though at times the sense is so condensed as to be quite difficult to follow. The opening lines, however, are unusually smooth and polished, and the address to Pope is in the poet's best manner:

> Pope, if like mine or Codrus' were thy style,
> The blood of vipers had not stained thy file.
> Merit less solid less despite had bred;
> They had not bit, and then they had not bled.
> Fame is a public mistress, none enjoys
> But more or less his rival's peace destroys;
> With fame in just proportion envy grows;
> The man that makes a character makes foes.
> Slight peevish insects round a genius rise,
> As a bright day awakes a world of flies;
> With hearty malice, but with feeble wing,
> (To show they live) they flutter and they sting.
> But as by depredations wasps proclaim
> The fairest fruit, so these the fairest fame.[27]

---

[e] Pope's first version read 'to Gay, to Young, to Swift'.

The second Epistle consists of a series of 'needful precepts how to write, and live'. Unfortunately Young himself by no means exemplified them all in his own work. It is said he carried out this rule:

> Write and re-write, blot out and write again,
> And for its swiftness ne'er applaud your pen.
> Leave to the jockeys that Newmarket praise;
> Slow runs the Pegasus that wins the bays.[28]

But it is extraordinary how all his labour ended in such unequal work, and it is a striking instance of parental blindness that so erratic a writer could lay down the principle:

> Excuse no fault; though beautiful, 'twill harm;
> One fault shocks more than twenty beauties charm.
> Our age demands correctness: Addison
> And you this commendable hurt have done.
> Now writers find, as once Achilles found,
> The whole is mortal if a part's unsound.[29]

His ideas were sound enough; it was his technique that was at fault. In other ways his practice followed his principles:

> If satire charms, strike faults, but spare the man.
> 'Tis dull to be as witty as you can.
> Satire recoils whenever charged too high;
> Round your own fame the fatal splinters fly.
> As the soft plume gives swiftness to the dart,
> Good breeding sends the satire to the heart.
> Painters and surgeons may the structure scan;
> Genius and morals be with you the man.
> Defaults in those alone should give offence;
> Who strikes the person, pleads his innocence . . .
> Let him be black, fair, tall, short, thin or fat,
> Dirty or clean, I find no theme in that.
> Is that called humour? It has this pretence,
> 'Tis neither virtue, breeding, wit or sense.
> Unless you boast the genius of a Swift,
> Beware of humour, the dull rogue's last shift.[30]

This was aimed, no doubt, at the dunces who made sport of poor Pope's deformities – but the warning could equally apply to Pope's own attacks on the infirmities of Lord Hervey or old John Dennis. As a satirist Young emerges as more estimable, but less effective, because he tried to be fair. The dunces' retort, *One Epistle to Mr Pope, occasioned by Two lately published*, written by Welsted and Moore Smythe, contained only one line of the mildest sarcasm at Young's expense,[f] and even that was qualified by an almost complimentary footnote on 'the Reverend Doctor Edward Young, who in this quarrel of the great contending powers in poesy has been courted by all sides. But some late incidents give a suspicion that he has privately acceded to the Treaty of Twickenham.'[31] Perhaps the mildness of this reaction pinpoints Young's weakness as a satirist: he did not hate, and he did not excite hatred. His satirical poems went as far as talent and wit could take them; they are brilliant, amusing and still well worth reading. But they lack the spice of personal passion that Pope added to the ingredients when he followed Young's recipe in his *Moral Essays*.

Meanwhile the poet continued his pursuit of the two will-o'-the-wisps of ecclesiastical preferment and the Wharton annuities. The Duke had been finally outlawed on 3 April, 1729[32] for high treason in joining the Spanish forces besieging Gibraltar, so that what remained of his trust-estates was forfeited to the Crown. This gave a new chance to Wharton's judgement-creditors to recover something from the wreck, and the suit that had begun in 1723 as *Stiles* v. *Wharton Dux* was revived as *Stiles* v. *the Attorney-General*, with 'your orator Edmund [*sic*] Young' among the minor creditors, still seeking payment of his £1200. The first hearing in the new case took place on 7 November, 1729,[33] but once again it dragged on interminably and another thirty years passed before the poet gained any benefit from his patron's careless munificence. On the preferment front one of the best livings in the gift of All Souls fell vacant in July 1729[34] and Young hurried to Oxford on the 4th[35] to canvass the votes of the other Fellows. The Rectory of Lockinge was the first important College preferment to become available since the three Rectories of Buckland, Barking and Elmly had been filled between December, 1723 and August, 1724, when Young was still hesitating on the brink of ordination. He spent ten days at the College and another week

[f] Even so Welsted apologized to Dodington in a letter dated 14 November, 1730 for this 'slight raillery' on Young. (H.M.C. Various, VI, 9.)

at the end of the month, during which one of the Fellows, Edmund Kinaston, wrote to Warden Niblett:

> Dr Young first acquainted me with the vacancy of Locking living, as likewise that he was a candidate to succeed. I told him I hoped matters would be made up among yourselves. I had last post another pressing letter from him, in answer to which, upon your appearing for the living, I have told him my thoughts this post, that his turn may soon come again and that if I was he, I should this time be easy; and farther that if I was called upon as a Fellow to act in this affair, I must declare for the Warden.[36]

Young came up to Oxford again at the end of August to attend the election, but in vain. On 5 September[37] the Warden was duly appointed and the poet once more disappointed.

Let down by both Carteret and All Souls, Young seems to have decided that his last hope was the King and he began a campaign in which he used every available approach, by petition, poetry – and the backstairs. George II had been out of the country from May, 1729 till 10 September, and his return, coming immediately after Young's repulse over Lockinge, may have seemed to offer a suitable opportunity for a new appeal. The poet therefore presented a written petition to the King, claiming to have lost £300 per annum by being in His Majesty's service;[g] he began another patriotic ode, 'occasioned by His Majesty's return . . . and the succeeding peace';[38] and he sought the help of the King's favourite, Mrs Howard. But he took far too long over his 'naval lyric' – it was 170 stanzas long – and by the time *Imperium Pelagi* came out on 6 April, 1730[39] not only were compliments like 'Returning George supplies the distant sun'[40] rather out-of-date but the Treaty of Seville, signed on 9 November, 1729, was already out of favour. It had been negotiated by Lord Townshend, Secretary of State for the Northern Department (and brother-in-law of Walpole), and came under heavy fire in Parliament as a breach of the Quadruple Alliance. The result was a new European crisis at the beginning of 1730, which brought a split in the government,

[g] My tentative explanation of this statement is that it refers to his missing the living of Lockinge. Did the other Fellows perhaps excuse their preferring the Warden by pointing to Young's royal chaplaincy and presumed chances of royal patronage?

with Townshend demanding action and Walpole preferring talks; and on 15 May Townshend resigned and retired from court to his turnips in Norfolk.

Imperium Pelagi was thus as unhappy in its timing as in its conception. It was a bigger, if not better, *Ocean* – more verses, longer lines and a variation of the theme that was even more open to the perils of bathos. For the subject this time was the merchant navy – indeed the alternative title was *The Merchant*[h] and the poet congratulated himself on being the first to hymn the glories of trade:

> Is 'merchant' an inglorious name?
> No, fit for Pindar such a theme;
> Too great for me – I pant beneath the weight.
> If loud as ocean's were my voice,
> If words and thoughts to court my choice
> Out-numbered sands, I could not reach its height.
>
> Merchants o'er proudest heroes reign;
> Those trade in blessing, these in pain,
> At slaughter swell and shout while nations groan.
> With purple monarchs merchants vie;
> If great to spend, what to supply?
> Priests pray for blessings; merchants pour them down.[41]

And he repeated his boast at the close:

> Thee, Trade, I first – who boast no store,
> Who owe thee nought – thus snatch from shore,
> The shore of prose where thou hast slumbered long,
> And send thy flag triumphant down
> The tide of time to sure renown.
> O bless my country! and thou pay'st my song.[42]

Presumably the poet also received a more practical payment for his song from the Duke of Chandos, to whom it was dedicated (not inappropriately, as he had done very well out of the business of supplies to Marlborough's army) and whose knowledge of 'the rare, illustrious art of being rich'[43] was tactfully extolled. But in the age of the East India Company and the American plantations there was more to commerce than simply making money. The poet praised trade not only for the

---

[h] *The Merchant* was the sub-title at the head of the text. The Dublin edition was issued under this name.

spread of peace and prosperity but for the expansion of empire. *The Close* with its boasts of 'this new, bold, moral, patriot strain', 'Britain's grandeur' and 'Empire's golden reign'[44] makes it clear that *Imperium Pelagi* was really a more appropriate title than *The Merchant*.

As in *Ocean*, the most valuable part of this ode was the preface, in which Young repeated his theory of original composition:

> We have many copies and translations that pass for originals. This Ode, I humbly conceive, is an original, though it professes imitation. No man can be like Pindar by imitating any of his particular works, any more than like Raphael by copying the Cartoons. The genius and spirit of such great men must be collected from the whole; and when thus we are possessed of it, we must exert its energy in subjects and designs of our own. Nothing is so un-Pindarical as following Pindar on the foot. Pindar is an original; and *he* must be so too, who would be like Pindar in that which is his greatest praise. Nothing so unlike as a close copy and a noble original.[45]

And, as with *Ocean*, Young's challenging words were ignored together with the verses to which they were attached.

It was probably at this stage, when he found his petition disregarded and his poem neglected, that Young turned in desperation to his friend Mrs Howard, writing her the notorious letter that is one of the biggest stumbling-blocks for his biographer. Not only do the various indications of the date appear self-contradictory, but the implications as to the poet's moral character are, on the face of it, sinister. Henrietta Howard was the King's *maîtresse-en-titre*, and here was the Reverend Dr Young soliciting her influence for his advancement in the Church:

> Madam,   Monday morning.
>   I know His Majesty's goodness to his servants and his love of justice in general so well that I am confident, if His Majesty knew my case, I should not have any cause to despair of his gracious favour to me.
>   Abilities – Good manners – Service – Age – Want – Suffering and Zeal for His Majesty.
>   These, Madam, are the proper points of consideration in the person that humbly hopes His Majesty's favour.

As to *abilities*, all I can presume to say is, I have done the best I could to improve them. As to *good manners*, I desire no favour if any just objection lies against them. As to *service*, I have been near seven years in His Majesty's and never omitted any duty in it, which few can say. As for *age*, I am turned of fifty. As for *want*, I have no manner of preferment. As for *sufferings*, I have lost £300 per annum by being in His Majesty's service; as I have shown in a representation which His Majesty has been so good to read and consider. As for *zeal*, I have written nothing without showing my duty to their Majesties, and some pieces are dedicated to them.

This, Madam, is the short and true state of my case. They that make their court to the Ministers, and not their Majesties, succeed better. If my case deserves some consideration and you can serve me in it, I humbly hope and believe you will. I shall, therefore, trouble you no further, but beg leave to subscribe myself, with truest respect and gratitude, Yours, etc.

P.S. I have some hope that my Lord Townshend is my friend. If, therefore, soon and before he leaves the court, you had any opportunity of mentioning me with that favour you have been so good to show, I think it would not fail of success; and if not, I shall owe you more than any.[46]

The key to the dating of this letter is the reference to Lord Townshend, who was evidently on the point of resignation. This would make it about the beginning of May, 1730; it could not in any case be much later since Young finally obtained preferment in July, and it could not be earlier if we are to explain his other statements, which demand as late a date as possible. Even so they appear almost impossible to reconcile. 'Near seven years' in His Majesty's service would take him back to the middle of 1723, whereas his service as chaplain to the Princess of Wales could hardly have begun before his ordination at the end of 1724 – a total of five and a half years. Young, however, was poetically vague about figures,[i] and if he simply counted the years from 1724 to 1730, the answer comes to seven. If 'turned of fifty' means in his fiftieth year, the correct date would be after mid-

---

[i] In a letter of January, 1747 he claimed twenty-four years' royal service – and in a letter of February to the same correspondent 'more than five-and-twenty'. (Pettit, 262; 268.)

1732, since he was born in July 1683. But he seems to have believed he was born in 1680 (in 1763 he began a letter 'as a person of 83'),[47] which would put him in his fiftieth year in May 1730.[j]

In the light of his circumstances at that date Young's letter to Mrs Howard is understandable – but is it pardonable? The case against him was vividly expressed by the pious poetess Hannah More, who was one of Young's most devoted admirers:

> I was dining in a Parliamentary party with Lord Castlereagh and he produced for our amusement in the evening some volumes of original letters, curiously preserved by Lady Castlereagh. My curiosity was immediately fixed by that of Dr Young. I professed my enthusiastic admiration of his *Night Thoughts* and begged to see and admire as a relic the original letter of such a man. My request was immediately granted with a significant smile; and what had I the mortification to read? *Horresco referens!* It was the most fawning, servile, mendicant letter, perhaps, that ever was penned by a clergyman, imploring the mistress of George II to exert her interest for his preferment.[48]

The revelation of this letter, unknown to Young's earlier biographers, came when the poet's reputation as a sublime and saintly moralist was at its height, and the shock and reaction was correspondingly severe. But would Young's contemporaries have felt the same? Mrs Howard held an official position at court in the Queen's household. Her behaviour was very proper and her friends, who included the most distinguished members of the aristocracy and all the wits,[k] gave out that her relationship with the King was merely platonic. Horace Walpole described her as 'discreet without being reserved; and having no bad qualities and being constant to her connections, she preserved uncommon respect to the end of her life'.[49] Pope wrote for her the lines *On a Certain Lady at Court*, which ended:

[j] When Young died in April, 1765, the parish register of Welwyn recorded him as 'in the 85th year of his age'. The same uncertainty is shown by his biographer; Croft gave his date of birth as 1681. The *Biographia Britannica*, 1684.

[k] Mrs Howard's villa at Marble Hill, Twickenham, was designed for her by Lords Burlington and Pembroke, the gardens planned by Pope and Lord Bathurst, and the duties of major-domo were undertaken in turn by Pope, Arbuthnot and Swift.

> 'Has she no faults, then (Envy says), Sir?'
> Yes, she has one, I must aver:
> When all the world conspires to praise her,
> The woman's deaf and does not hear.[50]

Was it really so scandalous for a clergyman, who had been a colleague in the service of the Princess, now Queen, to appeal to this much-respected and faultless lady whom all the world conspired to praise? After all, he had the example of the Dean of St Patrick's for it.[51] And if one reads the letter with an unprejudiced eye, it is not really so fawning and servile. There is no flattery of the lady at all, just a straightforward, almost blunt statement of the writer's case, however overstated and eccentric in expression. By the standards of his time there was nothing shameful or even unusual in Young's applying to Mrs Howard to bring his case to her master's notice.

With his usual bad luck or bad judgement Young appealed to Mrs Howard just when her influence was on the wane. After George II's accession Queen Caroline asserted her power over him and snubbed and humiliated the mistress. By 1730 her favour with the King was declining and she could do little for her friends. Yet it may be that she did manage to procure the offer of a post for Young all the same – the office of Poet Laureate. In the early 1730s Richard Rawlingson was gathering material for his 'Biographical notices of Oxford writers'[1] and his manuscript notes in the Bodleian Library accurately record the facts of Young's life up to 1731, with the addition of a detail hitherto unknown: 'recusavit officium Poetae Regiae mortuo Eusden 1730'[52] – he refused the post of Poet Laureate on the death of Laurence Eusden, which took place on 27 September, 1730. It would not have been a surprising choice; the Laureate's duties, in return for a stipend of £100 and a tierce of canary wine, were to write fulsome odes in honour of His Majesty's birthday and the New Year, and Young's recent lyric efforts were very much in the Laureate vein. Why then did he refuse? Was it that by

---

[1] Rawlinson noted, 'Of Dr Young I have an imperfect account from himself.' He also circulated a printed questionnaire for a continuation of Wood's *Athenae Oxonienses*, to which the Rev. Charles Wheatley, Vicar of Brent, Herts, replied on 19 January, 1737: 'Dr Young I know well and believe I could have interest enough with him to fill up an account of himself and his own writings.' (MS Rawlinson, Letters, 29, f. 445.)

September the offer was too late, as he had at last obtained preferment. At any rate on 3 December the laurel was given to Colley Cibber the comedian, whose odes were even more absurd than Young's; and the occasion was celebrated by the usual satirical *Session of the Poets*. The sketches of the candidates before the judgement seat of the goddess Dullness summed up the general opinion of the day:

> With torches, with flambeaux and abundance of fire
> Y——g entered the hall, but was bid to retire;
> She confessed that his plays might pass for good things,
> But his satire too much abounded with stings.[53]

By then, however, an event had taken place that brought about a major change in the poet's life. On 20 July, 1730[54] he was presented by his College to one of its best livings, the Rectory of Welwyn in Hertfordshire. He quickly settled down to the life of a country parson and it seemed that he had given up poetry. One anonymous ode was all that he published in the next ten years, and in 1741 the united publishers found it worth while to issue what they doubtless considered the definitive edition of his works. He retired at the height of his celebrity as one of the brightest luminaries of the Augustan constellation; and his personal reputation was as high as his poetic. His friends loved him for his good heart, while they laughed at him for his eccentricities. Whether or not Young was really the person described by Pope in his letter about the 'odemaker',[m] it could be believed by his friend and admirer Joseph Warton, who commented in his edition of Pope, 'It is said he meant Dr Young; and that he laughed at his frequent absence of mind, to which, but not with affectation, he was subject.'[55] Here then is Pope's story:

> My supper was as singular as my dinner. It was with a
> great poet and *odemaker*, that is a great poet out of his wits
> or out of his way. He came to me very hungry, not for want
> of a dinner (for that I should make no jest of) but having
> forgot to dine. He fell most furiously on the broiled relics of
> a shoulder of mutton, commonly called a blade-bone, he

[m] Sherburn assigns Pope's undated letter to 1716, before Young had published any odes or tragedies. It was first printed in the 'Letters to Ladies' section of Pope's *Works*, vol. V, Cooper, 1737.

professed he never tasted so exquisite a thing, begged me to tell him what the joint was, wondered he had never heard the name of this joint or seen it at other tables, and desired to know how he might direct his butcher to cut out the same for the future – and yet this man, so ignorant in modern butchery, has cut up half a dozen heroes and quartered five or six miserable lives in every tragedy he has written.[56]

Young's odes were indeed 'out of his way'; it was on his satires and dramas in the classic manner that his fame rested. Had he died, as he nearly did, in 1740, he would be remembered only as a minor Augustan. His retirement to Welwyn in 1730 closed a successful, but not outstanding, classic career.

CHAPTER 8

Welwyn Rectory

1730–1740

The presentation of Edward Young to the Rectory of Welwyn was a turning-point in his life. From the end of 1730 he had a home and a family of his own and a regular job in a small country community, instead of wandering between Oxford, London and the country homes of his friends. True, he had had a permanent base at All Souls for twenty-one years, but he had spent very little time there, as far as the surviving Buttery Books show, since 1720. Even when the Rev. Francis Offley, Rector of Welwyn, died on 14 June, 1730,[1] Young did not return to the College till 17 July,[2] three days before the meeting that appointed him to the vacancy; and three days later he left again. Two months later, on 25 September,[3] he came back for his final stay in College and remained nearly a month till 22 October, when he left All Souls for ever. On 3 November[4] he was instituted Rector of Welwyn by the Bishop of Lincoln.

Meanwhile he had taken an even more crucial step. On 4 August, 1730[5] – just a fortnight after his preferment to a living that was worth the respectable income of £300 p.a. and carried with it the Lordship of the Manor – he married the Lady Elizabeth Lee at the church of St Mary-at-Hill, near the Tower of London. Lady Betty was a widow with three young children and, according to her friend Mrs Pendarves, 'not a farthing to support her'.[6] Her husband, Colonel Francis Henry Lee,[a] had died on 26 March,[7] just over four months before her marriage to the poet; and the trouble was that he had invested all his money in buying his Colonelcy three years before and had not

[a] Francis Henry Lee, an officer in the 4th Foot, was first cousin of Lady Elizabeth Lee, whom he married on 31 August, 1717. Soon after, he obtained a Captaincy in the Grenadier Guards, but lost both his own and his wife's money in the South Sea slump in 1720. In June 1725 he was appointed Master of the Revels with an official residence in Somerset House. The salary was only £10 p.a., but the perquisites from his right of licensing plays enabled him to raise nearly £3000 to buy his Colonelcy in his old regiment, the 4th Foot, on 31 March, 1727. He died at Somerset House on 26 March, 1730.

had time to recoup. The sad story is set out in the undated petition for a pension that his widow presented to the King:

> That your petitioner is a daughter of the late Earl of Litchfield from whom she had a considerable fortune; that she married the above-said Col. Francis Henry Lee, who was at that time in very good circumstances, but suffering extremely in his fortune in the fatal South Sea year and having laid out upwards of £3000 for his post as Lieutenant-Colonel in your Majesty's service which (without your Majesty's great clemency and goodness) must be lost to his family, he has left your petitioner and three children in a condition no way suitable to her quality or his rank and in very strait circumstances.[8]

It is clear, then, that Young did not marry Lady Betty Lee for her fortune. On the contrary she may well have married him for *his* money – with three young children to support and no means of her own, a comfortable Rectory may have seemed attractive and Young, a famous poet accepted in the highest circles of society, by no means an unflattering proposal, even though not of the same 'quality' as herself. But why did Young, if he wished to get married, choose to take on three children as well as a wife? Was it a love-match? It might at first seem unlikely. The lady's husband was only four months dead and the couple were both of mature age. Young himself was now 47 and Lady Betty 36; moreover, according to her nephew, the lady-killing Lord Baltimore, she was 'so confounded ugly' that he 'hated to look at her'.[9] On the other hand she was described by the *Historical Register* for 1731 as a 'lady of excellent endowments and great sweetness of temper'.[10] The marriage on both sides was probably one of convenience at first; she needed a husband and a home for her children, he a housekeeper for his new domestic life. But there was a mutual attraction too – he had the glamour of a poet, she the glamour of royal blood. For Lady Betty was the grand-daughter of King Charles II. Her mother, Lady Charlotte Fitzroy, daughter of Charles and Lady Castlemaine, was married in her thirteenth year to Edward Henry Lee, the teenage son of Sir Francis Henry Lee of Ditchley, Oxfordshire, and cousin of Anne Lee who married Thomas Wharton.[b]

[b] Croft attributes Young's acquaintance with Lady Betty to the alleged connection between his father and Mrs Wharton. (Hill, III, 376.)

Edward Henry was duly rewarded with the title of Earl of Litchfield and with his Countess made considerable additions to the royal stock; six boys and four girls, out of eighteen, survived childhood. Lady Betty, her tenth child, was born on 26 May, 1694,[11] married in 1717 and had four children – Elizabeth, born in 1718; Charles Henry, two or three years younger; George Henry, who died in childhood in 1728; and Caroline, born about 1727 and named after the Queen. Thus when Young married her in 1730, his ready-made family consisted of a girl of 12, a boy of about 10 and the baby, Caroline.[c]

But whatever the motives for their marriage, love certainly grew between them and there is one anecdote that suggests that the union was one of affection from the beginning:

> Some time before his marriage, the Doctor walking in his garden at Welwyn with this lady and another, a servant came to tell him a gentleman wished to speak to him. 'Tell him,' says the Doctor, 'I am too happily engaged to change my situation.' The ladies insisted that he should go, as his visitor was a man of rank, his patron, and his friend; and as persuasion had no effect on him, they took him, one by the right hand and the other by the left, and led him to the garden gate. He laid his hand upon his heart and in that expressive manner for which he was so remarkable spoke the following lines:
>
> > Thus Adam looked, when from the garden driven,
> > And thus disputed orders sent from Heaven.
> > Like him I go, but yet to go am loth;
> > Like him I go, for angels drove us both.
> > Hard was his fate, but mine still more unkind;
> > His Eve went with him, but mine stays behind.[12]

This sentimental tale is not, of course, reliable evidence, as Young was already married before he went to Welwyn. Yet it might still be true, for the marriage appears to have been kept

---

[c] The ages of the children are not recorded and can only be inferred. Their parents married on 31 August, 1717 and Elizabeth was 18 when she died on 8 October, 1736. Charles became Page to the Princesses on 21 January, 1729; Page to the King, 27 October, 1736; Cornet of Horse, 29 October, 1739. This suggests birth about 1720. George, buried at St Mary-le-Strand on 24 March, 1728, is recorded as 'Child'. Caroline was still an 'infant' on 23 February, 1747, but by July, 1748, according to a lawsuit, she had 'attained her age of 21 years'.

secret and the publicly announced date of the wedding was over ten months later, 27 May, 1731![d]

Why did the couple conceal their marriage for so long? And why choose 27 May to announce it?[e] If it was a question of public decorum and possible disapproval of Lady Betty re-marrying so soon after her husband's death,[f] surely a year's mourning would have sufficed for form's sake? Or if it was because her claim for a pension might be prejudiced if it were known that she had found provision elsewhere, there was no further reason for concealment after 2 December, 1730,[13] when a royal warrant was issued for payment to her of a pension of £100 p.a. from 'midsummer last past'. Again, supposing that there were good reasons for keeping the secret till May, why could they not simply wait? There seems no reason why Young, having waited so many years to get married, should not have been patient a little longer, till everything was duly and properly arranged. Perhaps it was Lady Betty who was anxious to make sure of a supporter for her family, and Young was ready to oblige her.

Young went to take up his duties at Welwyn at the end of October.[14] His official residence was the Parsonage House, an Elizabethan half-timbered house still in existence but even then in need of repair. But evidently he did not consider it fit for his wife and family, for within three months, on 14 January, 1731,[15] he was recorded in the parish vestry book as paying Poor Rate 'for the late Mr Gelsthorp's house', and Poor Rate was paid by the tenant. It was a large house and property called 'Guessens', which had the advantage of being just across the road from the church and two doors away from the Swan Inn, where guests could be accommodated when the house itself was full. The lease of Guessens must have been arranged before the death of Gelsthorp, which occurred only six days before Young paid the rates, and he appears to have taken the house

---

[d] E.g. *Gentleman's Magazine*, May, 1731, lists under Marriages, '(May) 27, The Rev. Dr Young, an ingenious author, to the Hon. Lady Betty Leigh, sister to the E. of Litchfield'; *Grub-Street Journal*, 3 June, 1731, reported the marriage 'last Thursday', i.e. 27 May, etc.

[e] Could the fact that the bride's birthday was 26 May have any significance?

[f] Young himself, four months after Lady Betty's death, was seeking a new wife, but he took care to keep his courtship from 'taking air in this curious world sooner than it is decent for me to have it known'. (Pettit, 82.)

furnished.[g] Thus there seems no reason why Lady Betty and the
children should not have moved in by the end of 1730; but
presumably she avoided doing so until the marriage was openly
acknowledged in May, 1731. She still retained her first
husband's official lodgings in Somerset House, so there was no
housing problem in the meanwhile – and in fact she never
quitted these apartments, as it was understood (and indeed
reported in the papers a week after Col. Lee's death)[16] that her
young son was to have the succession to the post of Master of the
Revels, though the warrant of appointment was not issued till 22
October, 1731.[17] Possibly Young wished to do some repairs and
redecoration at Guessens before Lady Betty joined him and they
decided to postpone the announcement of their marriage till she
came to Welwyn – a theory which would fit in with the story of
his verses on Adam, if she paid a visit to Welwyn in the guise of
his betrothed. But all we can say for certain is that the poet took
from the start the house that was to be his home for the rest of
his life.

So began for Young a period of pastoral domesticity and
poetical quiescence that lasted for some ten years. Between them
the family was comfortably off, with Young's £200 pension and
Lady Betty's £100 to add to the £300 of the Rectory; and even
young Charles was able to contribute £10 a year after his
appointment as Master of the Revels – at the age of about 11![h]
Besides this the Litchfield relatives were ready to help and Lady
Betty's youngest brother, the Hon. Robert Lee, bought £2000 of
3% annuities of 1731[18] to hold in trust for his nephew. The
Wharton annuities, of course, still gave Young nothing but
trouble, and on 4 February, 1731[19] he had to go to London for
examination by the Master in Chancery, to whom he 'set forth at
large the considerations of the annuities' as well as the Duke's
bond. Philip Wharton himself was now in his extremity, living in

[g] The will of Mrs Sarah Persey, Gelsthorp's mistress, to whom he left his
properties including Guessens, described the house in April, 1737 as 'now in the
possession of Dr Edward Young, . . . together with all the affixed furniture and
utensils that are enjoyed by Dr Young in his lease'. (Somerset House: Boycott
207.)

[h] The authority for payment of his salary was not issued till 11 February, 1732,
backdated to the day of his father's death. The debenture was lost by his mother
and he did not finally receive payment till 21 December, 1733. (*Treasury Books,
1731–1734*, 316; 465.)

poverty on his Spanish army pay, humiliated by the military governor of Catalonia, dissipated, depressed and broken in health, and on 31 May, 1731 he died at the monastery of Poblet, aged only thirty-two. But his death did nothing to help sort out his affairs, as his outlawry had already abolished his rights.

During this time of settling in the Rector had the assistance of a curate, the Rev. William Lytton,[20] who had retired from the Rectory of Knebworth in 1730. Young was frequently absent from Welwyn, but he was not an absentee rector. He resided in the parish and an anonymous contributor to the *Gentleman's Magazine*, who seems to have known Young and Welwyn personally, wrote in 1782:

> He was regular in the performance of all its duties, both in public and in private. I have been told that before his time divine service was performed only on Sunday morning; but he likewise read prayers in the afternoon and on Wednesdays, Fridays and all holidays . . . His discourses were such as must convey information to the meanest, pleasure to the more improved understandings, and edification to both. Every night he read prayers to his own family, and every morning when there was no public service.[21]

On the other hand the evidence of the parish registers and the Bishop's annual transcripts suggests that he was careless in his formal administrative duties. Lytton signed the transcript in 1731; the churchwarden in 1732; churchwarden and clerk in 1733; and it is not till 1734 that we find the signature of 'Ed. Young, Rector'.[22] It is the pattern that one might expect; while personally pious and conscientious, Young was impractical and forgetful in his daily chores and left the business of the parish to his churchwardens, just as he left the business of his household to his wife. As he told another lady after Lady Betty's death, 'I never yet had any hand in family affairs and have no turn for them. All receipts and payments of moneys, etc., was the province of my wife.'[23] Lady Betty coped successfully with her housekeeping and family and also found time to support her husband's enthusiasm for improving his church. An expert needlewoman, she embroidered an altar-cloth with a gold fringe and the words 'I AM THE BREAD OF LIFE' in the middle, which was described by the *London Chronicle* in its obituary[24] of the poet as 'the most curious in this or any other kingdom'.[i]

So the Youngs settled down contentedly to the peaceful round of village life and a harmonious home at Guessens, with its big rambling rooms looking out on to the wide lawns that run down to the little river Mimram. On the far side there stretches a fine avenue of limes, said to have been planted by Young, who soon showed the true eighteenth-century taste for 'improvement', filling his garden with kiosks and inscriptions. Boswell, who visited Guessens with Dr Johnson in 1781, described it thus:

> We went into the garden, where we found a gravel walk, on each side of which was a row of trees, planted by Dr Young, which formed a handsome Gothic arch; Dr Johnson called it a fine grove. I beheld it with reverence. We sat some time in the summerhouse, on the outside wall of which was inscribed *Ambulantes in horto audiebant vocem Dei,* and in reference to a brook by which it is situated, *Vivendi recte qui prorogat horam,* etc.[25]

But even if the poet planted the lime trees immediately he occupied the house, they could hardly have been big enough by 1742 to support the tradition that he composed the *Night Thoughts* in the chequered moonlight of his lime walk. Undoubtedly, though, he walked and moralized for many hours in his garden, as he did beside the river at Oxford and in the woodlands of Eastbury. Twenty-five years later he wrote:

> A garden has ever had the praise and affection of the wise. What is requisite to make a wise and happy man but reflection and peace? And both are the natural growth of a garden. Nor is a garden only a promoter of a good man's happiness, but a picture of it, and in some sort shows him to himself. Its culture, order, fruitfulness and seclusion from the world, compared to the weeds, wildness and exposure of a common field, is no bad emblem of a good man compared to the multitude. A garden weeds the mind; it weeds it of wordly thoughts and sows celestial seed in their stead. For what see we there but what awakens in us our gratitude to Heaven? A garden to the virtuous is a paradise still extant, a paradise unlost.[26]

---

[i] Lady Betty's altar-cloth survived until the disastrous fire of Welwyn Church in 1953.

But while on the garden side of Guessens he was secluded from the world, the frontage runs along the road; and this was the main road from London to the North. London itself was only 25 miles away, a mere four hours' ride, and it was easy for him to go up to town for business or to attend the court, while many important friends dropped in to see him on their way to their northern estates. Though removed from the bustle of London and the learned company of Oxford, Young was by no means cut off at Welwyn.

Not that he had to go four hours' ride to find congenial company. His correspondence and his will show that he was on terms of close friendship with most of the local clergy and gentry, and many of those that he and Lady Betty met when they first arrived in Welwyn turned out to be literally lifelong friends. Such was George North, the curate of Codicote, who also acted as curate of Welwyn when needed. Though one of the most learned antiquaries of his day, he never moved from Codicote from 1729 till his death in 1772, his only preferment being to Vicar in 1743.[27] At Digswell, so close that the Welwyn parish boundary actually ran through his Rectory parlour, was Dr William Keate, brother of Sir Henry Hoo Keate of Kimpton; he succeeded to the baronetcy in 1744 and died at Kimpton in 1757.[28] At Tewin the Rector was Dr Henry Yarborough, who remained there till his death in 1776;[29] and at Ayot St Peter another Fellow of All Souls soon joined the neighbourhood in the person of Dr Ralph Freeman, Rector from 1732 to 1766.[30] Farther away at Hitchin was the Rev. Mark Hildesley from 1731 till his elevation to the Bishopric of Sodor and Man in 1755,[31] while at Hertford was an older man, the Rev. Daniel Hallows,[32] whose daughter became Young's housekeeper. It was the same with the local squirearchy. Nearest was the Searle family at Lockleys in Welwyn parish; at Digswell was Thomas Shallcross, who died in 1770;[33] at Stagenhoe, St Paul's Walden, from 1734 to 1767[34] was Giles Thornton Heysham, whose daughter was to marry Young's son; and at Lammer Park, Wheathampstead, was Sir Samuel Garrard, who died in 1761.[35] All these were later named trustees of Young's charity school. Another great friend was Sir Jeremy Sambrooke of Gubbins, North Mymms, where the poet used to stay; John Boteler of Watton Woodhall was named in his will; at Balls Park lived 'my friend Mr Harrison', MP for Hertford till his death in 1759;[36] while at Tewin were James Fleet and his wife, better known as Lady Cathcart, who ran through four husbands and died in 1789,[37] aged ninety-seven. In spite of her flighty record she had a kind heart and used to take Young's stepdaughter up to London for the season.

Beyond this immediate circle of neighbours extended all the family connections of the Youngs and the Lees. In the decade from 1730 to 1740 nearly all the news is of family events, of which the first important one was the birth of Young's own son on 20 June, 1732.[38] Lady Betty had gone up to London for the confinement and the child was thus born at Somerset House and baptized at St Mary-le-Strand on 16 July[39] with the name of Frederick, after his godfather, the Prince of Wales. The *Biographia Britannica* stated that 'for some years before the death of the late Prince of Wales our poet, who was in favour with that potentate, attended the court pretty constantly';[40] and this is by no means unlikely, since Dodington had become Frederick's chief adviser. Young's courting of the heir to the throne may have been, as Croft hinted,[41] what brought him into disfavour with the King, who loathed his son in the Hanoverian manner. But at the moment this did not matter and Young seemed content with his quiet retreat at Welwyn.

He continued to take an affectionate interest in the Harris family, where his nephew and niece were now growing up. John Harris had obtained a second Rectory at Ash, also in Surrey, in 1718[42] and duly moved there from Chiddingfold, marrying a second wife, who gave him another daughter, Ann. Doctor of Divinity since 1720 and Canon of Chichester since 1721, with his two livings and his Fellowship of Winchester, he was a more successful and prosperous cleric than his famous brother-in-law, and his children's careers were equally smooth. His son Richard proceeded from Winchester to New College in 1730, took his BA in 1733 and his MA and holy orders in 1737.[43] His daughter Jane in 1734[44] married the Rev. Walter Bigg, Fellow of Winchester and brother of the Warden, whom he had succeeded in the family living of Worting, Hants. On Lady Betty's side of the family the relations were, of course, of much higher social standing, but they still kept a fond eye on their young kinsmen in the poet's care. By the time she married Young, still more of her brothers and sisters had succumbed, including two elder brothers on military service as a Guards Colonel and a naval Captain. Thus the Earl of Litchfield at the time was the sixth-born son, George Henry, who was three years older than Lady Betty. Three more brothers were still living, Fitzroy Henry, born in 1699[45] and following the service tradition of the family in the Navy; Thomas, born 1703,[46] of Corpus Christi, Oxford; and the last of the brood, Robert, born in 1706; and there were two married sisters as well. At one remove were all the ducal cousins that resulted from King Charles's unwearied liaisons, the Fitzroys with their three Dukedoms of Cleveland, Grafton and Northumberland, and the Beauclerks with their Dukedom of St Albans; and these too come into the story of Young through his guardianship of the Lee children.

· All this adds up to a retirement from the world of poetry and society that was far from oblivion and solitude. The world, in fact, refused to believe that he had given up writing and attributed to him various probable and improbable works. Some wished to saddle him with the life of Philip Wharton, prefixed to a so-called collection of the Duke's works in 1732. More assigned to him the *Essay on Man*, which came out anonymously in 1733. Even Swift was not sure and wrote to Pope from Dublin on 1 May:

> All things in verse good and bad that London produces are printed here; among the rest the *Essay on Man*, which is understood to come from Dr Young. Nobody names you for it here (we are better judges and I do not rally). It is too philosophical for me; it is not equal, but that author, our friend, never wants some lines of excellent good sense.[48]

It was in this letter that Swift remarked that in his satires Young was not merry enough or angry enough. But whatever Swift thought, the satires were still in high repute and would-be satirists often invoked Young's name, like Thomas Newcomb who dedicated to him the first of his series on *The Manners of the Age*, 1733,[j] or Joseph Turner, who in 1738 wrote *An Epistle to Dr Young*, subtitled 'Of the Depravity of Human Nature'. A

---

[j] This consisted of thirteen moral satires in the manner of the *Universal Passion* and contained complimentary references to Young's sacred poetry and tragedies as well as his satires. Interestingly, Newcomb's Sixth Satire is dedicated to the Earl of Scarborough, the abortive patron of Young's *Satire II*.

different sort of tribute was a parody of his satiric style published
by Isaac Hawkins Browne in 1736. In *A Pipe of Tobacco* the theme
of smoking was treated in the manner of Pope, Swift, Thomson,
'Namby-Pamby' Philips, the Laureate Colley Cibber and Young:

> Critics, avaunt! Tobacco is my theme.
> Tremble like hornets at the blasting steam.
> And you, court-insects, flutter not too near
> Its light nor buzz within the scorching sphere.
> Pollio, with flame like thine my verse inspire,
> So shall the Muse from smoke elicit fire.
> Coxcombs prefer the tickling stink of snuff;
> Yet all their claim to wisdom is – a puff.
> Lord Fopling smokes not – for his teeth afraid;
> Sir Tawdry smokes not – for he wears brocade.
> Ladies, when pipes are brought, affect to swoon;
> They love no smoke except the smoke of town.
> But courtiers hate the puffing tribe; no matter
> Strange if they loved the breath that cannot flatter! . . .
> Yet crowds remain who still its worth proclaim,
> While some for pleasure smoke and some for fame:
> Fame, of our actions universal spring,
> For which we drink, eat, sleep, smoke – everything.[49]

But Young's satire-writing days were over and he never again
used the Heroic couplet. His only poetical publication during
the decade 1731–1740 was yet another patriotic naval ode, *The
Foreign Address*, which came out anonymously on 5 February,
1735[50] with the misleading attribution 'By a Sailor'.[k] It was no
more inspired than his previous lyrics and one breathes a sigh of
relief as he ends at last:

> But ah! 'tis past. I sink, I faint,
> Nor more can glow, or soar, or paint;
> The refluent raptures from my bosom roll.
> To heaven returns the sacred maid,
> And all her golden visions fade,
> Ne'er[l] to revisit my tumultuous soul.[51]

[k] The full title was *The Foreign Address, or the best Argument for Peace. Occasioned
by the British Fleet, and the Posture of Affairs, when the Parliament met, 1734.* Curll
printed a 'second edition' in his collection of Young's *Poetical Works,* 1741,
omitting eight verses.
[l] Actually the 'sacred maid' did revisit him once, twenty years later, bring back
eleven of the same verses for *The Sea-Piece,* 1755.

In 1735 came the first happy scene in what was to be the gloomy drama of the *Night Thoughts*. As recorded in the Welwyn parish register, it reads:

> Marriages: 1735 June 24. The honble. Mr Templeman & Mrs Elizabeth Lee.[52]

The bride was Young's seventeen-year-old stepdaughter Elizabeth, but the name of the groom was really Temple. Henry Temple was the elder son of the first Viscount Palmerston[53] and, according to a well-informed correspondent of the *Gentleman's Magazine*,[54] he first saw Elizabeth at court. While this is not unlikely, there is no need to ascribe their meeting to romantic chance, for Young had known the Temple family ever since 1719, when he met Lady Giffard and her relations at Sheen. His friendship with young Henry Temple dated, according to the *Night Thoughts*,[55] from that time. It would be only natural for his young friend, now about thirty, to meet his stepdaughter, and it would be a source of particular pleasure that they should get married.

But tragedy was waiting to spoil the family's happiness. The Lee stock does not seem to have been strong and marriage was to prove quickly fatal to all Young's stepchildren. A year later Elizabeth was attacked by consumption, and in the autumn of 1736[m] the young couple, accompanied by her mother and stepfather, crossed to France and began to make their way down to the warmer sun of the Riviera. But poor Elizabeth never reached their destination. On 8 October 1736[56] she died, aged eighteen,[n] and on the 10th she was buried in the Protestant cemetery at Lyons. A black marble tombstone, giving the date, her age, her ancestry and a moving Latin inscription, was set up in the courtyard of the Hôtel-Dieu by her grieving husband. Some more prosaic details can be found in the municipal archives of Lyons:

---

[m] The last record of Henry Temple's movements in his father's diary for 1736 was 11 July, when he went from Sheen to London.

[n] The only traces of Elizabeth's married life are (i) a note in Lord Palmerston's diary for 1736: 'May 15. Harry & wife came to Sheen'; (ii) the subscription list of Stephen Duck's *Poems on Several Occasions*, 1736, where her name figures with those of her husband and the rest of the Temples.

Madame Elizabeth Lee, daughter of Colonel Lee, aged about eighteen, wife of Henry Temple, English by birth, was buried at the Hôtel-Dieu at Lyons in the cemetery of the persons of the so-called Reformed religion of the Swiss nation, on the 10th of October 1736, at eleven o'clock at night, by order of the Provost of the Merchants.

Received 729 livres 12 sols.

(Signed) Para, priest-treasurer.[57]

Lord Palmerston's diary[58] noted laconically, 'Harry's wife died at Lyons;'[o] and his mourning son wrote some verses that were later printed as *Lines written at Lyons on the Death of his Wife*:

> Forgive, kind heaven, this lavish waste of tears,
> Whilst sins unwept remain in vast arrears . . .
> But ah! whilst yet the beauteous corse I view,
> Smiling in death, and take my last adieu,
> The impetuous streams no reasoning can restrain;
> Unchecked they run and scorn the stoic rein.
> What though her present state no sorrow knows,
> My heart adopts imaginary woes;
> Her grief, her anguish and her restless pain
> Still tear my breast and throb through every vein;
> My listening ear each moment hears her moan,
> And troubled fancy forms as oft a groan.[59]

Croft therefore was undoubtedly correct in stating that 'Mrs Temple died of a consumption at Lyons,[p] in her way to Nice.'[60] Yet somehow the myth arose that she was buried at Montpellier.

[o] This entry is found against 11 September! The words, 'Harry's wife died' also appear on 4 October. Presumably Lord Palmerston added these entries after he had got the news from France without bothering about the exact date – since both are *before* Elizabeth's death.

[p] This statement, and the words about the difficulties of the funeral, do not appear in Birkbeck Hill's edition of the *Lives of the Poets*, which is a reprint of the third edition, 1783. There Croft simply wrote 'Mrs Temple died . . . at Nice.' The corrected version appeared in Hawkins's edition of Johnson's *Works*, 1787, vol. IV, after the intervention of the second Lord Palmerston, Henry Temple's son by his second wife. (See Laetitia-Maria Hawkins, *Memoirs*, I, 170.) The draft of a letter from his mother to Johnson (in the Liebert collection, Yale) says, 'Narcissa . . . died of a consumption in Oct: 1736 at Lions . . . She was also buried at Lions by Dr Y and in holy ground; which was a privilege not easily obtained and was required to be done at the dead of night, and with the greatest privacy that could be.' This information was evidently conveyed to Croft through Hawkins. Croft's own copy of the 1783 *Lives*, with his manuscript corrections (BL.C.28.h.24) notes: 'By Lord P's communication the last edition of the *Lives* is corrected.

The *Biographia Britannica* in 1766 declared categorically, 'It is certain that his daughter is figured under the poetical name of Narcissa; in her last illness he carried her to Montpellier, . . . where she died.'[61] And in 1769 the French translator of the *Nights*, Pierre le Tourneur, glossed the words 'I bore her nearer to the sun' with the footnote, 'A Montpellier.' Young himself did not name the place in his famous description of his stepdaughters's end:

> Snatched ere thy prime! and in thy bridal hour!
> And when kind fortune, with thy lover, smiled!
> And when high flavoured thy fresh opening joys!
> And when blind man pronounced thy bliss complete!
> And on a foreign shore; where strangers wept,
> Strangers to thee, and more surprising still,
> Strangers to kindness, wept; their eyes let fall
> Inhuman tears, strange tears that trickled down
> From marble hearts. Obdurate tenderness ! . . .
> While nature melted, superstition raved;
> *That* mourned the dead, and *this* denied a grave . . .
> What could I do? What succour? What resource?
> With pious sacrilege a grave I stole;
> With impious piety that grave I wronged,
> Short in my duty, coward in my grief!
> More like her murderer than friend, I crept
> With soft-suspended step and, muffled deep
> In midnight darkness, *whispered* my last sigh –
> I whispered what should echo through their realms,
> Nor writ her name, whose tomb should pierce the skies.[63]

This scene, with the poet secretly laying Narcissa at midnight in a stolen grave, was illustrated in Le Tourneur's *Nuits d'Young* and copied throughout the Latin countries, becoming part of the mythology of European romanticism. The keeper of the King's Garden at Montpellier took advantage of the visits of curious English tourists to elaborate a circumstantial story of the Doctor bribing his predecessor to dig a grave in a solitary corner and 'raining tears'[64] as he carried the corpse, wrapped in a sheet, to her secret resting-place. In 1787 Lord Gardenstone noted in his *Travelling Memorandums*:

> In this garden was secretly buried Narcissa, on whose death Young raves with all the romantic wildness of poetical

phrenzy in his *Night Thoughts*. The spot, a little gloomy grove, is known; I saw it; it is indeed a *doleful shade*. Some generous and liberal-minded French persons of distinction lately made a contribution to erect a monumental tomb over this burial place. The proposal has occasioned serious contests, not yet settled. The orthodox are greatly offended that such a monument should be erected over *unhallowed ground* and to the memory of a heretical girl.[65]

Soon afterwards Lord Camelford[q] obtained permission to dig up the spot and found human bones, which 'put the authenticity of it beyond a doubt';[66] and the subscribers, led by Talma the tragedian, finally achieved their monument, simply inscribed 'Placandis Narcissae Manibus'.[67] The 'Tomb of Narcissa' became one of the sights of Montpellier.

A possible explanation of the rise of this legend may be seen in the curious coincidence of Young's account of Narcissa's burial and the equally secret interment of Lady Wildair in Farquhar's *Sir Harry Wildair*[r] at Montpellier. Farquhar's play was first produced in 1701; but a popular edition was printed in 1735 and it had a short revival in 1737. *Night III, Narcissa*, came out in 1742 and some confused memory of the two similar stories may have given the public the impression that Narcissa too died at Montpellier. It was by no means an unlikely destination; the University was famed for its medical school and the air, according to Smollett, was 'counted salutary in catarrhous consumptions, from its dryness and elasticity'.[68] It is strange that the playwright should have anticipated so closely the circumstances of Elizabeth's end, but there is no reason to doubt that Young's account, though poetically heightened, was basically true. Not only did Croft state, on the authority of Lord Palmerston, that 'her funeral was attended with the difficulties painted in such animated colours in Night the Third';[69] but his

---

[q] Gardenstone (*Memorandums*, I, 191) mentions meeting Lord Camelford at Montpellier. Others attribute the exhumation to the Duke of Gloucester.
[r] Noted by H. W. O'Connor, 'The Narcissa Episode in Young's Night Thoughts' (PMLA, XXXIV, 130–49). Lady Wildair's servant Dick relates: 'Those cursed barbarous devils, the French, would not let us bury her . . . She was a heretic woman and they would not let her corpse be put in their holy ground . . . (We) carried her out upon our own shoulders through a back door at midnight an laid her in a grave that I dug for her myself with my own hands.' (Farquhar, *Complete Works*, 1930, I, 172–3.)

corrector in the *Gentleman's Magazine*, 1782, confirmed the story:

> I well remember to have seen a letter to the Doctor from a
> gentleman who was present at the burial of Mrs Temple . . .
> recalling to his memory some circumstances attending it.
> The Doctor, grieved to be obliged to perform the last offices
> by stealth, proposed that the body should be embalmed and
> brought over to England; but Lady Betty objected. I mention
> this as a confutation of an idle story . . . that, when the Doctor
> was once asked why, since he so deeply lamented the
> obscurity of Mrs Temple's funeral, he had not brought over
> the corpse, he had answered 'I never thought of it.'[70]

Young's French biographer, M. Thomas, more zealous than Le
Tourneur to defend his country against the slur of inhumanity,
pointed out that burial by night was the normal regulation in the
case of heretics[s] and claimed that the poet's only ground for
complaint was the exorbitant fee paid to the city authorities.[t]
Was it just a case of the Provost of the Merchants taking
advantage of a distressed English milord – or perhaps of his
agitated and impractical father-in-law, if the grief-stricken
husband left the arrangements to Young? Or does it argue some
special arrangement, at a special price? Was it merely that a
Protestant ceremony was forbidden? Or did the poet, with
Temple and the other gentleman, really bury the poor girl by
night in an open grave prepared for someone else – and then
settle with the authorities by paying a large fine? This would at
least tally with the poet's rather hysterical memories and the cold
fact of the 726 pounds and 12 sous paid by order of the Provost.

After this tragedy the Youngs moved to Nice, where they spent
the winter, recovering from their grief in the Riviera sunshine.
They took a *bastide* or country house outside the town and Young
spent the time in daily walks beside the sea and discussions on
religion with the local *curé*. Three years later, in a letter to a friend
who was visiting Nice,[u] he indulged in some reminiscences of his
stay there:

[s] Nocturnal burial was not unknown in England; Young's friend William
Harrison's funeral took place at 10 p.m.

[t] Said to be equivalent to some £35 at the rates of that time.

[u] John Williams, former secretary of Richard West, Lord Chancellor of Ireland,
and rumoured lover of his wife. He may have met Young through Mrs West, whose
father, Gilbert Burnet, was Bishop of Salisbury when Young's father was Dean.

> When I was there, I contracted a great intimacy with the
> Mediterranean. Every day I made him a solemn visit. He
> roared very agreeably . . . If you visit my *quondam* habi-
> tation, you will pass a solemn assembly of cypresses; I have a
> great regard for their memory and welfare; they took up
> my quarrel against the sun[v] and often defended me from
> his insults, when he was much more furious than you now
> represent him.[71]

The letter ended with greetings from Lady Betty and himself to
an expatriate friend named Paterson, who had sent his
remembrances. James Paterson, a Scottish officer in the
Sardinian service, evidently liked to welcome British visitors[w]
and from the way Young teased his 'little wife'[x] about her
distaste for eunuchs, it is clear that an intimate friendship had
developed between them. The sun, the sea and good company
soothed the Youngs' sorrow and in the spring of 1737 they set
out to return to 'the rigid north'.

During their stay in Nice – if we may trust the reminiscences
of Temple's second wife – 'Dr Young employed himself in
composing a work; but unfortunately the manuscript was lost in
the journey back to England in the spring. As it had been put
into a trunk which was frequently opened, it was supposed that
the woman-servant, through ignorance, had thrown it out as a
bundle of waste paper at one of the inns.'[72] Young himself
confirmed this in 1762, when he told an inquirer: 'The second
part of the thing you speak of, I wrote at Lyons in France; where
by the carelessness of a servant it was left behind, nor could I
ever recover it.'[73] This sounds suggestive of the 'lost' second part
of his *True Estimate of Human Life*, though the sad events of
Lyons could hardly have been conducive to the expressed
purpose of the second Discourse, to correct the mistaken view
that this world is a vale of tears and to show that God enjoins us
to be happy. At any rate the work was lost and the travellers

[v] According to Mrs Temple (Liebert MS, Yale) Young 'used to say that he was
tired of the clear serene sky and bright sunshine, which was so constant at Nice
that winter, and that he longed to see an English rainy day'.

[w] He was warmly mentioned by Captain Augustus Hervey in 1747 (*Diary*, ed.
D. Erskine, 1953, 54) and Smollett in 1763 (*Travels*, 131). He rose to General and
became Governor of Nice in 1752. He died at Bath in 1765.

[x] Paterson was not married when the Youngs were at Nice; but they may have
met his bride, Deborah Bowdler of Bath, when they visited the Spa in 1737/8.

continued on their way back to England. When they reached
home we do not know.[y] At Easter, 10 April,[74] the Bishop's
transcript for Welwyn parish was signed by a new curate,
Thomas Gatis,[z] while Young's own signature does not appear in
the Vestry minutes till January, 1738. Fifteen years later the
poet told a German visitor that he 'caught a fever on the passage
from Calais to Dover, which brought him to the brink of the
grave';[75] and in 1758 he wrote to Richardson from Bath, 'I was
here twenty years ago.'[76] We may therefore conjecture that the
rest of 1737 was taken up with a serious illness, followed by
convalescence at Bath.

By Christmas Young was back at Welwyn, where he presided
at the vestry meeting on 5 January, 1738.[77] In February he
accompanied Temple to Broadlands, the Palmerston seat in
Hampshire, and in March his friend visited him at Welwyn.[78]
From then till Christmas such news as we have is only of the
family. On 12 September,[79] after waiting a decent two years,
Henry Temple took a second wife, Jane,[aa] daughter of Sir John
Barnard, who had been Lord Mayor of London the previous
year. Young's association with Temple was not interrupted by
this new marriage and the poet thus became acquainted with
Lady Barnard's family, the Godschalls of Sheen, of whom more
later. A week after Temple's wedding Lady Betty's aunt, the
Duchess of Northumberland,[bb] was buried in Westminster
Abbey and Young found himself involved, as the legal guardian
of little Caroline, in the tangled business of clarifying the
Duchess's eccentric will. Caroline's interest, as a 'devisee in
remainder' with her Litchfield and Beauclerk cousins, was
remote, but the business led to a new friendship for Young. The
Duchess left the Great Frogmore estate, near Windsor, worth
£20,000, in trust for her 15-year-old niece, Grace Parsons, on

[y] A rumour, mentioned on 19 January, by a Hertfordshire neighbour, the
Rev. Charles Wheatley, that Young had 'gone with his Lady to drink the waters
at Aix-le-Chapelle', seems to have no basis. (Pettit, 73, n.2.)
[z] Gatis was doing curate's work in the neighbourhood. His signature is also
found at Codicote and Ayot St Lawrence in 1736.
[aa] On 4 December, 1739 a son was born of this union, destined to be second
Viscount Palmerston and the father of the great Victorian Premier.
[bb] Mary Dutton married George Fitzroy, King Charles's third son by Lady
Castlemaine, as his second wife in 1715. A year later he died without legitimate
issue and she lived in great state at Frogmore till her death in 1738.

marriage, provided that she should live under the 'prudent care and management' of the Duchess's friend, Miss Grace Cole, and her father, Captain Cole, and not marry without their consent.[80] Meanwhile she was to receive the rent from the letting of Frogmore House, and this was the difficulty – the house was a white elephant without furniture. The matter was settled amicably, and Chelsea, where the Coles lived with their ward, became a regular port of call for the poet.

Lady Betty's son, Charles, by now had left the nest. On 27 October, 1736,[81] while the family was away in France, he was promoted from Page to Princess Amelia to Page of Honour to the King himself, and as such he spent December at Harwich, awaiting the King's return from Hanover. As Master of the Revels, however, he suffered a severe financial blow when Walpole, stung by Fielding's dramatic satires, forced the Stage Licensing Act through Parliament in June, 1737, giving the right of licensing all dramatic performances to the Lord Chamberlain. The rights of · the Revels Office had been threatened two years earlier by a similar bill proposed by Sir John Barnard, and Charles Lee (then about 15) and Lestrange Symes, the Comptroller of the Revels (who had been appointed under Charles II), had petitioned against that bill as an infringement of their rights.[82] That time they were saved by Barnard's decision to drop the bill rather than establish the arbitrary power of the Lord Chamberlain, as Walpole wished. But in 1737 there was no effective resistance to Walpole's own bill, and poor Charles was left with his £10 salary, his quarters in Somerset House and his empty title, but no more perquisites. The possibility that Young the dramatist might have to apply to his teenage stepson for a licence was now past.[cc]

At last in 1739 the information about Young himself becomes a little fuller. Four letters, all from Welwyn, in February, November and December, together with vestry signatures in July and October, indicate that he spent most of the year quietly at home. Two of the letters were addressed to John Williams on his travels, the first on 23 February to Lyons, the second on 23 November to Nice, already quoted. Williams evidently wrote

cc Young's plays were still occasionally performed; *The Revenge* on 19 and 20 January, 1736 and a special benefit by gentlemen amateurs on 2 May, 1737; *Busiris* on 3 March, 1736. (*London Stage*, III, 544–5; 557; 666.)

first from Lyons, seeking to revive his acquaintance with the poet and wishing him an early 'deanery or mitre'. But though perhaps it was the sight of Elizabeth's tomb that gave Williams the excuse to write, Young's reply avoided the painful memories of Lyons and he confined himself to rueful jokes about his prospects of preferment and safe subjects like books – Homer, Horace, Fénelon and his own contemporaries:

> Newton looked so far and so clearly into nature that he found himself under the necessity to clap a God at the head of it, in order to render anything accountable. As to Voltaire, he is content with the contemplation of his own parts, without looking for any other immortality than they shall give him.[83]

It was only in the letter to Nice, nine months later, that he allowed himself some reminiscences of his own journey and the less harrowing days at his *bastide* by the Mediterranean. The other two letters, on 7 and 18 December, were in answer to the irrepressible Edmund Curll, who had approached the poet in his retirement for a collected edition of his works, which, after ten years of virtual silence, the publishers had every reason to believe were now complete. The first merely acknowledged Curll's letter and complained of the apparent omission of the *Paraphrase on Job*.[84] Curll was evidently rather taken aback by the abruptness of his old victim's reply, for the poet's letter ran:

> Be assured I bear you no ill will; I heartily wish you all success in that undertaking, but am at present not at leisure to revise what I formerly writ.[85]

Why was he not at leisure to revise the edition of his collected works? Was it that he did not want dealings with Curll? Or that he was not really interested any more? Or was it that the fatal illness that was soon to carry off his wife had already become grave? In the *Night Thoughts* he painted the picture of a long slow sickness:

> She (for I know not yet her name in heaven)
> Not early, like Narcissa, left the scene,
> Nor sudden, like Philander. What avail?
> This seeming mitigation but inflames;
> This fancied medicine heightens the disease.

The longer known, the closer still she grew,
And gradual parting is a gradual death.
'Tis the grim tyrant's engine, which extorts
By tardy pressure's still-increasing weight
From hardest hearts confession of distress.
O the long, dark approach through years of pain,
Death's gallery! (might I dare to call it so)
With dismal doubt and sable terror hung;
Sick hope's pale lamp its only glimmering ray;
There fate my melancholy walk ordained,
Forbid self-love itself to flatter there.
How oft I gazed, prophetically sad!
How oft I saw her dead, while yet in smiles!
In smiles she sunk her grief to lessen mine;
She spoke me comfort, and increased my pain.
Like powerful armies trenching at a town,
By slow and silent, but resistless sap,
In his pale progress gently gaining ground,
Death urged his deadly siege. . .
. . . Many a night
He tore the pillow from beneath my head,
Tied down my sore attention to the shock,
By ceaseless depredations on a life
Dearer than that he left me . . .[86]

If this is a true picture – and it strikes one as sincere – Lady
Betty's long decline may well have reached a serious and anxious
stage by mid-December; for before the end of January she was
dead. She had evidently gone up to London for treatment, for
she died in her brother's home in Hanover Street on 29 January,
1740.[dd] After nearly ten years of happy domesticity the pattern
of Young's life was changed once more.

[dd] Reported in the London newspapers on 30 January, 1739/40. She was
buried at Welwyn in the chancel of the church; but the relevant entry by the ill-
educated clerk in the burial register – '1739 Jann: 29 the Right onerable Ladey
Elez: Young' – must refer to the date of her death rather than her actual burial.
The Bishop's transcript (unsigned) adds the words 'from London'.

CHAPTER 9

On the Brink

1740–1741

The change that followed Lady Betty's death was not so much in the poet's physical circumstances as in his spiritual. True, he was deprived of the services of his wife as manager of his household, which he had always left to her; but this was something that could be remedied by finding a new housekeeper – or a new wife. Otherwise his outward life continued as before; he went on living in the same house with his children and carried on with his duties as a country clergyman. Welwyn and Guessens, indeed, remained the background of his being for the rest of his life.

But the real wound was deeper. He had been sincerely attached to his wife and could hardly bear to describe his feelings at her loss. It was not till the end of the fifth *Night*, written in 1743, that he brought himself to the point, after telling of two lovers who perished together:

> A tear? – Can tears suffice? – But not for me.
> How vain our efforts! and our arts, how vain!
> The distant train of thought I took, to shun,
> Has thrown me on my fate – These died together,
> Happy in ruin, undivorced by death!
> Or ne'er to meet, or ne'er to part, is peace –
> Narcissa, pity bleeds at thought of thee;
> Yet thou wast only near me, not myself.
> Survive myself? – That cures all other woe . . .
> O the soft commerce! O the tender ties,
> Close-twisted with the fibres of the heart!
> Which, broken, break them and drain off the soul
> Of human joy, and make it pain to live –
> And is it then to live? When such friends part,
> 'Tis the survivor dies – My heart, no more.[1]

This passage demonstrates the change in him. The personal note, the 'parade of his bleeding heart', is typically romantic. Though it needed yet another blow of fate to open the floodgates, this was the death that meant most to him. Real

feeling broke through the veneer of polite classicism and brought
him back to poetry after ten years – but it was poetry of a different
kind, a kind new to his generation and truly original at last.

Though cynical critics have assumed that the poet, in venting
his griefs at such length, must have been hypocritical or at least
hyperbolical, the facts show that Young was indeed deeply
shaken by the loss of his partner. It was at this time that his long
correspondence with the Duchess of Portland began.[a] Now aged
twenty-four, Prior's 'noble, lovely, little Peggy'[2] was the daughter
of Edward Harley, second Earl of Oxford, the friend of Pope,
Swift and all the Augustan wits. Her mother, moreover, was an
old friend of Young's wife,[b] and the earliest letter of Young that
we have after Lady Betty's death (4 or 11 February) was
addressed to Lady Oxford, 'whom *she* justly held as her truest
friend'.[3] It announced that he was leaving London, but not for
home, as he could not bear the sight of it or indeed of her friends.
Next day he answered the condolences of the Duchess, thanking
her and the Duke for their notice of him in his distress and
wishing they might long continue 'a mutual comfort to each
other, which is a blessing few know how sufficiently to value, till it
is lost'.[4] He was 'going a little way out of town in hope of finding
some relief from change of place', and his next letter showed
where – East Sheen, the home of Henry Temple.

Now it was Temple's turn to comfort Young in his bereavement,
and he took the most practical step possible to restore the poet's
peace of mind by immediately seeking another wife for him.[c]
Among his neighbours at East Sheen was Nicholas Godschall, the

[a] These letters, now at Longleat, were arranged and indexed by the Duchess in
December, 1753. On 2 December Mrs Delany wrote: 'I have had great
entertainment from Dr Young's letters to the Duchess, which she has been settling
and read me above three score: they are, I think, the best collection of men's letters I
ever read: strong sense, fine sentiments, exalted piety; they are written with as much
ease and freedom as politeness can admit of to a great lady and the compliments are
delicate, without the least flattery ... and for wit and lively and uncommon
imagination he is most excellent.' (Llanover, III, 247.)

[b] Lady Betty's only known letter, 12 August, 1728, is addressed to Lady Oxford,
regretting she could not go to Bath, where she had hoped to enjoy 'agreeable deal of
dear Lady Oxford's company'. (Pettit, 77.)

[c] Temple's second wife, who was 'intimately acquainted' with the circumstances,
later wrote, 'Dr Young was deeply affected by the loss of his wife, as they had lived in
great friendship and harmony. He was a very easy, good-tempered man and very
much of a gentleman; but very unfit to be left quite alone or to manage his own
domestic affairs.' (Liebert MS.)

uncle of his own new wife, and one of the Godschalls' friends, a spinster of fifty named Judith Reynolds, was selected as a suitable candidate. She was well off, came of a county family of Suffolk and was sister to a judge.[d] Young was willing to take his friend's advice and by 21 May, after his return to Welwyn, things had advanced to the stage where he could write:

> Dearest Madam, I am detained here necessarily till Tuesday next. On Wednesday morning I propose the great happiness of waiting on you in Norfolk Street, and I hope in God we may then talk together to our mutual satisfaction on the most important point in human life. I wait with impatience for that hour.[5]

This was only four months after Lady Betty's death and may seem to make his protestations of grief ring a little hollow. But we should remember that Lady Betty herself had not scrupled actually to marry Young only four months after the death of Colonel Lee, and secondly that the poet was urgently seeking someone to look after his household and children rather than a new love. Nevertheless the suitor had qualms about letting his new courtship become public property so soon and he took elaborate precautions to keep the affair secret, with Temple and Godschall as eager accomplices. Miss Judith's brother was due to arrive at any moment from Ireland to take up his new appointment at the Court of Exchequer, but Young did not want him to be told till his own legal affairs had been cleared up. His twenty-year struggle to win payment of the Duke of Wharton's bond and annuities was boiling up again and on 26 April the Duke's creditors had demanded that 'the claim of Dr Young is to be considered as a gratuity or present only and ought to be postponed to their demands'.[6] But it was nearly a year before judgement was pronounced and two more before the case was finally settled.

Meanwhile he risked a visit to 'Mrs' Reynolds at her house in Norfolk Street at the end of May, and on 1 June he wrote again from East Sheen, suggesting another call if she could give him

---

[d] James Reynolds (1684–1747), Chief Justice of the Common Pleas of Ireland, had just been appointed a Baron of the Exchequer.

an appointment 'at an hour when no notice will be taken'; otherwise he was afraid to visit her again 'lest our acquaintance should take air in this curious world sooner than it is decent for me to have it known'.[7] Miss Judith replied kindly but coyly without appointing any rendezvous; her brother had now arrived from Ireland and as yet knew nothing. But Young pressed her again:

> Either, Madam, my inclination imposes on my judgment or, I think, a *second* visit cannot give suspicion ... Your brother is sometimes abroad and his servants with him; if his motions are at all regular, you can choose an hour for our purpose ... I desire you to direct your letters to Mr Temple and drop a blot on the superscription, and I shall be sure to have it unopened.[8]

But his 'dearest Madam' does not appear to have replied, for on 10 June Young wrote again, repeating his suggestion; and fearing that she might not have received his previous letter, he added, 'That this may be sure of coming to you, Mr Temple is so good as to deliver it himself.'[9] Miss Reynolds, however, remained unapproachable and Young perhaps began to think twice about courting such a coy old maid, for in his next letter he got down to business:

> A chief difficulty that presses me is a fear lest I expect more from you than you may be willing to undertake. Madam, the case stands thus, and Mr Temple told Mr Goodschall of it: I never yet had any hand in family affairs and have no turn for them; all receipts and payments of moneys, etc., was the province of my wife. How far this may suit with your temper or inclination I am at a loss to know and beg the favour of you to write freely to me on this point. For I think it not fair to desire anything of you after our meeting which was unmentioned before.[10]

The meeting, however, still proved elusive, even though Young, hearing she was going to Sheen in June, postponed a visit to Tunbridge Wells and called three times at the Godschalls' during her stay there. Finally he gave up and went off to Tunbridge at the end of the month. But he continued to write and she, with the safety of distance, ventured to encourage him again.

The poet had been unwell ever since his wife's death and at the Wells he hoped to find a cure. But the weather was bad and the results worse. On 2 July he told Miss Judith that, since coming there, he was 'much indisposed';[11] on 21 July his health was 'yet far from being re-established', and he added, 'The loss of a friend [i.e. his wife] brought this disorder on me, and I hope finding another may prove my cure';[12] on 3 August[13] the waters had not yet answered and the excessive rains had given him a sore throat. But his illness was much more serious than a sore throat. The following day[14] he wrote to Curll and his hand was so tremulous that it is clear he was already in the grip of the fever that nearly killed him. For ten days he was critically ill and only the skill of the famous Dr Mead[e] saved him.

> How late I shuddered on the brink! how late
> Life called for her last refuge in despair!
> That time is mine, O Mead, to thee I owe.[15]

This tribute, at the beginning of the second *Night*, was the only form of payment Young could make, for Mead never accepted a fee from a clergyman.

By 15 August he was able to write to the Duchess, who had invited him to stay with her, that the danger was over but he was 'sunk to the lowest. I am not, Madam, the person you invited; if you will admit this poor stranger whom you never saw before, I will wait on your Grace as soon as I can crawl so far.'[16] Two days later he gave Miss Reynolds a more detailed account of his long fever that had left him with a blister on his head and a weakness not to be expressed; and he added, 'Besides I am so struck with the news of poor Mr Temple [who was taken ill the very same day] that I know not what to do.'[17] Evidently she had written to warn him of the serious illness of his friend, and still worse was to come. On 18 August, the day after this letter was written, Henry Temple died; and by the 22nd Young had heard the shattering news:

> O Madam, what a loss is such a friend! – But I take your advice and indulge myself no farther ... Continue the charity of your correspondence; indeed I want consolation and hearing from you is a cordial.[18]

[e] Richard Mead (1673–1754), physician and book-collector, received a similar tribute from Pope.

This double shock, his own near-fatal illness and the sudden death of his friend, following so closely on the loss of his wife, left the poet a prey to the depression and insomnia that troubled him for the rest of his life and formed the physical background of his *Night Thoughts*. All he could do, as he told Miss Reynolds on 1 September was to 'pray for patience and resignation, of both which I had a most eminent example in my dearest friend Mr Temple'.[19]

Young's words about Temple and Temple's concern for Young, as shown in the Reynolds letters, prove that the young man was more to the poet than a mere ex-stepson-in-law, that despite the twenty-year difference in their ages he was indeed one of Young's closest friends. The tradition that this was the third of the deaths that inspired the *Night Thoughts*, that of his dear friend Philander, is vindicated by the facts. In the sleepless hours that followed the poet's own fever and this new grief his great poem was born.

The tragedy of their mutual friend seems to have brought Young and Judith Reynolds closer than hitherto. Her womanly understanding and sympathy revived his flagging enthusiasm for her, while she melted so far as to permit him to call again. The interview, at Norfolk Street on 25 September,[20] must have been encouraging, for Young wrote to her on 14 October[21] from Ditchley, the Oxfordshire seat of Lord Litchfield, that as soon as his brother-in-law returned from Bath, he proposed to talk to him about their affair. He hoped therefore that she could let him know more of the mind of her brother, who was now evidently in the secret. Mr Baron Reynolds's reaction was still far from certain and his approval was necessary – as was that of Lord Litchfield, apparently, in the case of Young. Though the suitor was nearing 60 and the lady was over 50, they still could not act without reference to the heads of their respective families!

Meanwhile, on the way to Ditchley, Young had paid his long-promised visit to the Portland country home at Bullstrode. Among the guests there was the brilliant Miss Elizabeth Robinson, later famous as Mrs Montagu, the 'Queen of the Blue-stockings', who told her sister on 23 September how she was looking forward to meeting Young, 'for I hear he is agreeable and indeed his private character is excellent'.[22]

She was not disappointed and on 8 October she reported:

> The poetical Dr Young is with us. I am much entertained
> with him; he is a very sensible man, has a lively imagination
> and strikes out very pretty things in his conversation; and
> though he has satirised the worst of our sex, he honours the
> best of them extremely and seems delighted with those who
> act and think reasonably ... Poor Dr Young has got a
> terrible cold, to my great mortification, for he is hoarse and
> can hardly be heard. A wise man of threescore loses a great
> deal by being only seen.[23]

In other letters she described how he 'starts new subjects of
conversation – and there is nothing so much wanted in the
country as the art of making the same people chase new topics
without change of persons';[24] how she intended to write after
dinner, but 'Dr Young came in and entertained my mental
faculties "with a feast of reason and a flow of soul" till six and left
me with a notion or two which I could not digest till tea came
in';[25] how 'he has nothing of the gall of satire in his conversation,
but many pretty thoughts and a particular regard for women
when they are good'.[26] Young's visit to Bullstrode, in fact, had
been a great success and he was invited to come again on his
way back from Lord Litchfield's. Leaving Ditchley early in
November, he revisited Oxford before returning to Bullstrode
for a week-end in the middle of the month and the Duchess was
so pleased with him that she commanded him to join the band of
her regular correspondents. His letter of thanks from London
on 25 November is an example of his ingenious mock-modesty:

> Though, Madam, I cannot add to the brilliancy of your
> letter-box, I can add to the variety of it. I present your
> Grace with a letter which stands eminently distinguished
> from all the rest and defy you to show me another in your
> whole collection in which it had been a merit to be short.[27]

Young stayed in London till 9 December,[28] spending the time
on visits to Miss Reynolds and the equally frustrating pursuit
of his Wharton claims, to which he referred ruefully on 4
December:

> Your Grace is so kind as to enquire if the Law goes on to
> my satisfaction. It goes on to my satisfaction, if I may be

allowed to talk in the language of fine gentlemen, who are
pleased to say they have received satisfaction when they are
run through the body.[29]

This letter also contained the first of a series of teasing
compliments to another of the Duchess's circle, Mrs Pendarves,
the former Mary Granville and future Mrs Delany. Niece of
Lord Lansdowne, sister of Bevil Granville and brought up by
her aunt, the wife of Sir John Stanley, she and Young must have
known each other for years, even before he married her friend
Lady Betty Lee. But now he began to show a special interest in
her and it is clear that the Duchess was pushing 'Penny' as her
candidate for second wife of her favourite poet. Nor was Young
unattracted. The affair with Miss Judith was languishing
through her continued failure to settle matters with her brother;
and Mary Pendarves, though poorer,[f] was ten years younger
and had the advantage in looks, intelligence and family. The
poet's first reference to her is an example of the rather tiresome
affectation of his style when he was being playful and flirtatious:

> I know your Grace starts as much at a pun as Mrs
> Pendarves at a spider. Sweet animal! why should it fright
> us? It was once a pretty girl, till Pallas gave her a rap with
> her thimble for embroidering as well as herself . . .
> However, as I am much inclined to apologise for Mrs
> Pendarves' only fault, I will venture to say she has some
> excuse for her antipathy, since it is but proper that she who
> inherits all the polite arts of that goddess should espouse
> her quarrels.[30]

Mrs Pendarves's aversion to spiders was evidently a family joke
among the Portland set, and in his Christmas letter from
Welwyn Young elaborated on the theme, which he introduced
with the words, 'I am glad to hear Mrs P. is proud of her
weaknesses. I shall now entertain some small hope that I may
not entirely be out of her favour.'[31] Obviously his thoughts were
turning towards Mrs Pendarves, and his letters to Miss Reynolds
at this time became increasingly impatient for a definite answer.

Although Young had been away from his home and parish for

---

[f] Her elderly Cornish husband, whom Lansdowne forced her to marry when
she was 17 and he near 60, died of a fit in 1724 and left no will, so that she had
nothing but her widow's jointure.

over six months, his return to Welwyn on 9 December[32] was sudden and unexpected, in response to an urgent summons from his stepson, who was now a cavalry officer, commissioned Cornet in October, 1739[33] in the Duke of Montagu's Horse. At Barnet, on the way down, he wrote to Miss Reynolds to explain his disappearance without taking leave, adding that he did not dare write to her from Welwyn, 'for the mistress of the Post there is a fine lady and great pryer into secrets, and I am not willing this affair should make a noise till it is more settled between us'.[34] The lady perhaps was offended, for when Young returned to town a month later and wrote inquiring about her brother's intentions towards her and begging to know his final determination, he received no reply. He waited ten days and then on 27 January he seems to have decided to terminate the affair, writing:

> The very great and very just esteem I have for you will not permit me to think any part of your conduct is such that you cannot perfectly justify it if you please. I shall therefore only say that I have, and ever shall have, the deepest sense of your many former favours.[35]

This rebuke provoked an apologetic reply from his 'dearest Madam', who pleaded an indisposition and begged him to 'think favourably' of her. But Young was tired of excuses and delays. With the despairing comment, 'I suppose your health permits you not, Madam, at present to give an answer to that letter of mine which was so long before it came to your hand',[36] he decided to return to Welwyn, after arranging for his town landlord to forward any letter from her so as to circumvent the postmistress's curiosity.

The end of the affair was in sight. But when it came, the *coup de grâce* came from her side – her brother did not approve. On 27 February, 1741 Young wrote his last letter to Judith Reynolds:

> I am heartily sorry for your brother's inflexibility. Your own conduct through this whole affair has given me the highest esteem of your virtue and prudence and lays me under the strongest obligations to be, to the last moment of my life, with the utmost gratitude, respect and affection, Dearest Madam, Your most obedient and most humble servant.[37]

With that, despite the suitor's protestations of lifelong devotion, Miss Reynolds vanished from his life. The 'affair' had lasted nine months without getting anywhere and in the circumstances disenchantment was bound to set in. Moreover he may have begun to suspect that the lady had certain faults, if we may believe John Fenn, a descendant by marriage who annotated the correspondence in 1781 and described her as 'a woman of good sense, but of a high spirit – charitable, if a promiscuous distribution of money may be called charity, but of an unforgiving disposition towards those who had ever offended her and tyrannical to all in any manner dependent upon her'.[38] It sounds as if the poet really had a lucky escape; and he wasted no tears on the occasion, turning his attention at once to the Duchess's choice, Mrs Pendarves, whose superior charms may have contributed to his disillusionment with his late friend Temple's candidate.

Young's visit to London in January had not been solely for the purpose of pursuing his 'Dearest Madam'; it was the Wharton suit that, as he put it, 'drags me to Town through bad weather and gangs of robbers, who infest Enfield Chase. But what can the fools expect from a man at law? I hope they will not beat me for my poverty, for I can honestly assure them that I have parted with my money to gentlemen who deserve hanging full as well as themselves, which they cannot take ill of me; at least, not so ill as if I had fooled it away in paying my debts or squandered it in charity.'[39] The case had now become an internecine battle between the Duke's later creditors, who were owed huge sums for goods and loans, and the poet, whose annuities and bond were prior in date but for less tangible services. On 16 December,[40] after Young had been called away to Welwyn, the Master in Chancery had reported that he did not find any pecuniary consideration for either the bond or the annuities, and as several of the Duke's lenders were still unpaid, he submitted to the court the question whether the demands of Dr Young, amounting to £365,[g] ought to take precedence over debts subsequent in time. The hearing was set for March and in January Young was so busy 'hunting money' that he could not

[g] This figure presumably represented the £350 that Wharton had acknowledged owing to Young, plus interest.

immediately pay his respects to the Duchess, who had now come up to her town house in Whitehall.

> 'But what have I to do with money?' he went on, 'Your Grace promised me what is much more valuable, the friendship of Mrs Pendarves. I thought that long ere this I should have known her very well, but I know her no more than I know your Grace – and you, Madam, of all female riddles are the most exquisite and impenetrable. Why was this favour so often promised? Was it to try my philosophy and see how well I could bear a disappointment? Or was it to try my taste and see how I could relish a jest? The jest is too poignant for my taste; the disappointment is too heavy for my philosophy.'[41]

After Young returned to Welwyn in February the Duchess continued her campaign by letter, claiming that Mrs Pendarves had 'all the perfections of her sex but none of the weaknesses', making Young protest that a fault or two was desirable. 'Gold without alloy will not work; it is quite unfit for the mint, and I fear Mrs. P. without a little more of the *mere mortal* in her will hardly receive that impression I am willing to make. Was admiration our only passion, the most shining excellencies would infallibly carry the day; but, Madam, there are other passions in the heart of man, and those more importunate.'[42] The Duchess's reply encouraged him to be still plainer in his hints, now that Miss Judith had been eliminated:

> Your Grace's endeavour to convince me of her worth is such another attempt as if you should strive to convince me of the truth of the Christian religion; both are equally unnecessary and equally imply your distrust of [my] judgment. But your Grace, like some other celebrated divines, will preach eternally on a text that needs no comment and leave quite unexplained what is truly mysterious. For instance, why has your friend, in spite of several advantageous offers, devoted herself to the criminal selfishness of a single life, when she knows it is her duty to diffuse happiness as much as possibly she can?[43]

A postscript announced meaningly that he would soon be calling on Her Grace and Mrs Pendarves.

The climax came on his next visit to London in March for the

judgement in the case of *Stiles* v. *the Attorney-General*, which had
begun eighteen years before as *Stiles* v. *Wharton Dux*. He sent the
Duchess an elaborately 'phantastical' letter, written, he said, 'as
most of our Wits do, purely for a dinner',[44] and he ventured to
suggest that Mrs Pendarves might be invited too. His first
engagement, however, was on 14 March, when the Lord
Chancellor, the Earl of Hardwicke, pronounced a Solomonic
decision on his claim:

> I cannot determine how far Dr Young is to be preferred
> to general creditors or postponed . . . as they are not before
> the court . . . As to the first annuity, I am of opinion that it is
> not a legal consideration; for though it may be a very good
> inducement to a person for his doing it, yet it will not
> amount to a valuable consideration in the eye of the law.
> But then Dr Young in his examination before the Master
> swears that he quitted the Exeter family and refused the
> £100 annuity, which had been offered him for his life,
> provided he would continue as tutor to Lord Burghley, and
> this merely upon the pressing solicitations of the Duke of
> Wharton and the assurances he gave him of providing for
> him in a much more ample manner. If this be the truth of
> the fact, and it is nowhere contradicted, it does certainly
> amount to a valuable consideration . . . Though the grant of
> the first annuity may be voluntary, taken singly, yet the
> recital in the second will alter the nature of it and turn it
> into a valuable consideration; for as there were arrears on
> the first, there is no doubt but this was a just and lawful debt
> and the promising not to sue for those arrears was a good
> consideration, and from that time the first annuity ceased to
> be a voluntary grant. The bond can never be supported in
> any other light than a voluntary one . . . I cannot consider
> this as a valuable consideration, for Dr Young cannot be
> supposed to be a candidate for a seat in the House of
> Commons upon any other view but serving his country, and
> the part the Duke of Wharton took in the affair can be
> considered no otherwise than a desire or request at most.[45]

The legal report goes on to state that 'the Doctor's annuities
were by the Lord Chancellor directed to be paid out of the
money remaining in the hands of the trustees . . . from the sale
of the trust-estates, so as not to disturb any payments . . . already
made, which are comprised in the Master's report, that was

confirmed in 1729'.[46] But two days later another of the Duke's
creditors 'brought in a bill suggesting fraud and corruption in
the arbitrators and praying that the award be set aside',[47] and it
was another two and a half years before Young finally obtained
his due.

With his material prospects now somewhat brighter the poet
at last took the plunge and before he left town at the end of
March he told the Duchess, 'I had the delight and reputation
yesterday morning of waiting on Mrs Pendarves; but what
followed – stands candidate for a place among your Grace's
mysteries and will not rashly be revealed.'[48] It remains a
mystery. But one may hazard a guess that at this meeting the
poet proposed and was gently but firmly refused. A long
postscript, comparing the female sex to the vine and woodbine
which are made to twine their branches with the rough oak and
elm, complained:

> Now, Madam, a lady of genius that abounds in arts and
> accomplishments, she can agreeably employ every hour by
> herself; she can stand alone; she is free from that weakness
> which lays other ladies under the natural necessity of an
> embrace, and being superior to her own sex, affects an
> independency of ours. I wish that this is not somewhat the
> case of your friend.[49]

From this time on his references to Mrs Pendarves, though
always admiring, were less frequent and less pressing. They
remained good friends, but he had evidently given up the idea
of marriage to her – or indeed to anyone else. After two refusals
Young resigned himself to a single life, looked after by lady
housekeepers.

With his problems, legal and personal, now settled, Young
retired to Welwyn and on 25 March[50] he for once signed the
Bishop's transcript of the Parish register. He spent most of the
spring and early summer at home, and perhaps it was in this
period of lonely quietude that he began to compose the *Night
Thoughts*. The death of the Duchess's father, Lord Oxford, on 16
June brought a new distress and inspired a letter of condolence
that anticipated the paradoxical moralizing of the *Nights*:

> Of God Almighty's manifold blessings to mankind his
> afflictions are the greatest. They will make us wise, or

nothing will. We cannot bear an uninterrupted prosperity prosperously; we cannot bear it without being a little intoxicated with the delicious cup, which will make our virtue reel, if not fall. Hence an ancient said as wisely as wittily, No man is so unhappy as he who never knew affliction.[51]

The same thought is to be found versified in the fifth *Night* –

How wretched is the man who never mourned![52]

and though he had certainly not yet advanced so far into his new poem, he must by then have been well launched into the first of the *Nights* at least.

Having escaped from the brink of death and hovered on the brink of marriage, Young was now on the brink of a new and greater poetical career – at the age of nearly sixty! And it is ironical that this was the year, in January, 1741, when the allied publishers at last issued what they doubtless expected to be the definitive collection of his *Poetical Works*. Curll had taken the initiative, but all the most reputable booksellers were associated with the venture – Tonson, Lintott, Gilliver and six others, most of whom had published the original editions – and the *Works* were produced in two handsome volumes, octavo, at the price of nine shillings. Even so Curll was up to his tricks again; in a preliminary note 'To the Reader' he quoted Young's letters to him as proof that the collection was published 'with his approbation and under his own direction'.[53] But as usual he did not quote them straight. Young's three short notes of 7 December, 1739, 18 December, 1739 and 4 August, 1740[54] were run together as a single letter under the date 9 December, 1739 and by judicious omissions and re-arrangement were made to give the impression that the poet had taken a keen interest in the edition instead of politely brushing it off. By leaving out the phrases '[I] have nothing more to say than this' (7 December, 1739) and 'Be assured I bear you no ill-will' (18 December, 1739) the whole tone was changed. Nor did the impudent editor, who claimed that 'a particular friend of the author's has reviewed and prepared all these pieces for the press',[55] pay any attention to the author's wishes that the *Epistle to Lord Lansdowne* and the *Oration on Codrington* should be omitted; 'this we cannot comply

with', he announced, 'as rendering our collection imperfect'.[56]
But this time Curll's knavery provoked no reaction from the
poet. Young had agreed to the publication but took no active
interest in it. The *Poetical Works* summed up the achievement of
his classical period, but he himself knew that he had passed that
stage.

CHAPTER 10

The Complaint

1741–1743

There is no reference to the *Night Thoughts* in Young's correspondence until almost the eve of the publication of *Night I* in May, 1742. But by then he had already finished the second *Night* and it is safe to assume that he had begun the poem by mid-1741, if not earlier. From the time of his brush with death in August, 1740 he suffered from prolonged bouts of insomnia and it was natural that in the long sleepless hours of darkness he should pass the time by putting into some sort of order his flood of memories and thoughts on 'life, death and immortality'. Gloom and death had always fascinated him and now he gave rein to his natural bent. The *Night Thoughts* really were night thoughts. An anonymous acquaintance confirmed it forty years later:

> I suppose it is generally known that Dr Young, after his first sleep, spent the greatest part of the night in meditation and in the composition of his works; and that he only had to *transcribe* them (if I may use that expression) when he arose, which was at an early hour.[1]

Young himself informed a Swiss visitor in 1751 that the poems were 'really composed in the still of the night, which was made still darker for him by suffering and sleeplessness';[2] and Joseph Spence was told, 'The title of *Night Thoughts* not affected; I never compose but a-nights or on horseback.'[3]

During the daytime and in social company he continued to be an agreeable and amusing companion. It was only during the nights, or when he was ill, that he became the figure of gloom so monotonously depicted by later generations. In August, 1741, for instance, possibly affected by the Duchess's grief for her father, he was overcome again by depression and made for Tunbridge Wells. From there he wrote apologetically to her on 5 August:

> There are but two distempers, and those very different, that bring people to this place, either redundancy or want of

spirits. The first makes people mad, the last, fools. The first,
I observe in this place, like persons bit by the tarantula,
dance immoderately, till the distemper flows off; the last,
like poor Job's friends, sit silent for seven days together, till
the water gives them utterance. The virtue of the water is
yet got no higher than my fingers' ends, which enables me
to write; but when it will arrive at my lips is uncertain.[4]

But he must have recovered fairly soon, as the Duchess's friend
Mrs Donnellan told Miss Robinson on 1 September, 'I conversed
much with Doctor Young, but I had not enough to satisfy me . . .
He enters into human nature, and both his thoughts and
expressions are new.'[5] Indeed he became quite gay, if we may
believe his next letter to Bullstrode, which alleged that Mrs
Donnellan's brother-in-law, Bishop Clayton, and he 'were rivals
at Tunbridge as to a married lady, till her husband in a jealous
fit came from town and snatched her from the impending
danger'.[6]

The Duchess had invited him to stay at Bullstrode again and
he protested humorously:

> To be courted by a Duchess in my old age is a very
> extraordinary fate. Should I tell it to my parishioners, they
> would never believe one word I spoke to them from the
> pulpit afterwards. I lie therefore under a terrible dilemma;
> I must either burst by stifling this secret or make atheists of
> my whole neighbourhood.[7]

Nevertheless it was not till mid-November, after several more
pressing invitations and reproofs, that he promised to 'render
himself at her Grace's tribunal' on Friday, 20th.[8] The Duchess
had another of her favourite divines, Dr Alured Clarke, the
Dean of Exeter,[a] staying at Bullstrode at the same time, as well as
her train of feminine stars, Mary Pendarves, her sister Anne
Dewes and that indefatigable letter-writer, Elizabeth Robinson,
who with her sharp insight and clever pen hit off the contrast
between the two clerics:

> We have a noble convocation of clergy here; Dr Young
> and the Dean of —— are very different characters, of

[a] Dr Alured Clarke (1696–1742) held not only the Deanery of Exeter, from
1741, but prebends of two other Cathedrals, Winchester (from 1723) and
Westminster (from 1731), all at the same time.

different genius, and consequently often of different opinions in argument. We are entertained and instructed by their disputes, which are upon many grave subjects, particularly metaphysics and morality. Dr Young maintains his superiority in all abstracted subjects and is the man of speculation; but to give a notion of the world and to point the motives of action of the ambitious and busy part of mankind, the little courtier excels. Dr Young has only studied himself, and in himself has found wisdom, integrity, benevolence and candour; but for intrigue and cabal he is utterly unacquainted with it.[9]

And after Young's departure on 19 December she summed up:

There is great pleasure in conversing with people of such a turn as Dr Young and Dr Clarke. For the first there is nothing of speculation, either in the terra firma of reason or the visionary province of fancy, into which he does not lead the imagination. In his conversation he examines everything, determines hardly anything, but leaves one's judgement at liberty. The other goes far into a subject and seldom leaves the conclusion of an argument unfinished.[10]

Young got back to Welwyn in time to spend Christmas at home with his family and his parish, as he always tried to do; and on 22 December he sent the Duchess a letter of thanks that was one of his horseback compositions:

As I write this to your Grace on horseback, you will forgive the many allusions you meet with to that animal. The first I shall saddle is Mrs Pendarves. I look on her understanding to be very sure-footed and perfectly acquainted with the road; and though her understanding could show a good sheer pair of heels and distance most companies it comes into, yet is it wisely content not to rob others of their good humour by seeing themselves undone . . . As for Miss Robinson, her understanding is of the best blood . . . but it is sometimes rather pleased to prance than run . . . As for Mrs Dewes, my horse says he has no more similes.[11]

But there were, of course, plenty more similes, for Young seems to have had an inexhaustible stock of ready images both as a writer and talker. For the ladies he exerted the lighter, social and whimsical side of his wit, though at the same time he was busy on the poem that illustrated the deeper and darker side of his nature.

As the year 1742 opened, the time was drawing near for the publication of the first of his *Night Thoughts*, but he made no mention of it to his friends, as he intended to publish anonymously. But on 3 May, in writing of the impending death-bed of his friend and sparring partner, the Dean of Exeter, he ventured to tease the Duchess a little:

> Last week a neighbour of poor Dr Clarke's, now in Huntingdonshire called on me. He told me our friend was still living and . . . retains his spirits and is cheerful under circumstances that fright the bystander . . . Dr Clarke's behaviour brings to my memory some lines which I have formerly read, whether it be in Fletcher perhaps your Grace can tell. After the author has represented a good man whose name is Philander on his death-bed behaving to the surprise of all about him, he adds –
>
>> As some tall tower, or lofty mountain's brow,
>> Detains the sun, illustrious from its height,
>> When rising vapours and descending shades
>> In damps and darkness drown the spacious vale,
>> *Philander* thus augustly reared his head,
>> Undamped by doubt, undarkened by despair;
>> At that black hour, which general horror sheds
>> On the low level of inglorious minds,
>> Sweet peace and heavenly hope and humble joy
>> Divinely beamed on his exalted soul
>> With incommunicable lustre bright.[12]

These lines were actually by Young himself and came from the second *Night*, of which, with one or two minor changes, they form the conclusion. The first *Night* had not yet come out, but it was on the point of appearing. On 31 May, 1742[13] an anonymous poem was published by Robert Dodsley with the title of *The Complaint: or Night-Thoughts on Life, Death & Immortality* – and on the same day Dr Alured Clarke died.

The first edition of the first part of this poem was published in folio and is therefore never found bound up with the other parts, which were all issued in quarto. Moreover the words *Night the First* are not found on the title-page till the second edition. But, as Professor Pettit has pointed out in his *Bibliography of*

Young's Night Thoughts, it is a mistake to suppose that it was originally conceived as a poem complete in itself; those words *do* occur at the head of the text,[14] and Young's quotation of the close of the second *Night* before the first had seen the light, confirms that he always intended a series – though perhaps not such a lengthy one as it eventually became. The first intention, if we may believe Benjamin Victor, was to complete it in three parts, to match the three deaths of his theme. But the extraordinary success of the first books encouraged both the writer and the publisher to carry on rather too long.

In spite of the author's anonymity the poem achieved a second edition, in quarto this time, on 31 July[15] – just two months after its first publication. *Night the First* now figured on the title-page, with an 'inscription' to Speaker Onslow,[b] and soon everyone was talking about it. Benjamin Victor, for instance, who met Young at Tunbridge Wells in July, was not aware of the poem till he returned to London, from which he sent Young an enthusiastic letter about 15 August:

> Since I left you, I have read a poem with a tremendous title, called *The Complaint, or Night Thoughts on Death and Eternity*. A melancholy unfashionable subject – but the reading of it gave me great pleasure; I found the thoughts quite new, and *Doctor Young* written in large characters in every page. I found by your bookseller, Mr Dodsley, that you have carefully concealed your name . . . but you are too good a writer to be able to conceal yourself from your admirers. I hear we are to have the happiness of reading two books more.[16]

He urged Young to add his name in order to 'call the attention of those readers who are led by mode'; but the poet did not, in fact, ever put his name to any of the nine books of *Night Thoughts* that were published over the next four years. His authorship, however, was no secret; like Victor, who boasted to a friend that he found out the author 'the first reading',[17] the public soon guessed his name – there was no one else who could write in such an individual way at that time.

It is not surprising that the poem was something of a

[b] Arthur Onslow (1691–1768) had been a Commoner at Winchester, 1706–7. Elected Speaker in 1727, he was re-elected four times, serving 33 years in all.

sensation, for both in form and spirit it proclaimed a revolt against the ruling Augustan fashion and a reversion to the richer music and fuller emotions of the Elizabethans. The author's joking reference to Fletcher is significant; he was well aware that his new style was rooted in the past, that his blank verse, his startling vocabulary, his personal involvement, his gloom, were in a different mode and mood from the classic clarity and detachment of his contemporaries – and of his own earlier works. Blank verse in itself was a kind of challenge to the establishment, even though there had been plenty of attempts since John Philips revived the Miltonic style in 1701. Most of these, however, were more concerned with the method than the content, mere exercises or parodies in 'Miltonicks', and even in a major poem like Thomson's *Seasons* the style was mainly imitative with all the tricks of inversion, pause and grandiloquence imposed on a language and spirit that were still recognizably Augustan. Young struck a definitely different note; in spite of all his admiration for Milton his blank verse was not at all Miltonic, and his emotional disturbance was far from Augustan.

The famous invocation that opens the first *Night* might well be taken for the work of an Elizabethan:

> Tired nature's sweet restorer, balmy sleep!
> He, like the world, his ready visit pays
> Where fortune smiles; the wretched he forsakes,
> Swift on his downy pinion flies from woe
> And lights on lids unsullied with a tear.
>   From short (as usual) and disturbed repose
> I wake – how happy they who wake no more!
> Yet that were vain, if dreams infest the grave.
> I wake, emerging from a sea of dreams
> Tumultuous, where my wrecked desponding thought
> From wave to wave of fancied misery
> At random drove, her helm of reason lost.
> Though now restored, 'tis only change of pain –
> A bitter change, severer for severe.
> The day too short for my distress; and night,
> Even in the zenith of her dark domain,
> Is sunshine to the colour of my fate.
>   Night, sable goddess, from her ebon throne
> In rayless majesty now stretches forth

> Her leaden sceptre o'er a slumbering world.
> Silence, how dead! and darkness, how profound!
> Nor eye nor listening ear an object finds;
> Creation sleeps. 'Tis as the general pulse
> Of life stood still and nature made a pause,
> An awful pause, prophetic of her end.
> And let her prophecy be soon fulfilled;
> Fate, drop the curtain! I can lose no more.[18]

Here indeed was a 'romantic revival' both in spirit and style, and it was followed by many other passages that show that magic quality which distinguishes poetry from verse. At last Young was giving his originality free rein. It was not in the theme, nor in the scenery of night. The *memento mori* was not new in English verse, nor was the nocturnal reflection – even among the Augustans Parnell had written a *Night-Piece on Death*. What was new, as Leslie Stephen pointed out, was that the poet was 'elaborately and deliberately pathetic'.[19] These were not the calm reflections of a philosophical Augustan but the agonized search for comfort of a suffering soul; and it was exactly his insistence on the personal instead of the general that marks his work as a new departure. It is the essence of romanticism to look inward and expose one's heart – and preferably a bleeding heart; to involve the reader in the writer's emotions instead of treating him to a detached and didactic description of an 'unfortunate lady' or an 'untimely tomb'. Young was didactic too; but his didacticism, his preaching on immortality, had a far greater impact than other poetical essays on this theme because it was not a cold and orderly exercise of logic but a struggle with himself, often confused, often repetitious, but all very human. He was preaching first to convince himself in the long hours of darkness, natural and spiritual, and it was this personal pathos that drew the readers into the argument. The further he gets from his grief, the less readable he becomes. Just as the first book of *Paradise Lost* is the most famous, so the first book of the *Night Thoughts* is the greatest. 'With its famous opening line, its rich note of romantic despair, its exquisite episodes, its sustained magnificence of phrase,' says Gosse, '[it] is one of the lesser treasures of the English language.'[20]

After the launching of his new poem Young suffered a renewed attack of his old complaint and resorted once more to

Tunbridge Wells. On 1 August he reported to the Duchess, 'I dare positively affirm that my head is giddy, but whether I stand on my head or my heels I will not presume to be quite so positive.'[21] But his patroness, who had decided that the poet of the *Night Thoughts* should have preferment, felt that he must not miss the opportunity of courting the influential personages then at Tunbridge. Meanwhile she sent her husband direct to the fountainheads of ecclesiastical patronage, the Duke of Newcastle and the Archbishop of Canterbury, on Young's behalf; and the Duke of Portland instructed him to follow up at once with a letter to the Primate. But 'intrigue and cabal', as Miss Robinson had noted, was not the poet's strong point and the Duchess had to scold him for his diffidence at Tunbridge, causing him to write apologetically on 21 August:

> As to my Lord Egmont . . . I thought I put myself in his way. It was not for me by making the first advance to take his Lordship into my patronage. But perhaps I was too shy. I assure your Grace I'll endeavour to mend for the future.[22]

As for the Archbishop, he had written immediately but it was 'such a letter as neither has received nor expected an answer'.[23]

This evidence throws rather a different light on the traditional picture of Young's indefatigable and servile pursuit of a Bishopric. As will be seen again and again in their later correspondence, it was the Duchess who made the running in the campaign for his preferment and he can hardly be blamed for following the Duke's instructions to write to the Archbishop and the Duchess's to lobby persons of influence. Once again, as with Lord Carteret, he had every reason to expect success, and once again some insuperable and inexplicable obstacle barred the way and forced him – and his patroness – into years of vain importunity.

One favour that the poet *did* ask of the Duchess was that she would introduce Caroline into London society. The girl was now about sixteen and had been in his care ever since she was a baby. He had a deep affection for her, for he loved children and once told the Duchess, 'I consider children as the next order of beings to the blessed angels.'[24] In the spring of 1742[25] he sent her up to London under the wing of his neighbour, Lady Cathcart of

Tewin, who had run through three husbands since Young first
arrived at Welwyn. Though now over fifty and thrice widowed,
Lady Cathcart probably gave the girl quite a gay time, for she
loved dancing and was seen taking part in a dance at Hertford
forty-four years after this time – in her ninety-fifth year! But as
the daughter of a brewer of Southwark, whose marriage to her
Lord had lasted only a year, she could not launch Caroline with
the same éclat as the Duchess of Portland – and after all Caroline
came of royal blood.

The year 1742 also saw the first step in the career of his own
child, Frederick, but Young did not need any ducal assistance, in
getting him a place at his own old school, Winchester. With his
brother-in-law, John Harris, and Harris's son-in-law, Walter
Bigg, both on the Governing Body, the family interest was quite
sufficient and Frederick's name duly appeared on the election
roll of scholars for 1742.[26] The Electors did not even bother to fill
in the required details of birthplace and baptism on the original
election roll. But when the boy's name was entered in the register,
these details were recorded – and all wrong! Frederick's
birthplace was given as Welwyn and his date of baptism as 14
September, 1732 instead of Somerset House and 16 July.[27] Did
Harris simply assume that he was born at Welwyn and guess at the
date of christening? There was no point in deliberately post-
dating the record unless it was put after Michaelmas, the crucial
date in Wiccamical reckoning. A mistake of three months instead
of two would have gained Frederick an extra year's grace when he
badly needed it at the end of his school career. But as it is, we can
only attribute the error to carelessness.

In October[28] the poet set out from Welwyn on his annual
autumn pilgrimage to Bullstrode. But this year he never got
there. He was caught by a rainstorm and wet through by the
time he reached St Albans, where he was forced to spend the
night. Next morning he was seized with such pains in his limbs
that he was obliged to return to Welwyn and take to his bed with
a fever that proved to be the start of another long illness. On 12
December[29] he was able to report that his danger was over but
his recovery slow, and so he did not venture out that winter.
Young was always susceptible to colds, but now that he was
approaching sixty, the results were more serious. However
brightly he might jest in his letters, these recurrent bouts of

influenza, with the consequent loss of spirits, appetite and sleep, were the depressing reality that explains the long-drawn-out gloom of the *Night Thoughts*. The composition of the poem gave him relief in the dark and endless hours of insomnia, and the persistence of his fevers may well account for the persistence of his poem, book after book, long after the first sharpness of his grief – and the first keenness of the public – had passed.

For the moment, however, the public was eager for more, and the second and third *Nights* were greeted with the same acclaim and enthusiasm as the first. They followed each other rapidly at the end of the year; *Night the Second*, dedicated to the Prime Minister, Lord Wilmington,[c] came out on 30 November, 1742[30] and *Night the Third*, dedicated to the Duchess of Portland, on 14 December.[31] By this time the original plan of three books had been abandoned and an advertisement in the third *Night* stated, 'Speedily will be published *Night the Fourth*', though it did not actually appear till three months later. A letter of 20 November to Sir Thomas Hanmer,[d] enclosing the first two *Nights*, spoke of 'other parts to follow'[32] and it must already have been clear that the poet's scheme would not be completed even in four books, as they would cover only two of the three dear departed. The first *Night* had been introductory; the second, entitled *On Time, Death, Friendship*, was devoted to Philander; the third was headed *Narcissa*; while the fourth was *The Christian Triumph*. The third death, that of his wife, was still unsung, and in the event it remained unsung till the sixth part. But it is unlikely that the poet had yet planned as far ahead as that. Rambling, repetitive, with no plan except the general drift of his argument, the poem was a faithful reflection of the feverish musings of grief and sickness. It has been said that Young wrote the *Night Thoughts* to counter the Bolingbrokian Deism that had betrayed Pope in his *Essay on Man*, and Warton noted in his *Essay on Pope*:

[c] The Earl of Wilmington had been Sir Spencer Compton, Speaker from 1715 to 1727; Young had already dedicated to him the fourth satire of *The Universal Passion*.

[d] On 12 January, 1742 Young reported a rumour that Hanmer had married Mrs Pendarves, but the Duchess 'divorced' them on 28 February. In wishing them happiness Young commented: 'There is but one objection against marriage, and that is one which the wise world amongst its ten thousand objections never makes; I mean that the husband and wife seldom die in one day, and then the survivor must necessarily be miserable.' (Pettit, 133; 135.)

Mr Walter Harte[e] assured me he had seen the pressing letter that Dr Young wrote to Mr Pope, urging him to write something on the side of revelation in order to take off the impressions of those doctrines which the *Essay on Man* were supposed to convey. He alluded to this in the conclusion of his first *Night Thought*:

> O had he pressed his theme, pursued the track
> Which opens out of darkness into day!
> O had he, mounted on his wing of fire,
> Soared where I sink and sung immortal man![33]

But for all this it is obvious that the original source of Young's inspiration was his personal grief, not the desire to set right Pope's philosophy. He himself declared in the preface to *Night IV* that 'this thing was entered on purely as a refuge under uneasiness'.[34] The two poems of Pope and Young illustrate the difference between the classic and romantic approach.

Perhaps it was the hint of Pope's deficiencies that annoyed the arrogant William Warburton, who had ingratiated himself with Pope three years earlier by a defence of the orthodoxy of the *Essay on Man*. For Warburton's was one of the few sour voices to greet the *Nights*. On 9 February, 1743 he wrote to Dr Doddridge, the hymn-writer:

> I hope the manuscript poem you mention in your last will be more in the Christian spirit than Dr Young's *Night Complaint*, a dismal rhapsody, and the more dismal for being full of poetical images, all frightful, without design or method; so that I have thought, as Mr Pope's motto to his *Essay on Man* was, 'Know yourself', so the motto to this should be 'Go hang yourself'. For what is any man to do else under that perturbation of mind the author seems to be in? . . . He appears rather to be under a poetical than a religious dilemma by the straining and heaving of his thoughts, which are so strangely affected that one would fancy he thought *album Graecum* better than an ordinary stool.[35]

In his edition of Pope's *Works* eight years later the future Bishop attributed his rather coarse joke to Pope himself. But we have

---

[e] Walter Harte (1709–1774), poet and friend of Pope, wrote an *Essay on Reason*, 1735. He too pressed Pope to write on the side of revelation but was told, 'No, you have already done it.' (Elwin, II, 269.)

other evidence as to how Pope, who was no bigot in his appreciation of poetry, reacted to his old friend's new departure. William Shenstone, the pastoral poet of the Leasowes, told Richard Graves in 1743:

> Dr Young's *Complaint* is the best thing that has come out this season (these twenty years, Pope says) except mine – for so *thinks* every author, who does not think proper to say so.[36]

From poets and public alike the welcome for the *Night Thoughts* was general and at least up to the fourth *Night* they looked forward eagerly to the sequel, like the poetess Mary Jones of Oxford[f] who in January, 1743 had 'seen two of the *Night Thoughts* and like 'em so well as to be impatient for a third. There are some noble *soul-awakening* things in 'em that make my blood run cold when I read 'em.'[37]

Night the Fourth, sub-titled *The Christian Triumph: containing our only cure for the fear of death*, came out on 10 March, 1743,[38] and then there was a pause. The new book was preceded by a short preface:

> As the occasion of this poem was real, not fictitious, so the method pursued in it was rather imposed by what spontaneously arose in author's mind on that occasion than meditated or designed. Which will appear very probable from the nature of it. For it differs from the common mode of poetry, which is from long narrations to draw short morals. Here, on the contrary, the narrative is short and the morality arising from it makes the bulk of the poem. The reason of it is that the facts mentioned did naturally pour these moral reflections on the thought of the writer.
>
> It is evident from the *First Night*, where three deaths are mentioned, that the plan is not yet completed; for two only of those three have yet been sung. But since this *Fourth Night* finishes one principal and important theme, naturally arising from all three, viz. the subduing our fear of death, it will be a proper pausing place for the reader, and the writer too. And it is uncertain whether Providence, or inclination, will permit him to go any farther.[39]

---

[f] Called the 'Chantress' by Dr Johnson, because she was the sister of the Chanter of Christ Church Cathedral, Oxford.

Dodsley therefore issued the fourth *Night* with a general title for the quarto set, and he also seized the opportunity to publish an octavo collected edition of the four *Nights*, still anonymous, which came out on 6 June.[40] The title-page called this the 'fifth edition', though in fact only the first and third *Nights* had so far passed through four editions. The publication of this collected edition makes a convenient point for us also to pause and consider various aspects of the work as far as it had proceeded.

If the poet had really stopped at this stage, even though he had not told the full story, the *Night Thoughts* might well have survived better in times that no longer have the patience to read long poems. There were five more books to come, getting longer and longer and ever more indigestible as they became more didactic. The later books, and especially the ninth *Night* with its astronomical vision of the universe, contain many magnificent passages, but they also contain much that is turgid and are not free from the poet's old failing of bathos. Young was a very unequal writer with as little judgement in his writings as in his dealings with the world. Joseph Warton remarked:

> So little sensible are we of our own imperfections that the very last time I saw Dr Young, he was severely censuring and ridiculing the false pomp of fustian writers and the nauseousness of bombast. I remember he said that such torrents of eloquence were muddy as well as noisy, and that these violent and tumultuous authors put him in mind of a passage of Milton, B. 2, v. 539:
>> Others, with vast Typhaean rage more fell,
>> Rend up both rocks and hills and ride the air
>> In whirlwind. Hell scarce holds the wild uproar.[41]

The dramatic and rhetorical style of the *Night Thoughts* – it is really one enormous soliloquy – laid it open to the dangers of bombast and its counterpart, anticlimax. But in the first book these failings hardly appeared.

In the first *Night* the rich originality of the language and the striking felicity of many of the lines –

> Prisoner of earth and pent beneath the moon[42]

or –

> And quite unparadise the realms of light[43]

or –

> The spider's most attenuated thread
> Is cord, is cable, to man's tender tie
> On earthly bliss; it breaks at every breeze,[44]

these seem the spontaneous inspiration of the moment, and
there are long passages in which this standard is kept up, like:

> This is the desert, this the solitude.
> How populous, how vital is the grave!
> This is creation's melancholy vault,
> The vale funereal, the sad cypress gloom,
> The land of apparitions, empty shades.
> All, all on earth is shadow; all beyond
> Is substance – the reverse is folly's creed.
> How solid all, where change shall be no more!
> This is the bud of being, the dim dawn,
> The twilight of our day, the vestibule;
> Life's theatre as yet is shut, and death
> Strong death alone can heave the massy bar,
> This gross impediment of clay remove
> And make us embryos of existence free,[45]

or the famous lines:

> Be wise today; 'tis madness to defer.
> Next day the fatal precedent will plead;
> Thus on, till wisdom is pushed out of life.
> Procrastination is the thief of time;
> Year after year it steals, till all are fled
> And to the mercies of a moment leaves
> The vast concerns of an eternal scene . . .
> All promise is poor dilatory man,
> And that through every stage. When young, indeed,
> In full content we sometimes nobly rest,
> Unanxious for ourselves, and only wish,
> As duteous sons, our fathers were more wise.
> At thirty man suspects himself a fool;
> Knows it at forty, and reforms his plan;
> At fifty chides his infamous delay,
> Pushes his prudent purpose to resolve,
> In all the magnanimity of thought
> Resolves, and re-resolves; then dies the same.[46]

In the 460 lines of the first book there is hardly a passage that falls much below this level; but in the second book the peculiarities of Young's style – the ingenuity, the paradoxes, the repetition, the images, the neologisms – already begin to seem less natural. There are still the striking lines –

> Lavish of lustrums, and yet fond of life,[47]

or (on man's fate) –

> Endless, hair-hung, breeze-shaken.[48]

There are still fine passages, like this on time:

> Ah, how unjust to nature, and himself,
> Is thoughtless, thankless, inconsistent man!
> Like children babbling nonsense in their sports,
> We censure nature for a span too short;
> That span too short we tax as tedious too . . .
> Blest leisure is our curse; like that of Cain,
> It makes us wander, wander earth around
> To fly that tyrant, thought. As Atlas groaned
> The world beneath, we groan beneath an hour.
> We cry for mercy to the next amusement . . .
> Yet when death kindly tenders us relief,
> We call him cruel – years to moments shrink,
> Ages to years. The telescope is turned.
> To man's false optics, from his folly false,
> Time in advance behind him hides his wings
> And seems to creep, decrepit with his age.
> Behold him, when past by! What then is seen
> But his broad pinions swifter than the winds?
> And all mankind, in contradiction strong,
> Rueful, aghast, cry out on his career.[49]

But sometimes the images become too ingenious and elaborate, as in these lines on thought and speech:

> Thoughts shut up want air
> And spoil, like bales unopened to the sun.
> Had thought been all, sweet speech had been denied;
> Speech, thought's canal! speech, thought's criterion too.
> Thought in the mine may come forth gold or dross;
> When coined in words, we know its real worth . . .
> Speech ventilates our intellectual fire;

> Speech burnishes our mental magazine,
> Brightens for ornament and whets for use.
> What numbers, sheathed in erudition, lie
> Plunged to the hilt in venerable tomes
> And rusted in, who might have borne an edge
> And played a sprightly beam, if born to speech.[50]

And at the end he plunges to the depths:

> 'Tis thought's exchange, which like the alternate push
> Of waves conflicting, breaks the learned scum
> And defecates the student's standing pool.[51]

Young's virtues were degenerating into mannerisms and straining for effect; and there was another ominous development in the second *Night*. Lorenzo, the gay wordly unbeliever, who had only been mentioned in passing in *Night I*, assumed a more important part and Young's soliloquy became a one-sided dialogue, in which Lorenzo's sceptical arguments were continually quoted, only to be demolished; as Gosse put it, he was 'an infidel lay-figure . . . who is for ever being knocked over and then placed on his feet again'.[52] Whenever Young brought in Lorenzo, he was arguing against others, not expressing his own feelings, and the verse suffered accordingly. Despite the rich and vigorous language the approach became more cerebral and lost its emotional force. After the death of Philander in *Night II* and Narcissa in *Night III*, Lorenzo figured more and more prominently as the poet turned from mourning to preaching, and the death of Lucia at the opening of *Night VI* was only an episode in the protracted disputation. Yet for all his ubiquity throughout the nine books Lorenzo has not the reality of the other characters; he stirs no feelings and we do not believe in him.

The others, Narcissa, Philander and Lucia, were identified by tradition with real persons – Young's stepdaughter Elizabeth, her husband Henry Temple, and her mother Lady Betty – and there seems no reason to doubt it. Young himself confirmed it to the earnest Swiss admirer who cross-questioned him in 1751 and reported, 'Lucia was his wife and the mother of Narcissa . . . Narcissa was married to Philander, the son of Lord Palmerston';[53] and in 1762 he wrote categorically to another inquirer, Mrs Anne Brett, 'Philander was both my son-in-law

and my friend.'[54] Yet floods of ink have been poured out on this
question, particularly by French and German scholars, and all
sorts of ingenious solutions have been put forward for the
puzzle of the poet's claim in the first *Night*:

> Death, great proprietor of all! 'tis thine
> To tread out empire and to quench the stars . . .
> Amid such mighty plunder, why exhaust
> Thy partial quiver on a mark so mean?
> Why thy peculiar rancour wreaked on me?
> Insatiate archer! could not one suffice?
> Thy shaft flew thrice, and thrice my peace was slain,
> And thrice, ere thrice yon moon had filled her horn.[55]

In other words the three deaths celebrated in the poem
occurred within three months. This is the stumbling-block for
those who wish to take the poet's words literally: Elizabeth died
over three years before her mother, and her husband six
months after. It was therefore necessary, like Young's French
biographer, to postulate another daughter, hitherto unknown,
to explain Narcissa or, like a German critic, to dismiss the factual
basis of the poem entirely.[g] But surely it is simpler to take it that
Young's account is a dramatized, not a literal, version of the
events; he asserted that 'the occasion was real' but not that the
episodes were absolutely factual. Poetic licence contracted and
altered the order of events to suit poetic requirements; but the
poet's descriptions retained enough other details to identify his
subjects.

The identification of Lucia has never been disputed and the
coincidence between the fate of Narcissa and the facts of
Elizabeth's end would prove her identity even without the
explicit statement of Young himself. But there is, on the face of
it, more difficulty in reconciling the description of Philander,

> For twenty summers ripening by my side,[56]

with Henry Temple, who married Elizabeth in 1735 and was

---

[g] M. Thomas in *Le Poète Edward Young* suggested a natural daughter, whom
the poet took to Montpellier after his wife's death. His candidate for Philander
was Young's old friend Thomas Tickell, who died at Bath just under three
months after Lady Betty, on 23 April, 1740. Professor Mutschmann of Marburg
in *Die Schlüssel zu Youngs Nachtgedanken* contended that Philander and Lorenzo
symbolized the good and bad sides of the poet himself.

only about 35 years old when he died. Young's letters to Lady Giffard show that he had indeed known the Temple family for twenty years, but in 1720 Henry was only a boy of 15 or so. Could he really be the friend

> Whose mind was moral as the preacher's tongue
> And strong to wield all science worth the name.
> How often we talked down the summer's sun
> And cooled our passions by the breezy stream!
> How often thawed and shortened winter's eve
> By conflict kind, that struck out latent truth,
> Best found, so sought.[57]

The discovery of Young's letters to Judith Reynolds revealed how close their friendship really was – and after all the boy grew up; the operative word is 'ripening'. Probably at first it was a tutor-pupil relationship, which developed with the years into the deep intellectual companionship that Young mourned.

Tradition is thus vindicated by our new knowledge; but though a valuable guide when supported by facts, it is not always reliable. Lorenzo was popularly rumoured to be modelled on the poet's own son Frederick, with whom he quarrelled bitterly in his last years. The obituary in the *Biographia Britannica* gave currency to this insinuation, which persisted even though Croft, a zealous friend and defender of Frederick, demonstrated its absurdity in his life of Young. Croft pointed out that when the poet drew the portrait of the finished infidel Lorenzo, his son was not yet 10 years old. Who then can Lorenzo have been? Was there a model or was he purely a lay-figure? The obvious candidate would be the Duke of Wharton; but Young had broken with Wharton twenty years before and the 'scorn and wonder of our days' had died in poverty and exile over ten years earlier. Most of Lorenzo's characteristics would fit any imaginary 'man of the world'; he was young, rich, blasé, rationalistic, witty, much-travelled, ambitious of glory, fond of women and night-life, a brilliant speaker in Parliament. But there were other more individual details – he was a friend of Philander as well as the poet; Narcissa was a favourite of his; his father was still living, and he had a young son, Florello, whose mother, the much-loved Clarissa, died in giving him birth; and surely Young must have had some real person in mind in the incident where Lorenzo, as a dilettante collector, was refused an export permit for some ancient works of art by the Pope! In the absence of any plausible tradition, however, it is useless to try to identify Lorenzo, nor would it be profitable. Perhaps he was a composite figure – which would explain his lifelessness.

At the end of the fourth *Night* Young claimed to have defeated the unbelieving Lorenzo and with him the fear of death. Determined to fight the rationalists on their own ground, he claimed reason as the basis of Christian belief:

> Reason the root, fair faith is but the flower,[58]

and in particular of his own faith:

> Wear I the blessed cross, by fortune stamped
> On passive nature before thought was born?
> My birth's blind bigot, fired with local zeal?
> No, reason re-baptized me when adult,
> Weighed true and false in her impartial scale.
> My heart became the convert of my head
> And made that choice, which once was but my fate.
> On argument alone my faith is built.[59]

Thus fortified, he no longer feared death:

> The knell, the shroud, the mattock and the grave,
> The deep damp vault, the darkness and the worm;
> These are the bugbears of a winter's eve,
> The terrors of the living, not the dead.
> Imagination's fool and error's wretch,
> Man makes a death which nature never made;
> Then on the point of his own fancy falls
> And feels a thousand deaths in fearing one.[60]

Indeed he longed for the –

> Happy day that breaks our chains;
> That manumits; that calls from exile home.[61]

After four books and over two thousand five hundred lines of poetical argument he had at last found tranquillity and it seemed quite likely that the *Night Thoughts* would cease there.

But death was preparing new shocks for him. Even before *Night IV* came out in March, 1743,[62] Young's brother-in-law, the second Earl of Litchfield, had died at the comparatively early age of fifty-two, on 15 February.[63] A fortnight later the Duchess of Portland lost her youngest daughter, Lady Fanny, a guiltless babe of less than two. Soon afterwards the poet himself again fell dangerously ill. On 2 June he told his patroness:

I have been confined to my bed for five weeks with the most acute distemper, and all the severities those butchers, surgeons, are able to inflict, I have gone through. Twenty nights I had not twenty hours sleep, nor am I yet at all come to my rest or strength, though, I bless Almighty God, they tell me I'm past all danger.[64]

It was the same pattern – long sleepless nights of pain, with death threatening himself and striking his friends – and the natural result was the resumption of the *Night Thoughts* or, as the poet entitled his fifth *Night, The Relapse.*

CHAPTER 11

The Relapse

1743–1746

The pause announced in the Preface to *Night IV* lasted just over nine months, from March to December, 1743; and apart from May, when he was bedridden after his operation, they were very active months for the poet, full of business and personal affairs. He had come up to London for the publication of the fourth *Night* in March, hoping at the same time to press his case for preferment and to present Caroline to the Duchess, having sent her in January to stay again with Lady Cathcart in Westminster, 'so that the child may be cured of starting at a human face'.[1] But his visit to London was both frustrating and bad for his health, and even his poem brought disappointment.

Night the Fourth was dedicated to the Hon. Philip Yorke, the elder son of the Earl of Hardwicke, the Lord Chancellor. The muse claimed to be 'much-indebted'[2] to him, but though Yorke was already an MP and FRS, he was only twenty-three and one cannot help suspecting that the dedication was really aimed at his father, who not only had pronounced in favour of Young in the Wharton judgement but was also a confidant of the Duke of Newcastle with his command of church preferment. Unfortunately the young man apparently failed to take the usual notice of the dedication and the poet was obliged to send him a reminder in the form of a private set of complimentary verses. In the covering letter he explained that because of his patron's known modesty he 'durst not venture to ask your permission of inscribing my Nightly Thoughts to you',[3] but he could not deny himself the satisfaction of privately expressing a panegyric on the young man's extraordinary qualities, and there followed seventeen lines of blank verse, extolling him as author of the brilliant *Athenian Letters*, which had enjoyed such a *succés d'estime* in 1741.[a] But

---

[a] The *Athenian Letters* were originally an academic exercise in which eleven writers took part, but Yorke and his brother Charles wrote the greater part and were generally given the credit. Only ten copies were printed for private circulation.

Young's flattery was as awkward in blank as in couplets and one wonders whether such lines as these achieved their object:

> O thou whom Athens, Lady of the Main,
> Empress of elegance, amongst her sons`
> May count, her lettered sons . . .
> . . . Well the great Atossa, famed
> First epistolograph, may boast the palm
> T'invent, but must from all her glory shrink
> When thy Cleander rears his beamy head,
> Refulgent o'er the letter-writing tribe.[4]

Young also called on the Duchess to condole with her on the death of little Lady Fanny and the illness of her son and heir, the Marquess of Titchfield; and next day on her instructions he waited on the Archbishop of Canterbury as fruitlessly as ever. But he did not have time to present Caroline to his patroness, for at the end of March he was obliged to flee from the noxious fogs of London. He retired to the seat of his neighbour, Sir Jeremy Sambrooke, at Gubbins Park, from which he wrote that owing to a violent cold, caught in town, he was 'neither in a merry nor in a philosophical mood. Water gruel spoils my mirth and an eternal cough interrupts my philosophy . . . I was blooded this day, and tomorrow begin running the gauntlet through all the rods of an apothecary's shop.'[5] He still hoped to return and introduce Caroline, whom he had left in town. But the 'apothecary's shop' did him no good and he returned to Welwyn for an operation at the end of April that kept him abed, sleepless and in pain, for five weeks.

By 2 June he was sufficiently recovered to write to the Duchess[6] and by mid-month to return to London for his annual court duty, though not in time for the issue on the 6th of Dodsley's octavo collection of the first four *Nights*, the so-called 'fifth edition'. It was popular enough to be re-issued before the end of the year as the 'sixth edition', which has misled biographers into speaking of six editions in six months. But even if it was not quite all that it sounds, the success was real enough, while the evidence of the separate editions shows that the most popular books were the most pathetic – the first moving 'complaint' and the third with the sentimental episode of Narcissa's grave. *Night II*, concerned with the virtuous but rather colourless Philander, sold more slowly than its successor, while *Night IV, The Christian Triumph*, achieved little apart from the collected editions.[b] What appealed to the public, in fact, was the romantic note, not the didactic.[c]

At the beginning of July he returned to Welwyn, but soon had to set out for Winchester with his son Frederick, now just eleven, who was admitted to the College on 30 July.[7] From now on the child would only see his home and father for a month a year, during the Whitsun holidays, as Welwyn was too far away for a Christmas exeat. But the poet still had his beloved Caroline, while Charles, though now in the Army, kept in close touch with the family. Late in September, in answer to the annual invitation to Bullstrode, Young wrote facetiously:

> I should have had the honour of waiting on you before now, had not a very melancholy accident happened to prevent me . . . There is a young man to whom I wish extremely well, nor is he altogether undeserving in himself, nor, I think, quite a stranger to your Grace. He is going to be married, and my hands are chosen to be embrued in the blood of his precious peace. The nuptials are to be the latter end of this week, at Putney.[8]

The young man was of course his stepson and the special invitation to Young to perform the ceremony was an example of the strong bonds of affection between the poet and his stepchildren. Charles Lee was by now quite independent, with £100 a year as Gentleman Usher to the Princess Amelia, £35–40 a year from his commission as Cornet in the Duke of Montagu's Horse and a private income of £60 a year from the £2000 trust fund held by his uncle Robert Lee, as well as his post as Master of the Revels with an official residence in Somerset House. His bride, the sixteen-year-old Martha D'Aranda, was the daughter of a wealthy widow of Putney and she brought him a marriage portion of £684.17s.6d.[9] The wedding actually took place at Richmond, Surrey, on 29 September,[10] and the previous day the

---

[b] Pettit's *Bibliography* records: *Night I*, one folio and four quarto editions (two being 'second') before the collected octavo; *Night II*, two quartos only; *Night III*, four quartos; *Night IV*, one quarto only.

[c] e.g. Mrs Catharine Cockburn, 12 June, 1744: 'There are many curious and just reflections, which are extremely affecting, as they seem to come from the very heart of the writer.' (*Works*, 1751.)

marriage settlement was signed under which Charles agreed, in consideration of Martha's dowry, to leave her £1000 if she should survive him. This condition can hardly have seemed very urgent to the youthful bride and groom – yet it was soon to give a great deal of trouble to his stepfather. For death was waiting once more in the wings to counter the happiness of this day.

After the wedding Young found time for a quick visit to Bullstrode, but at the end of October he had to be back in London for another round of the interminable Wharton suit. On the 29th he reported to the Duchess from Temple Bar:

> This day, by your friend Mr Murray's assistance, I carried just one half of my point; the other is referred to Prince Posterity. Mr Murray[d] has certainly learnt your Grace's art; for he helped me to the wing without cutting off the leg. For the matter stood thus: I had two annuities of different dates; that of the second date he sliced off for me with infinite address and dexterity, and left that of the first date still sticking to the Duke's estate . . . On Tuesday, Madam, I go to Welwyn for some writings necessary to the final conclusion of this matter, for the Chancellor's decree is not yet more than minuted and some trouble is to follow its being perfected, before a poor creature embarked in law for 24 years can come safe to land.[11]

But, alas for his hopes, just as he was thinking to have done with the law at last, fate was preparing a new involvement for him. In a sad postscript to a gay letter of 10 December,[12] in which he teased all the ladies of Bullstrode, he told them that Caroline's brother was dying of the smallpox – news that made only too appropriate the publication a few days later of *The Relapse* and the start of a long new series of *Night Thoughts*. Charles's death followed inexorably on 8 January, 1744.[13] A special messenger was sent down to Welwyn with the tragic news and Caroline hurried to Putney in a hired coach. On the 12th[14] Charles was buried beside his father in a vault at St Mary-le-Strand; and then, since the poor boy had naturally enough not yet made a will, there began a wrangle over his estate.

[d] William Murray (1705–93), the Solicitor-General, was well-known to the Portlands, having prepared an 'Outline of a Course of Legal Study' for the young Duke in 1730. He ended as Lord Chief Justice and Earl of Mansfield.

Back at Welwyn after the funeral Young tried hard to disguise his grief in a determinedly frivolous letter to the ladies of Bullstrode on 17 January. But he could not keep it up and finished, 'Caroline gives her duty to your Grace. Next to his poor wife, she is the greatest sufferer, an only sister and most beloved. Thus you see, Madam, though we begin gaily, we end otherwise. Death steals into the latter end of my letter.'[15] Soon after he had to go back to London again. 'Business only', he told the Duchess, 'brought me to town, and like an old ugly mistress as she is, she torments me in it. Poor Mr Lee's affairs, which are perplexed, oblige me to go tomorrow to his widow at Putney for two or three days.'[16] But the business was not to be settled so quickly and Young had to stay on in London, where he found the climate more and more trying. 'I'm going a mile or two in the country,' he wrote, 'I had almost as willingly have my head stuck upon Temple Bar as upon a pillow under it. I have had no sleep since I came to town, except a half hour nap in the pulpit this morning.'[17] He therefore moved out to Kew, staying at first with his old friend and fellow-poet Thomas Newcomb, from whose home he sent an urgent message on 19 March[18] to George North, now Vicar of Codicote, asking him to take care of the Easter services at Welwyn as he himself would be unavoidably absent till the middle of April. He found Kew a 'delicious spot' and 'being obliged to be near my gentle friends of Putney, till affairs are settled between us', he decided to take a lodging of his own there, a 'most elegant villa' according to an invitation he sent to the Duchess.[19] In the end he stayed there till nearly the end of May, when it was clear that he would have to go to law with his 'gentle friends' over Charles's estate.

The dispute was over the £1000 promised to Martha Lee if Charles should die first. Mrs D'Aranda had immediately taken charge as administratrix on behalf of her daughter, who was still a minor, and her accounts rendered to the Master in Chancery show that on the very day of Charles's death she collected all his ready money, including £4.18s.7d. 'by cash in Mrs Lee's hands' and £50.6s.6d. 'found in his Escrutore'.[20] Determined to see that her daughter should receive her full rights, she contended that the £1000 was a debt to be paid before the division of the residue of the estate in accordance with the rules of intestacy. Young's interest was to protect the rights of Caroline and his own

Frederick, who as sister and half-brother of Charles, were entitled to one fourth part each of the clear estate; and since the young man had left some £2400, it would make a considerable difference if the £1000 was deducted before division.

One pleasant interlude during this vexing time was a dinner with the Portlands at Whitehall on 16 April, where Young met the former Mary Pendarves with her new husband, Dr Delany. 'Dr Young . . . is vastly broke,' she reported to her sister, 'but he and D.D. took very kindly to one another.'[21] Eventually he escaped to Welwyn, from which he wrote ruefully on 29 May:

> The town is a great net, where honest men are caught like flies and know not how to disentangle their integrity; and where knaves sit like spiders, spending their vitals in spinning out snares of iniquity . . . As to the second sort of spiders, the blood-suckers, they nest chiefly in the Inns of Court and Westminster Hall. Two or three of these lately seized on me at once and played their part so well that it is almost incredible to think how much I am reduced . . . And now, Madam, is it not a most melancholy consideration that I must soon be re-entangled in this horrid cobweb of the town?[22]

The poet's new entanglement with the law was to take another two and a half years before a decision was finally reached.

It was not only legal business, however, that took him to town. On 30 March, 1744,[23] while he was at Kew, the sixth *Night* was published and by June the seventh was ready for publication. But things were not going smoothly even with his poems. The previous November[24] Dodsley, encouraged by the success of the collected edition, had bought the copyright of the first five parts of the *Night Thoughts* for 160 guineas, and on 16 December[25] he had brought out *Night the Fifth, The Relapse*, with a specially engraved frontispiece by Vertue, showing a robed figure leaning on a tombstone in a moonlit churchyard that is usually supposed to be Welwyn. But although Young personally approved it on a visit to Vertue in October, it was an imaginary evocation of the scene rather than an exact representation of Young's haunt and it forms an early specimen of 'romantic apparatus'. In spite of the attraction of the frontispiece, however, the sales of *Night V*[c] hung fire. Though the poet at last brought himself to speak of his wife's death, it was only at the very end of over a thousand lines of religious argument; and the same applies to *Night VI*, where the moving passage on Lucia[f] at the opening failed to weigh with the new sentimental public against over eight hundred lines of *The Infidel Reclaimed*. The learned Miss Carter reported hearing a lady exclaim, 'What, will that man never have done complaining?'[26] and the poet Shenstone was even less respectful:

> I have an old aunt that visits me sometimes . . . She shall fetch a long-winded sigh with Dr Young for a wager; though I see *his* Suspiria are not yet finished. He has *relapsed* into 'Night the Fifth'. I take his case to be wind in a great measure and would advise him to take rhubarb in powder, with a little nutmeg grated amongst it, as I do.[27]

Even the adoring ladies of Bullstrode were critical and Mrs Delany told her sister on 4 January, 1744, 'I believe I told you the judgment of this house about the *Fifth Night*; 'tis not so dark as some of his former, but has not so much merit as his last, though many thoughts and lines in it are charming.'[28]

The crisis came over the publication of *Night the Seventh*, the second part of *The Infidel Reclaimed*, for at this stage Dodsley withdrew from the venture, which was doubtless becoming unprofitable. At any rate from now on the *Night Thoughts* had a new publisher, G. Hawkins, and – more important – a new printer, Samuel Richardson, who was soon to become one of the poet's dearest friends. Young was already an admirer of Richardson's novel *Pamela*, which the Duchess had lent him in 1741,[g] and Richardson was equally an admirer of Young. At that

---

[c] *Night V* was dedicated to Young's nephew by marriage, the third Earl of Litchfield, who had succeeded to the title the previous February, aged twenty-five. The lines clinch the question of Narcissa's identity:

> Think not unintroduced I force my way;
> Narcissa, not unknown, not unallied,
> By virtue or by blood, illustrious youth,
> To thee . . . asks admittance for the muse.   (Mitford, 80.)

[f] Quoted at the end of Chapter 8.

[g] Young's letter of thanks is dated 'Feby. 18, Six in ye evening': 'I this moment finished the history of *your* Pamela; I am extremely obliged to your Grace for introducing me to so agreeable an acquaintance . . . Is it not a shame at my age to own myself wiser, and I hope better, for conversing with a little minx of fifteen? . . . In a word 'tis an excellent book and the lady that feels no impression from it

time the novelist was busy writing *Clarissa* and as soon as he was brought into touch with the celebrated author of the *Night Thoughts*, he sought his advice about the plot, as he loved to do with all his literary friends. The first extant letter in their long correspondence was Young's reply, dated 20 June, 1744, when the printer must have been preparing for the issue of *Night the Seventh* on 23 July.[29] Evidently Richardson had sent an outline of the story to the poet, who as a tragedian strongly advised against those who urged a happy ending:

> Does Lovelace more than a proud, bold, graceless heart, long indulged in vice, would naturally do? No. Is it contrary to the common method of Providence to permit the best to suffer most? No. When the best so suffer, does it not most deeply affect the human heart? Yes. And is it not your business to affect the human heart as deeply as you can? Yes.[30]

After the appearance in July of *Night the Seventh, being the Second Part of the Infidel Reclaimed, containing the nature, proof and importance of Immortality*, Young generously told the printer that *Clarissa* would have 'many more readers than I can expect. And he that writes popularly and well does most good, and he that does most good is the best author.'[31] And in the same vein of disillusion he wrote to the Duchess, 'Though, Madam, I have not written *to* your Grace, I have written *for* your Grace and ordered a copy of it to your house in town a week ago. For if I have not written for your Grace, for whom have I written? Not for ten more in the kingdom.'[32] But though he clearly realized that the public's enthusiasm for his poem had waned, he was still writing on and was now, he told Richardson, 'pretty much engaged in the *Last Night*'.[33] The public, however, assumed that with the completion of seven *Nights* the poet must really have finished at last, like Miss Catherine Talbot[h] who wrote on 7 September to Miss Elizabeth Carter:

---

had best keep the secret.' (Pettit, 116–17.) He also admired the sequel, *Pamela in her Exalted Condition*, which came out in December, 1741. The MS index of Richardson's correspondence in the Victoria and Albert Museum lists a letter from Young expressing 'his high opinion of the last two volumes', but unfortunately the letter itself is missing.

[h] Catherine Talbot (1721–1770) was grand-daughter of a Bishop of Durham and ward of Thomas Secker, later Archbishop of Canterbury. She was one of the rising group of female intellectuals, like her learned friend Miss Carter (later to translate Epictetus), and had contributed to the *Athenian Letters*.

> Dr Young has now, I suppose, done with his *Night Thoughts*; he has given us one for every night of the week. I do not know whether you critics and fine folk will allow them to be poems; but this I am certain of, that they are excellent in their kind, though they may be of a kind peculiar to themselves. He shews us the Muse in her ancient dignity, when she inhabited temples and spoke an immortal language, long before sing-song came into being.[34]

And on 9 October Miss Carter replied:

> I really regret there are no more than seven nights in a week . . . But as greatly as I admire this book, and as trifling as most of the criticisms on it appear, I cannot help making one objection – that the author has given too gloomy a picture of life . . . Indeed this melancholy turn of thought runs through all of Dr Young's writings.[35]

Young's old friend Aaron Hill, however, probably reflected the general reaction more truly when he commented to Richardson on 24 July:

> As to Dr Young, I know and love the merit of his moral meanings, but am sorry that he overflows his banks and will not remind himself (when he has said enough upon his subject) that it is then high time to stop. He has beauties scattered up and down in his *Complaints* that, had he not so separated them by lengths of cooling interval, had been capable of carrying into future ages such a fire as few past ones ever equalled. What a pity that want should be derived from superfluity![36]

That autumn the poet had his usual share of illness and suffering; yet he always managed to keep his letters lively and cheerful. He joked about his pains, commiserating with Lady Peterborough on her indisposition, 'which, by the way, puts me in mind of my own, which I had really forgot. But now I remember it, my head aches mightily, and from eating a load of unripe fruit I have been for a whole week in a good deal of pain.'[37] He joked about a military cousin of his, General Columbine,[i] formerly

---

[i] Francis Columbine (1680–1746) was son of Brigadier-General Ventris Columbine; but his relationship to Young is not known. The father began his career as page to Sir William Temple in Holland and came over with William III. Francis was commissioned Ensign, 1695; went with the 10th Foot to Gibraltar, 1730; and became Lieutenant-General and Governor of Gibraltar, 1739.

Governor of Gibraltar, now a neighbour of the Duchess at Hillingdon and not much to her taste, protesting that he was 'fit to make a Prince'[38] and the 'sort of a man, . . . that inspired a Homer'.[39] He joked about Stephen Duck, when the Wiltshire thresher-poet came specially to Welwyn to be married by his old friend:[j] 'I blessed Mr Stephen Duck yesterday with a third wife; they were pleased to come to Welwyn for that benediction. How long they may think fit to repute it such is uncertain.'[40] And when the Duchess insisted on his joining her house-party at Bullstrode in the depths of November in spite of his rheumatism, he finally agreed so as to give her 'ocular demonstration'[41] of the reality of pain, in which, he protested, she did not seem to believe. Nor were his complaints only physical; on 8 December he told Richardson that he had been 'much out of order, and a good deal in your way. My nerves were so tender that a door clapped or a dog running by me on a sudden gave me a shock, which I thank God I did not understand before.'[42] But a stay at Bullstrode always did him good and he was now much better.

By now the poet and the novelist were fast friends, exchanging not only literary ideas but symptoms and news, such as the death of old Sir John Stanley, who had helped Young's father over his Newmarket duty as long ago as 1699. But their writings were still the most important thing, and while Young consulted the printer about the sales and advertisements of his latest *Night*, Richardson fished for the critical assistance of the poet:

> You do me great honour in remembering what takes up the leisure time of such a scribbler as I am . . . I have not gone so far as I thought to have done by this time. Then the unexpected success that attended the other thing, instead of encouraging me, has made me so diffident! And I have run into such a length, and am such a sorry pruner, though greatly luxuriant, that I am apt to add three pages for one I take away! Altogether I am frequently out of conceit with it. Then I have nobody that I can presume to advise with on such a subject . . . For though I remember your kind hint

---

[j] Among Duck's patrons were the Temples, who all subscribed (including Elizabeth) to his *Poems*, 1736. Lord Palmerston instituted an annual threshers' feast in his honour at his birthplace, Charlton, Wilts.

that a folio may be short and a duodecimo long, yet cannot
have I the vanity to take comfort from the first without I had
such a judge as I have in my eye, to put me into heart by
pointing out to me where it may be best contracted. But this
would be a great presumption and vanity to hope for.[43]

Young replied that he proposed to be in town soon after
Christmas to print the eighth *Night*, 'for my indisposition has
been such as rather to promote than hinder thinking'.[44] He
hoped for Richardson's critical comments on the poem and
would be glad to return the favour in kind, if the novel could
be read to him, as his eyes were now too weak for reading.
From now on the two writers consulted each other on
everything and the influence of Richardson can be traced in all
Young's works to come.

The poet returned to Welwyn for Christmas, but not without
a typical misadventure, when his servant Tom lost the way.
This man, whose shaggy appearance made the Duchess say he
looked like an ancient Briton, fell asleep as they rode along and
led his absent-minded master miles out of his way before the
stumbling of his horse woke him up; so that the 27-mile
journey took them two days.[45] After Christmas Young delayed
his visit to London and the publication of *Night the Eighth* was
deferred till 7 March, 1745.[46] He took Caroline with him, but
the climate of the city had its usual adverse effect on his health
and he soon retired to the country again.

At the beginning of April, however, he ventured to the villa
of his old friend Dodington at Hammersmith,[k] where he
conferred with the Oxford poetess, Mary Jones, about the
plans for a memorial in Westminster Abbey to Lord Aubrey
Beauclerk, a gallant naval officer who died of wounds in the
attack on Cartagena in 1741. Lord Aubrey was the eighth son
of the Duke of St Albans, whose father was King Charles II,
and he was thus a cousin of Lady Betty; Young was no doubt
asked as a relative to compose the verse epitaph for his

---

[k] Dodington was now Treasurer of the Navy in Pelham's 'Broad Bottom'
ministry. His agent, the poet James Ralph, remembered once meeting Young
at Hammersmith: 'The Doctor happening to go out into the garden, Mr
Dodington observed to him on his return that it was a dreadful night, as in
truth it was, there being a violent storm of rain and wind. "No, sir, (replied the
Doctor) it is a very fine night. The *Lord* is abroad!"' (Hill-Powell, IV, 60, n. 2.)

monument, while Miss Jones, a friend of the family, was to write an inscription in prose.[1] She told a friend on 3 February that she was going to town the following month 'to have a conference with no less a person than Dr Young upon an affair that is to endure for ever' and thus 'grow immortal';[47] and on 2 April she announced that in two days she was to 'go to Hammersmith about this business of immortality'.[48] But it cannot be said that Young's ten lines of tame heroics are immortal in any way except for their place in the Abbey.[m] He probably stayed with Dodington over Easter, moving on to Richardson's country house at North End, Fulham, in the second half of April. For when he returned to Welwyn on 1 May, he told his friend that his house was 'full of friends that congratulate my return to life; till now I knew not that report had buried me!'[49]

Caroline had preceded him home with a new housekeeper, Mrs Liston, recommended by the Richardsons. 'Caroline is pleased with her,' Young reported, 'but not so much as with someone who has doubled his favours on her at the first interview and made her apprehensible of the consequences of so warm an attack.'[50] The military metaphor was quite appropriate, for Caroline's suitor was a young Army officer by the name of William Haviland. At that time he was a Captain in the 27th Inniskillings, which was not considered a suitable match for such a well-connected young lady. But her stepfather could not be severe and he told the Duchess on 19 May:

> I believe the thing is past retrieve; by my direction she has written to Lord Litchfield to acquaint him with it ... Caroline gives her humble duty and looks like a fool, as she ought to do. If she performs as well every part of her duty in a married state, she will make the best of what, I fear, is but a bargain.[51]

On 18 June[52] he had to go up to town again for his court duty, but once more he begged a bed of Richardson and in the end he

---

[1] Mary Jones also printed a long poem in memory of Lord Aubrey, ending with a compliment to Young, in her *Miscellanies*, Oxford, 1750. Among her subscribers was Young, who took a royal paper copy.

[m] The verses were published in a posthumous collection of scraps, issued as Volume VI of Young's *Works* in 1778. The reviewer in the *Gentleman's Magazine* commented, 'This epitaph has always seemed to us a *chef d'œuvre* of the kind.' (*GM*, XLVIII, 484.)

stayed right through July, busy with law business and the Duchess's campaign for his preferment. At last at the beginning of August he was able to 'disengage from the briars' of the town and escape to Tunbridge Wells, from which he wrote to the Duchess on 21 August:

> As to poor Caroline, I fear the affair proceeds. I made her write to my Lord Litchfield and she received a letter from him that became the prudence of his character and the nearness of his relation, but I fear it had too little effect. All I can bring her to is that she will not marry him in his present circumstances, and in that I am persuaded I may rely on her.[53]

The same letter describes Tunbridge and its 'pack of comedians'. But for others Young himself was one of the most amusing 'characters' of the spa. Mrs Montagu was there and sent the Duchess several lively letters in which she made affectionate fun of the Doctor's eccentricities. The first was dated 27 August:

> I have great joy in Dr Young, whom I disturbed in a reverie, and at first he started, then bowed, then fell back into a surprise, then began a speech, relapsed into his astonishment two or three times . . . I told him your Grace desired he would write longer letters, to which he cried 'Ha!' most emphatically, and I leave you to interpret what it meant. He has made a friendship with one person here whom I believe you would not imagine to have been made for his bosom friend . . . You would not guess that this associate of the Doctor's was old *Cibber*! . . . The waters have raised his spirits to a fine pitch, as your Grace will imagine when I tell you how sublime an answer he made to a very vulgar question. I asked him how long he stayed at the Wells? He said, 'as long as my rival stayed!' I was astonished how one who made no pretensions to anything could have a rival, so I asked him for an explanation: he said he would stay as long as the *sun* did![54]

Young's absence of mind was notorious, and Mrs Montagu added the tale of a typical gaffe when he met a lady whose face he had evidently forgotten and caused much merriment, when she mentioned her husband's name, by asking her where his wife was. But she also admired his wit and his wisdom, as her letter of 3 September shows:

I am extremely happy in Dr Young's company; he has dined with me sometimes and the other day rode out with me; he carried me into places suited to the genius of his muse, sublime, grand and with a pleasing gloom diffused over them. There I tasted the pleasure of his conversation in its full force; his expressions all bear the stamp of novelty and his thoughts of sterling sense. I think he is in perfect good health; he practices a kind of philosophical abstinence but seems not obliged to any rules of physic. All the ladies court him, more because they hear he is a genius than that they know him to be such. I tell him I am jealous of some ladies that follow him; he says he trusts my pride will preserve me from jealousy. The Doctor is a true philosopher and sees how one vice corrects another till an animal made up of ten thousand bad qualities, by 'th'eternal art educing good from ill', grows to be a social creature, tolerable to live with.[55]

On 17 September it was Young's turn to give his version:

As for poor Colley, his impudence diverts me and his morals shall not hurt me, though by the way he is more of a fool than knave and, like other fools, is a wit . . . Mrs M's 'many people and little company' is prettily and truly said; but let her not complain, she shines the more, she has often held me by the ear till all about her were annihilated and in a numerous assembly there was neither company nor person but herself . . . She has an excellent and uncommon capacity, which ambition a little precipitates and prejudice sometimes misleads, but time and experience may make her a finished character, for I think her heart is sound.[56]

But the lady had the last word after Young's departure in the last week of September:

I have been in the vapours these two days on account of Dr Young's leaving us. He was so good as to let me have his company very often and we used to ride, walk and take sweet counsel together. A few days before he went away he carried Mrs Rolt[n] (of Hertfordshire) and myself to

---

[n] Mrs Rolt, born Anne Calvert, was related distantly to Young. In June, 1746 the poet referred to her husband as 'my cousin Rolt', but the connection came through his wife, since Lady Betty Young's eldest sister married Lord Baltimore, head of the Calvert family.

Tonbridge, five miles from hence, where we were to see some fine old ruins; but the manner of the journey was admirable . . . First rode the Doctor on a tall steed, decently caparisoned in dark grey;° next ambled Mrs Rolt on a hackney horse, lean as the famed Rozinante but in shape much resembling Sancho's ass; then followed your humble servant on a milk-white palfrey . . . I rode on in safety and at leisure to observe the company, especially the two figures that brought up the rear. The first was my servant, valiantly armed with two uncharged pistols . . . The last was the Doctor's man, whose uncombed hair so resembled the mane of the horse he rode, one could not help imagining they were of kin and wishing that for the honour of the family they had had one comb betwixt them; on his head was a velvet cap, much resembling a black saucepan, and on his side hung a little basket . . . We took this progress to see the ruins of an old castle, but first our divine would visit the churchyard, where we read that folks were born and died, the natural, moral and physical history of mankind . . . Mrs Rolt and I jumped over a stile into the parson's field and from thence, allured by the sight of golden pippins, we made an attempt to break into the holy man's orchard. He came most courteously to us and invited us to his apple-trees; to show our moderation we each of us gathered two mellow codlings, one of which I put in my pocket, from whence it sent forth a smell that I uncharitably supposed to proceed from the Doctor's servant, as he waited behind me at dinner . . . After dinner we walked to the old castle . . . It was late in the evening before we got home, but the silver Cynthia . . . cast such a light on the earth as showed its beauties in a soft and gentle light. The night silenced all but our divine Doctor, who sometimes uttered things fit to be spoken in a season when all nature seems to be hushed and hearkening. I followed, gathering wisdom as I went, till I found by my horse's stumbling that I was in a bad road and that the blind was leading the blind; so I placed my servant between the Doctor and myself, which he not perceiving went on in a most philosophical strain to the great amazement of my poor clown of a servant, who not being wrought up to any pitch of enthusiasm nor making any answer at all to all the fine things he heard, the Doctor,

° Mrs Montagu sent the Duchess a fan with Dr Young's picture in his riding accoutrements.

wondering I was dumb and grieving I was so stupid, looked round, declared his surprise and desired the man to trot on before; and thus did we return to Tunbridge Wells.[57]

From Tunbridge Young had written to Richardson about the proofs of his ninth and last *Night*, which was now ready though, as he said, 'As 'tis a time of year in which nothing can be published, the world has no cause as yet to *complain*.'[58] In the end it did not come out till January, 1746, postponed by the crisis of the '45 Rebellion. The Young Pretender had raised the standard of rebellion on 19 August and within a month he entered Edinburgh in triumph. The danger became really serious with the rout of General Cope at Prestonpans on 21 September, and it was probably after this that Young began the verses which were annexed to the ninth *Night* under the title of *Thoughts occasioned by the Present Juncture*. These lines were dated October, 1745 and were evidently written during another stay with Richardson at North End. When he left Tunbridge at the end of September he intended to go to Bullstrode, with a night or two at Richardson's on the way. But on 25 October he was still at North End, from which he apologized to the Duchess that 'writers, like other sinners, when they have once given way to the first temptation, are carried farther than they designed'.[59] This was true enough, for the *Thoughts* ran to less than 545 lines and consisted of a singularly inappropriate appeal to the Duke of Newcastle – who by his skill in the corrupt management of Parliament had held office since 1717[P] – to save Britain from the 'Pope-bred Princeling' by leading a moral revival in public life.

> Know then from me,
> As governed well or ill, states sink or rise;
> State ministers, as upright or corrupt,
> Are balm or poison in a nation's veins . . .
> 'Tis fixed, by fate irrevocably fixed:
> Virtue and vice are empire's life and death.[60]

Thus Young proclaimed in the 'Statesman's Creed';[q] but by the time it saw the light the crisis was over.

[P] Newcastle was to continue in office (with interruptions of two days in 1746 and eight months in 1756–7) until 1762.

[q] Young also made a more practical contribution to the cause by giving £50 to a local volunteer defence association.

November was the most anxious month, particularly for the Portlands, who owned large estates around Carlisle, as the Pretender had advanced into England and laid siege to the town on the 8th. Young, still lingering in London, tried to comfort the Duchess with his doctrine of trials being blessings in disguise, God's way of 'reducing us to the relish of moderate goods':

> When a Highlander's broadsword is waved over the head of a fine lady, her radiant eyes are opened, she sees that to be true which before appeared incredible. If he will suffer that fair neck and shoulders to continue their acquaintance a little longer, she finds it possible to make a shift to spend one evening, with some tolerable degree of content, without opera, ball, assembly or gallant.[61]

At the end of November he followed up his letter personally and at last arrived at Bullstrode, as he told Richardson, 'after a very wet journey above and below'. But in spite of all the anxieties of the time his greatest excitement was still the progress of *Clarissa* – 'What a heart have you to draw in Clarissa's final determination! The more I think of that occasion, the more am I smitten with it.'[62] – and he even tried his hand at composing a letter for her himself. On 3 December the novelist replied tactfully:

> I am greatly obliged to you for your admirable additions to the letter I sent you, but believe I shall insert them rather nearer the hour of her death . . . Such noble, such exalted sentiments and expressions will adorn her last hours, when above the world and above the resentments she acknowledges in this piece. And only they are too exalted for the rest of the work, or they are entirely conformable to the frame I have designed she shall then be in.[63]

The two writers were now collaborators.

On 7 December the poet returned home from Bullstrode and his letter of thanks to his hostess contained another saga of misadventure with poor Tom:

> My man was ill of a fever; therefore, when we came to St Albans, he desired I would stop a minute, that he might take something, being ill; and as he said he thought his blood was much inflamed, I stopped and left him the liberty of having what he pleased; on which he drank half a pint of

hot brandy. Then we put on apace and by the time we had rid four miles, his horse stumbled, though it was the rider drank the brandy. On the jolt Tom waked and cried, 'Sir, I have dropped the bag!' I was in a passion at his negligence and told him I should then have nothing for dinner. 'No, sir,' says he with great joy, 'the venison is here; I only have dropped your leather bags.' Now, Madam, in those bags was nothing but my shirts, wigs, shoes, razors, &c: in short, my whole travelling estate. On being a little disgusted even at that loss, he told me to be sure somebody must pick it up and no doubt would bring it after us; and then trotted on with great tranquillity of mind. Whilst I was considering how I should best manage the handle of my whip to knock him off his horse and leave him to be picked up by the next comer, with my bags, a servant from [the] honest landlord at the Red Lion overtook me with what was lost; which was left on a horse-block in his inn-yard. Now judge, Madam, if I stand in need of Highlanders in order to be undone. How long it may be before they strip me of my shirt, which I so happily recovered, Heaven only knows.[64]

Actually the danger of the Highlanders had already passed. Two days before, on 'Black Friday', 6 December, 1745, the news of the rebels' arrival in Derby had caused panic in the City; but on that very day the Prince turned back and began the long, grim road to Culloden.

Life gradually returned to normal. 'The *times* and the weather will mend,'[65] Young told Richardson on 19 December, and after vainly inviting his friend to Welwyn for Christmas he accepted the other's hospitality again when he went up to town in January to see the last *Night* through the press. *The Consolation* was published on 29 January, 1746[66] and the poet's greatest work was at last completed. The ninth and last book of the *Night Thoughts* was 2434 lines long, not counting the annexed *Thoughts on the Present Juncture* – only a hundred lines shorter than all the first four *Nights* together. No wonder the sales fell off! Many copies, of course, were bought to make up complete quarto sets of the *Nights*; and the smaller collected editions were becoming popular. Dodsley produced an octavo volume of the first six *Nights* – all he had published – in March, 1746,ʳ and another in 1747;[67]

ʳ This was in fact a made-up volume, consisting of the remainder of the 'sixth' edition of *Nights I–IV* (2nd collected edition) with *Nights V–VI* added. Even the

Hawkins published the corresponding octavo of *Nights VII–IX* in 1748;[68] and both issued new editions of their parts in 1749.[69] But until 1750,[70] when the first combined collection of all the nine *Nights* was published jointly by Dodsley and Andrew Millar,[s] the latter books of the poem lagged badly behind the earlier ones. From that time on there were innumerable editions of the complete *Night Thoughts*, but one cannot escape the conclusion that, though the later books make up the bulk of the poem, it was the first three or four that 'carried' it.

Not only the evidence of the editions but contemporary comments show that it was the romantic side of Young's work, rather than his religious arguments, that really appealed to the public. From the moment that he 'relapsed' into the fifth *Night* the 'power of the *Pathetick*'[71] that so moved Boswell played less and less part in his verses and the argumentative element loomed larger and longer all the time – so much so that in the prefaces to *Nights VI* and *VII* the poet made a summary of his arguments. After the beginnng of the sixth book, where he described his wife's death, he was no longer concerned with the emotions that had been the genesis and inspiration of his work. The last book, where night comes once more to the fore with a 'Moral Survey of the Nocturnal Heavens' and a 'Night Address to the Deity', contains some fine passages of imagination and the poet's astronomical vision of a journey into infinite space strikes a strangely modern chord. But it is all simply too long. No poet could keep up the required pitch of inspiration for nearly 9000 lines, nor could many readers stand it if he did. This is not to say that any of the *Night Thoughts* are dull. On the contrary you can dip into almost any page and find lines that strike you and make you think. The energy of his thought and language is

---

date, '1743', was unchanged; but an advertisement on 16 March, 1746 said, 'Those who have the first four in 8vo may have the fifth and sixth alone.' (*G.A.*, 15 March, 1745/6.) Dodsley had purchased the copyright on 26 January, 1745 and immediately prosecuted John Wesley for piracy in printing 144 pages of extracts in his *Collection of Moral and Sacred Poems*, 1744. On 8 February, 1745 Wesley paid Dodsley £20 and a cheque for £30 and signed a promise not to reprint the *Nights*. (Colorado, no. 5, 9.) (Incidentally he had also printed extracts from *The Last Day*, the *Paraphrase on Job* and the first two satires of *Love of Fame*.)

[s] Millar purchased the author's rights in the last three *Nights* (and the *Paraphrase on Job*) on 7 April, 1749 for sixty guineas – the same price as Dodsley had paid for *Night VI* alone.

astonishing; he never leaves you quiet; ideas and images of all sorts crowd each page. There are none of those pedestrian passages such as one finds in the longer poems of Wordsworth; but though Young's verse is certainly not prosaic, in the later books he seldom rises to true poetry and one is reminded that this is the same author that wrote those brilliant satires on *Love of Fame*. Take for instance this passage from *Night VIII*:

> Wit, how delicious to man's dainty taste!
> 'Tis precious as the vehicle of sense,
> But as its substitute a dire disease.
> Pernicious talent! flattered by the world,
> By the blind world, which thinks the talent rare.
> Wisdom is rare, Lorenzo; wit abounds;
> Passion can give it; sometimes wine inspires
> The lucky flash; and madness rarely fails . . .
> Chance often hits it; and to pique thee more,
> See dullness blundering on vivacities . . .
> But wisdom, awful wisdom, which inspects,
> Discerns, compares, weighs, separates, infers,
> Seizes the right and holds it to the last,
> How rare! In senates, synods, sought in vain
> Or if there found, 'tis sacred to the few;
> While a lewd prostitute to multitudes,
> Frequent as fatal, wit. In civil life
> Wit makes an enterpriser; sense, a man.
> Wit hates authority, commotion loves
> And thinks herself the lightning of the storm.
> In states 'tis dangerous, in religion death.
> Shall wit turn Christian, when the dull believe?
> Sense is our helmet, wit is but the plume;
> The plume exposes, 'tis our helmet saves.
> Sense is the diamond, weighty, solid, sound;
> When cut by wit, it casts a brighter beam,
> Yet, wit apart, it is a diamond still.
> Wit, widowed of good sense, is worse than nought;
> It hoists more sail to run against a rock.
> Thus a half-Chesterfield is quite a fool,
> Whom dull fools scorn and bless their want of wit.[72]

Young loved a paradox, and his poem is a paradox in itself, for in spite of its enormous length it is often expressed so concisely, so epigrammatically, so elliptically as to be quite difficult to follow. Young's fault is not that he is long-winded in the sense in which we normally use the term, that is, saying a few things in an inordinate number of words; it is rather that he is repetitious, saying a large number of things several times in a variety of words and on a variety of occasions. Repetition, of course, can be exceedingly effective as a poetical device, as in this example from *Night IX* of Young at his most sombre:

> What is the world itself? Thy world – a grave.
> Where is the dust that has not been alive?
> The spade, the plough, disturb our ancestors;
> From human mould we reap our daily bread.
> The globe around earth's hollow surface shakes
> And is the ceiling of her sleeping sons.
> O'er devastation we blind revels keep;
> Whole buried towns support the dancer's heel . . .
> As nature wide, our ruins spread. Man's death
> Inhabits all things – but the thought of man.[73]

But Young never knew where to stop. 'What a pity that want should be derived from superfluity', as Aaron Hill remarked; or as Gray put it, 'The fault of Young in his *Night Thoughts* was redundancy of thought.'[74] But that is no reason for dismissing the whole work, and the fairest summing-up was perhaps that of Coleridge in 1811: 'Young . . . was not a poet to be read through at once. His love of point and wit often put an end to his pathos and sublimity; but there were parts in him which must be immortal. He [Mr Coleridge] loved to read a page of Young and walk out to think of him.'[75]

CHAPTER 12

Caroline and Clarissa
1746–1749

By the time that Young's patriotic verses on the *Present Juncture*
were printed with the ninth *Night* at the end of January, 1746[1]
the threat of invasion had passed and the Pretender had retired
to Scotland. But there the rebellion still flourished and was a
source of particular anxiety to the household at Welwyn, for
Captain Haviland was with General Blakeney in Stirling and
Stirling was besieged by the Jacobites. On 17 January Hawley's
relief force had been beaten at Falkirk and Young ruefully
remarked to the Duchess on 2 February that as Caroline's lover
was in Stirling Castle, 'she has a chance of being a widow before
she is a wife'.[2] Actually it was on that very day that the castle was
relieved by the young Duke of Cumberland. But the campaign
was not yet over and it was a long time before poor Caroline saw
again the man on whom she had set her heart.

She had other reasons for depression too. She had been in
London for the holidays but had to spend them by the sick-bed of
her sister-in-law Martha, now married to her second husband,
Dr William Coxe.[a] Welwyn was threatened by an epidemic of
smallpox, which, as her stepfather anxiously said, had been very
fatal to her family. And she had offended the touchy Mr
Richardson by failing to call on him in town, especially when he
had presented her with a new and splendidly-bound copy of
Pamela. Young made her excuses and assured the novelist of her
admiration, adding that she was too much of a woman not to like
the gift still more for being so well-dressed; and early in March[3]
he saw Richardson personally, when he paid a short visit to court
as a Lent preacher. But the printer had already forgiven her and
sent her a new present, Hervey's *Meditations among the Tombs*,
which did not do much to cheer her up. As Young reported on
19 March, 'she is far from well, but no symptoms of the disease
we would particularly guard against. The disorder hangs chiefly

---

[a] Dr Coxe was physician to the King's household.

on her spirits and she told me, after she had dipped into your book that she fancied flowers and tombs were (though seeming so remote) as near in nature as in that author's composition.'[4] Finally the poor girl was sent up to London at the end of April[5] to be inoculated against the smallpox, which made her ill, but fortunately not fatally so.

Young himself was not much better. His hurried trip to London was perhaps too strenuous – court duty, overseeing the publication of the collected *Nights I–VI*, visits to the Portlands and Richardson and to Chelsea, where he called on the Cole family and their ward, Miss Parsons, to condole with them on the death of Captain Cole, who had been buried on 1 March.[6] He also breakfasted at Chelsea with a young poet, Joseph Warton,[b] the son of his old friend Thomas Warton, who as Professor of Poetry at Oxford had written verses in praise of Young's *Last Day*. On his return to Welwyn he developed a fever and throughout April he was 'much out of order' with a 'great laziness and lowness'.[7] In May, on the orders of Dr Mead, he began drinking the waters of Welwyn's own chalybeate springs 'for the recovery of my strength, which is much impaired';[8] but his recovery was so thrown back in June by a severe cold that he could not get to London to start his annual court duty on the 17th.[9] Nor was the news of his friends any more cheerful; the health of Grace Cole, the late Captain's daughter, was giving cause for anxiety, while Mrs Rolt, his companion on last summer's Tonbridge jaunt, was seriously ill and desperately worried about her children being left to the care of their drunken and spendthrift father.[c]

By the end of June, however, the poet was sufficiently recovered to carry out his chaplain's duty at court and, while there, he visited both Chelsea and North End. At the latter he listened to some new chapters of *Clarissa* and assured the author, 'I wish you would lessen your apprehensions of length. If all fixes and satisfies attention, the longer the better.'[10] At Chelsea

[b] On 18 March Joseph reported this meeting to his brother Thomas, quoted a remark of Young's that 'Proper distrust of all mankind is one of the most prudential maxims' and added, 'I spent two or three hours very agreeably & in conversation he is a very sensible and entertaining man.' (Pettit, 224, n. 2.) Joseph Spence was also there.

[c] In this year an agreement was drawn up between Thomas Rolt, of Sacombe, Herts, his wife and his creditors for £3000; and in 1747 an Act of Parliament vested his property in trust for his family.

he again called on the stricken Cole household, worried that an heiress like Grace Parsons should have no protection but the ailing Miss Cole,[d] and he urged her to accept the Duchess of Portland's invitation to Bullstrode. Then on 16 July he hastened home 'as to a pillow'.[11]

Next day[12] he presided at a parish vestry meeting, where he took the first step in a new line of activity. After the prolonged and stupendous effort of the *Night Thoughts* he was not contemplating any new literary work. His creative energy was turned into other channels and he embarked on a programme of building and improvement of his church, his home and his parish in general. The meeting voted to sell the old church bells (which had been lying about the churchyard ever since a gale blew down the old belfry over eighty years before) to raise money for a new bell turret. By 11 November the Rector was able to tell Richardson that he was 'composing, but it is in wood and stone, for I am building a steeple to my church'.[13] He did not, however, seek to make a reality of the frontispiece of *Night IV* with its Gothic spire; his turret was in the normal eighteenth-century style, octagonal with a low-pitched roof. This was the first step in what grew into an ambitious plan for developing Welwyn as a fashionable spa, prompted by Mead's prescription of the local chalybeate springs, of which Young wrote on 11 November:

> The waters here are not new things, they were in great vogue fifty years ago; but an eminent physician of this place dying, by degrees they were forgot . . . They are the same as Tunbridge and I myself have found from them just the same effect.[14]

Certainly Welwyn's steel-water did him good, and in November, on Richardson's advice, he took to drinking tar-water too.[e] 'Tar

---

[d] It is not clear why Grace Parsons was so 'naked of defence'. Her father, Sir William Parsons, was still living and possibly her elder brother John, who took orders. Her younger brother, an army officer, was perhaps the danger; he was transported for highway robbery and forgery and, when he returned to England in 1751, hanged.

[e] The virtues of tar-water were recommended by Bishop Berkeley in his *Siris*, 1744, followed by Prior's *Narrative of the Success of Tar-water in curing a great number and variety of distempers*, 1746. After reading Prior, Young asked Richardson on 16 November to send him six gallons. On 11 January, 1747 he wrote of its 'wonderful effects'; and in May he went so far as to prescribe it for a lady with a cancerous breast, which resulted in a 'bloody discharge'. (Pettit, 248; 261; 275.)

by winter and steel by summer' became his rule and for at least a year he was free from further illness. Yet when he received his usual invitation to Bullstrode that autumn, he made excuse after excuse and one suspects that his new hobby of building had something to do with his inability to leave Welwyn. On 10 August[15] his curate had just been preferred and he was 'tied by the leg' till he could find another; on 23 September[16] he was still hoping to get some neighbouring cleric to take one Sunday for him; on 28 October[17] he had found a curate but was required as a Justice of the Peace to deal with an outbreak of foot-and-mouth disease; on 23 November[18] there was an epidemic of pleurisy as well; and on 5 December he wrote:

> I once saw a poor deserter shot in Hyde Park. Six musketeers were employed in this melancholy office; the three first, stooping, shot at his breast and then the other three shot over them at his head and killed him after he was dead. Such, Madam, is your request supported by Mrs Delany's . . . But . . . though I am in fact a deserter, yet am I an innocent one; or rather I am not a deserter but taken prisoner by the enemy and detained in chains, which I am willing to break, but the links are too strong and too many. For first, Madam, next week's fast insists on my stay; secondly, your friend Mr West, who is patron to my curate, calls him to town; and lastly, my little house is full of London guests, with whom I am on the foot of some form and therefore can neither dislodge nor abandon them.[19]

His unwillingness to leave home, however, did not mean that he went without company. His letters of 1746 were full of visitors, some passing like Whiston the prophet, some visiting like his London friends, and some staying for long periods like his ex-housekeeper's young sister or Charles Lee's little godson, later famed as the actor Charles Lee Lewes,[f] who recollected 'the Doctor's attachment to me when only five years of age, his often taking me with him to his house at Welwyn in Hertfordshire, where I stayed occasionally many weeks together.'[20] But there

---

[f] Lewes's *Memoirs* said that his father, a Welshman, was a hosier of Bond Street, who also acted as postman. He had, however, a good classical education and was thus 'well qualified for the conversation of such an enlightened character' as Dr Young, with whom he was 'honoured by being in intimate friendship'. (I, 9–12.)

was one London friend whom Young kept inviting in vain. On 17 July he wrote: 'I should welcome a Richardson as returning day. In a word, I love you and delight in your conversation, which permits me to think of something more than what I see, a favour which the conversation of very few others will indulge.'[21] In November[22] he brought in Caroline to reinforce his plea with an invitation to Mrs Richardson and one of the daughters. But the novelist was even harder to stir than the poet.

In the end Young was dragged to town by the law in December, but he cut the trip as short as possible and did not even have time to see Richardson. On 17 December he wrote to the Duchess from a coffee-house where he was 'waiting for a rascally attorney who, having robbed me already of all my money, would now rob me of my time'.[23] The dispute over Charles Lee's estate was now approaching its climax and on 3 February, 1747 Young reported that 'Mr Murray is my counsel, and always shall be so, for he gave me excellent advice when he bid me expect nothing.'[24] The hearing was fixed for 23 February, but meanwhile another legal complication arose that concerned Caroline. The Duchess of Northumberland's legacy to her niece, Grace Parsons, held in trust for her as long as she lived under the guardianship of the Coles and did not marry without their consent, included Frogmore House, Windsor, which was proving a white elephant. But it could not be sold without the consent of all the 'devisees in remainder', of whom Caroline was one. Captain Cole was now dead and his daughter had suffered a nervous breakdown from grief.[g] The Duchess of Portland had therefore taken Miss Parsons under her wing at Bullstrode and the move to sell Great Frogmore was perhaps due to her having already found a suitable match for the young heiress.[h] As Caroline was a minor, Young was involved as her guardian, but fortunately nothing more was needed than her formal agreement to the sale.[i]

[g] The death of her mother, only seven months after her father, was the last straw. Mrs Cole died about 14 October (buried at Chelsea, 17th); Young on 16 October replied to the Duchess's news of Miss Cole's loss of reason owing to filial affection. (Pettit, 241.)

[h] Grace Parsons was married on 28 May, 1747 to Thomas Lambard of Sevenoaks, Kent, who was 42 years old. Her fortune was given in the *Gentleman's Magazine* notice of the marriage as £30,000. (*G.M.*, XVII, 247.)

[i] Great Frogmore was sold in August, 1748 for £2500 to Edward Walpole, second son of Sir Robert.

The case of *Carolina Lee and Frederick Young, infants, by Dr Edward Young, their next friend, plaintiffs, versus Elizabeth D'Aranda, widow, and William Coxe, doctor of physick, and Martha his wife,*[j] *defendants* (known for short as *Lee* v. *D'Aranda*) was heard on 23 and 24 February by Lord Chancellor Hardwicke, who decreed that 'the defendant Martha, wife of the defendant Dr Coxe, is not entitled to the sum of £1000 . . . and also to her distributary share . . . in case such distributary share shall amount to £1000 or any greater sum'.[25] He directed that an audit of the estate should be made by the Master in Chancery, but it took two full years before the Master's report was finally issued on 3 March, 1749.[26] The schedules attached to the report show that Charles's stepfather made him an allowance and lent him money on occasion; the widow D'Aranda's disbursements as administratrix included 'Paid to Dr Young in discharge of two notes of the intestates, £30.10s.', while the young husband's ill-spelt book of accounts[k] recorded 'Memorandum Receiv'd the interest of Dr Young to Cristmas 1742'.[27] Charles in his turn helped Caroline and noted 'Lent my sister ten guineas and a half.' The Master's final conclusion was that the boy's clear estate came to just over £2400, leaving £2255 after the deduction of costs. His widow's portion thus worked out at more than the promised £1000 and the other half was left for distribution between Caroline and Frederick, a useful sum of over £560 each. But by 1749 it was too late to be of much help to poor Caroline.

After the Lee case Young turned his mind to the more congenial avocations of literature. For his own part he was engaged in preparing the octavo collected edition of *Nights VII–IX*, to be printed by Richardson and published by Hawkins to correspond to Dodsley's edition of the first six *Nights*, also a new edition of the *True Estimate* for Lintott, also printed by Richardson. But his real interest was not his own but his friend's work, *Clarissa*, of which he had written on 11 November, 1746:

[j] Eleven days later, 7 March, 1747, Martha gave birth to her first son, William Coxe. Both William (d. 1828) and her younger son Peter (d. 1844) find a place in *D.N.B.*, the first as a historian, the other as a poet.

[k] Charles Lee's pocket memorandum book opened on 10 November, 1743 with the entry, 'Begun the Lodgings at too Guinea's p Week' and ended on 7 December with the purchase of two lottery tickets. (*PAPS*, vol. 107, no. 2, 158–9.)

I consider Clarissa as my last amour; I am as tender of
her welfare as I am sensible of her charms. This amour
differs from all other in one respect – I should rejoice to
have all the world my rivals in it.[28]

And on 11 January, 1747 he replied to the novelist's regrets at
being in 'great and unusual arrear' with his letters:

You make an apology for not writing. I write because I'm
at leisure; you forbear because you are not; and both these
are equally right, so that your apology wants an apology . . .
Clarissa is my rival, and such a rival I can bear; she'll pay me
what you owe me, though you should owe the correspondence of an age.[29]

With the coming of the spring and the 'chalybeate season' the
poet pressed his friend to come and finish his novel in the peace
of Welwyn. But despite Richardson's half-promises he never
managed it, though Young tried desperately throughout the
summer to stir him with the lures of the season, the fine weather,
a vacation, the small distance, the benefit to his health, the
gratification of a friend, regard to a promise and perhaps the
company of Mr Cibber. Meanwhile Young himself was being
equally elusive with the Duchess and ventured to counter her
summons to Bullstrode with an invitation to the Portlands to
visit Welwyn: 'I am but four hours from you and it may be some
amusement to you to laugh at a country parson.'[30] The Duchess
persisted, but on his return from court duty at Kensington in
June a new obstacle arose:

My schemes are quite broken. I cannot go to Tunbridge,
though a ten years habit and my health requires it. Miss Lee
is gone to Ditchley and has left my family on my hands,
which I cannot leave without detriment.[31]

From this it appears that Caroline, now aged about eighteen,
was acting as his housekeeper. Mrs Liston had not lasted long;
she came in May, 1745 and about September of the same year
Young was thanking Richardson for his 'little acquaintance with
her'.[32] But before Mrs Liston there must have been another
housekeeper, and a letter of 16 April, 1747 provides the clue to
her identity:

A young woman – now about twenty-one – of good birth
and better principles was some years in my family. About
two years ago her much elder sister, who had long been
governess of my family and me, married, settled in town
and carried her younger sister with her. A young
apothecary in good business and circumstances courted
her, won her affections, mutual vows of marriage were
passed. Things standing thus, she came down for a month
or two to me the latter end of last autumn; the thing was
kept warm by letters every post; I invited, nay, pressed him
to come down to her, knowing the pain of absent lovers; but
business, he said, hindered him. She returned to town in
high expectations just before I was last there; the spark
visited her, but his behaviour was cold; she burst into tears;
on which he said, 'My dearest, I understand those tears;
they upbraid me, and so far they agree with my own
sentiments; I upbraid myself. You feel, I see, the force of
love and therefore will the more easily pardon the same
weakness in another. I feel it to distraction, but ask ten
thousand pardons, 'tis for another person. I courted her
some years ago, but she absolutely refused me, which
occasioned the fatal step I have taken with you. But since
you have been in the country, I have received intimations
that she has thought better of it. The temptation is
irresistible, and therefore we must part.' And so he took his
leave.[33]

This 'melancholy but true tale' – almost worthy of Richardson –
not only illustrates the poet's goodness of heart but throws light
on his domestic arrangements. After Lady Betty's death the
'governess' looked after the household as well as the children,
while her teenage sister was a companion for Caroline. She was a
spinster lady, Miss Letitia Battell, daughter of the late Rector of
the adjoining parish of Digswell; but at the age of 50 she became
the second wife of Alexander Ward of Charles Street,
Westminster, and moved to London, taking along her sister
Isabella, daughter of her father's second marriage and the
unhappy heroine of Young's story. On her marriage in 1745,[34]
therefore, the poet took on Mrs Liston, and when the latter left
Caroline took over the household.

As long as Caroline was away, therefore, Young was confined
to Welwyn. On 10 September[35] he told the Duchess that he did

not expect her back till next month, when Lord Litchfield would be coming to town to welcome his uncle Fitzroy back to England and would bring Caroline with him. Caroline had doubtless been invited to Ditchley, the Lee family seat, so that Lord Litchfield could bring pressure on her to give up her unsuitable attachment to a mere Army Captain. Not that the family had any objection to the army *per se*; there was in fact a strong service tradition among the Lees (as indeed among all the bastard branches of royalty), but their connections enabled them to rise more rapidly than poor Captain Haviland. Caroline's father had risen from Ensign in 1713 to Lieutenant-Colonel in 1727; two of her uncles, who died aged 32 and 29, had been a Colonel of the Foot Guards and Captain of HMS *Litchfield*; and Uncle Fitzroy, now the senior surviving member of the family, was on the point of promotion to Rear-Admiral.[1] As a senior officer as well as the eldest living uncle of Lord Litchfield his opinion about Caroline's case was evidently desired by the young Earl. But for the moment his ship was delayed and everyone had to wait.

During this interval the Duchess managed to tempt the poet as far as St Albans to meet her on her way back from Welbeck – with the usual fatal results. The following day, he told her, he was 'seized with a sore throat', which ended in a fever;[36] and in a letter to Dodsley on 16 October[37] he talked of having been near death. On the 25th he compared Bullstrode, with its wholesome air, to the Pool of Bethesda, which he was too crippled by rheumatism to reach. 'Even the very hand I write with is a cripple', he complained, but was able to add:

> I heard yesterday from Miss Lee; she is still at Ditchley. Her lover, who has been two years at Inverness, is coming to town to meet her; but so long as absence has given her time to reflect and she seems to me disinclined to give him the meeting, unless it can be on terms which prudence can justify; and I much question if such terms are to be had,

[1] The Commodore's promotion had in fact been suspended, till complaints of his conduct as Commander-in-Chief of the Leeward Islands had been investigated. Commodore Legge, sent out in December, 1746 to relieve him and arrange a court-martial, did not find sufficient grounds for his trial and Lee's promotion was confirmed. Described as a man of debauched habits and a foul tongue, he is said to have been the original of Smollett's Commodore Trunnion (*DNB*). His will, dated 1744, left £100 to his niece Caroline; but the by time of his death, 18 April, 1751, she was herself dead.

though General Blakeney professes for him the greatest
friendship and has promised to recommend him to Mr
Pelham and the King. She is a young creature of a sweet
temper and good sense, and as cordially as I wish her
happiness, I should rejoice if I could flatter myself that your
Grace, as occasion offers, would give her the credit and
advantage of your countenance in life.[38]

A fortnight later, in a letter reporting the arrival of Commodore
Lee aboard the 'Suffolk', he followed up this hint by expatiating
on the high character he had heard of Mrs Lambard from her
new neighbours in Kent, where he considered her 'as a lovely
vine planted by your happy hand'.[39] But if Young was hoping
that the Duchess would be able to achieve a similar feat of
matchmaking with Caroline as with Grace Parsons, he did not
know his stepdaughter's resolution.

By 22 November Caroline was back home, but Young was so
racked by rheumatism, 'my days more than ever painful, my
nights almost insupportable',[40] that he could not take advantage
of the chance to get away. The Duchess did all she could,
offering her chaise to bring him to Bullstrode, arranging for a
supply of tar-water and promising some special powders for his
pains. But as he could not face the rough cross-country journey,
she forwarded the medicine via Mrs Ward of Westminster, his
former housekeeper, and fortunately it soon brought him relief.
By 27 December he was hoping for 'some permanent good
effects',[41] and by the end of January, 1748 he was fit enough to
travel to London, where he stayed with Mrs Ward in Charles
Street. Thanks to the powders, he told his patroness, he was
'better, but not quite free from pain; and hardly expect to be so
till I am powder myself'.[42]

His business in London was the publication on 30 January[43] of
Hawkins's octavo edition of the last three *Nights*, printed by
Richardson 'under the inspection' of the author. The printer
himself had at last brought out the first two volumes of *Clarissa*
on 1 December, 1747, with the enthusiastic encouragement of
the poet. Writing to Young on 19 November to advise him of the
imminence of the publication, he apologized for his failure to
visit Welwyn and went on:

I have a very great fault in being will-less ... What

contentions, what disputes have I involved myself in with my poor Clarissa through my own diffidence and for want of a will! I wish I had never consulted anybody but Dr Young, who so kindly vouchsafed me his ear and sometimes his opinion . . . Miss Lee may venture (if you and she have patience) to read these two to you. But Lovelace afterwards is so vile a fellow that, if I publish any more, I don't know (so much have some hypercritics put me out of conceit with my work) whether she, of whose delicacy I have the highest opinion, can see it as from you or me.[44]

Young hastened to re-assure him:

> Miss Lee is in haste to read it and I am all ear. Be not concerned about Lovelace. 'Tis the likeness, not the morality, of a character we call for. A sign-post angel can by no means come into competition with the devils of Michael Angelo.[45]

He also announced the good news to the Duchess:

> A second work by the author of *Pamela* will be published in a fortnight and I fancy your Grace will find amusement in it, if, I mean, your taste is for a melancholy tale. I have heard it formerly, and not without a tear; but, as I remember, your Grace laughs at fiction. If so, I must visit others to see them weep. Fictitious tears are detestable, tears from fiction are not so.[46]

Though he had seen the book in manuscript, the poet never tired of it and in January he told the author, 'I have read or heard *Clarissa* thrice, and the last kiss was the sweetest,' while Caroline was 'entered already' in the school of Clarissa and hoped to be placed 'in the middle class'.[47] All he could do to thank Richardson was to present him with a copy of the newly-published *Night Thoughts*.

In February Young hastened home, but he had to return to London on duty as a Lent preacher at the Chapel Royal on 23 March.[48] The Duchess suggested that he should come up a little earlier in order to attend a private performance of *The Revenge* by a company of her friends,[m] but he could not get away because

---

[m] The Earl of Bute, afterwards Prime Minister, took part in this performance. Lady Mary Wortley Montagu wrote to her daughter, the Countess of Bute in May, 1748: 'I remember very well the play of *The Revenge*, having been once

of the many 'real tragedies' in his parish that winter. When he
went up on duty, he took Caroline with him and this time she
did meet his patroness. But it was too late for the Duchess to do
anything for her. After their return in April Young reported:

> Miss Lee has acquainted Lord Litchfield and her uncle
> the Admiral of her determination to marry, so the matter is
> past retrieve, though against the pressing advice of us all.
> I wish Count Saxe found our officers as irresistible as
> they are found to be at home. This irresistible hero is at
> Portsmouth, taking leave of his friend General Blakeney
> ... I expect him here at his return. He is purchasing a
> majority; the bargain is agreed between the parties and the
> Duke's[n] leave is waited for and expected very soon. The
> man seems to me to be a plain and honest man and I can see
> not much she could fall in love with unless it is his integrity,
> which, methinks, should have more charms for an old
> philosopher than for a young lady.[49]

So Caroline won her battle to be allowed to marry the man of
her own choice – nor was her choice a bad one. Whatever it was
in the 30-year-old William Haviland that attracted *her*, General
Blakeney clearly appreciated the military abilities that eventually
carried him to the highest ranks of the army;[o] while his non-
military qualities cannot have been negligible, for he became
both neighbour and intimate friend of Edmund Burke, who was
not a man to tolerate dullards.

After seeing off Blakeney, Haviland came to stay at Welwyn
till the wedding. But when this would take place was uncertain,
as there were still some legal points to clear up in the D'Aranda

---

acquainted with a party that intended to represent it, not one of which is now
alive ... I suppose Lord Bute was Alonzo by the magnificence of his dress.'
(Halsband, II, 400–1.) Bute's daughter, Lady Louisa Stuart, said in her
reminiscences that the production was organized by the Duchess of Queensberry
and performed three times. (*Selections from her MSS.*, 1899, 39.)

[n] Either the Duke of Richmond, who commanded Haviland's regiment, or the
Duke of Cumberland as Commander-in-Chief.

[o] William Haviland (1718–84) was born in Ireland, son of an army officer.
Though Young refers to him henceforward as 'the Major', his Majority did not
come through till 1750. He became Lieutenant-Colonel in 1752, took his
regiment to America 1757 and commanded a large force in the operations
against Montreal 1759. His resourcefulness and mechanical talent, especially his
invention of the pontoon, contributed to Britain's victories in America and
Canada, and he was promoted full General.

case; nor could Young get away to Bullstrode till all was settled. Fortunately the law moved more quickly than hitherto. On 3 June the Master in Chancery conferred with the lawyers on the audit of Charles's estate; on the 13th the interrogatories were settled; on the 18th[50] the documents were filed; and although the Master's final report was not made for another nine months, the couple were able to get married on 12 July.[51] The ceremony was performed at Welwyn by the Rector, who, according to Mrs Montagu, made a settlement of 'uncommon liberality'[52] on his stepdaughter. Caroline had been in his care for more than seventeen years, ever since she was a baby, and the poet loved her as his own child. Now she too left Guessens and Young was all alone except for the Whitsun holidays of his son.

Perhaps because of this his friend Richardson at last made up his mind to face the four hours' journey to Welwyn. Young was reluctant to leave home till Caroline had finally left for Scotland and on 25 September he once more put off the Duchess because 'Mrs Haviland is now in town, putting her goods on board for the North; but she returns to me next week for some – as yet – uncertain time; I suppose it depends on the Major's being commanded to his post.'[53] While she was away, Richardson came down to keep him company, as he mentioned in the same letter:

> If, Madam, Mrs Lambard is still with you, I beg my best compliments and let her know that her friend Mr Richardson left me but on Saturday last, and that she may expect to see before Christmas part of her own amiable picture in the remaining part of *Clarissa*. I know your Grace has no great esteem of this author; therefore in a letter to you I shall suppress my admiration of him and will only, instead of panegyrist, turn prophet and let your Grace know that your great grandchildren will read, and not without tears, the sheets which are now in the press. They will pay their grandmamma's debt to this poor injured man, and injured in a point which would touch him most nearly, if he knew your Grace and knew your opinion of him.[54]

Unluckily Young prefaced his message to Mrs Lambard with the mention of a rumour 'lately heard' of matrimonial discord between her and her husband, 'and with this particular circumstance that, though the fact was true, yet Mrs Lambard to all her acquaintances declared the contrary'. His incautious juxtaposition of the visit of Richardson with the report of Mrs Lambard's unhappiness evidently led the Duchess to put two and two together as to the source of the rumour, since Richardson, who in his sentimental way had regarded Grace Parsons 'as one of my own children',[55] was known to have disapproved of the match, arranged by the Duchess, with a man twice her age. The Duchess wrote a sharp rejoinder, complaining of the novelist's impertinence and ill-nature, and poor Young had to try and pour oil on the waters that he had so artlessly troubled.

Meanwhile Caroline set out to join her husband's regiment in Scotland and by 3 November[56] her stepfather was able to send a letter to welcome his 'dearest child' to her new home in Dundee. But the regiment was already on the move for Ireland and Young's letter had to be forwarded to Glasgow. Amidst his devout wishes for her happiness the forlorn poet asked her always to remember that she had a friend at Welwyn and to come to him as soon as she could; while he left the news of the neighbourhood to Mrs Ward and 'July',[P] who were still with him. Evidently the family's old governess and her sister, Caroline's playmate, had come to stay at Guessens to see her off and were looking after the Rector till he could find a new housekeeper. His letters to Caroline over the next few weeks show that he was missing her as much as she was missing Welwyn: 'I am obliged to you for talking with such a relish of Welwyn and shall set you down for a little hypocrite if you do not see it as soon as possibly you can.'[57] But all he could do was to offer religious comfort and try to arrange introductions for her to the society of Dublin, like Mrs Delany and the Duchess's sister-in-law, Lady Isabella Monck.

Mrs Ward returned to London in November and Young seems to have accompanied her, as he wrote to the Duchess from Charles Street on 22 November, giving her news of Caroline and promising to talk seriously to Richardson, though he stoutly asserted that 'if I find him guilty either of impertinence or ill-nature, I shall have a less opinion of mankind than I had before,

---

[P] 'Miss July', as she was called in a later letter (Pettit, 323), was presumably a nickname for Mrs Ward's young sister, Isabella Battell.

for I own I conceived him to be as incapable of either as any man on earth'.[58] On his return to Welwyn in mid-December he reported on the result of his talks:

> He and your Grace, I find, from the beginning were of different sentiments, though I dare say of equal good intention; you for, he against the match; he against it from the great inequality of age; your Grace for it from, I suppose, such an opinion of the young lady's temper and prudence as rendered the objection of no weight. You prophesied good and he ill; and now you are both for verifying your several prophecies ... Mr Lambard being often in the Tunbridge season at the Wells and she never, though much enquired after, gave, I find, some ground for suspicion, but whether a just ground or not they themselves alone can tell.[59]

Actually the explanation was simple; Mrs Lambard was expecting a baby, which had in fact been born before this letter was written. When he heard of it in January, 1749, Young commented:

> I rejoice that Mrs Lambard has made her spouse so agreeable a present. Such presents are great peacemakers where peace is wanted and pour fresh oil into the lamp of love where it burns the brightest. I heartily hope my friend Richardson was a false prophet; prophets of old had two provinces, one was to foretell, the other was to instruct. Though he may have failed in the first, yet he has not in the last.[60]

And with that he launched into a panegyric on his friend's new novel, of which the last three volumes had appeared in December:

> Has your Grace read his Clarissa? What a beautiful brat of the brain is there! ... That romance will probably do more good than a body of divinity. If all printers could turn such authors, I would turn printer in order to be instrumental in promoting such benefit to mankind. And yet, Madam, this excellent offspring of the imagination was in danger of having been stifled in its birth, or[q] at least of having been made a changeling. I think your Grace knows

[q] Young wrote 'of at least of' – an obvious slip of the pen.

Mr Lyttelton; he, Mr Fielding, Cibber, etc., all of them pressed the author very importunately to make his story end happily. But does not your Grace think that it is infinitely better as it is? It does end happily, most happily, for Clarissa in the sense of all who do not terminate their notions of happiness at the grave.[61]

The Duchess, however, who did not admire fiction anyway, was not to be appeased so easily and forgive a printer for daring to contradict her. It took another ten months and all the poet's persuasiveness to get her to relent. But it is to the honour of both of them that Young did not waver for a moment in the support of his humbler friend, while the Duchess treated the poet with increasing favour and respect, even honouring his home with a ducal visit in the autumn.

'Clarissa has put Pamela's nose out of joint,'[62] Young had proclaimed when the second two volumes came out in April, 1748, and now that the work was complete he took every opportunity to sing its praises. When Mrs Delany wrote from Ireland to ask his opinion of the novel, he answered at length on 9 February:

> I know no work that discovers more excellence of both head and heart together in the writer than this. What entertainment! What instruction! It might perhaps sound oddly if I should say that the Bench of Bishops might go to school to the writer of a romance; and yet, I think, there are but few who might not be both the wiser and better for reading it . . . I conceive that *Clarissa* may not improperly be called *The Whole Duty of Woman* . . . In the last volume my friend (pardon the vanity), my *friend* Mr Richardson has performed the difficult task of making a deathbed an object of envy, I think more effectually than any that have gone before him. In a word, I look on it as a work of true and uncommon genius, and like all such the more it is read, the more it will be liked, so that as yet its reputation, though great, is as yet but in its minority. And I verily believe it will be read with profit and admiration as long as the mutable language in which it is written is able to convey its precious contents to our posterity.[63]

Having forgotten Mrs Delany's Irish address, Young sent this letter via Richardson, so that the novelist could read his eulogy before forwarding it to Ireland. But this roundabout method of despatch caused it to be either lost or delayed, for Mrs Delany never replied, giving Young much concern as he had ended with a request that Mrs Delany should give Caroline the 'comfort, credit and instruction' of her acquaintance in Ireland. Perhaps he also muddled things by telling her that he believed the Havilands had already arrived, whereas on 26 February[64] he still had time to send a hasty 'bon voyage' note to Glasgow, adding that in Dublin the next winter Caroline might meet Mrs Delany. Again, on 9 April,[65] when the Havilands had reached their new post at Drogheda, he mentioned Mrs Delany living 'not two miles out of Dublin', and on 7 May[66] he told the Duchess how worried he was at hearing nothing from her friend. But the Delanys were by then preparing for an extended visit to England and in the end it was Young who met them, not Caroline. On 10 July, after a visit to town, where he saw both the Duchess and Richardson and consulted his lawyers about the still-unfinished D'Aranda case, the poet wrote in his last surviving letter to his 'dear child':

> I hear you are got to Dublin; I am sorry Mrs Delany is not there nor likely to be there all this summer. I saw her and the Dean at the Duchess of Portland's last week and found they were taking a house in town, so that their stay will not be short.[67]

He added a little local gossip, though he left this mostly to 'Miss July', and ended with the plea, 'Let me hear from you as soon as conveniently you can; for considering your present condition no friend but must have some solicitude about you.' The words 'present condition' must surely mean that Caroline was pregnant and Young's deep parental anxiety shows touchingly through the undemonstrative phrasing.

Though Caroline was now far away, life at Guessens was not too lonely, for there were always plenty of visitors and among them that autumn were both his most assiduous correspondents. Richardson came down in mid-August[68] with his friend John Grover,[r] a Parliamentary official, and stayed for four days,

---

[r] Grover was Clerk of the Committee of Elections to the Commons and already well known to Young, with whom he corresponded. He died immediately after his visit to Welwyn, on 1 September, of a fever from an 'overheating walk to Ember Court', the seat of Speaker Onslow. His unexpected death left his affairs 'greatly disordered'; so Richardson took Grover's maiden sister under his wing, and on 10 September Young sent to Richardson five guineas to help to support her. (Pettit, 328.)

which prevented Young from accepting the Duchess's summons to meet her at Stevenage on her way up to the Portlands' Nottinghamshire property at Welbeck. In his letter of thanks to the Doctor and all the neighbours who had entertained them, the novelist begged his friend to put him right with the Duchess over the Lambard affair, though not without complaints of Mrs Lambard's neglect of him; and this the poet at once undertook. Once again he was prevented – by a 'coachful of ladies' – from meeting his patroness at St Albans on her way back, so he enclosed Richardson's letter with the comment:

> My friend Mr Richardson, your Grace will perceive, is very
> uneasy and, I am confident, is very honest. If therefore on
> the perusal you can furnish me, at your Grace's leisure, with
> anything of consolation to him, I shall rejoice . . . for I know
> poor Richardson's great delicacy is quite in pain about it.[69]

He greatly desired therefore to talk to her and only wished that she and the Duke could come to Welwyn, as he dared not leave home so late in the year in his state of health. This appeal was effective, for the Duchess arranged a special visit to Welwyn to allow him an opportunity to speak more largely on the subject of Richardson, of whom he asserted, 'I am fully confident that on a clearing-up it will not be in your Grace's power not to have a value for him.'[70]

The Portlands duly came to Welwyn for the week-end, 29 September to 2 October, during which time, Young reported afterwards to his friend, 'I had full time to talk over your affair. But she was a little on the reserve and told me she would write to me fully when she had heard from Mrs Lambard, to whom she would write as soon as she got home; which is now near ten days, but I have not yet had the expected letter.'[71] In the end it was another fortnight before he could forward to his anxious friend part of a letter from the Duchess, 'which, though very short, I hope may give you some satisfaction',[72] and he added in a postscript, 'I have had a letter from Mrs Lambard that may make Mr Richardson perfectly easy; nor has he been neglected as he imagined, for the only time she has been in town since she married, which was but a very little while, she went to his house in town.' These explanations were accepted by the printer, who thanked his friend most heartily for his trouble and promised to 'make himself easy upon it'. But he could not resist some rather querulous self-justification and complaint that his wife, 'who was so greatly obliged to Miss Parsons for her declared value for her, should never be favoured with one line or the least notice from Mrs Lambard';[73] and he was clearly highly dubious about the lady's alleged call at his house. The feminine side of Richardson, which contributed so much to his novels, could be tiresome in real life. As Young said, in thanking the Duchess for her paragraph about Mrs Lambard, 'Poor Richardson is a low-spirited man and not only deserves but wants satisfactions.'[74] But at least a reconciliation had been effected between his two friends of such different social station and Young must have been happy at the result of his efforts at mediation, which had lasted nearly a year.

But if the poet was happy at the end of October, his happiness was short-lived. Early in November death struck another crushing blow at his affections, for on the 13th[75] Caroline Haviland was buried at Drogheda. We do not know the cause; but Mrs Delany reported that she died suddenly in her coach between Drogheda and Dublin,[76] and one can only suppose that her death was connected with her pregnancy. Her stepfather, said Mrs Delany, was 'in great trouble'; but there is not one word about this tragedy in his letters of December, 1749. With the advantage of hindsight one can perhaps detect an unusual fervency in his wishes for the recovery of the Duchess's son, Lord Titchfield, on 16 November,[77] and on 26 December he thanked her for an unspecified 'kind enquiry'.[78] Probably the loss of his 'dearest child' was too painful for him to bear speaking of it. Though his fame is based upon the public exposure of his griefs and bereavements, we must remember that it was four years before he could face describing the death of his beloved wife at the end of *Night V*.

So passed, unsung, the last of the poet's three stepchildren, all of whom he had blessed in marriage and all of whom he had seen dead within a few months – Elizabeth after fifteen months of married life, Charles after three, and now Caroline after sixteen. 'She is a good girl, though no Clarissa,'[79] the poet had told Mrs Delany; he did not know that she too would so soon have a tragic end.

CHAPTER 13

Duchess v. Duke

1746–1748

Two recurrent themes of Young's correspondence during the *Night Thoughts* period have been left for separate treatment – the question of his ecclesiastical preferment and the growth of his poetical fame. They make a surprising contrast: the former, constantly discussed and pressed by his ducal patroness, got absolutely nowhere in six years; the latter, reflected in an occasional paragraph to Richardson about new editions, spread of its own momentum throughout Europe. It was not so much a case of a prophet without honour in his own country as in his own profession; the English public gave Young the widest possible recognition, but not so the Church of England. This is the mystery – a mystery to Young himself, as to posterity – which will be examined in the present chapter.

The story began, as we have seen, immediately after the publication of the first *Night* in 1742, when the Duke of Portland spoke to the Duke of Newcastle and the Archbishop of Canterbury in the poet's favour and instructed him to write to the Primate. This Young did; but the Duchess criticized his diffidence both in his writing and his lobbying of influential acquaintances at Tunbridge that year. The second *Night* was duly dedicated to the new Prime Minister, Lord Wilmington, but he was a somewhat ineffectual figure and all matters of patronage remained firmly in the hands of the Duke of Newcastle. *Night III* was gratefully inscribed to the Duchess of Portland; and *Night IV*, in March, 1743, to the Hon. Philip Yorke, son of the Lord Chancellor. It was at this stage that the poet made his notorious plaint about the court's neglect:

> Ah me! the dire effect
> Of loitering here, of death defrauded long!
> Of old so gracious (and let that suffice)
> My very master knows me not.———
> Shall I dare say, peculiar is the fate?
> I've been so long remembered, I'm forgot.

An object ever pressing dims the sight
And hides behind its ardour to be seen.
When in his courtiers' ears I pour my plaint,
They drink it as the nectar of the great
And squeeze my hand and beg me come tomorrow.
Refusal, canst thou wear a smoother form? . . .
Twice told the period spent on stubborn Troy,
Court favour, yet untaken, I besiege –
Ambition's ill-judged effort to be rich.
Alas, ambition makes my little less,
Embittering the possessed. Why wish for more?
Wishing, of all employments, is the worst;
Philosophy's reverse and health's decay.
Were I as plump as stalled theology,
Wishing would waste me to this shade again . . .
Wishing, that constant hectic of a fool,
Caught at a court; purged off by purer air
And simpler diet – gifts of rural life.
Blest be that hand divine which gently laid
My heart at rest beneath this humble shed . . .
If this song lives, posterity shall know
One, though in Britain born, with courtiers bred,
Who thought ev'n gold might come a day too late,
Nor on his subtle deathbed planned his scheme
For future vacancies in church or state;
Some avocation deeming it – to die,
Unbit by rage canine of dying rich;
Guilt's blunder and the loudest laugh of hell.[1]

Young was often his own worst enemy. The satirical picture of
his twenty-year siege of the court has been seized on as literal
truth by his critics, who point out that this striking denunciation
of ambition was followed by five years of intensive campaigning
for a mitre or at least a stall. Actually, when he wrote those lines
he had not even been in orders for twenty years and twelve years
of quiescence, from his appointment to Welwyn till the
publication of *Night I*, divided his first siege of Lord Carteret
from his new siege of the Duke of Newcastle – in which the
running was made by the Duchess of Portland. As with his
griefs, so with his disappointments; the occasion was real, but
the poetic details were not strictly true.

Young must have written those lines in the autumn of 1742

after the high hopes raised by the Portlands' intervention had subsided into disillusion. No doubt he sincerely meant it when he said:

> Here on a single plank thrown safe ashore,
> I hear the tumult of the distant throng
> As that of seas remote or dying storms.[2]

But he had reckoned without the obstinacy of the Duchess, who was not used to having her wishes thwarted or ignored. It was no good his being resigned if she intended that he should be preferred; and when he went up to London to see to the publication of these very verses, an interview with his patroness was followed the next day by a call on the Archbishop! But all the Archbishop could do was to present the Doctor 'with his own good wishes in the handsomest manner' since 'nothing was to be done without the Duke of Newcastle or Lord Carteret'.[3] After this check the Duchess advised Young not to set his hopes too high and he replied philosophically, 'What God Almighty is pleased to give I shall receive with the greatest gratitude, nor shall I repine at what he is pleased to deny.'[4] But it is clear that he and his patroness still expected *something* and the subject of preferment continued to exercise their pens. On 25 August, 1743 'a thousand thanks' to her husband for all his favours, 'particularly for his last',[5] suggests that Portland had again intervened; and some cut or partially deleted letters of September with a sardonic quotation from Seneca indicate that his intervention had again failed. Young tried to make a joke of it:

> But . . . since you condescend in your last letter to ask me for a translation, pray, Madam, to what Bishopric? . . . However, if your Grace only means to enquire whether I understand Seneca as well as yourself, . . . I take his meaning to be that he is a fool that is seeking preferment at my time of day and that success – should I have it – would only convince me that it deserved not so much trouble in the pursuit.[6]

Nevertheless, for all his Senecan philosophy, this was the only period when Young showed impatience rather than resignation. In his next few letters the poet urged on his patroness rather than vice versa, protesting, for example, on 10 December:

If your Grace defers till the great world is settled, I shall
wear a mitre in the millennium. The Duke of Newcastle is
our Pope. Ecclesiasticals are under his thumb and he is as
fixed as St Pauls by his own weight in spite of all the
revolutions of the little court buildings round about him.[7]

It was true enough. The government reshuffle that followed the
retirement of Wilmington in August had made no difference to
the position of Newcastle, whose brother, Henry Pelham, had
succeeded to the Premiership. On 17 January, 1744[8] Young
mentioned casually that he had heard there were some Prebends
and Deaneries vacant; and in February, while leaving absolutely
to the Duchess's judgement the timing of her approach to her
'excellent cousin' (Newcastle was first cousin to her mother), he
ventured to suggest, 'I should think that a promise is like money,
it carries interest and the sooner it is procured, the richer in
hope we should be.'[9] In March he sought to attract the new
Prime Minister's attention by dedicating to him *Night the Sixth*.
But the Duchess was busy having a baby[a] and it was not until 14
May that she took up the cudgels again and wrote to Newcastle:

> Your Grace is no stranger to the desire I have long had of
> serving Doctor Young, as I have taken the liberty before of
> applying to you in his favour by my Lord. His character is
> so universally honoured and so well known to your Grace
> that it is unnecessary for me to say anything on that head,
> and you are a much better judge of his abilities than I can
> pretend to be. I know him to be a most worthy man and
> have long had a sincere esteem for him and shall take it as
> a particular obligation to myself if your Grace will obtain
> for him the first Prebend that shall become vacant in
> Westminster, Windor or Christ Church.[10]

The Duke made a soothing reply – and there the matter rested
for a year.

Night VII followed in mid-July, but without any dedication,
unless one counts as such the introductory lines in memory of
the poet's friend Pope who had died on 30 May:[b]

---

[a] Lord Edward Bentinck was born on 31 March, 1744.

[b] Pope and Young kept up their friendship to the end. In his *Conjectures on
Original Composition* Young recollected having heard Pope 'talk over an epic plan
a few weeks before his decease'. (*Conjectures*, 344.)

Pope, who couldst make immortals, art thou dead?[11]

Nor was there any dedication in *Night VIII*, which appeared in March, 1745. But whether there was any significance in these omissions it is hard to say. The 'inscriptions' of the *Night Thoughts* were very different from the lengthy panegyrics of Young's earlier works; the poet was rather conferring an honour than seeking a favour in putting the patron's name on the title-page of so sublime a poem. Onslow the Speaker (*Night I*) and Pelham the Premier (*Night VI*) received no mention in the text, while Wilmington was given one puzzling line late in *Night II*:

A Wilmington goes slower than the sun.[12]

Philip Yorke got the first three lines of *Night IV* from the 'much-indebted muse', but the longest compliments – and those only six and nine lines respectively – were reserved for the poet's own patroness, the Duchess of Portland (*Night III*), and his own nephew, the Earl of Litchfield (*Night V*). He could surely have found eminent names for the title-pages of *Night VII* and *VIII*. But perhaps he felt it was hardly worth while.

The fame of the *Night Thoughts* re-awakened interest, as best-sellers do, in Young's other works and the year 1744 saw the first of a long series of revivals of his best tragedy, *The Revenge*, which established it in the regular repertory of the playhouses for the next hundred years. Hitherto the occasional performances of this play had been mainly by amateurs and only seven altogether have been recorded between the first run in April, 1721 and Quin's production at Covent Garden in November, 1744.[13] But the latter had a greater success than the original production and Quin's portrayal of Zanga, the villainous Moor, set the example for a century of star actors who made it a favourite role. Altogether the play ran for twelve nights between 12 November, 1744 and 19 March, 1745.[14] The Young band-wagon was beginning to roll[c] – but only as far as his writings were concerned.

Almost exactly a year after her first letter to the Duke of Newcastle the Duchess of Portland wrote him a polite reminder

[c] There was also a performance at the Haymarket on 24 April, 1745.

and sent a copy to Young, who replied gratefully but with a
certain cynicism on 19 May that she 'should not have been at the
trouble of transcribing your letter to your cousin. Though seeing
is believing, yet faith is.believing too; but your Grace takes me for
an infidel. I wish the Ministry did, and then I might have a better
chance.'[15] This was a hit at the free-thinking divines who had
been so favoured by Queen Caroline, like his Tunbridge friend,
Bishop Clayton, who was eventually prosecuted for doctrines
contrary to the Thirty-nine Articles.[d] His cynicism was justified,
for this time the Duke attempted evasive action by simply not
replying, till the Duchess fired a second salvo a fortnight later with
the sarcastic comment, 'I am apt to believe you did not receive
my letter by my not having heard from your Grace since.'[16]
Meanwhile she was pulling every string and had enlisted the aid
of the Solicitor-General, William Murray, who had been Young's
counsel in the Wharton suit. On 18 June Murray wrote her a
cautiously encouraging letter that ended, 'If I was the Doctor
under your protection, I would not despair of Windsor, at least
not in prose, whatever I did in verse when the night inspired
melancholy thoughts.'[17]

When at last the Duchess received a reply from Newcastle in
July, she forwarded it to Young with a list of queries. But it is
difficult to believe that even the poet, vague as he was about
figures, could have been responsible for the overstatement in her
next letter to the Duke on 15 July, which asserted that 'Doctor
Young's is a peculiar case, having been a Chaplain to this King full
thirty years without having received the smallest preferment, and
whose worth and abilities undoubtedly deserved a much earlier
notice.'[18] As Young was not ordained till 1725, he must surely
have written 'twenty' and been misread. At any rate this letter,
reinforced with flanking attacks by the Duke of Portland on the
Archbishop and by the Duchess on the Premier, procured for
Young an audience with Newcastle, which he described in a letter
from Tunbridge Wells on 21 August:

> The Duke of N. received me with great complaisance,
> ministerially kind, took me by the thumb as cordially as if he

---

[d] This letter also contained a wry joke about the Duchess's one-year-old son,
Lord Edward, being 'born a Bishop'. He followed this up in later letters with
rather misleading greetings to 'my good Lord Archbishop', meaning the baby.

designed it should go for payment in full. In a word,
Madam, with great civility . . . he told me the King had
made some promises, and that he – the Duke, I mean – had
his own pre-engagements, but that he would certainly do
what he could; so that if nothing is done, he has kindly
prepared me for it.[19]

Young realized he had been brushed off again and commented:

Half the evil of life is nothing but an ill-judged
expectation of good, and really at my time of life I know not
what is most eligible, a late success or an early despair. But
there is one success which fate cannot rob me of, which is a
consciousness of your Grace's and my Lord Duke's sincere
endeavour to befriend me. This, Madam, I shall always
enjoy and consider Welwyn as my Bishopric when I think
upon it.[20]

Young was willing to give up the chase, but not so his friends.
At Tunbridge he met John Roberts, the Prime Minister's
secretary, who encouraged new hopes and importunities. This
revived the whole business and no fewer than six entries at the
end of 1745 in the Duchess's index of Young's letters, all
deleted, can be read as 'On his preferment'.[21] These were
evidently destroyed as of no later interest, but the general trend
is clear enough – the Duchess determinedly pulling every string,
the poet following up half-reluctantly, the great world
encouraging them, and only the Duke of Newcastle proving the
ultimate, slippery but irremovable stumbling-block. *Night the
Ninth and Last* was on the stocks at the time and when it finally
appeared in January, 1746 it was 'inscribed' to the Duke. Young
did not, however, stain the culmination of his great work with
worldly flattery; there is not a word about the Duke in all the
2434 lines of the book and the only hint of the poet's
preoccupation is another assertion of resignation in the opening
lines:

As when a traveller, a long day past
In painful search of what he cannot find,
At night's approach, content with the next cot,
There ruminates a while his labour lost;
Then cheers his heart with what his fate affords
And chants his sonnet to deceive the time

Till the due season calls him to repose;
Thus I, long-travelled in the ways of men
And dancing with the rest the giddy maze
Where disappointment smiles at hope's career,
Warned by the languor of life's evening ray,
At length have housed me in a humble shed
Where, future wandering banished from my thought
And waiting, patient, the sweet hour of rest,
I chase the moments with a serious song.[22]

The crisis of the '45 Rebellion, however, inspired him to his patriotic *Thoughts on the Present Juncture* and these he did address to

Holles, immortal in far more than fame![23]

The tone, though, was more admonitory than flattering:

Let greatness prove its title to be great . . .
Let not the ties of personal regard
Betray the nation's trust to feeble hands,[24]

and so on; while the close reminds his Grace of the Last Day:

Where statesmen and their monarchs (names of awe
And distance here) shall rank with common men,
Yet own their glory never dawned before.[25]

Whether this was the sort of thing the Duke liked to hear may be doubted, and Young's next letter to his patroness spoke of his dullness in preparing his petitions.[26] The Duchess, however, was still lobbying 'persons of power' with the assistance of Murray, for by now the mystery of Newcastle's refusal to budge was becoming a matter of personal pique to her and of hurt curiosity to the poet. On 12 June he complained to her:

When I last saw his Grace of N——, he told me he had two or three to provide for before me. Three are just now preferred, but perhaps his two or three, like Falstaff's men in buckram, may grow to nine or ten. For what fictions in the extravagance of poetry can exceed the wonderful realities in humble life?[27]

The Duchess must have told him to put his point direct to the Duke, for on 4 July Young sent a plaintive plea to Newcastle, claiming that both the Archbishops were ready to bear testimony in his favour and begging the Minister to reflect 'how severe it is for one of very long service and known attachment to his Majesty, after promises from those that hold them most sacred and after all methods taken to recommend himself to your Grace's patronage, the intercession of friends and his own attempts in letters . . . – and at the very latter end of life, when distant expectations are no expectations – . . . to be thrown far backward in my hopes.'[28] But a fortnight later he was talking of rebukes to his ambition 'which should . . . make me wiser than to aim at anything more than humble content for the future'.[29]

The death, however, of Nicholas Clagett, Bishop of Exeter, on 8 December, 1746 sent the Duchess into action again and she hinted that 'a friend of [hers] would be considered if any removals beneath were occasioned by Bishop Clagett's death'.[30] After waiting for a month, Young wrote on 11 January a humble reminder to Newcastle of his promises, adding:

> I have been, my Lord Duke, twenty-four years on duty. My children, both as to age and service, wear mitres. And the Duchess of Portland has told me (what I hope is true) that your Grace will be kind.[31]

The story was continued in a letter to the Duchess on 20 January:

> From this golden dream I was awaked by the thunder of Mr Roberts' letter, which indeed did not kill me but filled me with great astonishment, as being utterly at a loss how to reconcile his storm and your Grace's sunshine together. This astonishment was scarce over when your Grace filled me with new, by taking a dead cause in hand, for dead in all appearances it seemed to me.[32]

The Duchess insisted; another letter to the Duke was to be written at once, putting Young's case more forcibly, and sent to her at once for forwarding with a covering note from herself. The poet did so, but commented diffidently, 'As you are my oracle, I have obeyed your commands, but I consider my letter only as a carriage for your Grace's artillery. 'Tis your influence must do all the execution.'[33] His statement, which he despatched to his patroness by courier, repeated his case, only raising his years of service as 'Chaplain to his Majesty (Prince and King)' from the January figure of twenty-four to 'more than twenty-five'! The Duchess forwarded it to Newcastle's secretary, Andrew Stone, and Young remarked on 3 February:

> If that will not do, nothing will, and I resign my chimerical expectations, which it is a shame I should have retained so long. I consider it as a sort of a curse on the clergy that the nature of their provision in *this* life keeps them generally gaping after preferment so long that they forget the next ... As I must soon resign in much more material points, I bless God I am resigned in this. I humbly thank your Grace for your kind wishes and endeavours and shall call off my thoughts from so dead a scent to other game. I shall send them to take a turn, not among the stalls, but among the tombs of Westminster Abbey. There ambition will go out as a taper in a damp vault.[34]

Three weeks later, when he went up to town for the Lee lawsuit, he reaffirmed his determination to resign himself, declaring, 'After this to sue would be mean in any that wanted not bread; it would be mean at any time of life, but monstrous at mine. I am therefore fully resolved to stir no further, which is only taking pains to be despised';[35] and he repeated it in the words, 'Your hearing nothing from Mr Stone is a decisive answer. I will expose myself no more.'[36] And yet he did. On 1 March he called on the Duchess to thank her for her 'zeal to befriend' him; and on the 3rd he wrote once more to the Duke of Newcastle, pouring out his full feeling of humiliation at the shabby way he had been treated:

> I am ... the *only person* living that has served above twenty years for nothing; the *only person* who served His Majesty when Prince, that was not preferred; and I believe the *only person* that is in a worse situation with your Grace than he was four years ago ... This ... seems somewhat hard; but this is not the worst. I am confident your Grace does not consider that not only my fortune and family, but my character too, feels the stroke of my being thus overlooked. It is not only my loss but my reproach and infamy. For what must the world think of me who by so professed and eminent a patron of worth and learning am thrown aside? And that too, when all possible efforts of various kinds have been made to procure his favour, and when both the Archbishops and Mr Pelham are ready to

second the Duchess of Portland's intercession with your
Grace . . . For these reasons I am not . . . more sorry than
ashamed of a repulse. That your Grace would not brand me
is, in effect, the favour I presume to ask and therefore I
most humbly hope your Grace will reconsider my case.[37]

This final, desperate fling was ignored like the rest, and three
months later[38] Young informed the Duchess with wry humour
that he would apply again for preferment when Lord Titchfield
(her son and heir, just going to Westminster School) was Prime
Minister,[e] and not before. The Duchess, however, did not let
things rest that long.

To set against the frustrations and disappointments of this
long and fruitless agitation were the compensations of the poet's
ever-growing celebrity. The octavo collections of the *Night
Thoughts* were spreading his name among every stratum of the
reading public, even the humblest; his tragedy of *The Revenge*
was becoming a popular stock-piece, performed again in the
autumn of 1746[39] not only at Covent Garden but at the gala
opening of the remodelled theatre in Goodman's Fields; even
his old sermon, the *True Estimate of Human Life*, was reprinted in
1747. He was also approached by Sir William Bunbury,[f] the
nephew of Sir Thomas Hanmer, about the possibility of
producing his suppressed tragedy of *The Brothers*. Though this
project did not materialize for some years, it illustrates the
interest now taken in all Young's writings; and this interest was
not confined to Britain. In March, 1746,[42] immediately after the
completion of his great work, the first German review appeared
in the *Göttingische Anzeigen*, which praised the 'nightothoughts of
D. Younge', and in the following June the *Neue Zeitungen* of
Leipzig hailed it as a masterpiece.

Young may not, of course, have been aware as yet of the
international extension of his fame. But he must have seen a
tribute of a different sort that appeared in the *Gentleman's
Magazine* for September, 1747. This was a parody under the title

[e] He was in fact twice Prime Minister, as Duke of Portland; in 1783 with Fox
and North as his Secretaries of State, and again from 1807 to 1809 with Canning
and Castlereagh.

[f] Sir Thomas Hanmer died on 7 May, 1746 and Sir William, as his heir, must
have found the manuscript of *The Brothers*, which Young had lent to Sir Thomas,
among his uncle's papers.

New Night Thoughts on Death, written by a Wykehamist of a younger generation named William Whitehead.[g] Young's highly idiosyncratic style was an easy mark and Whitehead managed to hit off many of his characteristics with that amusing touch of exaggeration that makes parody one of the most illuminating forms of criticism. But there was no malice in Whitehead's mockery and the closing lines show that he had a real respect for the poet and the work he was imitating:

> O Night! dark Night! wrap'd round with Stygian gloom,
> Thy riding-hood opaque! wrought by the hands
> Of Clotho and of Atropos! those hands
> Which spin my thread of life – so near its end!
> Ah! wherefore, silent Goddess, dost thou now
> Alarm with terrors? Silence sounds alarms
> To me, and darkness dazzles my weak mind.
> Hark! 'tis the *Death-Watch*! Posts themselves can speak
> His awful language. Stop, insatiate worm!
> I feel thy summons; to my fellow-worms
> Thou bidst me hasten: I obey thy call.
> For wherefore should I live? Vain life to me
> Is but a tatter'd garment, a patch'd rag
> That ill defends me from the cold of age . . .
> What's life? What's death? – thus coveted, and fear'd?
> Life is a fleeting shadow – Death no more.
> Death's a dark-lanthorn; Life a candle's end
> Stuck on a save-all, soon to end in stink . . .
> Death chases life, and stops it ere it reach
> The topmost round of Fortune's restless wheel.
> Wheel! Life's a wheel, and each man is the ass
> That turns it round, receiving in the end
> But water, or rank thistles, for his pains.
>   And yet, Lorenzo, if consider'd well,
> A life of labour is a life of ease;
> Pain gives true joy, and want is luxury.
> Pleasure, not chaste, is like an opera tune;
> Makes man not man, and castrates real joy.
> Would you be merry? Search the charnel-house,
> Where Death inhabits; give the King of fears

---

[g] William Whitehead (1715–1785), the son of a Cambridge baker, was at Winchester, 1728–35, where he won a poetry prize offered by Lord Peterborough and judged by Pope. In 1757 he succeeded Colley Cibber as Poet Laureate.

A midnight ball and lead up *Holbein's Dance.*
How weak, yet strong! how easy, yet severe,
Are Laughter's chains, which thrall a willing world!
The noisy idiot shakes her bells at all,
Nor e'en the Bible, or the poet, spares:
Fools banter Heaven itself, O *Young* – and thee.[43]

Here are all Young's tricks of style – his paradoxes, his rhetorical questions and exclamations, his riot of images, some macabre and some absurd, his self-pity, his delight in the grave. All that is missing is the inspiration of the poet at his best.

On 10 October, 1747 Archbishop Potter died and the question of the poet's preferment was resuscitated in spite of his resolution not to stir again. At that time he was seriously ill and not contemplating promotion in this world. But the Duchess was still smarting from the slighting of her explicit wishes, and on 4 November she sent him the following imperious missive:

> I have been so often disappointed in the great desire I have of serving you that I should almost despair that anything would be done, were there not so great a number of vacancies. But as I am determined not to be made a fool of any longer in that point, I will not write any more but should be glad you would acquaint Mr Roberts that if they have a mind to *please me*, they must either make you Dean of Winchester or Residentiary of St Paul's; nothing less will I accept or I must insist upon your sending this letter to Mr Roberts as my unalterable determination.[44]

In the face of this positive command the poet had little choice but to forward the letter, which he gave on 8 November to the local MP to hand to the Prime Minister's secretary. Three weeks later he reported that he had not heard one syllable from Roberts,[h] but had just received a letter from another hand, 'which puts an end to the affair', adding, 'I find this comfort in my disappointment that it makes my sincere gratitude to your Grace appear to me less mercenary than otherwise it might have

---

[h] Early in December Young wrote again to Roberts, asking him to return the Duchess's letter. Roberts replied that he had passed it to Stone, the Duke of Newcastle's secretary, and would return it as soon as he got it back. It was retained, however, in Newcastle's files and thus became the only one of all the Duchess's letters to the poet to escape burning with the rest of his papers at his death. (Pettit, 294–5.)

done.'[45] Yet it was another six months before the Duchess finally admitted defeat. On 4 June, 1748 Young wrote to thank her for her 'very kind letter, which has set my heart at rest from the uneasiness of foolish expectation and suspense', and he repeated, 'Your Grace's endeavours were not the less kind for being unsuccessful, and to the kindness of a friend our gratitude is due, and not to his success.'[46] And so at last the subject was dropped.

It may well seem that this dreary story of solicitation and disappointment has been treated with unnecessary fullness; but the whole evidence must be put on record if we are to judge the poet fairly in one of the most criticized aspects of his career. It has become the accepted thing to portray Young as one who (to quote *The Stuffed Owl*) 'hunted preferment as a pig hunts truffles',[47] while hypocritically proclaiming his contempt for worldly things.[i] But the real trouble was not so much that he was always chasing preferment as that he never obtained it. Can he really be blamed for following up Lord Carteret's express promise of 1724? Or for obeying the encouragement of the Duke and Duchess of Portland from 1742? If either approach had borne the expected fruit, he would not have had to persist; and in the latter case it was the Duchess that persisted rather than the poet. The only time that he actually received preferment – from his own College in 1730 – nothing more was heard from him for twelve years, and then only because he had written a major work of religious poetry which his patroness thought deserved reward. Another pause of ten years followed the final fade-out of the Duchess's campaign; and his final appeal to Newcastle in 1758, after the elevation of his friend Secker to the throne of Canterbury, seems to have been prompted by curiosity rather than expectation. His eventual appointment as Clerk of the Closet to the Princess Dowager of Wales in 1761 was unexpected and unsolicited.

If we compare Young's record with that of his contemporaries – like his classmate at Winchester, Cobden, who held plural livings with two canonries and the Archdeaconry of London, or

---

[i] e.g. the reviews of Pettit's *Correspondence of Edward Young*: 'a sycophant to his patrons ... and a clergyman always soliciting for ecclesiastical appointments' (*T.L.S.*, 14 April, 1972); 'this persistent sycophant, ... this miserable time-server' (Hugh Trevor-Roper, *The Listener*, 13 April, 1972).

his friend Jonathan Swift, whose Deanery did not prevent his soliciting the favour of Mrs Howard – it is clear that the conventional portrait of him as an insatiable and servile preferment-hunter is far from justified. There was no such suggestion in his own time; it was a later generation, which knew him only as the great moralist, the author of the sublime *Night Thoughts*, that was shocked to find him sinking to solicitation. Young seems to be judged by a different standard from his contemporaries and one can only suppose it was because he had been set up on a higher pedestal. The common faults of his age, flattery and string-pulling, were in him blown up to major sins; the very lack of success which caused him to repeat his solicitations was turned against him as evidence of greedy importunity; his vain pursuit of *one* preferment, at long-separated intervals, was somehow interpreted as a ceaseless hunt for preferment after preferment. It is ironical that one who was a byword among his friends for his unworldliness, for his hopeless innocence of 'intrigue and cabal', should now have become a byword for exactly the opposite.

More puzzling than the posthumous effects of his disappointment is the contemporary cause of it. *Why* did he never gain any recognition of his services to religion, even when backed by the highest in the land? It was not only his ducal friends, the Portlands, that supported him. His professional merits were vouched for by both the Archbishops, not to mention the Prime Minister, while the public had greeted with enthusiasm his contributions to Christian poetry – good Church of England Christianity too. On the strength of his poetry alone he would have been an ornament to the Bench of Bishops; the Germans found it incredible that the English Church could leave such a man without a mitre. As Gosse put it, 'it would be easy to show . . . that he really was, to an eminent degree, what Hobbes calls an "episcopable" person, and that his talents, his address, his loyalty and his moral force were qualities which not only might, but for the honour of the English Church should, have been publicly acknowledged by preferment.'[48]

What then was the insurmountable obstacle to his advancement that made even the Duke of Newcastle steadfastly resist the most importunate pressure of the Portlands? Various theories have been put forward, the most circumstantial by Benjamin

Victor in commenting on Young's *Centaur Not Fabulous* in 1756:

> How wise, how just are these thoughts! how powerfully
> conveyed! Experience [he says] is not the growth of action,
> but of reflection on it. True, too true, my dear Doctor – for to
> that one hasty action, to which you were tempted by your
> false friend Pope, to visit Bolingbroke at Dawley farm[j] (with
> whom you stayed a week and returned enraptured with him,
> at a time when he was in a paper war with Walpole, your
> patron), it was from the reflection on *that action* you reaped
> *experience* which plainly discovered your error; for to that
> false step alone it is owing that you will go to the grave
> without the title of *Right Reverend Father in God Edward Lord
> Bishop of* ———. I was intimate with Dr Young at that time
> and told him of his danger. And to what was this sacrifice
> made? To the enchanting wit of Bolingbroke![49]

Victor is a highly unreliable witness and this letter is full of
demonstrable inaccuracies on other points; but this story might
be true. Indeed it sounds typical of Young's innocence, though
it would hardly explain Newcastle's continued obstinacy after
Walpole's fall. In the 1740s, with the full force of the Portland
interest behind him and at the height of his fame as a poet and
divine, what could stop his advancement? Yet for nearly twenty
years he got nowhere – until suddenly, with a new reign, he was
given the consolation prize of the Clerkship of the Closet to the
Princess Dowager – at the instance of the Duchess of Portland! It
is here that we must seek the answer to the riddle, the mystery
that the poet himself was so curious to solve. In 1761 the Duke
of Newcastle was still clinging to office and patronage; indeed he
was Prime Minister. Why should he yield at so late a stage to the
Duchess's desire? The great change in the situation was that
there was a new King, and the only feasible explanation of the
Duke's stubborn resistance hitherto to the utmost pressure of
the great is the opposition of one still greater, King George II
himself. In October 1760 death removed this barrier, and in
January, 1761 the poet was offered the first suitable preferment.

If we accept this theory, that George II laid a personal and
life-long proscription on the poet, we still have to seek the

---

[j] Bolingbroke was granted a pardon and returned from exile in 1723. In 1725
he was allowed to inherit and buy property and he settled at Dawley, near
Uxbridge.

reason for so relentless a hostility. Croft alleged that whenever the King was approached on Young's behalf, he replied curtly, 'He has a pension.' But why in those days of pluralities and sinecures a pension should preclude any further advancement is not obvious. Croft could only guess: 'The neglect of Young is by some ascribed to his having attached himself to the Prince of Wales, and to his having preached an offensive sermon[k] at St James's.'[50] Whether it was his attendance, in the train of Dodington, on the King's detested heir or some gaffe like bursting into tears when he could not keep the attention of his royal audience, it is clear that poor Young himself had no idea of the reason nor suspicion that the stumbling-block to his advancement was irremovable except by death. Britain, and even Europe, might ring with his name; but George II, who had no use for 'boets and bainters', remained unmoved.

[k] George II was touchy about reflections on his moral behaviour. Young's old classmate, Edward Cobden, was dismissed from his royal chaplaincy in 1748 for a sermon tactlessly entitled *A Persuasive to Chastity.*

CHAPTER 14

A Female Superintendent
1748–1751

After the summer of 1748, when the Duchess finally abandoned her campaign for Young's preferment and Caroline married and left home, the poet's life settled into the pattern that it was to keep till his death seventeen years later. At sixty-five he had no further prospect, and no real desire, of moving from Welwyn and he devoted himself to plans for the improvement and development of his village; while his domestic problems were solved by the appointment of Mary Hallows, who devotedly ran his household for the rest of his life.

Significantly, he had taken the first steps in his development schemes about 1746, although the Duchess was then still harrying the Duke of Newcastle for his translation. In 1745[1] Young began to pay Land Tax on Guessens, and since this was the responsibility of the landlord, not tenant, he must by then have bought his home.[a] Next year (to judge by the rise in his Window Tax by six windows in 1747) he proceeded to enlarge his house; after which he embarked on the new turret for his church. By October, 1747[2] the turret was near enough to completion for the vestry to vote £5 towards the finishing of it; and in 1748, perhaps in connection with Caroline's wedding, the Rector inaugurated a programme of dances and functions that he hoped would turn Welwyn, with its chalybeate springs, into a new Tunbridge Wells. The fifth edition of Defoe's *Tour through . . . Great Britain*, revised and brought up to date by Richardson in 1753, said the spa at Welwyn had been 'newly revived' by Dr

---

[a] The Vestry books show Land Tax (paid by the landlord), Poor Rate and Window Tax (paid by the tenant). Up to her death in 1743 Young's landlady, Sarah Persey, paid Land Tax 'for that where Dr Young lives'; in 1744 her sister paid; but from May, 1745 Young himself paid the Land Tax on Guessens, though the description remained as before. In 1749 the Window Tax wording changed to 'Dr Young for his own house', but Land Tax and Poor Rate continued the old formula till 1753. One can only conclude that, though Young bought Guessens in 1745, the clerks simply copied the previous entries for several years after.

Young 'within these six years',[3] and the date is confirmed by the appearance in the *London Magazine* for September, 1748 of *Welwyn Spaw, a Cantata* by 'Mr N——h' (presumably George North of Codicote), advertising the place as a gay health resort:

> See joy and social mirth go round!
> The sprightly nymphs, th'enamoured swains
> Make it exceed Arcadia's plains,
> While thus they trip the flowery ground;
> Health, harmony and love uniting,
> All, all-delightful, all-inviting.[4]

A year later there was a regular assembly, for on 10 July, 1749 Young wrote to Caroline in Ireland:

> This is our Assembly Day, but we are extremely thin from its falling in with the Assizes at Hertford ... The Miss Heyshams[b] were much mortified last Assembly from being eclipsed by a sister of Lady Marchmont, by all very greatly and very justly admired.[5]

In 1751 the ladies of Welwyn 'promoted public breakfasting, and the charitable tanner of the town accommodated them with his barn to promote their good purposes; so that, notwithstanding the fragrance of the tanner's vats all around them, the resort of company is increasing beyond the donor's expectations'.[6] The tanner, John Shotbolt,[c] was Young's next-door neighbour and became a close friend of the poet and Richardson, who teased him about his bachelor status. On 18 December, 1751 Richardson joked about the bachelor's tanyard where a hundred ladies at a time 'have been obliged to him for a floor to bound upon',[7] and on 21 June, 1752 he again talked of a hundred ladies, 'collected through the country, every summer Thursday, hopping about in his shed'.[8] The spa, in fact, became so popular that Young eventually had some proper Assembly Rooms built, an elegant T-shaped building that still survives in battered shape, and beside it he laid out a bowling-green. With the provision of these amenities the poet's project flourished for

---

[b] Elizabeth, Anne and Jane, daughters of one of the local gentry, Giles Thornton Heysham of Stagenhoe, St Paul's Walden. Elizabeth afterwards married Young's son Frederick.

[c] Shotbolt took over the tannery in September, 1747 and lived at a house then known as 'Stalkers', now as 'Ivy Cottage', next door to Guessens.

many years and as late as 1789 the Hon. John Byng recorded in his diary, 'The Welwyn Assemblies, though continued, are not so frequented as formerly, when all the world danced . . . till August there.'[9]

Another project that lasted many years after the poet's death was his charity school, founded in 1749. There already existed a small school, run by the parish clerk, and on 29 December, 1748[10] a new schoolmaster, Thomas Pentlow, was appointed by the vestry.[d] This may have given the Rector the idea or the opportunity of setting up something bigger and more permanent, a regular foundation for 16 boys. The 'Orders to be observed in this Charity School as given by the Rev. Dr Young, Founder thereof, in the Year of Our Lord 1749'[11] included the teaching of reading, writing and arithmetic 'to fit them for Apprentices and other services'; age limits 7 to 14; free school clothes; hours 7 to 11 in summer, 8 to 11 and 1 to 4 p.m. in winter; expulsion for three days' absence in one month, or for swearing, disorderly behaviour or 'virmin'; and of course prayers morning and evening and catechism on Thursday and Saturday afternoons. Three years later, at Easter 1752,[12] the Rector was given leave to 'erect a School House on the piece of ground called the Anchor Pightle', which adjoined the churchyard. And so began yet another building project, till the new school was 'entered upon to be occupied for the use of the Master and boys on Monday, April the 7, 1755'.[13] What with the additions to Guessens, the church turret, the assembly rooms and the school, these years were full of 'composition in wood and stone' and it is clear that Young expected to live out the remainder of his life in Welwyn.

One factor that must have helped him to settle down contentedly was the finding of a satisfactory housekeeper. The first reference to Mary Hallows came in his letter to Caroline on 8 January, 1749: 'I like Mrs Hallows very well. She desires her humble service to you.'[14] This suggests that she was known to Caroline, who may have chosen her before leaving Welwyn to join her husband in October, 1748. His former housekeeper,

[d] The minutes record that 'Thos Pentlow do take in charge the school late in possession of Thos Lee deceased and the care of the parish accounts as the aforesaid Thos Lee did, with his allowances the school with 10 shillings per annum.'

Mrs Ward, was still staying at Welwyn on 3 November,[15] but perhaps she was helping to show the ways of the Young household to her successor. At any rate from the beginning of 1749 till his death the poet was devotedly – too devotedly – looked after by this middle-aged spinster,[c] who was 39 when she joined Young's ménage. Like Mrs Ward she was a gentlewoman, the daughter of a deceased local clergyman, and as such she was treated with respect both by her employer and his famous guests, sitting at table with them and appearing more like a relation than a servant. Her father, the Rev. Daniel Hallows, Vicar of All Saints, Hertford, from 1701 to 1741, had left her a very small private income and the poet 'never degraded her by paying her wages',[16] leaving her instead a handsome legacy – which caused some tongues to wag.

Mrs Hallows rapidly became a favourite of the Doctor and soon established herself as an important member of the family. Besides running the house she became a sort of secretary-companion, often acting as his amanuensis when his hands were too swollen with rheumatism or reading to him for hours when his eyes were too inflamed. Richardson sometimes wrote to her when he wanted to be sure of an answer from his absent-minded friend, and in general she made a most favourable impression on Young's guests, even of the highest rank. Less than a year after her appointment she had to cope with visits not only from the famous novelist but also the Duke and Duchess of Portland and she passed the test with flying colours, aided no doubt by Mrs Ward, who was staying at Guessens at the same time. On 9 September, 1749,[17] after his short visit, Richardson presented her with a copy of *Clarissa*; and in October[18] Young thanked the Duchess on her behalf for Her Grace's kind mention of her. This was the time when Young was working hard to reconcile the Duchess and the printer in their difference over Mrs Lambard, and Richardson was pathetically grateful, writing in October, 'If

---

[c] She was known as 'Mrs' Hallows by courtesy, and this may have misled Dr Johnson, who called her 'a clergyman's widow' (Hill-Powell, V, 270), and Croft, who stated in his *Life of Young* (1780): 'Upon enquiring for his housekeeper, I learned that she was buried two days before I reached the town of her abode' (Hill, III, 391). After Young's death she returned to Hertford, but she did not in fact die till 1790. Her mother, however, also lived on at Hertford till February, 1777, so if Croft visited the town at that time, enquiring for 'Mrs Hallows', it would explain his unlucky mistake.

you, or Mrs Hallows (to whom, I beg, my sincere respects) have any commission to give either to my wife or self, you will greatly oblige us both.'[19] From this time on Young's letters regularly included his housekeeper's greetings to his correspondents. She was already an accepted part of the family.

Young's dependence on her became even greater after the death of poor Caroline in November, for now the family was reduced to one, his own son Frederick, who was only home from Winchester for a month each year at Whitsun. His friends, of course, rallied round to help and comfort him, none more than Richardson, who not only undertook all the proof-correcting of the first complete edition of the *Night Thoughts*,[f] but sent him a New Year present of a privately-printed copy of *Clarissa's Meditations*, 'collected from the Sacred Books and adapted to the different stages of a deep distress'.[20] The *Night Thoughts* were ready in December, when Young gratefully ordered a presentation copy, bound 'after the best manner',[21] for his friend; but Millar, like the canny Scot he was, held back publication till the octavo edition of *Nights VII–IX*, of which he had bought the copyright, should be sold out. Then on 22 January, 1750[22] the complete *Night Thoughts* came out at last in a single volume, which proved so popular that further editions were soon under preparation.

Among those who hailed the complete work was Richardson, who wrote during the printing:

> I am expecting down the last proof of the new edition, in one volume, of your noble work. A noble work it is indeed! I never before read it in series ... But now printing the whole, it is not possible for me to express my admiration of it. You must not, sir, shut up your next to divine labours here. You will not. Do you consider that this work stands alone, absolutely alone? A monument of God's goodness to you in such gifts, such talents, as must exalt human nature and amend it at the same time.[23]

But he had a problem. When he was first preparing the collected

---

[f] Published in partnership by Dodsley and Millar, who had purchased the copyright of *Nights VII–IX* on 7 April, 1749 for 60 guineas, together with the *Paraphrase on Job*, which was included in the volume. Actually it had been unofficially anticipated by Peter Wilson of Dublin, who printed the nine *Nights* in one volume, 12mo, in 1747.

edition in September, 1749, he had put a query to the poet:

> On reprinting your *Night Thoughts* in one volume 12mo,
> which I am desirous to put to press myself, . . . I find that
> the preface to the fourth *Night* is temporary. I imagine you
> will make some little alteration in the latter part of it, as it
> leaves the reader doubtful whether you will proceed with
> the excellent work, when the whole is before him
> complete.[24]

Young immediately replied that the Preface might be entirely
omitted, and so it was in the first edition, both in duodecimo
and octavo. But Richardson was still not satisfied and on 5
September, 1750 he returned to the question in a letter to Mrs
Hallows:

> In reprinting in small his *Night Thoughts*, I think that part
> of the first preface, if he approves of it, should stand to all
> future editions, which is not temporary. In the last edition
> there is no preface at all. I had taken notice to the Doctor
> that the latter part of it was proper only to the work as
> published in parts before the whole was completed. Upon
> which the Doctor directed the whole to be omitted; and, I
> thought, intended to give a new preface. But not reminding
> him of it, it passed without any. And, if the Doctor has
> no objection, I would put to the new small edition the
> following first part of what he had at first prefixed. Which I
> transcribe, lest he should not have it by him.[25]

Young was away from home at the time, but the fact that
Richardson should write to his housekeeper about his literary
business shows the importance of her standing in his affairs.
Perhaps the printer was also relying on her to extract an answer
from his absent-minded friend, and not without justification, for
the poet replied promptly on his return home, giving his
'absolute consent' to Richardson's suggestion. Since then all the
innumerable editions of the *Night Thoughts* have included, as a
general preface to the whole work, the first paragraph of the
original preface to *Night IV*.

Meanwhile the printer kept the poet supplied with other
reading matter which, thanks to Mrs Hallows, he was able to
enjoy in spite of a bad eye. *Clarissa's Meditations* (of which
Richardson sent a second copy to Mrs Hallows, 'to whom I wish

all happiness, in which I am sure is included yours')²⁶ was much appreciated by Young, who urged the author to publish it as a 'pious stratagem' to convert those who would never read the Bible. In April he ordered the *Universal History* in twenty volumes, and then there was Johnson's *Rambler*. In August Cave, the publisher of the *Rambler*, reported to Richardson that he had had 'letters of approbation from Dr Young, Dr Hartley, Dr Sharpe, Miss C——, &c, &c, most of them, like you, setting them in a rank equal, and some superior, to the *Spectators*.'²⁷ Young's admiration for the *Rambler*ᵍ was also noted by Boswell:

> Some of these more solemn papers, I doubt not, particularly attracted the notice of Dr Young, the author of the *Night Thoughts*, of whom my estimation is such as to reckon his applause an honour even to Johnson. I have seen some volumes of Dr Young's copy of the *Rambler*, in which he has marked the passages which he thought particularly excellent by folding down a corner of the page; and such as he rated in a super-eminent degree are marked by double folds.ʰ I am sorry that some of the volumes are lost. Johnson was pleased when told of the minute attention with which Young had signified his approbation of his Essays.²⁸

One suspects that the poet was also behind a more practical gesture of appreciation, for Cave added, 'Soon after, Mr Dodington sent a letter directed to the *Rambler*, inviting him to his house when he should be disposed to enlarge his acquaintance.'²⁹ Johnson, however, wary of patrons, did not take up this approach, and so he did not meet Young for another nine years.

September, 1750 was a busy month for Young. We do not know where he had gone when Richardson wrote to Mrs Hallows about the new edition of the *Night Thoughts*. But after his return on the 14th he soon set out again, this time for

---

ᵍ Young also admired *Rasselas*, which he called 'a mass of sense'. (*Johnsoniana*, 1836, 327.)

ʰ Croft also noted this habit of Young's: 'The attention Young bestowed on the perusal of books is not unworthy imitation. When any passage pleased him, he appears to have folded down the leaf. On these passages he bestowed a second reading . . . Many of his books, which I have seen, are by those notes of approbation so swelled beyond their real bulk, that they will not shut.' (Hill, III, 392.)

Winchester to try to help his son in the New College election. Frederick, who had been at the school since 1743, was now approaching 18 and it was vital for him to gain a good place on the roll if he was to have a chance of a New College fellowship. He had proved himself a better scholar than his father, rising to the top form, Sixth Book, by 1747 and to the top of the school by 1749; and in the 1750 examination he duly won first place.[30] But for all that he was only third on the roll, as the first two places were taken up by Founder's Kin. All that could be done now was to wait hopefully for vacancies and Frederick's father, who had been busy lobbying the electors, returned home, stopping on the way for a few days' 'business' in Surrey. His explanatory letter of 21 October[31] to the Duchess does not elucidate his business and we can only guess that perhaps he was visiting his brother-in-law, John Harris, who had long since moved from Chiddingfold to his second living at Ash, Surrey. The visit may have been connected with the plaque erected in Chiddingfold church to the memory of his mother, which includes a quotation from his third *Night*. Though there is no mention of Harris in Young's known correspondence till the death of his 'brother' in 1759, we know from their wills that the two kept up their family friendship all their lives and Young in his bereavement may have turned for comfort to his sister's family.[i] Young's letters never went into details that were not of interest to the particular correspondent to whom he was writing, and the only reason for mentioning his son to the Duchess was to account for his journey to Winchester.

On his return home again at the beginning of October Young wrote to Speaker Onslow, who was planning to meet his son from Cambridge at Welwyn. Richardson, a protégé of the Speaker, had first suggested the visit in July and Young at once sent an invitation, pressing his friend to come along, too:

> Tell him that you will bear him company . . . It will do far
> more to carry my point than the enclosed. For I bribe high
> (if a Speaker of the House can be bribed); I bribe with fifty

[i] Harris's second wife had died in December, 1748. His son Richard held two Hampshire livings and in 1748 succeeded (without dispute) to his father's Fellowship of Winchester College. His daughter Jane was wife of another Fellow of Winchester, Walter Bigg, Rector of Worting, Hants, and they had a son, Lovelace, born in 1741.

miles of his conversation, with whom posterity will converse with pleasure.[32]

Eventually Onslow fixed October for his visit and after some deferments that caused Young to ask anxiously, 'Why tarry the wheels of his chariot?'[33] he arrived on Monday the 22nd and stayed till the end of the week. Richardson accompanied him, but had to be accommodated at Shotbolt's house next door, where he found time to compose two letters for his new novel, *Grandison*. The visit was a great success and had important literary results, for their discussions 'on original and on moral composition'[34] were the genesis of one of Young's best works, the *Conjectures on Original Composition*. The Speaker was so pleased that he promised Young a gift for his new altar, the next of the Bibles presented each year to the Chair; and in December[35] the Rector wrote to Richardson, saying his altar was now finished and enquiring tactfully whether the Speaker had remembered about the Bible. In a long letter on 2 January, 1751 the printer not only reassured him on this point but told how at Ember Court, where he had spent Christmas, the Speaker 'wished for you often' and 'always with delight mentions his excursion to Welwyn and your kind treatment of him there'.[36] Nor did he forget to make due acknowledgement to Young's housekeeper, or rather housekeepers, for Mrs Ward was helping Mrs Hallows at Guessens while she looked for a house of her own, having left London after her husband's death in May, 1750.

Young's next care was to find a pair of handsome gilt candlesticks for his altar, to match the noble Bible, which Baskett the binder said would soon be scarce, indeed probably never reprinted in imperial size.[j] The poet's dream of Welwyn Spa was taking shape and the church was a central part of it. But the spa was not the only attraction to draw visitors to Welwyn. Young himself was now an object of pilgrimage. The little town saw not only the Rector's famous friends, Duchesses and Speakers, Bluestocking ladies and novelists, but a stream of humbler

---

[j] After Young's death the churchwardens of Welwyn gave a receipt for the legacy of a 1717 Bible in Turkey leather, a 1749 Common Prayer, some damask cloths and needlework (including Lady Betty's altar-cloth), and a flagon, chalice, salver and offertory plate in silver gilt – but, strangely enough, no candlesticks.

aspirants in literature and religion, clergy and poets who came
to pay their respects and seek his advice. Nor did they come
from this country only – in February, 1751 he received the first
pilgrim from Europe, a young poet of the Swiss School called
Vincenz Bernhard von Tscharner.[k] Ever since the 'Nightothoughts' had been reviewed in the *Göttingische Anzeigen* in
March, 1746 the enthusiasm for Young's works had been
spreading among the Germans; Klopstock and Lessing, Gleim
and Uz, were discussing the poem in their letters, and several
others were busy with translations. The first published
translation from the *Nights* appeared in the *Neue Critische Briefe*
of Zürich in 1749,[37] two extracts from *Night IV* in blank verse
attributed to Bodmer himself, while Tscharner made a German
hexameter version during his stay in London, though he never
printed it.

Tscharner had written to Young in January, asking
permission to call with a friend and a copy of the *Night Thoughts*,
about which he wished to ask the author some questions. Young
replied on the 27th[38] that he would be glad to see them and
answer their questions, but not that week, as he was engaged and
his house was full of company. In due course, in late February or
early March, Tscharner and Count Sternberg came to Welwyn
and stayed for four days at the Swan Inn, two doors from
Guessens. A long letter from Tscharner to Haller on 15 March
reported the results of his cross-examination of the author of
the *Night Thoughts* and confirmed the identities of Lucia as the
poet's wife, Narcissa as her daughter and Philander as Narcissa's
husband and Lord Palmerston's son. But the most interesting
part of the letter is its picture of the poet at home:

> I have just visited Dr Young, the author of the *Night
> Thoughts*, and spent four days in the company of this
> amiable old gentleman . . . He lives twenty-five miles from
> London in a very agreeable retreat, where he enjoys all the
> pleasures of a perfectly free and peaceful life, pleasures of
> which his past afflictions make him doubly sensible.
> Everything that surrounds him is arranged with a certain

[k] Tscharner (1728–78) was one of the group of Swiss poets led by Johann
Jakob Bodmer, author of the epic *Noah*, and Count Albrecht von Haller, who
was a poet as well as as a professor of medicine and botany and edited the
Göttingische gelehrte Anzeigen.

taste of decent regularity and a very uniform, but very
pleasing, simplicity. He himself is gay in his conversation,
moderate in his sentiments and above all extremely discreet
in his judgements on his neighbours. He is, in a word, a
living example of the social virtues, an example that is more
persuasive than any books. I was so strongly charmed with
all his actions and with the open disposition that proclaims
his goodness of heart and tranquillity of soul, that I find
I have been drawn into a recital of his praises without
realising it.[39]

Such were a foreign visitor's impressions of Young and his
household in 1751. Croft, of course, sneered that the poet was
prepared for the visit. So it is instructive to compare this
description with the reminiscences of one who knew the
household from inside for twenty years, his servant Thomas
Wells. Though related fifty years after his master's death, the
account given by Wells to a correspondent of the *Monthly
Magazine* in 1816 is accurate wherever we can check it and rings
true in itself; even the mistakes were such as might honestly arise
from the old man's mixed memories or local accent, like 'Ishams'
for Heyshams. His recollections were recounted in the form of a
dialogue:

Do you remember Dr Young?
Yes – very well – nobody better. I worked and assisted in
his family ever since I can remember. I used to help fetch
his cows when I was but four years old (1745) and was
twenty-four when he died. Dr Young and Mrs Hallows, his
housekeeper, used to laugh at me, when a little boy, for
trying to make myself useful.
What did you do in the family?
I used to help the servant clean the knives and forks, and
to go on errands – and it was my business to mix the tar-
water, of which Dr Young used to drink a pint at 11 o'clock
every day. The servant put some tar into a quart-pot, with a
pint of water, and I used to pour it backwards and forwards
for two hours, in order to mix it and make it fine, till it was
as clear as wine. This I did every day for many years.
What were his complaints?
He had a complaint in the stomach, and he took it to give
him an appetite and to strengthen his inside – and he used

to say the tar-water was his best doctor and no other doctor could do him any good.

Did he keep a good table?

Yes, and I remember he was very fond of suet-pudding and had the suet cut in large pieces; and I have eat many a piece of his pudding after it came from his table.

Did he keep a carriage?

Not till he grew old and feeble; but he used to ride much on horseback before that time.

What was the number of his family?

He had a son and a daughter, and his housekeeper, Mrs Hallows, sat at his table and was his companion at home and abroad. Once, as he was sitting on a bench in the churchyard with Mrs Hallows, and I was carrying something to them, I overheard the Doctor say to her, jokingly, 'Here you and I are; do we sit like man and wife, or w—re and rogue.' He was apt to joke and say good-natured things, but never talked nonsense or romanced. He always spoke freely before me and was very cheerful and pleasant.[40]

Wells went off the rails a little when asked if Young kept much company – a question outside his personal experience. He was sound enough on the local gentry, the Heyshams, Dr Yarborough, Dr Persey and Dr Smith, and even on the Duchess of Portland, Dr and Mrs Delany, and 'Mr Richardson from London, a punchy, full-bellied gentleman'; but he added the Archbishop of Canterbury, once or twice a year, and also Dr Johnson, who certainly did not visit Welwyn till after Young's death. Perhaps Wells was confused with Johnson's call on Frederick in 1781, for his description is vivid and convincing – 'a very large gentleman, who used to take snuff with his hand out of his pocket . . . Dr Johnson smelt strong of snuff and used to talk very gruff, and we considered him a very high larned man.'

The catechism then went on:

Did the Doctor employ much of his time in writing?

He used to be called up in summer and winter at half past eight. His first walk was in his garden between the horse-chestnut trees. After breakfast he invariably passed some hours in his study. In an evening he used to extend his walk among some lime-trees at the top of his garden and sit on a white bench and view the stars; and I have often carried him something in a pint pot to drink.

Was he generally esteemed by the people?

Dr Young was beloved by everyone all round the country, far and near; and everyone used to take great notice of him and visit him.

What was his stature?

He was a middle-sized and well-made man – full face – fresh colour like a rose – neat in his dress – wore a brown wig – had piercing black eyes – and was pleasant and collected in his manners, but irritable in his temper, though not habitually passionate.[41]

Wells denied the anecdotes of the poet's absence of mind and gloomy character; and he called Mrs Hallows 'a jolly, handsome woman'. In the churchyard there were memorials set up by the Doctor to a favourite servant called Rogers and to his cook, Mary Lewes, who was often called up to attend him in the night, when he felt himself inclined to write. And he might have added two more such memorials, one on a thresher – 'Here lies my friend Edward Parker the Thresher, who discharged his duty in the *barn* with the same integrity as he did in the church'[42] – and the other, dated 1749, on a labourer 'industrious in low estate', which began 'If fond of what is rare, attend! Here lies an honest man, of perfect piety, of lamblike patience, my friend James Barker.'[43] Young was not ashamed to proclaim the humblest as his friends, and in return the people of Welwyn loved him.

But for all the veneration there was also gossip about the Rector's eccentricities. The surprising thing really is that there was so little of it about his relations with his favourite, that 'jolly, handsome woman', Mary Hallows. Amid all the posthumous smears on Young's character there is no suggestion of immorality, except for a story in the diary of one of his greatest admirers, James Boswell. In 1772 Boswell stopped for breakfast and a shave at Stevenage:

Wilson, our barber there, had married a woman of Welwyn in Hertfordshire, six miles from this place, so knew or pretended to know the celebrated Dr Young ... He said the Doctor kept a mistress, a likely woman who lived with him till he died; that he left this woman all he could, and that their connection was well known. I think it is Ranger who says, 'Your grave men are always the greatest whoremasters' ... But Dr Young was much more than a grave man; a man to whom all Nature appeared under the darkest shade, a man of the deepest theology and most sublime ideas of futurity. That such a man should keep a mistress seems hardly credible.[44]

Fascinated by the strange possibilities of human character, Boswell, who had 'for some time thought of writing an essay on the genius and writings of Dr Young',[45] passed on the barber's tale to his friends, who all dismissed it offhand. Bishop Percy said it was mere scandal, 'just as one should say that Dr Johnson keeps Mrs Williams';[46] and Johnson himself, when asked if there was any improper connection between them, answered, 'No, sir, no more than between two statues. He was past fourscore and she a very coarse woman. She read to him and, I suppose, made his coffee and frothed his chocolate and did such things as an old man wishes to have done for him.'[47]

Certainly there was no such suspicion on the part of Young's friends and guests. They sent their respects to Mrs Hallows and, far from disapproving of his domestic arrangements, commended them highly. Years later Mrs Montagu reminded the Duchess about the poet's housekeeper:

> Our friend Dr Young in his old age contrived the best; he had always some matron clothed in grey, who sat at the head of his table in decent sort, helped the guests, took care that the Doctor should not forget he was at dinner; and when the tablecloth was taken away, the sober gentlewoman shrunk back into her muslin hood and with composed serenity of countenance listened to the conversation of the company. With the same affability and discretion she poured out the coffee and made the tea, and such was her temper and deportment she was fit to have been High Priestess in the temple of the Great Apollo, if he had wanted a domestic establishment. Never did I see her disturbed in any of her great offices of carving, helping to sauce or sweetening the coffee, by any of the sublime or witty things Dr Young uttered. Often have I dropped the bit of chicken off my fork by a sudden start at something new and ingenious said by our friend, while she with a steady hand and sober mind divided the leg of the goose from the side, and other things that equally required an undivided attention. Such a placid personage is a great blessing to a philosopher.[48]

It sounds an ideal arrangement, almost too good to be true – and so, alas, it proved. From other sources we hear soon of other, less placid qualities in the Doctor's 'female superintendent of affairs'.[49] The appointment of Mary Hallows undoubtedly solved for Young the problem of comfort and companionship after the departure of Caroline; but in the end her régime was to bring him more distress than contentment.

CHAPTER 15

Revival

In the spring of 1751 Young took two important steps, both attributable to the influence of Richardson. After a fallow period of five years he took up his pen again in April[1] with two complimentary epigrams on his friend's latest work in progress, *Sir Charles Grandison*; and in the same month[2] he opened an account with Gosling's Bank in Fleet Street. Francis Gosling was a bookseller who had taken up banking and among his clients was his colleague Richardson, who doubtless advised the poet to bank there as well. Certainly it was time, as the poet's holdings of stocks were by that time considerable, over £10,000 worth of Old and New South Sea annuities, bank annuities and consolidated stock. For all his impracticality Young had amassed quite a fortune, thanks to his frugal handling of the respectable income from his rectory, pension and literary earnings. As he told the Duchess of Portland, he was 'far from want'.[3]

By July the fever of writing had gripped him again and on the 30th he wrote to Richardson, 'Have you leisure or appetite to read so long a prayer? If you have, what think you of it?'[4] His friend had both and replied two days later:

> What do I think of it? Why, I think of it as a piece of inspiration. But let me ask you, sir, what did you intend I should do with it? I have a character, Dr Bartlett, whom my Sir Charles reveres for his piety, good sense, grey hairs, sweetness of manners; who might be desired by Sir Charles, on the very occasion, to compose such a prayer for him. And how would it illustrate the character of that sound divine; whom I am afraid to make write, for fear I should not keep up the character given him. And how would it adorn and exalt my work![5]

But Young's ideas were tumbling over themselves again and a week later he wrote back excitedly:

I beg you to burn the prayer I sent you, ... for what I now send you is better. I would print it ... On second thoughts I will not print it unless you and some one of your friends, most judicious in these matters, are sincerely of opinion that it will do good ... It is written by Mrs Hallows, and partly her composition (for she is really a good divine), and you know how to correct ladies – but men too. And I beg, sir, in the most serious manner, your honest critique on what I send. For I write to the heart, and you are master of the heart and therefore the properest judge in England on this occasion ... I fear I am not enough popularly plain ... (P.S.) A prayer for Sir Charles must have less of severe self-condemnation and more of gratitude in it. This is not a prayer for a good man; if it was, it would not suit my design, which in effect is a satire on the present age.[6]

Meanwhile the Duchess was pressing him to stay with her and on 29 September[7] he was obliged to confess that he was 'printing a piece of prose' and therefore had to stay in town to correct the press. He hoped to bring it with him personally, or he would send it to her – and to her alone, as it was to be anonymous – as soon as possible. But as usual he was rushing ahead too fast. He was in Welwyn when he wrote that letter; in Welwyn on 17 October[8] for a vestry meeting; and it was not till 23 November[9] that he begged a bed of Richardson for the night, returning to Welwyn immediately. On 10 December he wrote urgently to the printer, suggesting that they should meet for dinner at Barnet, half-way between Welwyn and London, together with Millar the publisher, 'for in the first place I have been ill and cannot possibly go to town, and in the next place I cannot close what I have under my hand without consulting you on a remarkable particular in it'.[10] They were to name the day and he would be waiting at the Mitre with Shotbolt. His next letter, however, dated 15 December, was somewhat crestfallen:

Mr Shotbolt and I dined at Barnet yesterday. I was surprised and most ashamed at reading your letter; the most inexcusable blunder was occasioned by my misunderstanding Mr Millar's. You came out of love and with some inconvenience; I shall dare see your face no more.[11]

The poet had muddled the date of their rendezvous! This needless hitch seems to have taken the wind out of his sails, for though Richardson answered forgivingly on the 18th,[12] admitting that the notice was too short and offering to meet Young anywhere he liked in January, the urgency was gone. On Christmas Eve the poet invited the 'Barnet party' to Welwyn, adding 'Choose your own time; to me it is entirely indifferent';[13] and on 9 January, 1752 he dropped the whole idea:

> My hopes of consulting you on what I had written are over, as to the present; for from a cold I have such an indisposition in my eyes, I can't read without pain.[14]

So in the fiasco of Barnet petered out the affair of the prayer. The flood of thoughts and second thoughts, overflowing its banks as ever, made Young keep changing and deferring publication. Nor was it ever published – unless it formed the germ of the *Centaur not Fabulous*.

Perhaps the reason for the fading of his interest in the prayer was the flowering of a new enthusiasm, a return to his old love, the theatre. For several years he had been in desultory correspondence with Sir William Bunbury, the nephew of his old friend Sir Thomas Hanmer, about the possible production of his suppressed tragedy of 1724, *The Brothers*. The manuscript presentation copy of this play prepared for Henrietta Duchess of Marlborough had for some reason remained in the author's possession and he evidently lent it to Sir Thomas. On Sir Thomas's death in 1746 his estate was inherited by Sir William, who must have found the manuscript among his uncle's papers. In 1747[15] Sir William, who was a clergyman, approached the author about a revival of the tragedy for charity and Young suggested that he should visit Welwyn with Garrick to read the play together. But the following March Young heard a rumour that threw him into one of his panics:

> I hear a report that, by your permission, my play is destined for the stage. Sir, I do not, I cannot, believe it. It was on other conditions the play was entrusted with Sir T. Hanmer, and afterwards (at your request) with you. I had full promise from both of you that it should go no further without my consent . . . I therefore entreat you by Justice, Honour, Friendship and even Compassion . . . to put me out of pain from apprehension of future contingencies by restoring the trifle.[16]

Sir William replied soothingly and on 25 March Young apologized that 'the eagerness of my letter was owing to my surprise at the report and the violence of the asseverations that accompanied it; and. I hope you will not construe it as a meditated distrust of your honour'.[17] Perhaps to make amends, the poet now gave the manuscript to his admirer, for a note on the flyleaf reads, 'Presented by Dr Young to Sir William Bunbury, 1748.'[18] But for the moment Sir William dropped the idea, though he did not abandon it – in April, 1750[19] Young heard rumours that the Duchess had promised to second Bunbury in pressing the author to bring his old tragedy on the stage. Nothing more, however, came of it for two years, till after the abandonment of the prayer.

The cold and eye-trouble in January, 1752 that put paid to the prayer was followed by crippling rheumatism, which he still had not shaken off by 26 May, when he told the Duchess he was 'so swelled in my hands that I can scarce write';[20] while a month later his hand was still 'as big as two'[21] and his pains so frequent and severe that he feared he would only be a burden to her, not a guest, if he accepted her invitation to Bullstrode. In July[22] the practical Duchess found him some drops that immediately relieved his distress and by August[23] he was able to report that he was pretty well.

Meanwhile he had enjoyed the comfort of a visit from Richardson, who came down to Welwyn for the night of 13 June[24] with Gosling, the banker. Richardson's bread-and-butter letter to Mrs Hallows[a] shows that he was still hankering after the prayer – 'The Doctor was so kind as to say he would oblige me with a little part of a manuscript, and I promised to return it if I made not use of it to his liking'[25] – but one can only hazard a guess that Gosling's reassuring account of the state of Young's bank balance may have moved him to write on 23 June[26] to Sir William Bunbury, mentioning the public appeal on behalf of the Society for the Propagation of the Gospel[b] and asking if Garrick

---

[a] Richardson sent her a snuff-box and a compliment: 'My wife . . . often says, "How happy is the Doctor in Mrs Hallows! How happy is Mrs Hallows at the feet of such a Gamaliel!" While I shake my head and whisper, "It is owing to such good women as these, Bett, that so many of your sex are unprovided for, and that there are so many widowers and bachelors."' (Pettit, 381.)

[b] Young had been a member of the S.P.G. since 1742.

would be willing to act 'the tragedy in your hands' early the next winter for the benefit of that charity, to which he would donate the author's profits.

The time was certainly ripe for the revival of his play, for his reputation as a dramatist had never been so high. The success of the *Night Thoughts* had revived interest in his plays and *The Revenge* had become a popular stock-piece that could be relied on to draw good houses on special occasions. In 1748,[27] for instance, it was chosen by the new theatre in James Street for the first performance in England of a new actor, Keale from Fort St George. He took the part, of course, of Zanga, which was coming to be regarded as a sort of touchstone of an actor's talent, like Hamlet in our own days. That winter Quin repeated his Zanga at Covent Garden, while Keale played it at the Haymarket in May, 1749.[28] In 1751 Young's name came even more prominently before the theatre-going public with rival performances at the two great theatres of Covent Garden and Drury Lane. Quin put on his production with a new leading lady, the beautiful Mrs Cibber, as Leonora for three nights in the spring; and in the autumn Drury Lane countered with Mossop as Zanga and an even more sensational Leonora, the 'irresistible Bellamy'. This production ran for eight nights between October, 1751 and March, 1752[29] and its success[c] may have given the author the idea of a big picking for charity.

Bunbury passed Young's message to Garrick and on 28 July the actor replied:

> I have taken some pains to be at liberty to act the Doctor's play the ensuing season, but it is impossible for me now to fix the performance of it before or after Christmas. I can only say that it shall not be acted at a bad time . . . I intend to wait upon Dr Young the beginning of next week, and then I hope to be satisfied of his intentions. I could wish that he may have the copy of his play with him, that if he should come to a resolution of having it acted, I may carry it with me into Yorkshire.[30]

After reading *The Brothers*, Garrick wrote enthusiastically from Yorkshire to his friend Somerset Draper:

[c] The prompter, Richard Cross, was not so enthusiastic, commenting in his notes, 'Havard (Alonzo) played well, but the play appeared as it is wrote, dull.' (*London Stage*, IV, 265.)

Dr Young's play will do – greatly. It is much the best
modern play we have, and written with great tragic force
... At my return ... I am to spend half a day with him at
Welwyn. The Doctor seemed desirous to wash his hands of
the play and to give it up to my care and direction.[31]

Clearly he thought he had a scoop, for at the end of August[32] he
warned his brother George to tell nobody about the play or his
meeting with Young, now fixed for the following week.[d] On his
way home he stopped for half a day at the 'Swan' at Welwyn and
the negotiations for the production were settled. Young then
settled down to revising the play and on 14 November he wrote
to Richardson, proposing a flying visit:

I have a tragedy which I am desirous of reading to you.
For (on this occasion) it is your misfortune that you can
think and feel, which few men can. And I should be
inexcusable to let it come abroad without that advantage I
hope from your hearing it.[33]

The play was evidently still on the secret list, as he asked
Richardson in a postscript to say nothing of it.

Garrick, however, was careful to arrange some preliminary
publicity for Young by starting the new season with a revival on
21 September[34] of Drury Lane's successful production of *The
Revenge* with Mossop and Miss Bellamy. A week later[35] Covent
Garden played into his hands with a rival production, starring a
new actor from Dublin, Giffard, as Zanga; and over the next
months the two versions alternated with three performances
each. Young's name as a dramatist could scarcely have had a
better advertisement or one more provocative of the public's
interest.[e] All the pre-conditions for a smash hit seemed to be
fulfilled – a new tragedy by a celebrated and popular poet,
staged and played by the most famous actor-manager of the day,
supported by a brilliant and sensational leading lady, George-
Anne Bellamy. The author reckoned that his profits should

[d] Owing to the reform of the calendar, when eleven days were dropped
between 2 and 14 September, 1752, the meeting took place at a date that was
technically in the second half of the month.

[e] As a poet his international fame was manifested in 1752 by the publication
not only of two German translations of the *Night Thoughts*, by Ebert at Brunswick
and by Kayser at Hanover, but of an *Ode to Young* by the 'German Milton'
himself, Klopstock.

amount to some £1000. Early in 1753 he went up to London to stay with his friend Richardson for the rehearsals and the performance itself.

But behind the scenes things were not so smooth, for George-Anne was something of a handful. Now aged about twenty-five, she owed her name to a pretence and a mistake. Her tempestuous life began in Lisbon, where her real father, Lord Tyrawley,[f] persuaded an obliging sea-captain to marry her mother and give the baby a surname, while the local priest muddled her Christian name of Georgiana. A convent in Boulogne did nothing to subdue her spirit and her father, finding her grown into a beauty, introduced her into aristocratic society, where she mixed with peers and poets, including Young, and became a close friend, it seems, of Caroline Lee. But having forfeited her allowance by joining her mother, she took to the stage and achieved her first starring role at seventeen at Covent Garden. Various amorous adventures interrupted her career and Garrick refused her at Drury Lane; so she crossed to Dublin where, thanks to an aristocratic aunt, she soon became the rage, much to Garrick's mortification. In 1748 she returned to Covent Garden and finally crossed over to Drury Lane, appearing with Garrick in 1750 as Juliet with sensational success. But, however irresistible to the public, she proved a continual thorn in the manager's side. What happened over *The Brothers* was related thirty years later in her ghost-written imitation of Cibber's autobiography, the *Apology for the Life of George-Anne Bellamy*, which cannot pretend to much historical reliability. Nevertheless it makes lively reading and the story of Young sounds typical enough:

> I had unintentionally offended him [Garrick] by sending to Dr Young to beg the favour of a reading of his new piece, *The Brothers*, during my illness ... Mr Garrick sent me a part in [another] piece, which I declined accepting. This gave him great offence and provoked him to write to me in the following terms: 'Since you have humbugged the town, I suppose you think you are able to do whatever you please.

[f] James O'Hara, second Lord Tyrawley (1690–1773), was a soldier turned diplomat. From 1728 to 1741 he was Ambassador to Portugal, where he was highly popular but also, according to Walpole, 'singularly licentious', returning to England with 'three wives and fourteen children'. (Lewis, XVIII, 104.)

The liberty you have taken in asking to peruse Dr Young's piece is unwarrantable.' ... I informed him that I had not meant to infringe upon his authority. It arose entirely from my acquaintance with the author ... But that, notwith-standing I was to be governed with the greatest ease by complacency, yet no power on earth should rule me with a rod of iron.

Upon my appearing in the green-room for the first time after the before-mentioned letters had passed, the manager accosted me with, 'Ah, ah ah, madam, you are come at last. It was unfortunate for us that the Doctor insisted on your being his heroine.' To this I readily assented, as I really thought with him that Mrs Pritchard would have appeared in the character to much more advantage ... And being thus conscious of my inability, I was ready to give up the part. Here the Doctor cried out, 'No! no!', which did not seem to please the Manager ...

When the piece was read, I objected to a line which I imagined came with but an ill grace from the mouth of a lady ... 'I will speak to you in thunder.' ... The author replied that he thought it the most forcible line in the piece. To which I answered that it would be much more so if he joined lightning to it. Hearing this, he began to wax warm and declared that the performance then reading was the *best* he had ever written. I could not now resist saying, 'I fear, Doctor, ... I cannot help reminding you of a tragedy called *The Revenge*.' My having given the Doctor's thunder a companion had set the risible features of the performers in motion. This unfortunately increased the agitation I had put him into by not allowing him to be able to judge the merit of his own compositions and threw him into the most extravagant passion.

I now repented of my petulance to the Doctor, as I had the highest esteem for him and had lived in the strictest intimacy with his daughter. I therefore went up to him and, taking him by the hand, requested that he would not only forgive me for what I had said, but that he would likewise recall to his memory those divine precepts in his *Night Thoughts*; lest, by thus giving way to such immoderate anger, he should convince us that even *he* only knew and gave us the theory, without being master of the practical part. The Doctor thanked me cordially for the rebuke and, striding two or three times across the room, apparently ... in much distress ... he took his pen and to the astonishment of Mr Garrick struck out the line which had occasioned the contest.[g] He then sat down, as composed as if nothing had happened. But what greatly added to my triumph and to the surprise of the Manager, who well knew the Doctor's tenacious disposition, was his inviting himself home to dine with me. This mark of reconciliation you may be assured, I received with pleasure; and Mr Quin coming to town that day, he joined us. A more happy trio, I believe, never sat down to table together.[36]

The first night was on 3 March, 1753. Cross, the prompter, recorded that it 'went off with great applause, only a little laughing at Simson for his dress, or manner, I can't tell';[37] and the receipts were satisfactory, £220. But this was not, of course, part of Young's profits, for the author only got the benefit of every third night, which was advertised as 'for a public benefaction'.[38] Young's charitable intentions were proclaimed in an unauthorized epilogue, which Garrick substituted for the author's own serious one, and it is hardly surprising that the Doctor was offended when he heard Mrs Clive deliver the following lines, written by Mallet, in her broadest manner:

> To woman, sure, the most severe affliction
> Is from these fellows point-blank contradiction.
> Our Bard, without – I wish he would appear –
> Ud! I would give it him – but you shall hear.
> Good sir! quoth I, and curtsied as I spoke,
> Our pit, you know, expects and loves a joke –
> 'Twere fit to humour them; for, right or wrong,
> True Britons never like the same thing long . . .
> He humm'd and ha'd; then, waking from his dream,
> Cried I must preach to you his moral scheme.
> A scheme, forsooth, to benefit the nation!
> Some queer odd whim of pious propagation!
> Lord! talk so here – the man must be a widgeon –
> Drury may propagate – but not religion.[39]

---

[g] George-Anne's story is not confirmed by a manuscript prompt-copy in the Philbrick Library, Los Altos Hills, California, which I have been kindly permitted to examine. This copy, which appears to be a first draft with many MS corrections (three in Young's hand), does not contain the 'thunder' line at all, though it appeared in the first edition, published during the play's run. It might be that Young wished to insert this line in the acting copy but was dissuaded by George-Anne's protest, though he retained it in the printed version.

Young's own 'historical epilogue' began:

> An Epilogue, through custom, is your right,
> But ne'er perhaps was *needful* till this night.
> Tonight the virtuous falls, the guilty flies;
> Guilt's dreadful close our narrow scene denies.[40]

It was in fact a short history lesson on the wicked brother's ultimate downfall, for the moralist could not allow the guilty to get away with it. But, as the *Biographia Dramatica* remarked, it was an acknowledgement that the tragedy was 'imperfect in its catastrophe'[41] if the author had to finish the story in a postscript.

The *Biographia* also criticized the play as 'undramatical in its conduct'[42] and reported that it was coldly received; while Arthur Murphy in the *Gray's Inn Journal* rebuked the 'propensity which the small critics discovered at the representation of this piece to attach themselves to every trivial circumstance which could have the least tendency to excite their mirth'.[43] By the fifth night the play was clearly in trouble and an elaborate puff in the form of a *Letter from Mr Booth in the Shades to Dr Young* was printed with Young's epilogue in the *Public Advertiser* of the 10th.[44] In this Booth, who was to have starred in the original production thirty years before, forgives Young for withdrawing his play and waiting till Garrick could play the lead, and adds that there will be a performance in the shades by all the old actors – as soon as Curll can steal a copy for them! On the 12th[45] the play itself was published by Dodsley, who had also written the prologue. But in spite of all the publicity the houses remained thin and to add to the difficulties Garrick was taken ill on the second benefit night, 12 March. At that moment the author's profits amounted to no more than £300 and it was clear that they would come nowhere near his expectations. Young therefore decided he would not wait for the final result and made his donation at once, on 12 March.[46] Richardson told the story to Lady Bradshaigh:[h]

> The Doctor, you have heard, intended the benefit accruing to an author to go to the Society for Propagating the Gospel. He, finding it did not answer his expectations as

---

[h] The editress of Richardson's correspondence, Mrs Barbauld, in her inimitable way, dated this letter 24 February, 1753 – two weeks *before* the first performance!

to profits, took them to himself (not £400) and gave a thousand guineas to that society. I had some talk with him on this great action. 'I always,' said he, 'intended to do something handsome by this society. Had I deferred it to my demise, I should have given away my son's money. All the world are inclined to pleasure; I myself love pleasure as much as any man; could I have given myself a greater by disposing of the same sum to a different use, I should have done it.'[47]

However the poet might seek to laugh off his motives, it was a magnanimous gesture of sincerity. Young was sometimes accused of parsimony, but that was only where expense on himself was concerned; where his heart was engaged, he could be most generous – as Caroline, as well as the S.P.G., could witness. In the end his gesture cost him some £650, for the management of the theatre also did their best for the cause by advertising the next performance as the eighth instead of seventh, so that the last night – really the eighth – was again a charity benefit.

But the fact was that theatrical tastes had changed in the thirty years since *The Brothers* was first put in rehearsal and the public now wanted less splendidly rhetorical stuff. Richardson might be shocked: 'Will it be hereafter believed that the *Earl of Essex* had a run,[i] and that a play of the author of the *Night Thoughts* was acted to thin houses but just eight nights?'[48] Murphy, writing in the *Gray's Inn Journal* on the last night, 17 March, might speak of Young, 'justly celebrated among the foremost successors of Shakespeare and Otway',[49] adding another wreath to his garland; and Shenstone, reading the play in his retreat of the Leasowes, might tell Graves that he found it 'a noble tragedy, abounding ... with refined sentiments and elevated expressions'[50] and assure Lady Luxborough, 'I am not blind to many of its faults; Dr Young must be Dr Young; but I have read no tragedy of late years that has affected me so much.'[51] But the proof of a play is in the performance, and the public had turned *The Brothers* down. The big scene, the trial of the rival princes

---

[i] *The Earl of Essex* was written by Henry Jones (1721–70), an Irish bricklayer patronized by Lord Chesterfield. It was produced at Covent Garden on 21 February, 1753 and ran seventeen nights, bringing Jones £500 – a success which led to his ruin through drink.

before their father, King Philip of Macedon, was praised by all for its variety of eloquence. But the *Monthly Review* found the story 'less happily chosen' and the plot 'less animated with interesting business' than in his other plays – indeed, 'almost a cold and unaffecting performance'.[52] Tom Davies summed it up in his *Memoirs of the Life of David Garrick*:

> The great fault of this writer was his custom of seeking for pearls and diamonds when less costly materials would have served his purpose much better. Shakespeare is not more fond of a quibble than Young is of a bright thought. Long descriptions of misery, with all its attributes, in scenes of the greatest anxiety and distress, is a forgetfulness of situation to seek after prettiness and brilliancy of expression.[53]

The play has never been performed again; and as it turned out to be not so much based on Livy as closely modelled on a lesser work of a lesser French dramatist – the *Persée et Démétrius* of Thomas Corneille[j] we may be excused from a critical consideration of a piece that is not only an imitation but quite, quite dead.

After the failure of *The Brothers* Young retired to Welwyn, where he seems to have stayed quietly till nearly the end of the year. Only one or two letters have survived, but regular signatures of the vestry minutes indicate that he seldom, if ever, left his parish, while a story in the *Memoirs of the Author of Indian Antiquities* by Thomas Maurice[k] confirms his presence in September, as well as exemplifying his 'good heart' and freedom from conventional snobbery. Maurice's father was the Headmaster of Christ's Hospital, Hertford, from 1737 to 1762 and had struck up a friendship with the Rector of Welwyn on the common ground of 'those botanical and horticultural pursuits which were the delight of my father in his hours of leisure'.[54] The Headmaster's wife had a companion, a girl of 18, with whom, after her death, the widower fell in love. But his friends

---

[j] See *The Story on which the new Tragedy is founded*, Reeve, 1753.

[k] Maurice (1754–1824) used as a child to visit Welwyn with his father. He recalled, 'At a very early period I could recite select passages from the best English poets . . . I once astonished the author of the *Night Thoughts* by an emphatic enunciation of several passages of his inimitable work on his own bowling-green at Welwyn.' (Maurice, 24.)

objected to such a lowly and unsuitable union and the Rector of
Hertford refused to marry them. In the end the marriage was
performed by the Rector of Stevenage on 21 September, 1753[55]
and among those invited to the wedding dinner was the Rector
of Welwyn. Maurice continued:

> Indisposition prevented his accepting the invitation. He
> however requested to see the new-married pair in their
> return through Welwyn to Hertford, and I have often
> heard my good mother speak with grateful delight of the
> kind and courteous attention paid them by the venerable
> bard, both on that occasion and afterwards. Dr Young
> indeed, my memoranda inform me, was a very different
> character from what might be conjectured from the general
> gloomy strain of the *Night Thoughts*, being, when in health, a
> man of very social habits and the animating soul of every
> company with whom he intermixed.[56]

Young's cheerfulness in company, indeed, quite offended the
more solemn of his admirers, who wished the author of the
Night Thoughts to behave always in character with his poem. Miss
Carter, we are told, 'was much disappointed in his conversation.
It appeared to her light, trifling and full of puns';[57] while Miss
Laetitia-Matilda Hawkins[1] complained in her *Memoirs*:

> The place of Young's residence was visited, a short time
> after his death, by a friend of my father's, who was curious
> to see the scenery in which he had framed his mind. It bore
> no analogy to his cast of thought; and from a servant
> who had lived with him he learned that no two things could
> have less of affinity than Young's habits of life and his
> meditations . . . His gravity was hardly enough for a
> gownsman of any description.[58]

Actually the 'rectorial grounds of Welwyn', which 'owed not a
little of the taste and arrangement which they displayed to the
joint efforts'[59] of the poet and the headmaster, were full of
reminders of mortality, like the 'deception' inscribed *Invisibilia
non decipiunt* and the sun-dial, about which Boswell repeated
Bennet Langton's story as 'an instance at once of his pensive
turn of mind and his cheerfulness of temper: "Here (said he,

---

[1] Daughter of Sir John Hawkins, Johnson's 'unclubbable' friend and
biographer.

when they were walking in his garden) I had put a handsome sun-dial with this inscription, *Eheu fugaces!*, which (speaking with a smile) was sadly verified, for by the next morning my dial had been carried off.'"[60] .

During this time his great interest was the progress of Richardson's new novel, *Sir Charles Grandison*. On 20 September, 1753, after receiving an advance copy of the first four volumes,''' he sent his thanks and added, 'You keep me in awe by your good sense: I dare therefore say but little. Yet must I say what is extraordinary to be said, the wisest man in England may be wiser for reading a romance.'[61] At the beginning of December[62] he went up to London to stay with the novelist in order to consult the famous Dr Heberden about a 'moving pain' near his heart with wind and indigestion, and he doubtless saw the next two volumes of *Grandison*, which were published on 11 December. By that date the poet was back at home, feeling much better, and a week later he told Richardson that he was 'reading Sir Charles the second time and like it much more than before'; that he believed that 'not one half of your revenue of fame is yet come in . . . and I am persuaded that apologies will be made you for the defective applause which you have hitherto received.'[63] The seventh and last volume appeared in March, 1754 and was greeted with a long and impetuous paean of praise:''

> Joy to you, dear sir, and joy to the world; you have done great things for it. And I will venture to affirm that no-one shall read you without either benefit or – guilt. Pray ask Mr Cibber from me, where now are the *fine gentlemen* of the stage? . . . When the pulpit fails, other expedients are necessary. I look on you as a peculiar instrument of Providence, adjusted to the peculiar exigence of the times, in which all would be *fine gentlemen* and only are at a loss to know what that means. While they read, perhaps, from pure vanity, they do not read in vain and are betrayed into benefit, while mere amusement is their pursuit.[64]

''' These volumes were not actually published till 13 November.
'' Young was reading it with Shotbolt and had reached 'the scene where little Emily comes to confession . . . It is, I think, in the highest degree natural, tender, exquisite and original. I am got no further in the volume, but could not forbear turning my own and my neighbour's thanks, the first post, for a favour so delightful.' (Pettit, 401–2.)

Two entries in Young's bank account at this time, mentioning
the name of Frederick Young, are a reminder that the poet's son
had come of age in 1753 and was now legally competent to
handle his own affairs. On 19 March, 1754,[65] the proceeds of
the sale of £622 worth of 3% stocks by 'F(rancis)G(osling)
Att(orne)y to Fredk Young' were credited to his father's
account, and on 22 April just under £75, being the half-yearly
interest on Frederick's 3% holdings, was likewise paid over to
the poet. Frederick was now up at Balliol College, Oxford, as a
gentleman-commoner, having suffered the same fate as his
father and been superannuated from Winchester. In Frederick's
case, however, fortune was more unjust. Top of the school by
1749, he headed the New College election roll in September,
1750 and again in 1751;[66] but each time two Founder's Kin took
precedence. Worse, there was an extraordinary block in the
vacancies, with not a single admission to the College in 1751. As
the boy was nineteen, he had to leave that summer and there was
nothing for it but to go up to some other college as a Commoner
while he waited and hoped for a vacancy before the next
election. So in October, 1751 his father sent him to Oxford with
a presentation copy of the *Night Thoughts*[67] for the Master of
Balliol, Dr Theophilus Leigh.° Frederick was duly admitted as a
Commoner on 4 November, matriculated on the 12th,[68] and
remained at Balliol for the next seven years. Only two New
College vacancies occurred before September, 1752 and they, of
course, were taken up by the Founder's Kin.

Unfortunately the freedom of a gentleman-commoner's life at
Oxford seems to have gone to Frederick's head, especially after
he came of age. In his first year, 1752, his absences from College
corresponded with reasonable vacations, a month at Christmas,
another at Easter and four months in the long vacation, from
May to October. But from 23 February, 1753 he absented
himself for nearly a year, not returning to Balliol till 11 January,
1754.[69] During this period he reached his majority and the bank
records suggest that his father may – unwisely – have given him
a handsome twenty-first birthday present, for interest of £75 for
six months at 3% implies a capital holding of £5000. Frederick's

° Dr Leigh was Master of Balliol for sixty years, 1726–1785. His brother was at
All Souls with Young.

later record shows that he was an incurable spendthrift and the payment of nearly £700 to his father in the spring of 1754, when he had at last returned to his studies, makes one suspect that the poet must have paid off a number of large debts, incurred by his son during his prolonged holiday.[p] But the prodigal's repentance did not last long. After five months at Oxford, from January to June, 1754,[70] Frederick disappeared from the College again, this time for over a year.

It was at this time that Young began a new work, an attack on the morals of modern society that was eventually published as *The Centaur not Fabulous*, and one cannot help wondering whether it was inspired by the unfortunate behaviour of his son. On 29 June Richardson told Mrs Delany of a mysterious visit to town by the poet:

> Dr Young is another uncontrollable, therefore un-accountable. He had been in town, somewhere behind the Royal Exchange, for three weeks, without letting me know a syllable of the matter till the very day that, ready booted (Friday last week), he called in Salisbury Court, leaving word (I was out) that he was very desirous of seeing me at Welwyn.[q] I wish that he is not concerned in some plot, by this privacy to one of his sincerest friends. He is an absent man, you know, Madam, and if he be in a plot, it will not be long a secret. Of this we may be sure, it will not be against the state.[71]

Whether he had some private business reason for his secret stay behind the Royal Exchange, and whether it was connected with Frederick, we can only guess. But it is certain that part of the time was spent on the first draft of the *Centaur*, for on 14 July he told Richardson:

> I have a thing I would send immediately to the press; it's about the length of five sermons; and as I am distant from

[p] Young also paid considerable sums at this time to Charles Godwyn, Fellow and Bursar of Balliol, who was Senior Dean when Frederick came up to Oxford and may have been his Tutor. The unusually large amounts paid – 9 Feb., £50; 16 Feb., £40; 1 March, £66 – indicate debts much greater than the normal College expenses.

[q] Mrs Delany replied from Ireland, 20 July, 1754: 'I am glad you find a *man* can be an uncontrollable creature as well as a woman . . . Had he a tenth part of the value for me that I have for him, I should have seen him (though only in his boots) whilst I was in England.' (Barbauld, IV, 91–2.)

town, it can go on but slowly. I would fain show it you before I put it out of my hands; I put it in my pocket for that purpose when I called at your door . . . I print myself, because I cannot stay to talk with booksellers and they are not at hand.[72]

Richardson hastened down to Welwyn on the 17th to discuss the new project and on his way back was accompanied by Young as far as Barnet, where this time their talks over dinner bore fruit.[73]

What followed is very well documented with a flood of short letters making changes, additions, new ideas, changes of mind, and leaving all the practical details, even of punctuation, to be sorted out by the writer's patient and efficient friend. Young told him to blot, add, alter as he pleased; and the printer retorted with questions about size, page, type, price, etc. By 28 July[74] the piece had lengthened to five or six sermons; he would print it himself and let a bookseller handle it; besides, he might want to suppress it at the last moment; he would send it for printing letter by letter, dedication first. On 1 August[75] he agreed to Richardson's suggestions; but on the 5th he had second thoughts. Because of the length of the letters he would publish them one by one; 'though this publishing the letters separately is a sudden thought, yet for many reasons I am fond of it, unless you have one that can knock them all on the head'.[76] The printer knocked them on the head the same day with a long helpful letter explaining the difficulty of fixing a price for separate pamphlets, raising the questions of the publisher and anonymity, and questioning the wisdom of too clear a satirical dedication:

> Everybody will guess to whom the dedication is made, by Lady T——. Would you be careless on that head, should the piece be guessed to be yours? Mr Winnington once told me that Lady T—— was vindictive and jealous of being in print.[77]

Young took the hint and the book was dedicated to 'the Lady xxxxxx'.

On 11 August Young had another 'sudden thought', a satirical frontispiece, for which he apparently enclosed a sketch, saying:

> If you knew any proper artist in that way, I wish you would show him the grotesque picture of a Centaur in my

Dedication. If I could have a cut of it, I would prefix it to the letters. It would, I think, have two good effects. 1st, it would carry the reader with more appetite through the dedication, as letting him into the meaning of the odd picture before him. 2ly, it would look as if there was more occasion for the dedication (which is pretty long) than there seems to be at present.[78] And he added, I wish I knew Hogarth, or your friend Mr Hyman.[r]

Young's ideas were in spate again. 'When the pulpit fails, other expedients are necessary', he had told Richardson; just as the readers of *Grandison* might be 'betrayed into benefit', he hoped with the trick of his Centaur to 'cheat people into their own good'.[79] In October he was still engaged on the fifth letter, for it included a lament for his old friend Sir Jeremy Sambrooke, who died on 4 October[80] – a death that Young described to the Duchess as 'a great loss to the living, but a most happy release to himself'.[81] In mid-October another hasty conference was held with Richardson at their half-way house, Barnet, to which the poet brought a companion, the Rev. Mark Hildesley, Vicar of Hitchin, who six months later was appointed Bishop of Sodor and Man. Hildesley was a friend and correspondent of Richardson, to whom he sent his reminiscences of Young in 1760:

> The friendship of so valuable a person, in every respect, I was ever indeed ambitious to obtain and cultivate whilst he was my neighbour for upwards of twenty years; and for that end have often intruded upon him . . . The impertinence of my frequent visits to him (for impertinent must that liberty be deemed which in so many years failed to receive the encouragement of ever seeing him once at my house, beyond the threshold of my door), however, was amply rewarded: forasmuch as I can truly say that he never received me but with agreeable open complacency, and I never left him but with profitable pleasure and improvement. He was, one way or other, the most modest, the most patient of contradiction and the most informing and

[r] Young probably meant Joseph Highmore (1692–1780), who had done a series of twelve illustrations for *Pamela* as well as portraits of the novelist and his wife. He evidently confused the name with that of Francis Hayman, who designed a frontispiece for the collected *Night Thoughts*.

entertaining of any man (at least of any man who had so just
pretensions to pertinacity and reserve) I ever conversed
with.[82]

A few weeks after Barnet Young went up to London and
Richardson took the opportunity to introduce him to his painter
friend Highmore, whom the poet had mentioned in connection
with the frontispiece for the *Centaur*. The meeting was a great
success and Richardson quickly took advantage of it, writing to
the painter the same night:

> I have obtained of Dr Young what none of his friends
> have hitherto been able to obtain – that he will sit to the
> pencil. The pleasure he has received this evening at your
> house, and particularly in your conversation, has greatly
> contributed to his assent ... Be pleased to give me your
> time, the sooner the better, lest he should change his mind
> or not stay in town long enough to have it finished. He
> insists upon my attending him and thinks he shall not have
> patience to sit it out.[83]

Highmore made due haste and the portrait was achieved – the
only authentic picture of the poet, now hanging in the hall of his
old College, All Souls. A note by the painter at the foot of
Richardson's letter says, 'Dr Young paid for it, 1st Decr 1754.'[84]
The novelist, overwhelmed by his friend's gesture, wrote in
grateful protest on 17 December that even Mrs Hallows, who 'is
prepared to think all you do is right ... in this instance will, I
hope, think it possible that Dr Young can be once wrong.'[85] But
he still was not allowed to pay.

Perhaps it was during this visit that Young finished the
Centaur, for the conclusion is dated 'Nov. 29, 1754'. But even
then he could not stop and he added a postscript defending the
mixture of 'levity with solemnity', ending:

> So earnestly desirous am I of waking him [the infidel]
> from that dream ... that if nothing can do it but my own
> disgrace, my own buffoonery, as perhaps he will think it, I
> rejoice to fall so low. If he will but laugh *with* me at *himself*,
> he is freely welcome to laugh *at* me.[86]

The postscript was inspired by the objections of a friend who
feared he might expose himself to censure or ridicule. This

sounds very like Richardson, who on 21 January, 1755 apologetically suggested that 'the reader is not sufficiently prepared in that dedication for the solemn and elevated subjects of the following letters' and that a few pages might with advantage be cancelled 'lest the serious mind should be sorry for some condescending levities and images, and lest the lighter minds should take hold of such to avoid the force of the diviner parts'.[87] This was rather to miss the point, which was to trick the frivolous into reading the morality, but Young accepted his friend's amendments and followed up with a flurry of corrections, to be made without delay and regardless of expense, as another edition was 'precarious'.[88] And so at last on 4 March, 1755[89] *The Centaur not Fabulous*, now swollen to 378 pages, was published anonymously by Millar and the Dodsleys.[s]

It was a curious title,[t] and a curious work, which has been well described as a sort of *Night Thoughts* in prose. The five letters[u] on 'the Life in Vogue' were in effect a series of highly rhetorical sermons on the vanity of fashionable pleasures and their corollary, infidelity, with a special attack on the doctrines of Bolingbroke, whose posthumous works, edited by Mallet, had come out in five volumes in 1753–4. Nothing that Young wrote could be dull, but in this work he set out deliberately to amuse, to try and catch the attention of those who would never read a sermon. The extraordinary title, illustrated by the grotesque frontispiece, was explained thus:

> You will probably ask why the Centaur is prefixed as a title. The *Men of Pleasure*, the licentious and profligate, are the subject of these letters and in such, as in the fabled Centaur, the brute runs away with the man; therefore I call them Centaurs. And farther I call them Centaurs *not fabulous* because by their scarce half-human conduct and character that enigmatical and purely ideal figure of the ancients is not unriddled only, but realized.[90]

[s] On 29 August, 1755 the publishers paid £100 each to Young's bank account.
[t] Perhaps inspired by Christopher Smart's April fool's hoax in 1751 in the *Gentleman's Magazine* (XXI, 153), giving an 'authentic account of the surprising Centaur', to be exhibited at Charing Cross – on 1 April!
[u] The second and subsequent editions were divided into *six* letters by splitting the fifth.

The humour was rather laboured; wit, not humour, was Young's line. But the book was received with favour, reaching a second edition on 18 April[91] and a third on 17 November.[92] The *Scots Magazine* of March[93] quoted it as having great power and the *Monthly Review* of May found 'many proofs of a brilliant imagination', though 'no great judgement';[94] adding that, though the book was anonymous, few readers would be at a loss to discover the author's name. Young's friends, like Miss Talbot, found it 'well worth reading'.[95] But others were cooler, like Dr Thomas Blackwell from Scotland, who wrote that 'some fine thoughts in Dr Young's Centaurs are déparés by the tumid style; it is half verse, half prose, cut and empoulé like the *Night Thoughts*.'[96] A regular attack was mounted in November in *Three Letters concerning Systematic Taste exemplified in the Centaur not Fabulous*, and in February, 1756 Lady Echlin, the sister of Richardson's romantic Lady Bradshaigh, told him indignantly:

> I have read that good book, *The Centaur not Fabulous*. Sorry am I to know it is a melancholy truth; but I did not think there were so many monsters in human shape as I now believe there are, from the bad reception that excellent lesson meets with in the world. Can they be rational creatures who ridicule the author and impudently call the reverend doctor a madman?[97]

The *Centaur* was a tract for the times, Young's own times, not for posterity. Though the adoring Germans at once issued a translation and the more discriminating French later extracted from it some *pensées*, it never pretended to literary immortality and, once the immediate impact had passed, it was never separately reprinted. The five 'letters' are addressed to a friend who had asked Young to write about the 'reigning passion for pleasure',[98] and though some later passages suggest Richardson as the addressee – particularly Letter IV with 'that piece of devotion you desired on your friend's account',[99] the *Devout thoughts of a Retired Penitent*, which looks like a rehash of the abortive Prayer of 1751 – the earlier references to the friend's dissolute sister with her gay favourites and 'grey pretty fellows'[100] indicate that he was a composite character. This 'sister' sounds much like 'Lady T———', to whom the *Centaur* was dedicated and it is plausibly suggested that she was the notorious Lady Townshend,[v] niece of Young's neighbour, George Harrison of Balls Park near Welwyn, which she inherited on her uncle's death in 1759. Was it perhaps George Harrison of Balls who suggested the subject to Young? He fits the description – a friend, a 'coaeval' and an intimate of Sir Jeremy Sambrooke – and the 'sister' could have been camouflage for his niece.

It can hardly be doubted that in this attack on the corrupting influence of society's passion for pleasure, 'ranging from the gaming-house to brothels',[101] the poet's son was very much in his mind. Four days after it was published, on 8 March, 1755, Mrs Montagu wrote to her sister Sarah:

> I have just got Dr Young's new work called the *Centaur*; I have not yet looked into it, but I expect to find two species in the book as well as the title, for the Doctor's Pegasus is half horse, half ass. I remember you had heard some things to the disadvantage of Dr Young's character in regard to his behaviour towards his son; I believe if you enquire farther you will find that the young man is a worthless irreclaimable profligate. Mr Richardson (the author) has been concerned in their affairs and he acquits the father of any blame and charges the son very heavily.[102]

At that date Frederick had again been absent from Oxford for nearly nine months, and Mrs Montagu's words confirm what Gosling's records suggest, that he had been leading a life of wild and reckless extravagance.

The poet has been much blamed for his quarrel with his son and Croft, as Frederick's friend and self-appointed champion, set the tone. The earlier accounts made Young a stern father, but with justification: the obituary in the *Annual Register* referred to 'his son, whose boyish follies were long obnoxious to paternal severity',[103] while the *Biographia Britannica* alleged, on the authority of the mysterious Dr Eyre,[w] that at Balliol Frederick

---

[v] Ethelreda or Audrey, daughter of Edward Harrison of Balls, married Charles, 3rd Viscount Townshend, in 1723. She was the 'Bellaston' of Fielding's *Tom Jones*.

[w] Described by the *Biographia* as 'Dr Eyre of Gray's Inn, who was his [Young's] school-fellow at Winchester.' Probably the Rev. Dr Robert Eyre (1690–1775), who, though a cleric, kept a study in Gray's Inn. (PRO, Prob. 11/1004/9.) He entered Winchester in 1702, the year that Young left, and so just qualifies as a school-fellow. He was a Fellow of All Souls from 1712 to 1724, when the College presented him to the Rectory of Buckland, Surrey. He took his DD in 1735.

'misbehaved himself so much as to be forbidden the college',[104] and added that this misconduct so displeased his father that the old gentleman never after suffered him to come into his sight. But Croft, while admitting that Frederick caused his father 'uneasiness' with follies 'blameable in a boy', not only denied that he experienced any 'dismission from his college either lasting or temporary' but put the blame for his delinquencies on his father. 'Young was a poet,' he commented, 'poets, with reverence be it spoken, do not make the best parents,' and he went on to sneer that 'fancy and imagination . . . always stoop unwillingly to the low level of common duties'.[105] In his original manuscript, according to Isaac D'Israeli, he elaborated on this theme in a passage that was struck out by Dr Johnson:

> While the poet's eye was glancing 'from earth to heaven', he totally overlooked the lady whom he married and who soon became the object of his contempt; and not only his wife, but his only son, who, when he returned home for the vacation from Winchester school, was only admitted into the presence of his poetical father on the first and on the last day, and whose unhappy life is attributed to this unnatural neglect.[106]

Though D'Israeli's paraphrase is suspect (the same passage absurdly associates Mrs Hallows with the composition of the *Night Thoughts*), it must be remembered that Croft implied that his source was Frederick himself and the vacation story might be a distorted version of something told him in one of their sessions at the White Hart Tavern, Holborn, some twenty-five years after his schooldays. Was Frederick's misbehaviour at Oxford the result of some hidden grievance against his father dating from his time at Winchester? If so, it could only be from absent-mindedness on his father's part; the idea of cold and contemptuous neglect does not fit in at all with the rest of the picture, in which a fond love of children was prominent. This was the same man who was so much loved by his stepchildren.

While Frederick was at school, of course, his father would not see him except for a month at Whitsuntide; and if we examine the record of Young's Whitsun doings from the boy's first holidays in 1744, we find that he may well have had to leave his son to himself most of the time in the earlier years. The holidays customarily started on the Monday before Whitsunday, so that in 1744 they ran from 7 May to early June; but that May Young was entangled in the toils of the law over his stepson's estate, only escaping from town on the 26th and, as he told the Duchess on the 29th,[107] soon to be re-entangled. In 1745 the holidays were late, from 27 May for most of June, which meant that for the second half of Frederick's stay his father had to be away for his tour of duty as Chaplain to the King. The Whitsun period of 1746 was spoilt by serious illness; at the end of the holidays, on 12 June,[108] Young reported so severe a relapse that he could not go to London for his court duty. The following year the vacation coincided with the month of June, so Kensington duty interfered again. Then came 1748, filled with the preparations for Caroline's wedding, not to mention urgent law business; on 4 June,[109] in the middle of the holidays, Young had the bride and groom staying with him and probably paid more attention to them than to his son. In 1749 and 1750 the poet appears to have been at Welwyn all through the vacation; but by that time a new figure was dominating the household, Mrs Hallows. These facts suggest a possible cause of tension in Frederick's feelings towards his father. To a homesick and motherless child it might have seemed like neglect when in his first and most sensitive years of boarding-school his father always was going away during his one precious month at home; and later there could have been unconscious jealousy of Caroline and even more of the housekeeper. Dr Johnson told Boswell in 1773:

> The cause of the quarrel between Young and his son . . . was that his son insisted Young should turn away a clergyman's widow, who lived with him and who, having acquired great influence over the father, was saucy to the son. Dr Johnson said she could not conceal her resentment at him for saying to Young that 'an old man should not resign himself to the management of anybody'.[110]

That may have been the final straw – but the quarrel was by no means final yet. On 18 July, 1755[111] Frederick returned to Balliol after thirteen months' absence, if not rustication, and for the next three years his residence at the university was perfectly regular. On 8 October[112] he took his first degree as

Student in Civil Law, figuring from then on in the Buttery Books among the BA Commoners of the college as 'Dominus Young'. With his return to his studies and a steadier life the quarrel with his father was evidently patched up. But, alas, the 'Centaur' in Frederick was only suppressed, not dead.

CHAPTER 16

The Card

1755–1757

Neither *The Brothers* nor the *Centaur*, though respectfully received, had added any new dimension to Young's celebrity. He was still thought of, first and foremost, as the poet of the *Night Thoughts*, while his secondary claims to fame, as dramatist and satirist, rested on his older works, *The Revenge* and *The Universal Passion*. *The Brothers* was never revived, but *The Revenge* continued to hold the stage with further revivals in 1755 and 1756,[1] and in the latter year[2] even *Busiris* got an airing.[a] The satires, too, were still remembered; a Dublin satire of 1754, *A Dish of Chocolate for the Times*, was addressed to Young, and in the same year Arthur Murphy in the *Gray's Inn Journal* described an 'Election in Parnassus':

> Horace, Boileau and Mr Pope were made the Represen-
> tatives for Satire . . . As soon as the election was over, Mr
> Pope thanked the constituents for the honour conferred
> upon him and signified his inclination to take his seat for
> Ethics, to which he was recommended by the Lord Viscount
> Bolingbroke, and the voters came to a resolution to fill up
> the vacancy by putting up the famous Dr Young, though in
> his absence.[3]

But if his new works did not really increase his reputation, they increased the bulk of his works and the booksellers began to urge him to let them publish a new collected edition – the first, in 1741, having proved somewhat premature.

Young's enormous celebrity, however, provoked other reactions besides applause. While the normal response to the *Nights* was that of the young Edmund Burke, who scribbled in the Dublin edition of 1755:

---

[a] In November, 1755 Zanga was once again chosen as the vehicle for a new actor, Clarke, at Covent Garden. A benefit performance of *Busiris* at Covent Garden in March, 1756 was advertised as 'not acted these thirty years'. (*London Stage*, IV, 511; 533.)

> Jove claimed the verse old Homer sung,
> But God himself inspired Dr Young,[4]

there were others who disapproved of his gloom. In 1754 Henry Jones, the bricklayer-poet whose *Earl of Essex* had outshone *The Brothers*, took it upon himself to rebuke the tendencies of the *Night Thoughts* in *The Relief, or Day Thoughts.*[b] While denouncing Young's religious attitude and his romantic scenery, Jones did his best to imitate Young's style in twenty-five pages of turgid blank verse. The 'new wave' of melancholy, which by now included Gray's *Elegy*, provoked him to the following purple protest:

> Why all this solemn apparatus? why?
> Why all this din about a worm's concerns? . . .
> The awful temples, tombs and tolling clocks;
> The midnight damps that drop from weeping yews
> Beneath th' eclipsed moon (the screech-owl's haunt),
> Drenching the locks of some night-watching pilgrim
> Who sits, in dismal meditation wrapt
> And brainsick horror, o'er yon mouldering grave.
> . . . Thus hideous Melancholy dips
> Her pencil still in dark, delusive tints
> And paints the face of things – detested group!
> A landscape fit for Hell; the work of Fiends![5]

But the fulminations of Mr Jones were quite ineffectual in combating the rising popularity of the romantic 'apparatus' or turning back the 'fiends' from their dark musings to the broad classic daylight. Such attacks on Young were a recognition of his position as leader of the new movement.

A different kind of attack, personal rather than literary, was made on him in 1755 in a satirical two-volume novel called *The Card*. This was written by one John Kidgell, who is supposed to have been one of Young's curates. Certainly the novel shows a close acquaintance with the habits and character of the poet and his housekeeper, who figure under the pseudonyms of Dr Elwes

---

[b] Other *Day Thoughts* appeared in 1753, with the alternative title of *The Vindication*, by the Rev. Joseph Burroughs, attacking the melancholy of *Night I*:
> Too great fondness for the night has cast
> On your whole soul a dark, habitual gloom.

and Mrs Fusby.[c] But the Welwyn parish registers show no evidence of such a curate, whereas his signature appears on 16 April, 1752[6] as curate of the neighbouring parish of Ayot St Peter. Supply work was done by whoever was available in the neighbourhood and it seems likely therefore that Kidgell just did occasional duty at Welwyn when he was in the district – a theory supported by the novel itself, in which the curate for Elwes comes from another parish. In this capacity he must have observed the old man's eccentricities and decided to add them as spice to his *Card*.

For the novel is not primarily about Young, though the adventures of Dr Elwes as a travelling tutor take up several chapters of the first volume; in the second there is only one passing reference to the Doctor at the very end. The action is purely imaginary, for Young never went abroad as a tutor in his life; Kidgell simply took the character and invented ridiculous situations to illustrate it. It is the caricature of his nature and habits, and those of his housekeeper, that is interesting. Here we get the 'worm's eye view', exaggerated, of course, but illuminating. Kidgell was clearly a sharp observer and his later career[d] shows that his scruples were not likely to stand in the way of his satire.

Yet, on the whole, Young comes out of the ordeal pretty well; for all the mockery there is still respect and a sort of affection. The Doctor is described as 'a clergyman of great learning and humanity', though his knowledge was not 'the knowledge of the

---

[c] The identification of Young with Elwes is made explicit in a parody, which begins:

> Valence, inconstant lovely fair eloper!
> Yet why inconstant? for inconstancy
> Is but the absence of the constant mind . . .

and ends:

> Fair fugitive! and fugitive as fair!
> And fair as fugitive! implored, return
> And *be* the thing you *seem*. Alas! alas!
> My very mistress knows me not!

(Kidgell, I, 241)

[d] Born 1722, Kidgell was educated at Winchester and Oxford, graduating in 1747. His Hertfordshire curacy may have been his first appointment. Soon after *The Card* he obtained various country rectories, but his desire for a London living led him to act for his patron, the Earl of March, in secretly procuring a copy of Wilkes's *Essay on Woman*, which enabled the government to prosecute their enemy. Kidgell's *Narrative* in defence of his actions only served to blast his reputation and, being deep in debt, he had to flee the country.

world';[7] he was 'naturally good-humoured and could be occasionally droll and jocular; had sometimes a singularity, but always a benevolence of aspect';[8] and the story ends with a sort of apology to 'one who, in his general character, was an honour to his profession, having painfully acquired learning and virtuously adorned it with integrity. The minute particulars which relate to the Doctor, it is hoped, will not give offence to those of his venerable order who have his *merit* without his foibles. It is the property of *little* failings to be ridiculed.'[9]

The satirist's venom was directed against poor Mrs Hallows, who is described thus:

> This female superintendent of affairs had by artful management obtained the degree of a favourite. She had carefully studied *his* humour and caprice and generally knew how to direct him according to *her own*: but where she found him positive, had the address to coincide with his opinion. She fancied herself to *know* more than she really did, had somewhat of an inclination to be thought *younger* than she was. Censorious of her neighbours and austere to the servants of the family, but to the Doctor himself complacent and demure. She was in the general air of her deportment affectedly scrupulous and formal . . . and was *incontestably a virgin.*[10]

The curate seems to have had quite a different impression of Mrs Hallows from that of the Doctor's guests, whereas the picture of Young himself is reasonably consistent, whether in Kidgell or Pope or Mrs Montagu. In *The Card* he is shown as unworldly, absent-minded, changeable, parsimonious, jealous, vain of his Latin, susceptible, impractical, moralizing; but at the same time virtuous, honourable, gentle, compassionate, good-humoured, benevolent and patient. Of his foibles only his parsimony and his jealousy could be classed as faults; the rest are the failings of a poetical mind, while his virtues are those of a good heart. Mrs Hallows, on the other hand, is portrayed as sly, censorious, bossy, affected, ill-educated, uncontrolled, drunken, hysterical, quarrelsome, lying – a whole catalogue of unpleasant vices. Clearly she must have had a quarrel with Kidgell – and, the novel suggests, with another curate, who sounds like George North, Young's learned neighbour of Codicote. It is certain that later on she was at daggers drawn with Young's last curate, John Jones, not to mention his son Frederick. Thus, while making allowance for the rancour of enmity, one cannot altogether dismiss Kidgell's charges against the house-keeper or acquit the poet of letting his favourite assume too much authority in his domestic affairs. In Kidgell's day the Doctor could apparently still repress her when he wished; but as her domination became ever more unchecked, the arrangement became less and less happy, at least for those in any way under her authority.

The 'universal dread' that Mrs Hallows inspired in 'the inferior order of ecclesiastics'[11] may well have been the cause that obliged Young twice in these years (September, 1755[12] and May, 1756[13]) to apologize to the Duchess for not visiting her on the grounds that he had no curate. Young's friends, however, had no qualms about the sober matron who presided at the Doctor's table and since he would not visit them, they flocked to him. On 28 May, 1755 Mrs Delany called with a party from Earl Cowper's seat at Cole Green, arriving soon after nine at Welwyn, 'where we were regaled with excellent bread and butter and tea, and *more excellent conversation*'.[14] Another regular visitor was Bennet Langton,[c] later one of Johnson's circle, who in July sent the poet some writings and some oysters, both of which Young acknowledged with appreciation as 'peculiar natives of Lincolnshire'.[15] Boswell reported about these visits:

> Mr Langton, who frequently visited him, informs me that there was an air of benevolence in his manner, but that he could obtain from him less information than he had hoped to receive from one who had lived so much in intercourse with the brightest men of what has been called the Augustan Age of England; and that he showed a degree of eager curiosity concerning the common occurrences that were then passing, which appeared somewhat remarkable in a man of such intellectual stores, of such an advanced age, and who had retired from life with declared disappointment in his expectations.[16]

Langton in fact wished to pump Young, but instead Young pumped Langton. He did not live in the past with his memories

---

[c] Langton (1737–1801) came of the old family of Langtons of Langton, Lincs. Young was evidently an old friend of the family, as his PS ran, 'Pray my best respects to your father, mother, uncle, Mr & Mrs Battell.' The Rev. Ralph Battell, Rector of Somersby, Lincs, was a brother of Young's former housekeeper, Mrs Ward.

but still took a lively interest in the present. In August[17] he was still revising the highly topical *Centaur* for its third edition, while in September the political news inspired him to send to Richardson some verses written 'to support my own spirits'.[18] Though the peace patched up in 1748 at Aix-la-Chapelle had not yet officially broken down, Britain and France were already fighting in America and Admiral Hawke was cruising in the Bay of Biscay with orders to intercept a French squadron from Cadiz. The naval news unfortunately roused Young to resuscitate his old ode of 1735, *The Foreign Address*,[f] on 20 September[19] he sent his friend a poem of thirteen stanzas entitled *The Sailor's Song of the South*, 'occasioned by the rumour of a war' – and eleven of the stanzas were taken, with minor alterations, from the *Address*. The *Song* was published anonymously by Dodsley in folio on 2 October[20] as 'a new ballad'. But Young was still not satisfied and on 26 November[21] a revised and enlarged edition, in quarto, was issued under the title of *A Sea-Piece*.[g] This consisted of two odes, the first, subtitled *The British Sailor's Exultation*, being more or less the same as the *Song*; the second, *The Sailor's Prayer before Engagement*, consisted of seventeen entirely new verses. But, alas, Young's lyric taste was as pitiful as ever. The new ode, being a prayer, was a shade less embarrassing than the jingoism of the *Exultation*:

> In sudden night and ponderous balls
> And floods of flame the tempest falls,
> When braved Britannia's awful Senate lours.[22]

But it is an extraordinary instance of Young's critical blindness that he should take the trouble to revive and revise such stuff, not just once but twice in two months.

Young's spirits must have needed more support at the

---

[f] According to the *Public Advertiser* of 7 Aug., 1755 *The Foreign Address*, 'occasioned by the British Fleet and the present Posture of Affairs', was published that day 'with two Copper-plate Songs, in honour of the British Flag'. This may have reminded Young of the poem and inspired his attempt at a revised version.

[g] In the authorized *Works of the Author of the Night Thoughts*, 1757, Young added a nine-stanza *Dedication to Mr Voltaire*, which recalled their encounter at Eastbury. Both the *Sea-Piece* and *The Foreign Address* were reprinted in Bell's edition of Young's *Poetical Works*, 1784, and most subsequent collections include both, with rather confusing results.

beginning of 1756, for the theme of most of his letters was illness or death. The Duchess's mother, Lady Oxford, had died on 9 December, 1755[23] and Young himself was now suffering again from his teeth, which had begun to trouble him the previous year. A dental surgeon called Galleni had been recommended to him and the first results were encouraging. But they did not last long and in the spring of 1756 the poet had to go up to London for another operation at Richardson's town house. On 23 April[24] the novelist, who on Young's recommendation had also undergone the ministrations of Galleni, inquired whether the dentist had had more success with his friend than with himself, as his own teeth were 'leaving him apace' after much expense of pain, money and time. But Young's experience was equally disheartening:

> As Juvenal says of a boxing match, I think it is a blessing *paucis cum dentibus* to escape out of the hands of Galleni; mine have been distempered ever since and rather worse than before.[25]

On the same date, 27 April, he wrote an even more painful letter to the Duchess on the death of her daughter Lady Margaret; her other children too were dangerously ill and on 2 May he tried to comfort her with the thought that she had 'the very best cordials under any distress – a good head, a good heart and a good friend',[27] – Mrs Delany, who was staying to help. By 29 July the children were better, but Mrs Delany was ill. So was an old College friend, Thomas Colborn,[h] a Norfolk clergyman, whom he was expecting to stay with him, while he himself had had a dangerous fever. And Welwyn had its deathbeds too:

> Nothing is more to be envied than the death of the good. Last night I buried a most valuable woman, and her as profligate husband, now on his deathbed, I shall bury very soon. He was her death by his unkindness and his own by his debauchery. The difference of their last hours, to which I have been privy, carries in it an instruction which no words can express.[28]

[h] Colborn was at Corpus Christi College, Oxford, with Young, 1704–7. In 1756 his daughter appealed through Richardson to 'her papa's dear Dr Young' to use his influence with the Portlands on behalf of a young clergyman. In reply Young invited Colborn to Welwyn; but ill health prevented him coming and he died in 1762 without their meeting again. (Pettit, 429; 563.)

The village's tales of this deathbed, however, were less instructive. The man was Benjamin Fletcher, the local attorney, and he had married Anne, the widow of Sarah Persey's son George, probably for her money, as George had inherited the extensive estates left to his mother by her lover, Robert Gelsthorp, which had included Guessens.[i] Fletcher's ill repute lingered after his death and Young's last curate, John Jones, who was a great collector of gossip, recorded several scandalous tales, which incidentally illustrate the simplicity of the Rector. Fletcher was the steward of the manor of Welwyn Rectory and also Young's personal lawyer, 'unhappily for the Doctor and the parish'. He had no scruples about destroying court records and 'played a thousand other tricks', but his last trick is hardly credible: 'At last, even on his deathbed, [he] most artfully bit the Doctor himself, as he had done many times before, and receiving communion at his hands (to which the Doctor had by all means exhorted the wretch) picked his pocket of above twenty pounds.'[29]

By the autumn, however, Young had recovered from his maladies and literary matters again became prominent in his correspondence. In October Robert Dodsley modestly submitted his tragedy *Cleone* 'at the bar of so hallowed and experienced a judge'.[30] Though he had published many of the best poems of the time, including the *Night Thoughts*, and the most famous anthology of contemporary verse,[j] Dodsley had hitherto ventured only on light entertainments himself. *Cleone* was his first attempt at serious drama and he therefore turned for guidance to Young as the most revered and authoritative tragedian of the age. The poet replied with his wonted courtesy and kindness – as he did to all, friends or strangers,[k] who bombarded him with their poetical attempts. But his real

---

[i] Gelsthorp left Sarah lands in four parishes, plus all his personal possessions. George Persey, surgeon, inherited from his mother in 1743, married Anne Carter in 1745, and died in 1751. His widow then married Benjamin Fletcher. (Branch Johnson, 12; 22.)

[j] Dodsley's *Collection* was still in course of publication, the sixth and last volume coming out in 1758.

[k] E.g. James Elphinston (1721–1809), an eccentric Scot who invented his own system of phonetic spelling, 'Inglish Orthography Epittomized' and in 1791 published his *Forty years Correspondence between Geniusses ov boath Sexes and James Elphinston*, in which he printed his letters to and from Young, beginning in December, 1753. (Pettit, 398–9.)

enthusiasm was kept for Richardson. All the summer he pressed the Richardsons to visit Welwyn and at last, at the end of October, they came. The novelist's thanks after his return came in the form of a 'monstrous present' of books for Young and Mrs Hallows, together with a 'copy of the translation of the German verses you wished to have'.[31] The latter – Klopstock's *Ode on the Death of Clarissa*, not his verses *To Young* – had been brought to England by a young officer of the King of Denmark's Grenadiers, Major Bernhard von Hohorst. This 'worthy and pious man' followed up with a personal visit to Welwyn in January 1757 to see 'the author of the *Night Thoughts*, . . . whom he and his countrymen of taste and seriousness[1] very greatly admire'.[32] Young found the Major 'a very agreeable and, I believe, a very valuable man',[33] and Richardson answered that Hohorst 'is full of gratitude for your kind reception of him; speaks of you with love, reverence and admiration, as he before did of your works'.[34] But this latest pilgrim from Germany did not long enjoy 'the pleasure of saying, when he is abroad, that he has seen and conversed with Dr Young';[35] by November, when Young wrote to Klopstock himself, poor Hohorst was dead of a fever.

Among the subjects discussed during Richardson's visit to Welwyn was a collected edition of Young's works, for on 15 December, 1756 the printer mentioned to Mrs Dewes, the sister of Mrs Delany, that 'Dr Young . . . is about to give the world a collection of his works, at the entreaty of booksellers who have a property in them, in four twelves volumes. His *Love of Fame, The Universal Passion*, if the world were to be cured of its follies by satires, would be read to good purpose.'[36] Richardson was the printer of this edition; but as there is no reference to this major undertaking in their correspondence – except perhaps for a mysterious postscript to a letter of Young's on 20 January, 1757

[1] In 1755 William Mason wrote to Gray of his meeting with 'Madame Belch' of Hamburg: 'She asked me who was the famous poet that writ the *Nitt Toats*. I replied Dr Young. She begged leave to drink his health in a glass of sweet wine, adding that he was her favourite English author. We toasted the Doctor. Upon which, having a mind to give a Parnassian toast, I asked Mme Belch if she had ever read *La Petite Elegie dans la Coemeterie Rustique*. C'est beaucoup jolie, je vous assure. . . . Oui, Monsieur, (replied Mme Belch), je lu, et elle est bien jolie et melancolique; mais elle ne touche point la cœur comme mes tres chers *Nitt Toats*.' (Birley, 107–8.)

– one must assume that all the details had been personally settled in October. The postscript said merely, 'For the admirable addition to my last poetry all thanks are due.'[37] But what additions Richardson can have made is hard to see, unless Young simply meant the punctuation. The only additions in this edition were the nine stanzas of the *Dedication to Mr Voltaire*, prefixed to the *Sea-Piece*, and that was certainly Young's own work. Otherwise, far from adding, the poet pruned ruthlessly, declaring in his 'Advertisement':

> I think the following pieces in four volumes to be the most excusable of all that I have formerly written; and I wish less apology was needful for these. As there is no recalling what is got abroad, the pieces here republished I have revised and corrected, and rendered them as pardonable as it was in my power to do.[38]

This edition, in fact, which came out on 21 May, 1757[39] under the title of *The Works of the Author of the Night Thoughts* and under the imprint of no less than fifteen booksellers, was a selection rather than a collection. It represented the author's own judgement on his works and omits a considerable number of the poems printed by Curll in his two-volume edition of the *Poetical Works* in 1741.

Both the inclusions and the omissions are instructive. The contents are as follows: in the first volume, *The Last Day*, *The Force of Religion*, *The Universal Passion*, the two *Epistles to Pope*, the *Paraphrase on Job*, and his odes *To the King*, *Ocean* and the *Sea-Piece*; volume II contained his three tragedies; volumes III and IV, the *Night Thoughts* and the *Centaur*. It will be observed that he left out *all* his occasional pieces, together with all the dedications apart from those that form part of the verse. This might seem both logical and sensible, since the essence of an 'occasional' poem is that it is written for a particular occasion and not for all time; and dedications in that age were equally occasional, being written for the strictly practical motive of eliciting, or sometimes giving thanks for, patronage. But Croft chose to put the most sinister interpretation on the 'suppression' of Young's dedication of *The Revenge* to the Duke of Wharton and of his panegyric of Walpole in *The Instalment*; he did not note that the poet also 'suppressed' his encomium of Addison in his *Letter to Tickell* and his dedications to such blameless patronesses as Queen Anne and the Countess of Salisbury. After quoting Young's preface and exclaiming 'Shall the gates of repentance be shut .only against literary sinners?',[40] Croft exercised all his ingenuity in shutting those gates by imputing the basest motives for every omission. Even the reduction of the number of verses in *Ocean* and the dropping of the harmless *Wish* were not allowed to evince literary judgement. Few, said Croft, would have suspected Young of forming such a wish, and few would then confess 'something like their shame'[41] by suppressing it; while the merciful disappearance of *Imperium Pelagi* was described as a case in which he 'deliberately refused to own'[42] his earlier work. Croft was adept at the technique of the smear.

These four volumes, then, contained all that the poet considered worthy of the reputation of the author of the *Night Thoughts*. In his selectivity he compared very favourably with most of his contemporaries, who filled out their collections with all the petty occasional and familiar poems, of no general interest, that they had ever written. In our own day it is the accepted practice for poets to be selective in their collections and Young merely anticipated modern practice. The basis of his choice is easy to understand and justify – his moral and religious poems with the prose sequel of the *Centaur*, his tragedies, his satires and a much-deflated selection of his lyrics. Nowadays we would be rather more ruthless, cutting out his deplorable sea-pieces altogether with the vapid *Force of Religion*, the unnecessary *Paraphrase on Job* and the outmoded *Centaur*. But unless the selection were to be confined to 'beauties' and purple passages only, an editor would be bound to leave the nine *Nights*, the three tragedies, the nine satires and *The Last Day*.[1] Add to these his subsequent prose excursion in criticism, the *Conjectures*, and you would have a considerable residue worthy of modern notice. Considering the natural reluctance of any author to abandon his own brain-children, *The Works of*

---

[1] Brian Hepworth, editor of *Edward Young, selected poems* (Carcanet Press, 1975), prints extracts from *The Last Day*, *The Force of Religion*, *A Paraphrase on Job*, *Busiris*, *The Revenge*, *Love of Fame*, *Epistle I to Mr Pope*, the nine *Nights* and the *Conjectures*.

the Author of the Night Thoughts was a distinctly creditable production."

What was not creditable to the publisher nor fair to the author was to republish, after his death, the pieces that he himself had rejected. But the booksellers' thirst to make the most of their property led them to ignore his wishes. After a second edition of the four-volume *Works* in 1762 a fifth volume was published in 1767 and even, by scraping together all the dedications, the *Oratio Codringtoniana* and such stuff, a sixth in 1778. Thereafter most of Young's editors thought fit to print the complete works, though it was not till 1841 that *Cynthio* was tracked down and included by H. F. Cary, while the *Epistle to Bolingbroke*, unknown till 1961, entirely escaped the scavengers. Both these were occasional poems and therefore not appropriate for inclusion in his selected *Works*. Yet such is the lingering prejudice, engendered by Croft and buttressed by the authority of Johnson, that the rarity of the *Epistle* was explained in the auction catalogue as due to 'rigid suppression'[43] by the author after Bolingbroke's downfall! Even now the gates are shut against the repentant literary sinner.

" Horace Walpole commented to the Earl of Strafford, 5 July, 1757: 'I know nothing else new but a new edition of Dr Young's Works. If your Lordship thinks like me, who hold that even in his most frantic rhapsodies there are innumerable fine things, you will like to have this edition. (Lewis, XXXV, 284.)

CHAPTER 17

Original Composition
1757–1759

> I know not the merit or demerit of what I send; if it has
> merit, I beg you give it more. How much does the *Centaur*
> owe to you! If it has no merit, keep the secret and all is
> well.[1]

Thus the poet wrote to Richardson on 21 December, 1756; and
his friend, after glancing only at the first page, replied with
reassuring enthusiasm. The following Sunday Young followed
up in characteristic excitement, saying that he had added to the
letter; he would send for it in a week, to allow Richardson to
'favour it with some strokes'[2] of his pen; or, on second thoughts
(in a postscript) he would not send for it till he heard from his
friend. Though there is no specific mention of the subject of the
letter, it is clear that it was the first draft of the *Conjectures on
Original Composition*, which was written in the form of a letter to
the novelist. The introduction of that work indicated that its
origin lay in some questions by Speaker Onslow[a] 'on the serious
drama, at the same time when he desired our sentiments on
original and on moral composition'.[3] But if their discussion took
place when the Speaker and Richardson visited Welwyn in 1750,
why was it only now, over six years later, that Young was
inspired to take up the question?

The explanation could be the publication in April, 1756[4] of a
revolutionary book on the same theme, a book that was
dedicated to Young himself and might well have been discussed
by the two writers when the Richardsons came to stay at
Guessens in October. This was Joseph Warton's *Essay on the
Genius and Writings of Pope*, of which the argument was that
imitation of the classics was not the highest form of poetry, a
proposition that meant the demotion of Pope from his then
accepted pre-eminence among English poets. Joseph, as the son
of Young's friend Thomas Warton the elder, remembered

---

[a] Young identified him as 'your worthy patron and our common friend'.

frequently hearing Young 'speak with great disapprobation of the doctrine contained in this passage' – in Pope's Preface to his *Works*, 1717, that 'all that is left to us is to recommend our productions by the imitation of the Ancients' – 'with a view to which he wrote his discourse on Original Composition'.[5] In 1755 therefore Warton approached Young as the most appropriate patron of his anti-classic views, proposing to dedicate his anonymous *Essay* to the poet of the *Night Thoughts*. On 9 November[6] Young replied, accepting the honour, promising to keep Warton's secret and wishing him success. Warton's dedication was an open declaration of revolt[b] against the prevailing classicism:

> No love of singularity, no affectation of paradoxical opinions, gave rise to the following work. I revere the memory of Pope, I respect and honour his abilities; but I do not think him at the head of his profession. In other words, in that species of poetry wherein Pope excelled he is superior to all mankind: and I only say that this species of poetry is not the most excellent one of the art ... The *Epistles* on the Characters of men and women, and your sprightly satires, my good friend, are more frequently perused and quoted than the *L'Allegro* and *Il Penseroso* of Milton. Had you written only these satires, you would indeed have gained the title of a man of wit and a man of sense; but, I am confident, would not insist on being denominated a *poet* merely on their account.[7]

This verdict provoked Croft to quote Young's compliment to Pope at the end of *Night I*[c] and sneer, 'If Young accepted and approved the dedication, he countenanced this attack on the fame of him whom he invokes as his Muse ... Nay, even after Pope's death he says in *Night Seven*:

> Pope, who could'st make immortals, art thou dead?

---

[b] The revolt proved somewhat premature and Warton did not venture to publish the second volume for another twenty-five years, in 1782.

[c]   Man too he sung; immortal man I sing ...
O, had he pressed his theme, pursued the track,
Which opens out of darkness into day!
O, had he mounted on his wing of fire,
Soared where I sink and sung immortal man,
How had it blessed mankind, and rescued me!
                                                    (Mitford, I, 15.)

Either the *Essay*, then, was dedicated to a patron who disapproved its doctrine, which I have been told by the author was not the case; or Young in his old age bartered for a dedication an opinion entertained of his friend through all that part of life when he must have been best able to form opinions.'[8] But this surely is rather too disingenuous, even for Croft. In the first *Night* Young invoked Homer and Milton, and then the translator of Homer, regretting that he had *not* risen to higher themes, from Man to Immortal Man, which he would have done so much better than Young himself. He was expressing the wish that Pope had not stuck to a species of poetry – translation and imitation – which Young, like Warton, did not regard as the highest, and he was merely repeating publicly and poetically what he had said to Pope himself.[d] As for Croft's second charge, Pope could indeed 'make immortals' in his satires but that does not mean that Young thought satire the most excellent form of poetry. Nor can we agree that the poet, for all his seventy-three years, was past forming sensible opinions. He disproved it decisively by writing at this very time a piece of critical prose that has survived better than all his verse, and he disproved the charge of insincerity by maintaining in that piece an argument as critical of Pope as was Warton's *Essay*.

In January, 1757[9] Richardson had sent his observations on the draft, which by 24 February had become so overwritten that the author proposed a hasty visit to London to 'borrow one hour of you to hear me read the letter, as now by your assistance amended; for it is so transcribed that without some hints to you it will be unintelligible'.[10] The visit took place on Monday, 28 February,[11] and it was probably on this occasion that Samuel Johnson first met him. Sixteen years later in the remote fastness of Skye Johnson described the meeting to Boswell:

> The first time he saw Dr Young was at the house of Mr Richardson, the author of *Clarissa*. He was sent for, that the Doctor might read to him his *Conjectures on Original Composition*, which he did, and Dr Johnson made his remarks; and he was surprised to find Young receive as novelties what he thought very common maxims ... He said Young pressed him much to come to Welwyn. He

[d] See p. 184.

always intended it, but never went. He was sorry when
Young died.[12]

But then Young began to go off the boil. At the end of
March[13] he again begged a bed of Richardson for a night, but
this time because he was summoned to attest a point in Chancery
– probably in connection with the interminable Wharton suit,
since there was now some hope that the Duke's lead-mines might
pay off all his debts. On 10 May the printer inquired:

> How proceed you in your second letter? . . . How shall I
> rejoice to read in print such noble instances of the doctrine
> you advance in favour of the moderns! Surely, sir, this piece
> is the most spirited and original of all your truly spirited
> and original works. What memory, what recollection, does
> it display! With all the experience of years it has all the fire
> and (corrected) imagination of youth.[14]

The second letter was the trouble, as Young's reply shows:

> I have written a second letter, but it by no means pleases
> me – the subject is too common and I cannot keep out of
> the footsteps of my predecessors.[15]

As with the 'Prayer' of 1751, the writer had got stuck and laid his
work aside. For over a year the *Conjectures* dropped out almost
completely from his correspondence. Richardson inquired
anxiously about the second letter on 19 July[16] and repeated his
inquiry on the 26th,[17] but all that Young would vouchsafe on the
subject was a postscript on 30 July with a promise to speak of it
when he next saw him; 'I have great avocations and cannot
succeed to my wish.'[18] From then on nothing more is heard of
either letter till September, 1758 – and in fact the second never
saw the light. Frustration was followed by parochial problems,
and the solution of the latter by depression and illness.

During the summer of 1757, however, he was well enough and in
May he suggested that one of Richardson's daughters might enjoy
a holiday at Welwyn under the wing of that 'good, and not
unlettered, woman',[19] Mrs Hallows. The novelist eagerly accepted
the offer on behalf of Nancy, who was the sickly one of his brood,[c]

---

[c] Four daughters of Richardson's second marriage survived childhood. Mary,
Martha, Anne and Sarah, known as Polly, Patty, Nancy and Sally respectively, used
to help their father as amanuenses, Patty and Nancy being the favourites. Nancy
never married and, though sickly, outlived her sisters, dying in 1803.

and on 7 June[20] Mrs Hallows travelled up to London and brought Nancy back to sup at Guessens the same evening. Young took her riding, fed her on his fruits and no doubt introduced her to the pleasures of the Welwyn Assemblies; and her health showed gratifying improvement. Six weeks later the grateful father proposed to relieve Young of his trouble as soon as he could find someone to accompany Nancy home, as his 'unhappy tremors'[21] prevented him from fetching her himself. But the poet would have none of it:

> What you call our trouble is, indeed, our very great pleasure. Miss Nancy is a very agreeable and sensible companion; and my best fruits, which I from the first proposed as her chief entertainment, are not yet ripe. You must not rob her of them, nor us of her ... I myself will deliver her (God willing) safe into your hands, when the hour is come, which I trust is yet at a considerable distance; for indeed, indeed, she is as welcome to me as if she was my own.[22]

He was still missing Caroline; and how long he kept Nancy in the end we do not know. A letter to her father on 27 September[23] does not mention her, and by 23 October[24] he was once again in a deep depression.

The cause of his low spirits, accompanied as usual by long bouts of insomnia, was probably physical, for by August his worries over the curate problem had at last been solved. In that month he made an agreement with a new full-time curate to replace the temporary Mr Briggs, whose last signature in the parish register was on 11 January, 1757.[25] The new curate, introduced to the Rector by Richardson, was the Rev. John Jones, who was destined to stay with Young for the rest of his life. Like Mrs Hallows he contributed greatly to the easing of the old man's burdens by relieving him of most of his parochial duties; but like Mrs Hallows he did not contribute so much to the poet's happiness. Between them, in fact, these two helpers must often have made his life a misery, for they quarrelled violently. Mrs Hallows, if we may believe Kidgell, was the terror of the curates, while Jones, to judge from his own accumulations of papers, was an excitable, contentious and rather uncharitable character. Among these papers is his manuscript autobiography, begun at Welwyn on 21 December, 1765,[26] when he was vainly seeking for a new appointment after the death of Young. From his own record it would appear that he was either a very unfortunate or else a very difficult man. He was born at Carmarthen in 1700, and educated at Worcester College, Oxford, where he took his BA at the age of twenty-one. But though able, he was a poor man without influence and had to be contented with curacies until he was about forty. Meanwhile he added to his pittance with literary hackwork, making compilations for booksellers, and in this way made the acquaintance of Richardson. In 1741 he at last obtained a vicarage at Alconbury near Huntingdon, but found it 'poor and troublesome' with a ruinous house and after ten years he relinquished the living, disgusted with the 'brutish' inhabitants and perpetual 'squabbles'. In 1749 he published his best-known work under the title of *Free and Candid Disquisitions*, which stirred up considerable controversy in religious circles, and he sent a presentation copy to Young.[f] After Alconbury Jones was presented to the rectory of Bolnhurst in Bedfordshire, but this cannot have been much of an improvement except in prestige, as it was rated at only £9 a year. Moreover he found he was succeeding a Rector 'of strange turn, imperious and clamorous upon topics of little or no service towards the promoting of true religion', and he was as unhappy there as at Alconbury. In 1755 he got away for a time as curate of Everton, but returned to his rectory in the spring of 1756, where the rest of his stay was 'very uncomfortable'. But he 'chose not to say how he came to leave that parish, or his treatment from some of superior power'.

His story continued:

> In the time of my great distress the late celebrated Dr Young, into whose acquaintance I had some time before been introduced by his friend Mr S. Richardson, was pleased to give me an invitation to come over to be his

[f] Young told Richardson, 5 November, 1749: 'I am very much obliged to the authors of the *Candid Disquisitions* . . . both for their favour to me and their noble (and I hope useful) zeal for Christianity.' (Pettit, 338.) The book, which Jones was too timid to acknowledge, as it advocated revision of the liturgy, was long believed to be the work of his friend Archdeacon Blackburne. Hence perhaps Young's use of the plural.

assistant in the care of his parish of Welwyn. I removed
there at Michaelmas, 1757.[27]

It must have looked like a most promising arrangement for
both; Jones had found a haven and Young had found an
assistant who could also be a companion, a man of fifty-seven
who was not only a writer of original and stimulating ideas but
a most conscientious and hard-working priest. From some
other manuscript notes, headed 'Some particulars agreed upon
between the Rev. Dr Young and me in August, 1757'[28] it
appears that he bargained before accepting the curacy: the
Rector promised to assist or supply for Jones if he were ill or
absent; the Wednesday and Friday services, introduced by
Young, were to be dropped; and Jones was to have the use of a
horse for health or business purposes. His salary was fixed at
£20 a year, the same as Young paid to his other curates. On
these terms, which left him pretty free to come and go as he
liked, Jones took over the parish at the end of September and
moved into a lodging in the old Parsonage House.[g]

Having settled the question of his substitute, Young was free
to get away for a change, which he badly needed. On 23
October he told Richardson, 'My spirits fail me; I am very low
and am designing for the Bath as my last resource.'[29] His
friend at once offered to make all the arrangements, as his
daughter Polly was in Bath, married to a surgeon named
Ditcher. Though he personally had not benefited from Bath,
there was more hope for the poet since 'your nerves are good,
your constitution sound, and your muscular flesh is firm'.[30] He
also invited Young to come to Salisbury Court on the way and
suggested that Mrs Hallows should accompany him. So at the
beginning of November the poet set out, duly accompanied by
his indispensable housekeeper.

A few weeks before he left Welwyn,[31] Young received a
letter from a new German correspondent, the great Klopstock

---

[g] Briggs paid rates on the Parsonage House from 1754 to 1757. From 1755
there was no assessment for Poor Rate and he paid tax on only two windows,
while the Rector paid for 28. The formula was 'Dr Young for the Parsonage,
Mr Briggs for the House'. In 1758 Young paid as before for 28 windows, but
'Rev. Mr Jones for the House' was rated at three. Jones must have taken over
Briggs's apartment, slightly enlarged, and been excused all rates, as he never
paid Window Tax again.

himself.[h] Though it was five years since the German poet had
written his *Ode to Young*, it is evident that this was Klopstock's
first direct approach to his idol. It appears that he gave the letter
to be delivered to Young by a certain 'young Shoer', who had
already made the pilgrimage to Welwyn once before and had
been solemnly blessed on leaving. The German reverence and
high seriousness had a damping effect on Young's epistolary
style, and on 27 October he replied:

> What obligations do I lie under to you for your so kind,
> repeated and undeserved regards to a stranger – a stranger
> to your person, but not to your fame and merit. Poor
> Hohorst made me acquainted with that . . . And is he gone
> in the flower of youth? And am I still alive? Humanity
> obliges me to say that *I pity the dying*; and my age and
> infirmities oblige me to say that *I envy the dead* . . . You are so
> kind as to desire my friendship. Dear sir, you have my
> heart, and it would be one of the greatest blessings of my
> age if I could embrace you before I die . . . I rejoice in being
> able to write to one (how rarely to be found) who can relish
> thoughts unseasoned by the domineering interests of the
> world, that is, who can relish things a true taste of which
> renders empire and even genius, though equal to your own,
> insipid and of little worth. Adieu, worthy sir – adieu![32]

Klopstock's young wife Meta was another of Young's devoted
admirers and on 29 November she wrote to Richardson,
introducing herself and enclosing a letter for the poet. It was her
first effort in English, which, as she put it, 'it is very long ago that
I wished to do it'.[33] In his reply, dated 22 December, 1757,
Richardson told her he had transmitted the enclosure to Young,
who 'has been indisposed for two or three months past and has
been at Bath for four weeks for the recovery of his health'.[34] If
this statement is accurate,[i] Young must have travelled very
slowly, taking almost three weeks from Welwyn to Bath with,
one supposes, a long stop at Salisbury Court on the way. By 30

---

[h] Friedrich Gottlieb Klopstock (1724–1803), author of the *Messiah*, was the
leader of the Gottingen Poets' League (*Dichterbund*). His friend Ebert, Young's
most assiduous translator, led him to the study of English through the *Night
Thoughts*.

[i] The doubt is not about the accuracy of Richardson's statement, but that of his
editress's transcription. The *Auswahl aus Klopstocks nachgelassenen Briefwechsel*,
Leipzig, 1821 (I, 251), gives the words as 'for *some* weeks'.

December[35] the poet felt up to writing a short answer to the Klopstocks, apologizing for being too ill to reply at length; and on 3 January, 1758 he was able to tell Richardson:

> I bless God I at last find benefit from the waters, as to appetite, rest and spirits. I have now for three nights had pretty good rest, after two sleepless months; and I believe that persevering in the waters is the point, at least in my complaint. But at my time of day how dare I to complain of small things, on the brink of the grave and at the door of eternity. What a fall have I seen around me! I was here twenty years ago and scarce find one of that generation alive.[36]

The novelist replied with envious congratulations both to him and to Mrs Hallows on the success of her 'prayers and cares':

> What may we not promise ourselves from so sound and good a constitution; from your regularity and temperance; from the exercise you are enabled to take; and from the powers of such a mind invigorating the whole. A mind which can enjoy and even enlarge itself by that very sleeplessness which tears in pieces the health of others.[37]

Even so Young had to stay on at Bath till late April, and it was not till the 30th of that month that he wrote again from Welwyn.

During his convalescence Young had begun composing again, but it was a sermon, not the unfinished *Conjectures*, which exercised his pen at this time. His letter to Richardson on 30 April[38] enclosed the text, together with the draft of his proposed dedication to the King – was there anything *mean* in what he said of himself and his long service at court? On 2 May his friend replied tactfully:

> As to the dedication, I am far from thinking your mentioning length of service *mean*. Will it not rather be thought, or misunderstood, to carry with it something of complaint or even of reproach, and as if your neglecting your month for some years past were owing to resentment? I humbly think this part cannot be too delicately mentioned; especially as you have touched upon it with great feeling in more places than one, in your *Night Thoughts* so long ago – *My master knows me not*, &c; and nothing resulted from the just sensibility. Some of your

great admirers in that divine work thought you descended too much for the superiority you appeared in to them.[39]

Young's response was characteristic:

> A thousand thanks, my truest friend, for restoring me to common sense. I shall follow your advice in the Dedication and now, on reflection, think it monstrous that I stood in need of it . . . I could not forbear writing to you by this post, being pained with the thought of your thinking me a fool any longer.[40]

By 4 June[41] the proofs were ready, and in mid-month he went to stay for three days at Parson's Green, Richardson's new country home,[j] before going into waiting at Kensington Palace. The sermon was duly preached before His Majesty and the printed copies were sent out to the appropriate powers. It was much shorter than his previous printed discourses, only 9 pages as compared with 72 of the *True Estimate*, and the dedication contained no reference to his own case except in the final signature, 'Your Majesty's most dutiful subject and ancient servant'.[42] The title was *An Argument from Christ's Death*, and an advertisement sought to justify publication with his usual claim of originality – 'the writer not knowing that this argument has been made use of by others thought it excuseable to send it to the press'.[43]

It is clear, however, that Young's real motive for publishing the sermon was to remind the powers that be of his claims to preferment. Indeed he confessed as much to the Duchess on 9 July:

> I have lately by a Dedication taken on me to put His Majesty in mind of my long service, but I take for granted without any manner of effect. I perceive by your Grace that all hopes are over; but though hopes are over, my curiosity is not; that is rather increased . . . There must be some particular reason for my very particular fate, which reason, as I cannot possibly guess at it, I most ardently long to know.[44]

But why had he reverted to his old ambitions and complaints

---

[j] Richardson moved from North End, Fulham, which he had leased since 1739, to Parson's Green, also in Fulham parish, at the end of 1754.

after years of resignation and at the age of 75? One can only suppose that the extraordinary occurrence of the deaths of two Archbishops of Canterbury within twelve months[k] and the succession of an old acquaintance to the Primacy in the person of Thomas Secker[l] made him feel that with such a friend at court and a whole train of consequential moves pending in the church hierarchy he must surely be remembered at last. But, alas, the powers of patronage were not as innocent or enthusiastic as Mrs Klopstock, who wrote to Richardson on 6 May:

> I read lately in the newspapers that Dr Young was made Bishop of Bristol; I must think it is another Young. How could the King make him *only* Bishop! and Bishop of *Bristol* when the place of Canterbury is vacant! I think the King knows not at all that there is a Young that illustrates his reign.[15]

She was right in thinking that Bristol was another Young (his name was Philip), but not because Edward was being saved for higher things. The vacancy at Canterbury had already been filled, and the new Archbishop was not prepared to press the claims of merit or friendship against the implacable veto of the powers that be. On 8 July Secker acknowledged Young's reminder with as smooth a brush-off as any courtier could wish:

> Good Dr Young, I have long wondered that more suitable notice of your great merit hath not been taken by persons in power. But how to remedy the omission I see not. No encouragement hath ever been given me to mention things of this nature to His Majesty. And therefore, in all likelihood, the only consequence of doing it would be weakening the little influence which else I may possibly have on some other occasions. Your fortune and your reputation set you above the need of advancement, and your sentiments above that concern for it, on your own account, which, on that of the public, is sincerely felt by – Your loving brother, Tho. Cant.[16]

[k] Thomas Herring, Archbishop Potter's successor, died 13 March, 1757; and *his* successor, Matthew Hutton, died 18 March, 1758.

[l] Secker was confirmed as Primate on 21 April, 1758. Probably Young had met him at the Prince of Wales's court, for in the 1730s Secker had been Rector of St James's, Westminster, where Frederick had been a regular attendant. He tried to reconcile the King and the Prince and, though he failed, managed somehow to retain the favour of both.

After this rebuff all that Young could do was to make one last despairing appeal to the inevitable Duke of Newcastle, who was now Prime Minister:

> I was Chaplain to His Majesty even at Leicester House. All his other chaplains were preferred soon after His Majesty's accession. About ten years ago the Duke of Portland recommended me to your Grace. Your Grace was so good as to promise me your favour after two were preferred who stood before me. Soon after, your Grace bid me not wait on you, saying you would send for me when proper. Ever since I have been hoping for that honour. I lately presented a small performance to His Majesty in hopes that it might bring to his mind my long service; but I know that without your Grace's favour I have no hopes, nor dare I presume to ask that favour, having been denied it so long. How I came to lose it I cannot so much as conjecture ... I am not conscious of the least misbehaviour; I am not conscious of any word or deed that could give the least shadow [of] offence; and if I have given none, my fate is as unaccountable as it is singular. And it is so very singular that on closest enquiry I cannot learn that the like ever happened before; and probably never may again.[17]

And he ended with the pathetic postscript, 'Cannot, my honoured Lord Duke, a most gracious promise of ten years old and royal service of above thirty in some measure stand my friends?' It was the neglect, the inexplicable refusal of the least preferment, that hurt the poet's pride and made him persist in his applications long after he can have had any desire to leave Welwyn.

At this stage the Duchess of Portland evidently decided that if the King would not, she herself would do something for her favourite divine. For on 7 September Young wrote to her:

> Your Grace is extremely kind in the noble offer you are pleased to make me. Whether it is tenable with Welwyn or not I cannot tell; but be it so or not, your Grace's goodness lays me under an eternal obligation. If it should not be tenable with Welwyn, will your Grace pardon me if I ask a bold question? Can your great indulgence go so far as to give it to my son? ... My son, Madam, is a student at Balliol College in Oxford; he is between twenty-five and twenty-six years of age; I left the choice of his way of life to himself; he

chose Divinity; his tutor writes me word that he makes a
laudable progress in it and he will take orders very soon.[48]

It was three years since Frederick had returned to Oxford after
his quarrel with his father and during this period he had not
only taken his first degree but remained steadily in residence
with only short breaks at vacation times. On 13 July, 1757[49]
Young had rewarded him with a life annuity of £300 a year (a
safer provision than giving him stocks) and now the proud
parent was able to report that his son was about to graduate
and take orders. And yet in the end Frederick did neither. On
1 December, 1758[50] he vanished again from his College for
nearly two years; and nothing more was heard of the ducal
offer. Did Frederick baulk at the last minute, when brought
face to face with the reality of a potential parish? And was
Young offended at this disrespect to his patroness? All one can
say is that, if they quarrelled again on this occasion, it does not
seem to have been the final break. Eighteen months later
Young was to make another fruitless settlement with his son.

Meanwhile the poet had taken up the *Conjectures* again, and
on 11 September Richardson told Mrs Delany, 'Dr Young is
finely recovered and, if I *guess* right, will one day oblige the
world with a small piece on Original Writing and Writers.'[51]
He was not merely guessing; on 8 October Young sent him the
new version with the words, 'I have added, as you desired, Mr
Addison's death.'[52] The 'precious parcel' was delivered next
day by Shotbolt and on 11 October the novelist replied:

> I could not do anything else till I had run through it.
> *Run through it* I may well say – for my reading was rapid;
> and when I came to the end of it, I thirsted for more . . . I
> am charmed with what you have added of Mr Addison.
> What memory, what judgement, what force of writing,
> what unabated vigour of mind! Surely, sir, this spirited
> piece is the most spirited of all your spirited works.[53]

A gap of nearly two months followed, and on 6 December[54]
Young wrote anxiously to inquire after Richardson's health,
which Jones, after one of his trips to town, had reported as
indifferent. But it was only when Nancy wrote to Mrs Hallows
that he learnt of the dreadful accident in which a 'poor friend

and namesake'[55] of the printer was killed by his side[m] – enough to upset a less tremulous sensibility than Richardson's. In his letter of sympathy Young added, 'The leisure you have given me has occasioned me greatly to alter my scheme – which makes the review of my papers necessary . . . Please to let me have them by my servant; I propose returning them very soon.'[56] Impetuous as ever, he sent off this letter 'by man and horse, riding all night',[57] which gave poor nerve-racked Richardson a nasty fright till he opened it. On 18 December[58] the printer managed to reply with a longish letter, full of useful suggestions. Young, now in an access of enthusiasm, returned the manuscript in three days and ordered immediate printing. Both the friends were now suffering from insomnia, but as Richardson pointed out, 'When you sleep not, you are awake to noble purpose; I to none at all. My days are nothing but hours of dozings for want of nightly rest.'[59] Nevertheless he followed up on Boxing Day[60] with a long detailed letter, in which he suggested not only minor amendments of wording or style but whole new paragraphs – among them one to justify the inclusion of the grand moral lesson of Addison's end in a literary 'pastime', which the author described as 'miscellaneous in its nature, somewhat licentious in its conduct, and perhaps not over-important in its end'.[61] The novelist suggested comparing the Addison episode to 'monumental marble, scattered in a wide pleasure garden', which 'will call to recollection those who would never have gone to seek it in a churchyard walk of mournful yews'.[62] Young seized gratefully on the idea, but he was now in such a hurry that on 7 January, 1759[63] he pressed his friend to start printing the first part at once, while he was still finishing the rest. Spence was staying with him at the time and with the encouragement of the critic, who was 'struck with the vivacity' of the piece, and the assistance of Mrs Hallows, who wrote out the fair copy ('dictated to a female hand, the errors of which in spelling the composer will easily amend'), Young was able to send off the remaining part by 11 January.[64] Another long, conscientious and helpful communication from the printer on the 24th[65] was received with gratitude

---

[m] On 28 November Robert Richardson, attorney, was standing talking to Samuel Richardson at Charing Cross when a passing carriage collided with a stationary dray and drove it on to the pavement, where it hit Robert so violently as to kill him on the spot.

but less wholesale acceptance this time, the author explaining, 'As I have added much of my own, some of yours I have omitted.'[66]

By late April, 1759, the book was ready for publication and Young gave directions for complimentary copies to be sent to the Speaker, the Duchess of Portland, Dodington, Johnson, Dr Heberden" and the Bishop of Durham,'' but 'not saying by whom sent'.[67] For, as with all his later works, this was to be published anonymously to try the force of the piece without the advantage of his name. But the inimitable Young style gave him away at once and from the moment that the *Conjectures on Original Composition* was announced in the papers on 10 May, 1759[68] everyone spoke of him as the author. On the 24th Richardson wrote to him about the first reactions:

> I sent the books as you directed. The Speaker repeatedly thanks you and bid me tell you that he was highly pleased with the spirited performance. He read to me passages with which he was most struck and bid me tell you that he was beginning to read it again, which he should do with an avidity equal to that which at first possessed him. Mr Johnson is much pleased with it; he made a few observations on some passages, which I encouraged him to commit to paper and which he promised to do and send to you. Mr Millar tells me he has but very few left; so small a number as was printed, I wonder he has any. Mr Dodsley's must surely be near gone ... Dr Warburton commends highly the spirit of the piece and, with a few observations and explanations, subscribes to the merit of the whole. That good man, Mr Allen of Bath, is pleased with every line of it and warmly expressed to me, on a visit he made to me at Parson's Green, his approbation. Your promised succeeding letter is much wished for; is it, sir, in forwardness?[69]

In view of the book's success Richardson asked for the author's additions and revisions for a second edition. But Young modestly

---

" William Heberden (1710–1801) was a good classicist (he contributed to the *Athenian Letters*) as well as a famous medical practitioner and writer. He had become a close friend of Young from the time when the poet went to see him about his heart pain in December, 1753.

'' Richard Trevor (1707–71) was a Fellow of All Souls from 1727 to 1732 and from then till 1744 held a living in Huntingdonshire. But there is no evidence of any special friendship with Young apart from this presentation.

replied that he would not send his revised copy till he received
Johnson's letter and that he would give a lot for Warburton's
remarks too. The printer wrote urgently to Johnson, but advised
against waiting too long, as Millar had ordered an immediate
reprint of 1000; and he added:

> One of Dr Warburton's remarks was that the character of
> an original writer is not confined to subject but extends to
> manner; by this distinction, I presume, securing his friend
> Pope's originality. But he mentioned this with so much
> good humour that I should have been glad to have heard
> you both in conference upon the subject.[70]

Such a conference might indeed have been interesting, for while
Young commented mildly, '*Manner* (as Dr W. says) may be
original; but a *manner* different from that of the ancients, with
good judges, will run a great risk – a risk which a new *subject* will
escape',[71] Warburton was expressing himself with anything but
good humour in private. Jealously concerned to defend Pope
against Young's criticism of his being an imitator, he sneered in
a letter to Hurd on 17 May:

> I don't know whether you have seen Dr Young's
> *Conjectures on Original Composition*. He is the finest writer of
> nonsense of any of this age. And had he known that *original
> composition* consisted in the manner, and not in the matter,
> he had wrote with common sense, and perhaps very dully
> under so insufferable a burden. But the wisest and kindest
> part of his work is advising writers to be original and not
> imitators; that is, to be geniuses rather than blockheads, for
> I believe nothing but these rather different qualities made
> Virgil an original author and Blackmore an imitator; for
> they were certainly borrowers alike.[72]

The public, however, and the critics too were of a very
different opinion from the arrogant Warburton. Shenstone
wrote to Thomas Percy on 6 June that he must by all means read
the *Conjectures*, 'even though it should dissuade you, when you
have completed Ovid,[P] from undertaking any more translations.
I should not *murmur* at the effect, provided it stimulate you to
write originals.'[73] William Kenrick in the *Monthly Review* for

[P] Percy, the future editor of the *Reliques of Ancient English Poetry*, seems to have
abandoned his Ovid.

June disapproved of the 'equivocal, motley style' in a so-called letter but commended the doctrine as indicating 'a genius of the first rank':

> The striking allusions, bold metaphors and animated style of the poet distinguish this work, indeed, as much as if it had been divided into lines of ten or eleven syllables and been dignified with the title of blank verse . . . It must be nevertheless confessed that many of his observations on the merit of original writers and their imitators are new, striking and just . . . A daring spirit of liberty, an honest indignation at the meanness and servility of mere imitators, and a noble confidence in superior talents are the distinguishing characteristics of men of genius . . . The reader hath an instance in our author how far the executive and the speculative genius are compatible. In other words, he may see that taste and genius are not more necessary to form the writer than the critic; even in the latter capacity the letter-writer giving us very judicious specimens of his known and distinguished abilities.[74]

In the *Critical Review* the style as well as the theme won praise from a reviewer who is supposed by some editors to have been Goldsmith:[q]

> One of the oldest and bravest champions in the cause of literature has here resumed the gauntlet, and Dr Young, the only survivor of our Augustan age of writers, instead of growing languid with age, seems to gather strength by time and kindles as he runs. Strong imagery, frequent metaphor and a glowing imagination are generally the prerogatives of a youthful author; however, the writer in view seems to invert the order of nature and, as he grows old, his fancy seems to grow more luxuriant. To say the truth, his metaphors are too thick sown; he frequently drives them too far and often does not preserve their simplicity to the end . . . But wherever he falls short of perfection, his faults are the errors of genius; his manner peculiarly his own; and

[q] A MS note by Goldsmith in *The Present State of Polite Learning* identifies the following passage as referring to Young: 'I have heard an old poet of that glorious age say that a dinner with his Lordship [Lord Somers] has procured him invitations for the whole week following, that an airing in his patron's chariot has supplied him with a citizen's coach on every future occasion.' (*Collected Works*, ed. A. Friedman, 1966, I, 311.) Goldsmith probably met Young when working as a proof-reader for Richardson.

while his book serves by precept to direct us to original
composition, it serves to impel us by example ... As Dr
Young's manner of writing is peculiarly his own and has
already secured him an ample share of fame, we hope to see
some succeeding man of genius do justice to the integrity
of his life and the simplicity and piety of his manners;
for in this respect not Addison himself was, perhaps, his
superior.[75]

The *Conjectures*, as can be seen, was immediately recognized as
a pronouncement of major importance and it is fair to say that
the book forms a landmark in English – and indeed European –
literary criticism. His insistence on the superiority of originality
over imitation of classic models, of native genius over learning,
was shocking and inspiring. This led him to exalt Shakespeare
and Milton as the equals of Pindar and Homer and to degrade
Pope as one who not only practised but commended imitation.
Ben Jonson, in his view, was overloaded with learning; Dryden
lacked a heart; and Addison's *Cato*, though admirable when read
in the closet, failed to stir the necessary pity and terror in the
theatre. Rhyme he condemned as a 'Gothic demon',[76] suited
only to 'lesser poetry'. It was no wonder that such views, coming
from the last survivor of the Augustans, the friend of Addison
and Pope – and of Swift too, whom he sharply rebuked for the
cynicism of his Houyhnhnms – caused a sensation. The
Conjectures were a declaration of independence against the
tyranny of classicism and were generally recognized, and widely
acclaimed, as such. It has been argued that this work was not in
itself original, that such views were already current – as in
Warton's *Essay on Pope* – and that Young only summed up at the
critical moment the general trend of his time. But this is to
consider the *Conjectures* in isolation and overlook Young's other
works. The leaders in any revolution are those who at the right
moment express the feelings of the rising wave; but Young did
more than that – with his *Night Thoughts* he had set the wave of
romanticism in motion. With the *Conjectures* he was justifying
critically what before he had exemplified poetically; he was
confirming in theory what he had already demonstrated in
practice.

But it was not only Young's unique authority but his unique
vivacity that made his work so influential. Here was no dull

disquisition, but a lively letter to a friend, full of fascinating anecdotes as well as trenchant opinions. It was here that he told of his walk outside Dublin with Swift; of hearing Pope talk over the plan of an epic a few weeks before his death; above all, of the deathbed of Addison, as he had heard it from Tickell 'before his eyes were dry'.[77] Though he alleged that the revelation of this 'sacred deposit' was the chief inducement for his writing the piece, his exchanges with Richardson show that Addison really came into it quite late. But that is only another example of art improving on fact – the 'monumental marble', though set up later, was made the main objective of his visit to the pleasure garden of literature. To posterity, however, the Addison episode is incidental. What matters is the doctrine of 'genius', of innate originality being superior to classic indoctrination, of modern writers being able to rival or even surpass the 'ancients' of Greece and Rome. Moreover he asserted that if we all 'dive deep into our bosoms' and 'excite and cherish every spark of intellectual light and heat',[78] genius is not so uncommon; we should not let ourselves be browbeaten into diffidence by great examples or authorities. All this heady stuff was expressed in the usual torrent of images and epigrams, strewn as thickly as in the *Nights* and so condensed that one often has to read twice to appreciate the full meaning. The old man had lost nothing of his wit; the letter was written, as Mrs Delany put it, 'with the spirit of twenty-five rather than fourscore years of age'.[79]

The first part was devoted to the argument, the exaltation of genius at the expense of learning and imitation; the second part considered and reappraised the leading writers of modern England in the light of his newly-expounded criteria. Though to us, as heirs of the Romantic Revival, Young's break with ancient authority may not give the same excitement, the same sense of liberation and opportunity as it did to his contemporaries, the whole work can still be read with enjoyment and stimulation. Every page is full of provocative thoughts and highly quotable wit:

> We may as well grow good by another's virtue or fat by another's food, as famous by another's thought.[80]
>
> Nature herself sets the ladder; all wanting is our ambition to climb.[81]
>
> Rules, like crutches, are a needful aid to the lame, though an impediment to the strong.[82]

Copies surpass not their originals, as streams rise not higher than their spring.[83]

We may not go a-begging with gold in our purse. For there is a mine in man which must be dug deeply ere we can conjecture its contents.[84]

The sun as much exists in a cloudy day as in a clear.[85]

A man may be scarce less ignorant of his own powers than an oyster of its pearl or a rock of its diamond.[86]

Yet inevitably for the modern reader the most interesting part of the *Conjectures* is Young's judgement upon his contemporaries. In Pope he deplored both his practice of imitation and his use of rhyme:

Great things he has done; but he might have done greater. What a fall is it from Homer's numbers, free as air, lofty and harmonious as the spheres, into childish shackles and tinkling sounds . . . Had Milton never wrote, Pope had been less to blame; but when in Milton's genius Homer, as it were, personally rose to forbid Britons doing him that ignoble wrong, it is less pardonable by that effeminate decoration to put Achilles in petticoats a second time . . . How much nobler, if he had resisted the temptation of that Gothic demon which, modern poesy tasting, became mortal . . . Harmony as well as eloquence is essential to poesy; and a murder of his music is putting half Homer to death. Blank is a term of diminution; what we mean by blank verse is verse unfallen, uncurst; verse reclaimed, reinthroned in the true language of the gods . . . Would not . . . Pope have succeeded better in an original attempt? Talents untried are talents unknown. All that I know is that, contrary to these sentiments, he was not only an avowed professor of imitation but a zealous recommender of it also . . . Though Pope's noble Muse may boast her illustrious descent from Homer, Virgil, Horace, yet is an original author more nobly born . . . Therefore, though we stand much obliged for his giving us a Homer, yet had he doubled our obligation by giving us – a Pope. Had he a strong imagination and the true sublime? That granted, we might have had two Homers instead of one, if longer had been his life; for I heard the dying swan talk over an epic plan[r] a few weeks before his decease.[87]

[r] This was the projected epic on Brutus.

Young the moralist is even more severe on Swift:

> This writer has so satirized human nature as to give a
> demonstration in himself that it deserves to be satirized.
> But, say his wholesale admirers, few could so have written;
> true, and fewer would . . . Swift is not commended for this
> piece but this piece for Swift. He has given us some beauties
> which deserve all our praise; and our comfort is that his
> faults will not become common, for none can be guilty of
> them but who have wit as well as reputation to spare.[s] His
> wit had been less wild if his temper had not jostled his
> judgement. If his favourite Houyhnhnms could write and
> Swift had been one of them, every horse with him would
> have been an ass and he would have written a panegyric on
> mankind . . . Being born amongst men and, of consequence,
> piqued by many and peevish at more, he has blasphemed
> a nature little lower than that of angels. . . . The contempt
> of mankind is a vice. Therefore I wonder that, though
> forborne by others, the laughter-loving Swift was not
> reproved by the venerable Dean, who could sometimes be
> very grave.[88]

Young's real admiration was reserved for Addison:

> Among the brightest of the moderns Mr Addison must
> take his place . . . He had what Dryden and Jonson wanted,
> a warm and feeling heart; but being of a grave and bashful
> nature, through a philosophic reserve and a sort of moral
> prudery, he concealed it, where he should have let loose all
> his fire and have showed the most tender sensibilities of
> heart. At his celebrated *Cato* few tears are shed but Cato's
> own . . . Those two throbbing pulses of the drama, . . .
> terror and pity, neglected through the whole, leave our
> unmolested hearts at perfect peace. Thus the poet, like his
> hero, through mistaken excellence and virtue overstrained,
> becomes a sort of suicide, and that which is most dramatic
> in the drama dies . . . There is this similitude between the
> poet and the play; as this is more fit for the closet than the
> stage, so that shone brighter in private conversation than on
> the public scene.
>
> Addison wrote little in verse, much in sweet, elegant,

---

[s] Young had expressed a similar view to the Duchess on 8 December, 1751 in
commenting on Lord Orrery's *Remarks on Swift*: 'If he has used excellent talents
to a bad purpose, he himself is another Dr Swift.' (Pettit, 374.)

Virgilian prose . . . Addison's compositions are built with
the finest materials, in the taste of the ancients and (to speak
his own language) on truly classic ground; and though they
are the delight of the present age, yet I am persuaded that
they will receive more justice from posterity. I never read
him but I am struck with such a disheartening idea of
perfection that I drop my pen . . . And yet, . . . what is the
common language of the world, and even of his admirers,
concerning him? They call him an *elegant* writer; that
elegance which shines on the surface of his compositions
seems to dazzle their understanding and render it a little
blind to the depth of sentiment which lies beneath. Thus
(hard fate!) he loses reputation with them by doubling his
title to it. On subjects the most interesting and important no
author of his age has written with greater . . . weight; and
they who commend him for his elegance pay him such a
sort of compliment, by their abstemious praise, as they
would pay to Lucretia if they should commend her only for
her beauty.[89]

And here was how he compared the characters of his three
friends:

To distinguish this triumvirate from each other and, like
Newton, to discover the different colours in these genuine
and meridian rays of literary light, Swift is a singular wit, Pope
a correct poet, Addison a great author. Swift looked on wit as
the *jus divinum* to dominion and sway in the world and
considered as usurpation all power that was lodged in persons
of less sparkling understandings. This inclined him to
tyranny in wit. Pope was somewhat of his opinion, but was for
softening tyranny into lawful monarchy; yet were there some
acts of severity in his reign. Addison's crown was elective, he
reigned by the public voice. . . . But as good books are the
medicine of the mind, if we should dethrone these authors
and consider them not in their royal but their medicinal
capacity, might it not then be said that Addison prescribed a
wholesome and pleasant regimen, which was universally
relished and did much good; that Pope preferred a purgative
of satire, which, though wholesome, was too painful in its
operation; and that Swift insisted on a large dose of
ipecacuanha, which, though readily swallowed from the fame
of the physician, yet if the patient had any delicacy of taste, he
threw up the remedy instead of the disease?[90]

Only Young could write like this. Young, who had lived on equal terms with the great writers that he criticized, was the only man who could proclaim so boldly and effectively the new, iconoclastic doctrine. When we consider the date at which this manifesto of romanticism was written, we can see how the publication of the *Conjectures* was a milestone in literary history. But its interest is not only historic, it is intrinsic. It is a work that still deserves to be read for itself – and it is in fact the only work of Young to earn a new edition in the present century.[1]

[1] Edited by Edith Morley in Manchester University's *Modern Language Texts* (English Series), 1918; also reprinted in *English Critical Essays, XVI–XVIII Centuries*, edited by Edmund D. Jones in the World's Classics series, O.U.P., 1922; and in facsimile (first edition) by the Scolar Press, Leeds, 1966.

CHAPTER 18

The Polite Hermit

1759–1761

In spite of the brilliant success of the *Conjectures*, of which the second edition came out on 18 June, 1759,[1] Young never proceeded with the promised second letter in which he was to descend to the 'sublunary praise'[2] of Addison and consider how far he was an original. Instead he began to prepare for the inevitable and clear up his affairs. We do not know the purpose of a one-night visit by Richardson on 25 July;[3] but on 4 August[4] he wrote a will, leaving a legacy of £1500 for his charity-school. Soon, however, he thought better of it and on 4 September[5] John Jones wrote on his behalf to an attorney of St Neots, Huntingdonshire, called John Waller, about a deed of gift that the Doctor wished to execute, to establish a £1500 fund for a school trust. On 5 October[6] Jones enclosed a draft scheme for the establishment of the trust, of which the rough notes are preserved, giving the limits of the site, a list of trustees clerical and civil, and certain suggested rules such as: the Rector of Welwyn alone to have the nomination of the scholars; a curate of Welwyn not to be master at the same time; the master's salary to be at the Trustees' discretion; the master to be removed if he 'be not of good example to the children'; and if necessary (though 'contrary to the design of the Benefactor'), a tablet recording the benefaction. Six months later it had all been worked out in detail and the deed is dated 15 April, 1760.[7] It was another five months, however, before all the legal business was finally completed, partly owing to the illness of Mr Waller; but by 11 September all was finished. The whole business had taken just one year and at the end of it Jones noted the attorney's bill as 'very reasonable' and quoted the opinion of the Doctor that Waller was 'the reverse of the generality of his profession'.[8]

The continuance of the school that Young had founded in 1749 was thus ensured and in 1821 the terms of the benefaction were summarized by a local historian thus:

Dr Edward Young, formerly Rector of this parish, by deed dated 15th of April 1760 and enrolled in Chancery, convenanted with Sir Samuel Garrard, Bart., and others, trustees, that £1500 Old South Sea Annuities should be vested in them and that the same should be laid out in the purchase of land[a] to be settled upon the said trustees, to apply the issues and profits thereof 'towards maintaining, supporting and promoting a charity-school within the parish of Welwyn and for the meet and convenient clothing of 16 or more poor boys . . . and for thoroughly instructing and grounding them in the principles and duties of the Christian religion, as laid down in the Catechism of the Church of England, and to read, write and cast accounts'; and also to pay 10 shillings per annum to the Rector of Welwyn . . . for reading prayers and preaching a sermon (wherein the said Edward Young did expressly forbid any mention to be made of him) . . . at the time of the yearly meeting of the trustees. And he directed that his trustees should, after detaining 30 shillings towards their necessary charges and expenses, . . . apply the rest towards the salary of the schoolmaster . . . and for clothing the said poor boys and for books, paper and other necessaries; and for putting out one or more of them apprentices to some honest trade.[9]

In February, 1760,[10] while the legal arrangements for the school's future were being settled, Young began a revised will, his last. That winter he had received many admonitions of mortality. On 20 December[11] he had told the Duchess of the deaths of two neighbours, Mrs Sabine of Tewin and his friend George Harrison of Balls; but a loss that touched him more nearly was that which he reported on 10 January of 'an only brother, and an only niece, both within this last month'.[12] By 'brother' he meant brother-in-law and referred to John Harris, while the niece was Harris's daughter, Jane Bigg. Harris died on 13 December and was buried on the 17th[13] at Ash, where a monumental tablet records the main facts of his life, including

---

[a] Unfortunately the trustees neglected to invest in land and simply left the interest to accumulate for many years. About 1830 they sold the old stock and bought £1918 of 3% Consols, giving an income of £57 p.a. for the National School, with which Young's foundation was merged. (Cussans, *History of Hertfordshire*, 1877, Broadwater Hundred, 230.)

his two marriages. The identity of Young's niece, who he said had died of cancer, is confirmed by the mention in her father's will, dated 20 October, 1759, of his 'dearest daughter Bigg's complaint', which was 'of such a nature as probably will not suffer her to attend the execution of my will as executor as I had appointed her in my last.'[14] But the interesting provision was that by which he gave 'to my much esteemed friend and brother Dr Edward Young' twenty guineas 'to be laid out in a piece of plate with my own and his sister's arms, which I desire may always remain in his family as a token of that love and friendship which I hope and desire will always remain between his children and mine.'[15] Though there is no other reference to Harris in Young's letters, it is clear that their friendship had remained unbroken ever since the 1720s, when Young used to stay each summer at Chiddingfold.

In the case of his own will the confusion of dates indicates that he took it slowly and brooded over it. Though he started 'In the name of God and my most blessed Redeemer, Amen. I write this my last Will with my own hand Feby the 5th, 1760', it ended 'In witness and confirmation of this my Will I hereunto set my hand and seal this 25th of April 1760'; while a codicil of 1764 talked of the will 'made and published bearing date the 21 of June 1760'.[16] The contents of the will will be discussed later; for the moment, though witnessed by three village worthies, Robert Milward, churchwarden and gamekeeper of the Rector's manor, Thomas Pentlow, vestry-clerk and schoolmaster, and John Deards, collar-maker, the provisions were secret – or at least unknown to John Jones. On one point, however, Young anticipated a clause of his will, in which he requested that 'all my manuscript writings, whether in books or papers, immediately on my decease may be burnt, my book of accounts alone excepted.'[17] Early in 1760 he wrote to Richardson, asking him to send 'the parcel of sermons, which were packed up when I was in town',[18] so that he could commit them to the flames himself. It is said that some time before his death he also personally burnt some letters from Lady Mary Wortley Montagu on the grounds of their indecency. Perhaps he did so at this time too,[b] for Lady

---

[b] Another possible time was in June, 1763, when he read in the papers some letters of Lady Mary (who had died in 1762) 'in which are some things', he told the Duchess, 'to the publication of which, I am satisfied, that in her last hours she would not have given her consent'. (Pettit, 575.)

Mary was in his mind on 10 January,[19] when he contrasted her 'situation in marriage' with that of the Duchess's eldest daughter, who had married Viscount Weymouth in April, 1759 and was now happily settled at Longleat – luckily for the biographers of Young, since she inherited her mother's collection of the poet's letters, which are still safely preserved in the library there.

There was one other matter in which the poet sought to 'set his house in order' – his relations with his son. Frederick had been absent from Oxford ever since December, 1758,[20] when he disappeared soon after his father had begged the Duchess to transfer the offer of a living to him. On 29 July, 1760,[21] however, Frederick opened a bank account with Gosling's and the figures show that he began with a balance of £2400. Just over a week later he sold £1000 worth of 3% Consols, followed in a fortnight by a further £400. But on 12 September[22] he returned to Balliol and resided there in fits and starts for the next twelve months. It looks as if Frederick had once more run deep into debt during his prolonged absence and his father had again bailed him out on condition that he resumed his studies. The immediate drawing of such huge sums in August suggests that he was paying off his debts, and thereafter for a few months he drew no more. He still had another £1000 left in the bank and an assured income of £300 a year from his annuity – ample sums for a comfortable standard of living in the terms of those days.

But though the poet had now made his preparations for leaving the world, the world refused to leave him. Aspiring authors endlessly loaded him with presentation copies of their works, while his German translators, busy with ever more elaborate editions of the *Nights* and instant versions of the *Conjectures*,[c] bombarded him with earnest Teutonic questions as to the exact interpretation of his masterpiece, as in the letter from Hanover that Richardson passed on to him on 24 May, 1759 with the comment, 'In Germany they revere Dr Young in his works more than they do those of any other British genius.'[23]

---

[c] In 1760 Ebert produced the first volume of his revised and annotated edition of the *Night Thoughts* at Brunswick, while at Hanover Kayser issued a revised and extended version of his hexameter translation. Two translations of the *Conjectures* were published at Leipzig and Hamburg, and an adaptation of *The Revenge* at Vienna.

The Germans did indeed revere Dr Young and with scholarly thoroughness sought to check every puzzle of sense or fact. The poet, however, having indulged in poetic licence over the details, did not wish to be pinned down to exactitudes, so his answers were a little evasive. To an admirer like Klopstock, who did not pester him in this way, Young was much more responsive and on 7 February, 1759 he had made a special effort to condole with him on the death of his young wife Meta after only four years of married life:

> Pardon, dear sir, so long a silence after your so very kind letter; rheumatism robbed me of the use of my pen, which I can but very ill hold now . . . However, I cannot lay my pen aside without from my heart condoling your very, very great loss. I am too well qualified so to do, having not long ago undergone the same calamity – I say 'not long ago'; for though it is many years since, yet was the wound so deep that it seems even now recent and often bleeds as if it had been received but yesterday.[24]

Among the English admirers who sent him their poems in 1760[d] was George Keate, a versatile young lawyer of private means, who not only wrote verse but exhibited at the Royal Academy and was a collector of coins, shells and the like. On 29 May Young acknowledged the receipt of the blank verse *Ancient and Modern Rome*, which he said he had 'read over and over to myself and others with great pleasure'.[25] He added, 'I am glad to hear that you think the report of Voltaire's death is groundless.' Keate had lived in Geneva, where he formed an intimacy with Voltaire, and this connection with Young's old sparring-partner made a bond between them. In August Keate sent Young something of Voltaire's with his comments and in return Young ordered 'some sheets . . . from my dear friend Mr Richardson's press',[26] with his opinion of some of Voltaire's other performances, to be sent to Keate – presumably the *Dedication to Mr Voltaire*, first printed in his 1757 *Works*.

The last known letter from the poet to his 'dear friend' was dated 8 September, 1760, though it is probable that a number of

---

[d] Another was the pastoral poet John Scott, of Amwell, who sent Young his *Four Elegies, descriptive and moral*, which the recipient promised to recommend to all his friends. (Pettit, 515.)

later ones have been lost.' In this Young referred to some
unidentified literary business:

> I have received the papers – and how greatly am I
> concerned that I cannot take the advantage of the infinite
> pains you have taken for me. But every day puts it more
> and more out of my power. It is with difficulty that I can
> read what your friendship and genius and virtue has sent
> me. But still greater difficulty am I under sufficiently to
> thank you for it. To write is uneasy to me; must I despair of
> ever seeing you? Or have I that pleasure in life still to come?
> Success and peace be ever with you, Amen! Which is the
> natural style of those that have entered the intermediate
> state between this scene and the next. A dim apartment it is,
> which excludes action, but favours thought.[27]

It appears that Richardson was trying to get Young to write a
new work, for he wrote to Lady Bradshaigh on 10 August about
'a very desirable subject, on which I was free enough to engage
his pen'.[28] It is even possible that Young began it. For, according
to William Hayley in the preface to his tragedy *Marcella*, 'the
story was recommended to Young by the author of *Clarissa*. The
poet adopted it and wrote a single act; but this shared the fate of
his other unfinished manuscripts and, according to the direction
of his will, was committed to the flames. These particulars, with a
concise sketch of the story as related by Richardson, were
communicated to Mr Thornton[f] by the poet's very liberal and
amiable son, the neighbour and the much-esteemed relation of
my dear departed friend, who wished me to build a tragedy
upon this foundation.'[29]

The loss of the correspondence with Richardson during the
remaining few months of the novelist's life is to some extent
compensated by the re-appearance on the scene of Mrs

' A note about *Clarissa's Meditations*, 'a little piece hitherto [30 July, 1758]
unpublished' (M.M., XXXVII, 327), in Richardson's copies of his correspondence shows that he edited his letters in mid-1758. After that he probably had
neither the time nor the energy to preserve and copy all his correspondence so
carefully.

[f] John Thornton was related to Frederick through Giles Thornton, who
added the name Heysham on inheriting Stagenhoe, St Paul's Walden, near
Welwyn. Frederick married the eldest Heysham daughter. Both Hayley and
Cowper wrote poems in memory of John Thornton, celebrating his charity,
when he died in 1780.

Montagu. On her way north to join her husband in September she called in at Guessens and it is amusing to compare her first description of the meeting, sent to her husband on 19 September, with the later version written to Miss Anne Pitt on 30 November. The latter is rather elaborate and literary:

> I called on my old friend Dr Young at Welwyn and had the pleasure of conversing with so extraordinary a being as a polite hermit and a witty saint. He has quitted the dreams of Pindus, the Aonian swards, for the nymphs of Solyma; though they now direct his walk, his mind has still the gait and step of the gayer muses . . . My agreeable hermit invited me very much to proceed no further on my journey that day; But I considered the call at the hermitage was only to be an agreeable episode in my work and re-assumed the thread of my journey.[30]

But the letter to her husband is much more spontaneous and salty:

> I called on Dr Young at Welwyn and stayed about two hours with him. He received me with great cordiality and I think appears in better health than ever I saw him. His house is happily opposite to a churchyard, which is to him a fine prospect; he has taught his imagination to sport with skulls like the grave-digger in *Hamlet*. He invited me to stay all night, and if my impatience to see you had not impelled me on, I had been tempted to it. His conversation has always something in it very delightful; in the first place it is animated by the warmest benevolence, then his imagination soars above the material world. Some people would say his conversation is not natural; I say it is natural to him to be unnatural, that is, out of the ordinary course of things. It would be easier for him to give you a catalogue of the stars than an inventory of the household furniture he uses every day. The busy world may say what it pleases, but some men were made for speculation. Metaphysical men, like jars and flowerpots, make good furniture for a cabinet, though useless in the kitchen, the pantry and the dairy.[31]

Mrs Montagu's estimate of Young's conversation and manners was echoed and confirmed by the long, anonymous but well-informed article in the *Gentleman's Magazine* of 1782, provoked by the mistakes of Croft and written by someone with personal knowledge of the poet:

> He was very pleasant in conversation and extremely polite . . . Those . . . so intimately received as to be treated and considered as a part of his family, and that not only once and for a short time but oftener and for many months at a time, saw him always the same. He appeared neither as a 'man of sorrow' nor yet as a 'fellow of infinite jest' . . . The dignity of a great and a good mind appeared in all his actions and in all his words. He conversed on religious subjects with the cheerfulness of virtue; his piety was undebased by gloom or enthusiasm . . . His politeness was such as I never saw equalled; it was invariable. To his superiors in rank, to his equals and to his inferiors it differed only in the *degree* of elegance. I never heard him speak with roughness to his meanest servant; yet he well knew how to keep up his dignity and with all the majesty of superior worth to repress the bold and the forward. In conversation upon lively subjects he had a brilliancy of wit peculiar to himself . . . both *heightened* and *softened* by the great and amiable qualities of his soul. I have seen him ill and in pain, yet the serenity of his mind remained unruffled. I never heard a peevish expression fall from his lips, nor was he at such times less kindly and politely attentive to those around him than when in the company of strangers.[32]

The writer ended by saying that his only motive in writing was 'the sincerest and most disinterested veneration for the memory of a man who was a credit to religion and an honour to human nature',[33] and that the names of *poet* and *saint* were both applicable to him. The testimony of those who actually know Young is, as usual, strongly in his favour.

So the aged poet passed his days, his wordly affairs apparently settled, waiting serenely for the end. But death, instead of coming to him, struck down his old friends and brought him to a new work and – at last – preferment! The latter was a direct result of the death of the tough little King, George II, on 25 October, 1760. The fact that the Duke of Newcastle, hitherto so obstinate, was still in the saddle of patronage – in fact Prime Minister now – and that the offer of preferment came through the Duchess of Portland, whose utmost exertions of pressure and influence had previously got nowhere, surely prove that the

King himself had been the immovable stumbling-block to Young's hopes. But the poet himself had no suspicion of this and a letter to the Duchess on 20 November[34] contained no suggestion of a revival of those hopes. It is clear from his letter of 20 January, 1761 that the offer was unsolicited and a surprise:

> I have taken some hours to consider of the very kind offer your Grace is so good to make me. I am old and, I bless God, far from want; but as the honour is great and the duty small and such as need not take much from my parish, and especially as your Grace seems desirous I should accept it, I do accept it with great gratitude for your remembrance of one who might easily and naturally be forgotten. The honour indeed is great and in my sight greater still, as I succeed to so great and good a man.[35]

The post was that of Clerk of the Closet to the Princess Dowager, widow of Frederick, Prince of Wales and mother of the new King George III. The corrector of Croft states that Young's attachment to the Prince of Wales had given offence so well known that, when the new King struck the old man's name from the list of court chaplains, it caused astonishment and discontent in the Doctor's friends (though he never heard that it did so in himself), which was afterwards appeased by his being almost immediately appointed Clerk of the Closet to the Prince's widow. The previous holder, Dr Stephen Hales,[g] had died on 4 January, 1761 and the vacancy was the first suitable one since the old King's death. The appointment was gazetted in February[36] at a salary of £200 per annum[h] and his chaplaincy to the King now ceased.

Young was called to town for the occasion and was put up by the Duchess and an undated letter thanked her for the shelter and the elegant amusements:

> But how came I to emerge out of my own muddy element
> into such curious enquiries and polite converse in

---

[g] Stephen Hales (1677–1761) is remembered as a physiologist and inventor rather than a divine. In 1709 he was appointed perpetual curate of Teddington, where he set up his laboratory, which the Prince of Wales often visited. He was appointed Clerk of the Closet to the Prince's widow in 1751.

[h] Young's bank account shows his salary paid in from 21 January, 1762 at the rate of £190 p.a. 'by Edward Godfrey'. Perhaps Mr Godfrey charged a 5% fee. (MS Gosling, ledger N14, f. 294.)

your land of rarities? My collection is large, but it lies chiefly
in the churchyard, and a death's-head is the capital picture I
can boast. I little thought, a month ago, that I should have
been called out of my private path so late in life; but your
Grace was pleased to call me out of it in quest of honours.
Now the road to honours lies uphill and indeed the steep
ascent has put me a little out of breath; the natural appetite
of age is for rest, which I have fasted for at least a fortnight.
This has sunk me a little, but otherways, I bless God, I am
very well.[37]

His other friends wrote to congratulate him, and in thanking
Keate on 22 February he invited his young friend to Welwyn,
adding that he was 'pretty well, but not quite as well as I was forty
years ago; but I hope, through divine mercy, forty years hence to
be better still'.[38] Richardson passed on the news to Hildesley in
the Isle of Man and confirmed that the poet's health, and even his
eyesight, had improved:

> I have the great pleasure of congratulating you on Dr
> Young's good state of health and on his abated
> apprehension of the calamity he dreaded; as well as on a
> promotion that does equal honour to his acceptance and to
> the conferrer's, the royal conferrer's, choice and nomina-
> tion, . . . and upon the recommendation of His Majesty
> himself, as a noble peer assured me yesterday.[39]

Whether the noble peer's information was correct we do not
know. All that is sure about this belated preferment is that it came
to Young through the Duchess and it came to him as a surprise.

A week after the death of Dr Hales there occurred another
death that affected Young, for it caused him to take up his pen
again. On 10 January died Admiral Boscawen, the victor of
Lagos. It was not Young's naval enthusiasm, however, that
inspired him to verse on this occasion but the grief of the
Admiral's widow, who was associated with the 'Bluestocking'
movement, led by Mrs Montagu and the Duchess.[i] Twenty years
later Mrs Montagu informed Croft:

---

[i] Admiral Boscawen treated his wife's intellectual parties with breezy contempt
and Forbes's *Life of Beattie* makes him the originator of the term 'Bluestocking'.
Full dress was not insisted on and Benjamin Stillingfleet wore blue worsted
stockings instead of black silk, leading the Admiral to scoff at these 'bluestocking
parties'. (Forbes, I, 271.)

In regard to *Resignation* the matter which gave occasion to
that poem was simply this: Mrs Montagu having observed
that Mrs Boscawen in her great and just grief for the loss of
the Admiral seemed to find some consolation in reading
Dr Young's *Night Thoughts*, she wished to give her an
opportunity of conversing with him, having herself always .
thought his unbounded genius appeared to greater
advantage in the companion than the author. The Christian
was in him a character more inspired, more enraptured,
more sublime than the poet; and in his ordinary
conversation,
> letting down the golden chain from high,
> He drew his audience upward to the sky.

Mrs Montagu therefore proposed to Mrs Boscawen and
Mrs Carter[j] to go with her to Welwyn. It is unnecessary to
add that the visit answered every expectation.[40]

The visit took place in the second half of April, 1761, but the
contemporary evidence[k] suggests that Mrs Boscawen did not in
fact accompany the other 'two fair pilgrims', about whom Young
wrote to Mrs Montagu on the 9th. The 'Queen of the Blues' had
evidently made him some compliment on the lines of the 'witty
saint', for he protested, 'I hope they (the two fair pilgrims) are
too much Protestants to think there is anything sacred in the
shrine you speak of. I have too many sins beside to pretend I am
a saint. Was I a saint and could work miracles, I would reduce
you two ladies to the common level of your sex, being jealous for
the credit of my own, which has hitherto presumed to boast an
usurped superiority in the realms of genius and the lettered
world.'[41] Perhaps it was because he was not able to speak
personally to Mrs Boscawen that he wrote to her, at the other
ladies' urging, in the verses that eventually became his last
published work, *Resignation*.

Soon after their visit, on 9 June, Miss Carter wrote to Mrs
Montagu, asking if she had 'proceeded at all in a design so truly
worthy of you as attempting to make peace between Dr Young
and his son'.[42] The armistice, patched up in July, 1760, with a

---

[j] Elizabeth Carter (1717–1806) published an imposing translation of Epictetus
in 1758, to which Young subscribed.

[k] Mrs Scott, Mrs Montagu's sister, wrote on 28 November, 1761 that Young
wrote *Resignation* for Mrs Boscawen at the desire of her sister and Miss Carter,
when they visited him on their way to Tunbridge. (Pettit, 529.)

large bank deposit in Frederick's name and the young man's
return to Oxford, had evidently broken down once more; and
no wonder, for the prodigal had begun his tricks again at the
beginning of the new year. In January, 1761 Frederick sold a
further £200 Consols, and the same amount in February.[43] On
14 May another £100 went the same way – half of his remaining
capital gone in five months! Nor was his attendance at his studies
any more satisfactory; he was now twenty-eight and evidently
could not settle down. After his return to Balliol on 12
September, 1760[44] he resided for only two weeks; then two
weeks' absence, three weeks' residence, three weeks' absence,
four weeks in College, six weeks away over Christmas and the
New Year; and it was during this Christmas vacation that he
began selling his stocks again. And so it went on, with ever
shorter stays in College and a never-ending drain on the bank,
and one new delinquency too – he started to default on his
College bills. Hitherto his quarterly 'Battells' had been regularly
paid, even during his longest absences, but from March, 1761[45]
they remained unsettled till after his father's death.[1] Had his
father been paying up till then and was it part of the bargain that
Frederick should be responsible after Young had settled such a
generous sum on him? At any rate the breach this time seems to
have been final and, as far as we know, Mrs Montagu's efforts to
make peace bore no fruit. On 27 August[46] Frederick left Oxford
for good.

The break with his father and the looming spectre of
bankruptcy did little to slow down his prodigal career. In
September, 1761 he drew another £200 and his last £300
vanished, £100 at a time, by August, 1762.[47] On the 17th of that
month he sold the last remains of his stocks. But this time his
father refused to pick up the bits any more. On the 25th of the
previous month John Jones had reported to his friend, Dr
Birch[m] of the British Museum, with typically oblique caution,

---

[1] On 2 December, 1765 Frederick, having inherited Young's fortune, signed
the Bursar's book as having been repaid £10 Caution Money, i.e. he had paid off
his College debts.

[m] In 1759 Jones persuaded Young to lend Birch two folio letter-books of John
Dodington, Resident of Charles II at Venice, and in 1762 he got the poet to
present them to the Museum; he also extracted a third volume in 1764. Birch
himself received a presentation copy of the *Conjectures*, 2nd edition, 1759.
(Nichols, 614–15; 626.)

'There is thought to be an irremovable obstruction to his [Young's] happiness within his walls, as well as another without them; but the former is the more powerful and likely to continue so.'[48] In other words the influence of Mrs Hallows was stronger than that of Frederick and she may well have stiffened the old man's resolution not to give in again to his son's appeals for help. Whether there was any personal animosity between Young's housekeeper and his son, as alleged by Johnson, we can only surmise; but if in fact Frederick tried to insist that Mrs Hallows should be dismissed for her 'sauciness', it could have been the last straw. The poet might have told him to go away till he had apologized to the housekeeper, or alternatively the young man himself might have sworn never to return to Guessens as long as she was there. But whatever the clash of personalities between the two persons nearest him, the root cause of Young's estrangement from his son was clearly Frederick's utter and hopeless irresponsibility in money matters.

CHAPTER 19

Resignation

1761–1762

While Frederick continued his Gadarene rush to ruin, his father was busy composing for Mrs Boscawen those counsels of resignation of which he must surely have felt the need for himself. On 3 May, 1761 he sent what must have been the second draft to Mrs Montagu:

> You will be so good as to burn what I sent before and to recommend this to Mrs B. with the warmest good wishes of my heart. Your recommendation will enable this trifle, perhaps, to make some impression on her; which I send purely for an amusement, which in her case is of more use than anything else.[1]

Three weeks later he followed up with 'a paper which may be called a curiosity, as it is printed, but not for the public, only for your ease in perusing it'.[2] On 2 July he wrote about a 'something' that she was expecting, 'which will kiss your hand this week and if you are at the trouble of reading it over, you will find a sufficient excuse for my delay'.[3] By 30 July the final version was complete and he told Mrs Montagu at Tunbridge that he had 'ordered some stanzas to be sent you; they are of a cooling nature and may qualify your waters'.[4] Yet it was another month before the privately printed edition of *Resignation* was actually distributed to his friends.

The delay in the issue of the poem can be explained by the death on 4 July of Richardson, who was of course printing it. A note at the end of Part I runs: 'Whilst the author was writing this, he received the news of Mr Richardson's death';[5] and the published version of 1762 added, 'who was then printing the former part of the poem'.[6] It is difficult to reconcile the statements that Young was still writing the first part while Richardson was printing the 'former part' at the time of his death. But it looks as if the poet, because of his failing sight, ran off his various drafts in print and he might be referring to an earlier printed draft. The news of his friend's death set him off again and he added several verses on Richardson, so that yet another printing was required. But in his impatience Young ordered the revised copies to be sent out at the end of July without further proof-reading. Unhappily he now could no longer rely on his friend's efficiency and accuracy in correcting the proof and, when he finally received his copy on 2 September, he was obliged hastily to send out a series of apologetic notes of corrigenda,[a] starting:

> I was in too much haste and ordered a thing to be sent to you (which I suppose you have received) before I had read it myself. On reading it I find my distance from the press has occasioned many errors, so that in some parts I have had the impudence to present you with perfect nonsense.[7]

On the same day Mrs Montagu wrote to Miss Carter at Deal:

> I found on my table a poem on *Resignation* by Dr Young; he sent me a copy for you, which I will send by the Deal coach . . . You will be pleased, I think, with what he says of Voltaire; you know we exhorted him to attack a character whose authority is so pernicious. In vain do moralists attack the shadowy forms of vice, while the living temples of it are revered and admired.[8]

Another literary lady, Catherine Talbot, wrote to Young on 3 September from Lambeth, where she lived as ward of Archbishop Secker, to thank him for her copy. Though personally unknown to the poet, she was a friend of Richardson's and she referred to him when she said:

> To talk of a friend, with whom (during this short interval of life) we can no longer converse, is a pleasing indulgence of such feelings as are not inconsistent with the resignation you so admirably teach.[9]

She too was exercised by the problem of Voltaire, declaring, 'Your address to him in this poem must surely, if he has not laughed away all feeling, make him yet stop on the verge of eternity to look around, and even to look up'; and she ended by

---

[a] Two of these notes have survived, one addressed to Mrs Montagu, the other to an unknown male recipient, 'My dear and most honoured Sir'. (Pettit, 543.)

assuring the poet that, though unknown, she knew *him* very well, and had passed many of her most delightful hours with him – 'you have cost me many a tear, smoothed for me many a care, and impressed such thoughts upon my mind as I hope to thank you for a thousand ages hence'.[10]

This private edition of *Resignation*, printed solely for friends, differed considerably from the published edition of the following year and the poem will therefore be discussed when we come to the latter.

Meanwhile the Germans continued to send homage to the poet of the *Night Thoughts* and, while his own son rejected him, he was hailed as the 'spiritual father'[11] of his translator Ebert.[b] A teacher of English, Ebert had first published his prose translation in 1751–2[12] with such success that new editions were called for in 1753 and 1756, and he was now publishing a more elaborate edition with copious notes and the English text facing. In May, 1761 he sent the first volume of the new edition to the author,[c] who acknowledged it on 7 June, remarking 'I wish I understood the notes better than I do at present'.[13] Ebert followed up with an enormous and fulsome screed, which gives some idea of the extent of the Young-worship that was sweeping the German-speaking countries:

> All I can do here is to tell you for once by letter what I have been telling you in my thoughts almost every day these fifteen years past: that I revere in you one of the chosen vessels of God, ... one of those writers that applied the noblest talents to the noblest use and may be said ... with a genius as well *moral* as *original* to have cast out evil spirits and made a convert to virtue of a species of composition (poetry, and satire in particular) once most its foe.[14]

After a good deal more of this stuff the translator came down to earth:

> You will by this time have received the first volume of my new edition of your *Night Thoughts*. I began to translate

[b] Johann Arnold Ebert (1723–95), Professor of English at the Carolinum, Brunswick, was a friend of Klopstock and member of the 'Bremer Beiträge' group..

[c] On 12 November, 1761 Young presented this book to the Earl of Granville, formerly Lord Carteret, who understood German well. It is now in the British Library.

them about ten years ago, after having studied them for
four years almost night and day. I chose to attempt it in
prose rather than in verse, that I might render your
thoughts, if possible, in all their original energy without the
least alloy, with a scrupulous though not anxious exactness
. . . If I may trust to my sense of the beauties of the original.
and to the uncommonly favourable reception the translation has met with, I have not failed in my attempt. After
several editions there are now about 5000 copies of it and
together with them the glory of the immortal poet and the
solid advantages arising from the poem spread over all
Germany. Since that time I have translated also *The Last
Day, The Force of Religion, The True Estimate of Human Life,
The Centaur* (though there was already published another
translation, but a very indifferent one) and the *Two Epistles
to Mr Pope*. Your tragedies have likewise been translated,
but by another hand.[15]

He added that the *Satires* were to be annexed to the new,
annotated edition and explained that the lines frequently
quoted in the notes from Bodmer's epic *Noah* were imitations or
translations from the *Night Thoughts*, which the Swiss poet had
'excused somewhere in that work and at the same time publicly
declared his esteem and gratitude to his benefactor'. Other
quotations, though not actual imitations, earned their place 'as
well on account of their likeness as because the author more
than once confessed to me that during the course of his labour
he was often kindled and warmed by your flame . . . I mean Mr
Klopstock, our – more than Milton, our Shakespeare and Milton
united.'[16]

Next Ebert described how he had travelled to Copenhagen the
previous summer to visit Klopstock and Cramer, 'German
Chaplain to the King [of Denmark] and one of our best poets and
orators', and met 'several persons distinguished both by their rank
and merit, to whose favour my translation of your works served me
instead of an introduction and recommendation',[17] among them
the chief Minister, Baron Barnstorff, and the Countess of
Stolberg.

The latter, who had got your *Night Thoughts* almost by
heart, . . . desired me to invite you to do her the honour of
standing godfather to the child she was then big of; which

afterwards I was prevented to do by various avocations. About three weeks ago I received a letter from her amiable daughter, acquainting me in her mother's name that the night before, after having read with her almost the whole day your *Seventh Night*, she was happily delivered of a son; that she had invited the Queen Dowager, Baron Bernstorff . . . and you, sir, to be his sponsors at the font; and that she desired me to acquaint you with that news and to assure you that she was proud of having chosen the two greatest and worthiest men in the world she knew.[18]

Young replied on 29 June, thanking Ebert for his compliments and requesting him to tell the Countess that 'the surprising and very high honour she is pleased to do me shall be written on my tomb, which is not far off'.[19] But what he tactfully omitted to tell Ebert, who had really been rather dilatory about the whole business, was that Count Stolberg himself had written direct to the poet nearly three months before, and that he had answered on 12 April, accepting the peculiar honour, blessing his little Magnus Ernest Christian,[d] and wishing he was not divided from them 'by seas and lands and what is still worse, by an insurmountable mountain of near fourscore years'.[20]

When Young sat down to write to Ebert, he was unwell and ended with apologies for his brevity, but a postscript sending good wishes to Klopstock was much more lively and almost as long as the letter and included a description of the last days of Richardson:

Mr Richardson *vivit adhuc et vescitur aura aetherea*; but that hand, which has so written as to touch every heart, now so trembles that it can write no more. His years are drawing to an end, like a tale that is told – a tale which he can tell so very well. But he cannot wholly leave us; his *honest fame* defies the dart of Death.[21]

Five days later Richardson was dead, and one of the great influences on the German romantic movement had passed away. But Young still remained and his letters to Klopstock, Ebert, Stolberg and the rest were treated like relics.[e] Cramer had

---

[d] Two of the Stolbergs' sons became poets, but not Magnus.

[e] Even before Young's death one of his letters to Klopstock was published in J. C. Stockhausen's *Sammlung vermischter Briefe*, Part Two, Helmstädt, 1762 (2nd edition).

hailed him as 'a genius far sublimer than Milton and of all
human beings the nearest to David and the prophets';[22] and
there were other admirers besides those mentioned by Ebert,
like Lessing who called the *Nights* 'this masterpiece of one of the
sublimest poets',[23] or Wieland who said Young 'rises to the plane
of the very angels',[24] or the youthful Goethe who used the *Nights*
as his English reader. It was the fashion for all the rising poets to
'youngise', so much so that a reaction set in and Nicolai in 1761
reproached them for flocking weakly after a single genius; in the
last decade they were all revelling in anacreontic songs, but now
Young had come and all were full of complaint. There was a
constant battle of the reviews between the classical school of
Gottsched and the pioneers of the *Sturm und Drang* movement,
and the name of Young was a battle-cry of the romantics in
Europe even before he died.

Such tributes were perhaps some comfort to the poet in his
personal troubles – illness, the quarrel with his son, the loss of
Richardson and increasing worry over his curate. On 3
September, 1761 John Jones wrote to Spence:

> I have many times wondered why you never called upon
> us again at Welwyn. Dr Young, I am sure, would have been
> glad to have seen you and will still be so, every time you pass
> through this little hamlet. He told me lately that if he could
> see you, he would, or at least can, furnish you with ample
> materials ... relating to the life of his late friend, Mr
> Richardson, the poetical prose-writer.[25]

Jones ended with a hint of the trouble that was to burst into a
crisis the following year, 'God knows how long I shall continue at
Welwyn. . . . Please tell me privately in a letter if you can, upon
occasion, recommend a proper successor.' The curate had been
getting more and more dissatisfied with his situation at Welwyn.
Before taking up the curacy four years earlier he had bargained
for a free horse, free absence and no weekday services; he
wanted to be free to travel around as he wished. But it was not
working out, and on 2 April, 1760 he had prepared a formal
memorandum for submission to the Rector, reminding him of
these points, plus his promise to defray the cost of the carriage
of Jones's books to Welwyn, a hint of 'alleviation in the matter of
income, as this place is excessively dear', and grateful

remembrance of his declaration that 'whether he should live or die, I should find him my friend'.[26] Next day he noted that the Doctor had read the memorandum and 'allowed the whole to be very just, and returned the paper to me to keep'.[27] This kept Jones quiet for eighteen months, but by September, 1761 he was becoming restive again, especially as the old man was less and less able to take any part in the parish duties. The Rector's last signature in the vestry minutes was on 9 July, 1761,[28] after which the meetings were presided over by the local squire, Charles Gardiner of Lockleys.[f]

Another tribute, which probably pleased the poet more than all the paeans of Germany, came in October when his old friend Dodington sent him the draft of a poetical *Epistle to the Earl of Bute* for criticism and correction. Dodington had benefited like Young from the change of sovereign and the rise of Lord Bute, and in April he had at last been rewarded for his services to the Prince of Wales with the title of Baron Melcombe Regis. The *Epistle* was to be his public expression of gratitude to Bute and on 6 October Young replied that he was 'pleased and proud' to be given the task of correction and he sent his 'fancied amendments',[29] which were mainly verbal or metrical changes to improve the sense or rhythm or to heighten the effect.[g] Melcombe followed up with an ode, beginning 'Love thy country, wish it well',[h] and on 27 October he wrote from Hammersmith:

> You seemed to like the Ode I sent you for your amusement; I now send it you as a present. If you please to accept of it and are willing our friendship should be known when we are gone, you will be pleased to leave this among those of your papers which may possibly see the light by a posthumous publication. God send us health while we stay, and an easy journey.[30]

With this he enclosed a short verse epistle with the heading, *Lord Melcombe to his Friend, Dr Young:*[i]

[f] Gardiner was the son-in-law of Edward Searle, who died in 1743.

[g] The *Epistle* was not published till 1776, when Beckett printed it with an advertisement stating that the original MS, with Young's corrections, could be inspected at his shop. The printed copy shows Melcombe's original words in italics with Young's amendments as footnotes.

[h] Printed in the *Oxford Book of English Verse* under the title 'Shorten Sail'.

[i] In January, 1763 Young sent copies of these verses and the *Ode* to the Duchess of Portland as a New Year present, explaining that they were sent to him by Lord Melcombe 'scarce a month before his death'. (Pettit, 565.) Actually it was nine months before Melcombe trod the gloomy path; and the verses to Young had already been printed in the *Public Advertiser* on 23 August, 1762.

> Kind companion of my youth,
> Loved for genius, worth and truth,
> Take what friendship can impart,
> Tribute of a feeling heart.
> Take the Muse's latest spark,
> E'er we drop into the dark.
> He who parts and virtue gave
> Bade thee look beyond the grave:
> Genius soars and virtue guides
> Where the love of God presides.
> There's a gulf 'twixt us and God;
> Let the gloomy path be trod.
> Why stand shivering on the shore?
> Why not boldly venture o'er?
> Where unerring virtue guides,
> Let us brave the winds and tides.
> Safe through seas of doubts and fears
> Rides the bark which virtue steers.[31]

On 29 October Young replied to his 'dear and honoured Lord':

> The verses I sent you on Resignation were not designed
> for the public; but I find they are got into hands which will
> publish them when they dare, and I may not long keep
> them in awe. I will therefore publish it myself and to that
> end I have altered it much . . . Now the question, my Lord,
> is if the striking verses you are so kind as to have written to
> me might not with sufficient propriety be prefixed. I think
> there *happens* to be a peculiar propriety in it, considering
> the similar contents of both.[32]

Resignation was evidently proving popular enough to be worth pirating, even though it had not served its prime purpose, as he told the Duchess on 18 October that he was receiving 'very melancholy letters from my poor patient Mrs Boscawen, by which I find that I mistook my talent when I set up for a physician'.[33] But in the end the revised and enlarged edition did not appear till May, 1762, as the poet was seriously ill that winter. On 28 February, 1762 he told George Keate that he was 'just creeping out' after a long fever and thanked him for the present of his *Epistle from Lady Jane Grey to Lord Guilford Dudley*, which he found 'of the cordial kind and I think I am the better for it'.[34] A fortnight later he reported with wry humour to the Duchess:

I have been long ill, and since I see such numbers in this pretty severe season drop around me, a great blessing is it that I am still alive. I have made, Madam, a winter's campaign in my chamber; fought a long fever, which drew much blood from me; the physician stood by and saw the battle, and sometimes took part with the disease, though he had a subsidy from me . . . Fever and rheumatism are to me as formidable as France and Spain.[35]

At last, on 25 May,[36] the new public edition of *Resignation* was brought out anonymously by W. Owen and proved to be much longer than its predecessor. Whereas the private edition had consisted of five parts totalling 265 quatrains,[j] the 1762 version contained a total of 410 verses, though divided into only two parts and a postscript. But though he had added half as much again to the number of verses, it was mostly repetitive variations on his favourite theme of affliction as a blessing in disguise, sent to prepare us more readily to quit this world for the next.[k] *Resignation* was just another version of this argument and thus of no great value for what it said, and even less for how he said it, compared with the *Night Thoughts*. In spite of his recent denunciation of rhyme in the *Conjectures* he chose rhymed quatrains – the metre of the hymns of Tate and Addison – for his next, and last, poetical effort. It was the same mistake as he had made with his 'naval lyrics'; he took a metre suitable for a short song of praise and used it for a long reflective poem, with inevitably deflating effect. *Resignation* was generally regarded as (to quote the *Monthly Review* for June) 'a striking instance of the senescence of genius', and the critic, John Langhorne, went on:

The sentiments indeed are still characteristic of their author, but most of them are to be found in his *Night Thoughts* . . . The style also is like that of Dr Y——, but the resemblance is rather in its blemishes than its beauties.

[j] The title-page mentions a 'Funeral Epithalamium, occasioned by a new Marriage Act'; but this consists of eleven verses in Part III, containing an elaborate comparison of death to 'second nuptials'.

[k] On 27 May, 1762 Young repeated this advice to the Duchess of Portland, whose husband had died on 1 May: 'Of all the severe dispensations with which a good God is pleased to wean our affections from those objects which can never satisfy them, the most severe is the loss of those we love.' To judge by Young's next letter, on 1 June, the Duchess was more successful than Mrs Boscawen in practising resignation. (Pettit, 554; 556.)

> Here is the same fondness for antitheses and pointed
> expression, the same hunting down of figures and lowness
> of metaphors, . . . but little of their strength or harmony
> remains. He has also been unhappy in the choice of his
> metre. The Lyric Muse has always been unfavourable to
> him and to attempt her easy measures at this time of life was .
> an unfortunate determination.[37]

Only one critic ever disagreed with this verdict, but he was none
less than Dr Johnson:

> His last poem was the *Resignation*, in which he made, as he
> was accustomed, an experiment of a new mode of writing
> and succeeded better than in his *Ocean* or his *Merchant*. It
> was very falsely represented as a proof of decaying
> faculties. There is Young in every stanza, such as he often
> was in his highest vigour.[38]

There is indeed Young in every stanza, but it is not Young at
his best. Sometimes he even outdoes his worst:

> How proud the poet's billow swells!
>   The God! the God! his boast.
> A boast how vain! What wrecks abound!
>   Dead bards stench every coast.[39]

But while there is no particular merit in the content or form of
the poem, it remains interesting for the poet's comments on his
friends. First, the death of Richardson:

> Now need I, Madam, your support –
>   How exquisite the smart,
> How critically timed the news
>   Which strikes me to the heart! . . .
>
> When Heaven would kindly set us free
>   And earth's enchantment end,
> It takes the most effectual means
>   And robs us of a friend.[40]

The novelist's qualities were then summarized:

> To touch our passions' secret springs
>   Was his peculiar care;
> And deep his happy genius dived
>   In bosoms of the fair.

> Nature, which favours to the few
>   All art beyond imparts,
> To him presented at his birth
>   The key of human hearts.[41]

There were several compliments to Mrs Montagu and the phenomenon of feminine intellect challenging the supremacy of the male:

> The fruit of knowledge, golden fruit,
>   That once forbidden tree,
> Hedged in by surly man, is now
>   To Britain's daughters free.
>
> In Eve, we know, of fruit so fair
>   The noble thirst began,
> And they, like her, have caused a fall,
>   A fall of fame in man;
>
> And since of genius in our sex,
>   O Addison, with thee
> The sun is set, how I rejoice
>   This sister lamp to see![42]

And there was Young's last fling at his old sparring-partner, Voltaire, whose *Candide*, published in 1759, had provoked much indignation among the poet's circle:

> In youth, Voltaire, our foibles plead
>   For some indulgence due;
> Where heads are white, their thoughts and aims
>   Should change their colour too . . .
>
> What though your muse has nobly soared,
>   Is that our true sublime?
> Ours, hoary friend, is to prefer
>   Eternity to time.
>
> Why close a life so justly famed
>   With such bold trash as this?
> This for renown? Yes, such as makes
>   Obscurity a bliss.
>
> Your trash, with mine at open war,
>   Is obstinately bent,
> Like wits below, to sow your tares
>   Of gloom and discontent . . .

> Your works in our divided minds
>   Repugnant passions raise;
> Confound us with a double stroke;
>   We shudder whilst we praise.
>
> A curious web, as finely wrought
>   As genius can inspire,
> From a black bag of poison spun,
>   With horror we admire.
>
> Mean as it is, if this is read
>   With a disdainful air,
> I can't forgive so great a foe
>   To my dear friend Voltaire.
>
> Early I knew him, early praised,
>   And long to praise him late;
> His genius greatly I admire,
>   Nor would deplore his fate.[43]

Further on comes a passage that illustrates one of Young's greatest weaknesses; he would strike on a brilliant metaphor and then run it to death. The second of these stanzas is deliciously absurd, especially when it is realized that he is still addressing Voltaire:

> O how disordered our machine
>   When contradictions mix!
> When nature strikes no less than twelve
>   And folly points at six.[1]
>
> To mend the movements of your heart,
>   How great is my delight!
> Gently to wind your morals up
>   And set your hand aright.[44]

Just about the time of the publication of *Resignation* a different kind of resignation was troubling the poet. In February John Jones had fallen ill and, feeling 'the duty and confinement here to be too much',[45] he warned the Doctor that he would have to resign at Michaelmas. On 27 May he sent a formal letter

---

[1] This is a repetition of an image in *Night V*, 633–5:
>   Though grey our heads, our thoughts and aims are green;
>   Like damaged clocks, whose hand and bell dissent,
>   Folly sings six while nature points at twelve.

(Mitford, I, 96.)

reaffirming his decision because of his state of health and 'the unpromising aspect of some of my affairs'.[46] On 26 June he wrote to Birch that the Rector was in difficulties over finding a successor, 'for which reason he is at last, he says, resolved to advertise and even (which is much wondered at) to raise the salary considerably higher'.[47] £50 a year was the sum proposed, whereas Jones's predecessors, and he himself, had been content with £20. 'I never asked him to raise it for *me*,' added the curate virtuously, 'though I well knew it was not equal to the duty.' Finally, in a postscript, Jones gave the first veiled hint of personal objections to his master:

> I may mention . . . that in all likelihood the poor old gentleman will not find it a very easy matter, unless by dint of money and force upon himself, to procure a man that he can like for his next curate, nor one that will stay with him as long as I have done. Then his great age will recur to people's thoughts; and if he has foibles either in temper or conduct, they will sure not be forgotten on this occasion by those who know him, and those who do not will probably be upon guard.[48]

His next letter to Birch, on 25 July, was more open:

> The old gentleman here . . . seems to me to be in a pretty odd way of late, moping, dejected, self-willed and as if surrounded with some perplexing circumstances. Though I visit him pretty frequently for short intervals, I say very little to his affairs, not choosing to be a party concerned, especially in cases of so critical and tender a nature. There is much mystery in almost all his temporal affairs as well as in many of his speculative opinions. Whoever lives in this neighbourhood to see his exit will probably see and hear of some very strange things – time will show – I am afraid not greatly to his credit.[49]

He then went on with his cryptic words about the two 'irremovable obstructions' to the old man's happiness within and without his walls and added, 'He has this day been trying anew to engage me to stay with him. No lucrative views can tempt me to sacrifice my liberty or my health to such measures as are proposed here. Nor do I like to have to do with persons whose word and honour cannot be depended on. So much for this very odd and unhappy topic.'[50]

But in fact that was by no means all that Jones had to say about the topic – to himself. He had the habit of jotting down his thoughts on odd scraps of paper, the backs of book catalogues and such, and what is more, of keeping them; and these are still preserved with his other papers in Dr Williams' Library. Among them is a paper headed 'Some farther and more private reasons why I dó not choose to continue longer upon this C. of W.'[51] After mentioning the reasons given in his letter of 27 May he went on to 'add the following little mementos for my own satisfaction', in which he really let his sense of grievance go. The first section was concerned with the terms of their original agreement, i.e. (1) breach of several promises, viz. assistance in the discharge of duty, and supplies in absence; (2) weekday services not dropped and not performed by the Rector, 'though it is too well known that hardly any, or but very few, come to church on those days'; (3) the promise of a horse long forgotten; (4) 'In consideration of the dearness of the place &c., encouragements were given to me to come often to partake of the civilities of his table, being always welcome [he said] whenever I should come, with more such fair words, &c. (But I have long seen what such words they are come to; and their housekeeping is well known. Which is all I need say farther.)'

However, this was not the worst. As the prickly Mr Jones brooded over his grievances, his notes, mildly headed 'Certain qualities and circumstances not agreeable', became almost hysterical with the frenzy of secret denunciation:

> An haughty and imperious disposition – s[urli]ness and pride – high opinion of one's own worth and writings – expectations of great reverence and deference to be paid on that account – and impatience even of different judgement, much more of contradiction, &c. – disregard of others – making every aim and action centre in self – disregard to *truth*, *justice* and *common honesty* in many instances – unfair, mean, sneaking dealings, too obviously discerned and frequently complained of by many. And *real dues* not paid, nor promises kept – unless accidentally signed, &c. These and like things are reckoned infamous and are everywhere exploded. – Amazing parsimony and penuriousness – almost to a proverb. Addicted often to whims and humours – self-willed; obstinate in many cases to a great degree – addicted also (as I am well informed) to very bad language in his passions; and those passions are not infrequent – known to be addicted to

strong resentments; to bear a long grudge, and show it when
he can. Of a revengeful and unforgiving temper. Very
domineering over his inferiors.[52]

And finally, having filled his sheet, Jones continued up the
margin:

> A narrow contracted way of thinking – stiff and formal –
> affected grandeur, but attended with mean actions –
> morose; reserved; crafty.[53]

Under a third heading of 'Some unaccountable incivilities very
difficult to be borne'[54] the curate listed messages sent by the
Parish Clerk (one of Jones's *bêtes noires*) and such vague charges as
'disregard', 'inhumanity' and 'downright incivility and ill-
breeding'. But he got into his stride again over Mrs Hallows:

> The frantic qualities and behaviours of Mopsa (her
> unaccountable starts and whims, her insufferable imperti-
> nences, her continual intrusions, her conceited airs, her
> unbecoming pride, vanity, levity, &c, all the subject of
> common ridicule and contempt) might likewise be added;
> only that she is below notice. Yet wilful and unmannerly
> affronts cannot well be borne from such hands – nor even
> from the D. himself, though he should, as usual, take her
> part.[55]

The diatribe ended weakly with the note that 'many other things
might be added' and that he had thought of this for several years;
and a last scribble along the margin tilted at the 'disorderly parish
– many bad old customs and practices, &c – continual feuds and
contentions, &c'.[56]

Such were the bitter thoughts of John Jones on the night of 26
July, 1762.[57] In two months he would have to leave Welwyn, and
he had nowhere to go. Bolnehurst was too damp in winter and he
was thinking of taking a cottage somewhere near – and he actually
did rent one at Eynesbury at £6 a year. He was frantically trying
to convince himself that he was right to resign and that the
conditions at Welwyn were intolerable, especially with 'that
known artist in deceit Mrs. ————' asserting that the curacy,
with its furnished house, was worth £50. His Rectory at
Bolnehurst was only worth £9 p.a., and there was no doubt that he
was more secure at Welwyn. And so, when it came to the point, in
spite of all the alleged defects of the Rector's character, Jones was

prevailed upon to stay. On 13 August Young, after several rejections, applied once more to his curate, who noted, 'I think I must after all comply with his repeated applications'.[58] That evening he argued it out with himself on paper in a memorandum of 'Pro & Con';[59] and next day[60] he wrote to Young, promising to continue if his superior would alleviate his difficulties, including the expenses of the newly-rented house at Eynesbury. Five days later he recorded that the Doctor, after reading the minute of his difficulties, 'was pleased of his own accord to appoint my future salary to be at the rate of £45 a year',[61] plus payment of the Eynesbury rent.

So ended the great crisis of the curacy and from then on, despite his employer's faults and the frantic qualities of Mopsa, Jones remained with Young till the old man's death. To judge from the wide variety of addresses in his subsequent letters to Birch[62] and the number of other signatures in the Welwyn registers, he also won his point about absence and supplies; his doubled salary did not involve more assiduous duty. It is not surprising therefore that his next letter, dated 28 August, should have a triumphant, though still self-righteous, tone:

> How are matters altered since my letter to you . . . of the 25th past! You remember that I suggested to you about my resolution of leaving Welwyn, of which I had given very early notice to the worthy Doctor, that he might have sufficient time to provide. After repeated trials and repeated disappointments, though seven or eight offered, he thought proper to apply to me anew; and though lucrative motives could not, earnest importunities did, prevail with me at last to cheer up his dejected heart by promising to continue with him for some time longer at least, although my necessary measures in respect to other affairs are hereby disconcerted. But compassion and humanity will, I hope, ever dwell in my breast. By the way, I privately intimated to you that the Doctor is in various respects a very unhappy man. Few know so much as I do in these respects and have often observed with concern. If he would be advised by some that wish him well, he might yet be happy, though his state of health is lately much altered for the worse.[63]

How seriously should we take Jones's hostile dissection of Young's character in his secret denunciation of 26 July? Jones was

a querulous and quarrelsome Welshman with a 'chip on his
shoulder'; his autobiography is full of his clashes with his
parishioners at Alconbury and Bolnehurst, and his later
correspondence with Young's successor is described in the
catalogue of Dr Williams' Library as 'interesting and explosive'.[64]
It was inevitable that during his five and a half years as curate to
an aged and eccentric poet he should fall foul of his employer,
and still more of the housekeeper who was, according to Kidgell,
the terror of the curates. But, unlike Kidgell, who laughed at
Young's foibles and reserved his gall for Mrs Hallows, Jones
made a personal attack on the poet himself. About the only point
on which the two curates agreed was Young's parsimony.
Otherwise Jones's picture of the arrogant, dishonest, angry,
obstinate, selfish, unforgiving, domineering and crafty Young is
utterly opposed to Kidgell's benevolent, honourable, gentle,
changeable, patient, compassionate and impractical cleric. Had
Young's temper changed so much in the intervening seven years?
He was both ill and unhappy at the time, and age, infirmity and
distress at the breach with his son doubtless increased the
irritability mentioned by his servant, Tom Wells. Jones was clearly
an irritating man and his squabbling with Mrs Hallows would
touch a particularly sore and sensitive spot. But the charges of
dishonesty and incivility probably arose more from Young's
absent-mindedness and Jones's touchiness than from any
intentional craftiness or arrogance.

Once Jones got his rise, his ire was remarkably soothed and the
tone of his letter to Birch on 4 September was quite changed:

> My ancient gentleman here is still full of trouble, which
> moves my concern, though it moves only the secret laughter
> of many and some untoward surmises in disfavour of him
> and his household. The loss of a very large sum of money[m] is
> talked of, whereof this vill and neighbourhood is full. Some
> disbelieve, others say it is no wonder, where about eighteen
> or more servants are sometimes taken and dismissed in the
> course of a year. The gentleman himself is allowed by all to
> be far more harmless and easy in his family than someone
> else, who hath too much the lead in it.[65]

[m] A marginal note says 'Above £200'. Pettit notes that Gosling's Bank sent
Young £500 in 24 banknotes on 2 September. (Pettit, 561, n. 1.)

Now the curate became quite devoted, and on 1 January, 1763 he declared himself unwilling to desert his 'ancient gentleman', even though the confinement was greater than in any other parish of which he had had the care. But he could not help complaining:

> The mismanagement too well known unhappily continues and, still more unhappily, seems to be increasing, to the grief of friends and, I need not add, to the ridicule of others, who are not a few. What a pity! what a loss! But no advice will be taken, nor can it well be offered. Penuriousness and obstinacy are two bad things; and a disregard to the general judgment and friendly wishes of the wiser part of mankind, another. There seems to be no hope as long as the ascendency is so great.[66]

Young himself was now 'harmless and easy', while the blame was laid on Mrs Hallows; and this accords with the Kidgell version. Jones's outburst against the poet, which after all was not a considered verdict nor intended for others' eyes, may, I think, be dismissed as an exaggerated and reckless product of self-justification, a desperate defence of his own misjudgement, a search for causes of offence to bolster up his case for resignation, about which he was having serious doubts. While Young may not have been the saint pictured by Mrs Montagu, no one except this excitable and petulant Welshman ever accused him of such grave faults. Poor Mrs Hallows, on the other hand, really does seem to have had some unamiable qualities, as far as her inferiors and dependents were concerned. Though we must credit her with the excellent impression she made on all the visitors to Guessens, she quarrelled with both Kidgell and Jones and, it seems all too likely, with Frederick. But it was too late for anyone to contest the ascendency now. Resignation, in one sense or the other, was the only answer – to resign from the household, like Frederick, or to resign himself to it, like Mr Jones.

CHAPTER 20

The Dregs of Life
1762–1765

With the publication of *Resignation* Young's fifty-year career as an author came at last to a close at the age of 79. He believed himself even older and on 25 November, 1762, in reply to a letter and poem from his old friend Thomas Newcomb,[a] he wrote:

> My dear old friend,
> And now my only dear old friend, for your namesake Colborn is dead . . . I am pleased with the stanzas you sent me; there is nothing in them of *eighty-seven* . . . As for my own health, I do not love to complain; but one particular I must tell you, that my sight is so far gone as to lay me under the necessity of borrowing a hand to write this. God grant me grace under this darkness to see more clearly things invisible and eternal, those great things which you and I must soon be acquainted with. And why not rejoice at it? There is not a day of my long life that I desire to repeat, and at fourscore it is all *labour and sorrow*.[1]

And he added in a postscript, 'I am persuaded that you are mistaken as to your age; you write yourself eighty-seven, which cannot be the case; for I always thought myself older than you, and I want considerably of that age.' Five weeks later, writing to the Duchess on 2 January, 1763, he began with the words, 'As a person of eighty-three',[2] and this seems to have been the general belief as to his age, for his curate spoke of him the following year as 'about 84'.[3]

Among all the 'labour and sorrow' his growing blindness was a

[a] The friendship of Young and Newcomb began in 1703 at Corpus Christi College, Oxford, and survived the misunderstanding with Curll in 1717. Newcomb, a tireless versifier, frequently imitated or paraphrased Young, e.g. 1723, *The Last Judgment*; 1732, a series of satires on *The Manners of the Age* (the first dedicated to Young); 1757, *Mr Hervey's Contemplations, done into blank verse after the manner of Dr Young*; 1760, *The Retired Penitent, being a poetical version of Dr Young's Moral Contemplations* (i.e. the *Centaur*) published, according to the title-page, 'with the consent of that learned and eminent writer'.

source of special distress and his letters are full of references to it. On 24 August, 1762 he complained to the Duchess of 'dark days and sleepless nights',[4] explaining that his rheumatism had gone but his head and eyes were affected instead. To Keate he elaborated:

> Rheumatic pains of thirty years standing are entirely ceased, and have been so for half a year. The fatal consequence of which is that the malignity is fallen on my head and eyes, for which I have long undergone, and still undergo, severe discipline, and to very little purpose.[5]

'Books, my wonted refuge,' he told Keate on 2 December, 'are of no further use – *And wisdom at one entrance quite shut out*';[6] and on 4 January, 1763 he lamented his 'utter aversion to pen and ink'.[7] Yet, thanks to Mrs Hallows, who read and wrote for him, he continued to keep up a brisk correspondence on literary matters and the latest news. Though so many of his oldest friends were dying off – Richardson in 1761 and Colborn the following winter, the Duke of Portland on 1 May, 1762 and Dodington on 28 July – his letter-bag was still full. But now that reading was so difficult, company was all the more important and he was specially gratified by a visit in August, 1762[8] from the new young Duke of Portland, whom he had known since infancy, and from his new friend Keate in the late autumn.

Despite his infirmities his mind was as lively as ever and his friendship for Mrs Montagu did not inhibit him from criticizing her choice of Sunday evenings for her *conversaziones*, 'for religion has not met with greater enemies from any quarter than from philosophers, politicians and wits'.[9] He managed to read the poems which Keate regularly submitted to him,[b] and on 24 March, 1763 he wrote of the younger poet's latest offering, a blank verse description of *The Alps*, 'I like the poem much in general for the novelty of its subject and variety in its composition.'[10] Keate then proposed to dedicate it to the Doctor, who replied on 14 April that he was 'too vain to make any objection to it, but not so very vain as not to thank you for it'.[11] The poem was duly published by Dodsley in a handsome quarto with a large vignette of Swiss heroes on the title-page and an

[b] On 27 February, 1763 Young also acknowledged another offering from the eccentric Mr Elphinston, a poem on *Education*. (Pettit, 570.)

inscription to the 'genius, learning and virtues'[12] of Young. Though hardly inspired, it was not an inappropriate tribute to the leader of the revolt against classicism; at a time when the Alps were still generally regarded as 'horrid', the subject was, as Young said, novel and romantic.

The tone of his letters in the spring of 1763 suggests that his health and spirits were improving. On 14 April he was 'pretty well, but suspect myself to be a little older than I was';[13] and on 3 May he elaborated in his old whimsical manner:

> As to my health it is not so good as I could wish, but better than I ought to expect; it is so good as to demand my utmost thanks to God that 'tis no worse, but not so good as not to want a cordial under it, and I know of none more powerful than that which refreshes us from the face of a friend.[14]

But on 1 June he told Ebert that his sight was so bad that he could examine nothing, 'and if it was not, so bad at present is my health that I can attend to nothing'.[15] Nevertheless, the rest of the letter showed that his interest in books and writers was still keen and active:

> The late Earl of Granville, who was a perfect master of your tongue, having heard that you had translated the first part of the *Night Thoughts*, desired it of me and highly approved of your performance. I am obliged to you for translating the *Resignation*. I am sorry I did not furnish you with something more worthy such a patronage. . . . I will take care that Abbé Arnaud's character of my dear friend Mr Richardson shall be prefixed to his Works. Mr Warton's second part of *Pope* is in great readiness[c] and I believe you may see it soon.[16]

In July he was strong enough to venture to Tunbridge Wells, for the last time, and on the 19th[17] he told the Duchess, who had invited him to join her at Buxton, that he proposed to stay till the end of the season to treat his want of rest and appetite. But unfortunately Tunbridge did not answer that year. The weather was like the old days – 'much rain' – but not the social life – 'little company, no person of quality but Lady Abercorn'.[18] By 11

---

[c] In the event Part II of Warton's *Essay on Pope* did not appear till 1782.

September he was back at Welwyn, writing to Keate that he had all the infirmities of age 'and among others my sight is near gone, which troubles me, I fear, more than it ought to do'.[19] Even the short excursion to Lord Bute's new seat at Luton Hoo, nine miles away, was beyond him now and on 7 November[20] he wrote to excuse his failure to call, owing to the badness of his sight, on the patron who had obtained his preferment.[d] He did not leave Welwyn again.

As the last full year of the poet's life opened, Jones began to look around for other livings in view of the Doctor's great age, though he did not intend to leave him till his death. Young's treatment of him was now much appreciated and on 15 January, 1764 the curate wrote: 'The Doctor has thanked me for what I have done here, as others have done elsewhere. I overdid myself one summer here by instructing three times on Sundays.'[21] But he still wished to be free on weekdays and complained to Birch on 28 January that he could not get away:

> The whole duty of the parish here rests now upon my hands; the Doctor not being able to do any one thing therein; as neither has he for about two years past.[22]

Yet Jones was away on 23 February,[23] when the Rector of Datchworth stepped into the breach to perform a marriage in Welwyn; and on the 29th[24] he wrote from the Queen's Head in Gray's Inn Lane. Other letters of 1764[25] reveal the curate at Lincoln in July, Cambridge in August and Huntingdonshire in October; so the confinement cannot really have been too bad. He was now devoted to the Doctor. According to an account by one whose family spent some months at Welwyn in the summer of 1764 and knew Jones well, the curate 'usually spent two hours every evening with Dr Young in useful conversation and in reading to relieve Mrs Hallows (the good doctor's housekeeper), whose eyes were much impaired by constant reading'.[26] The readings doubtless included the latest offerings of the irrepressible Keate, which always had a cheering effect on the old man, though the present that he acknowledged on 12 February sounds more like a cheese than a poem:

---

[d] Bute resigned from the Premiership on 8 April, 1763 and finally retired from court on 28 September.

You seem to make me a king by your animal tribute. For two or three months I shall lay it up in my exchequer, of which I shall make my cat Chancellor, otherwise the rats will rebel and show that I have a very limited monarchy over them. They are of Wilkes's party, and I wish they were as far off. But I submit to my fate, for why should Edward's reign be less disturbed than George's? And why should rats be more loyal than men?

And now what is this kind of writing? It may be called the smile of the pen, to let you know that its master can fight age and infirmity and endeavour with Anacreon.

> Of little life the most to make
> And manage wisely the last stake.[27]

The jokes, perhaps, were not brilliant, but they were brave – and topical. In fact Young's failing sight seemed paradoxically to bring him closer to the daily world by making him read newspapers rather than books, and his last letters were full of sarcastic references to politics and politicians, Wilkes and the 'busy Duke' of Newcastle, rising prices and the newspapers themselves, which show that the satirist in him was by no means dead.

In March Keate sent Young some pre-Miltonic verses, together with the news that he was preparing for publication his elegy on the ruins of Netley Abbey near Southampton, an exercise in the increasingly fashionable style of melancholy and romantic scenery. This drew from Young some general reflections on the nature and practice of poetry:

Milton might possibly take his hint from the verses which you was so kind to send me; but there is a great difference between the beauty of the root and the flower that springs from it. You say this spring has produced nothing very considerable from the press. Every spring produces daisy authors, which true taste treads underfoot; but it is well if genius, like the aloes, vouchsafes to blossom once in fifty years. You say that your work has laid for some time dormant by you; that is not amiss, for by that means the fondness of a parent hardens into the impartiality of a judge, which is more a friend to the maturity of composition. After a sound nap your *Netley Abbey* may gather strength and vivacity and, though it went to sleep in perfect health, yet should I be glad to see what change is made in it.[28]

Encouraged, Keate sent the poem to him for his remarks, and on 22 March the old poet returned it with 'a few hints, possibly all wrong', adding, 'The melancholy cast and the moral tendency of the whole . . . have charms for me.'[29] But his suggestions were too late. By 3 April he had received the published version and, not at all put out, he sent his thanks:

> I take for granted that the hints I gave you were wrong. However, I should be glad to dispute with you on that point or on any other, provided Welwyn be the field of battle, the custom of which place is that the vanquished shall divide the smile with the conqueror and by that means, though demolished, in some measure to shine, like your Netley Abbey, in ruins.[30]

Meanwhile Young had been hoping for a visit not only from Keate but from the Duchess herself. On 13 March, 1764 he thanked her 'for the great honour you design me; . . . few pleasures are equal to seeing the face of those whom we know to wish us well'.[31] But on 28 June he was still 'disappointed in my hope' and expressed the wish that, if she were to repeat her last year's journey to Buxton, she would 'look on it as a point of curiosity to see one of the last age that is still alive'.[32] He ended this letter with a hit at the newspapers:

> The nature of a letter requires that I should now tell your Grace some news, but news is not the growth of the country. Indeed, if I would take the example of the public papers, I need not be silent on this head; but as venturing on lies would be evidently invading their peculiar property, I will content myself with the strictest truth, by assuring you that I am, with my whole heart, Your Grace's ever devoted and most obedient humble servant.[33]

Doctors were another of his favourite butts. In his letter of 7 August he rejoiced at the Duchess's recovery of health and spirits 'and that you have recovered them by the most pleasant as well as most effectual means, that is, by driving away from your physician as fast and as far as you can; which is the most likely way of leaving your disorder too behind you'.[34] As for his own health, he reported that he was suffering no severe pains, but had little appetite by day and very indifferent rest by night; and his eyes were growing worse and worse. But at least this time he had some news for her:

> This last week one Mr Keate of the Temple, an author both in prose and verse, favoured me with a visit for two or three days and told me that some little time ago he had the honour of dining with Mrs Montagu with about ten more, all or most of them writers; that the entertainment was very elegant, and that a celebrated Welsh harp added music to their wit.[35]

Apart from his eyes the poet's complaints – insomnia and lack of appetite – were the same as for the last twenty-five years and there was no particular reason to suppose that the end might be drawing near. But his will, written nearly five years before, was already partly out of date with the deaths of legatees like Richardson and Mrs Ward, and on 17 September he added a codicil, mainly to ensure that its execution should be carried out without any lawsuits. He added some more names to his list for mourning rings (including the Duchess and Miss Nancy Richardson) and a supplementary legacy for Mrs Hallows, together with a special, final plea addressed to her personally:

> It is my dying request that you would see all writings whatever, whether in papers or books (except my book of accounts), burnt and destroyed as soon as I am dead.[36]

This was stronger than his previous request to his executors 'in a particular manner' to burn all his manuscript writings. That might have referred only to his own unpublished work, but his new instructions applied to the writings of others too, and his faithful housekeeper carried out his wishes all too faithfully. The result is that Young's correspondence is very one-sided; while we have a good number of the letters written *by* him, we have practically none written *to* him except those of Richardson, who kept copies. The loss to posterity, if he still had among his papers the letters not only of Lady Mary Wortley Montagu but of his other friends like Addison, Steele, Pope, Swift and the rest, is sad to contemplate. But Young seems to have been determined that his death should be accompanied by as little as possible in the way of the posthumous vanities of the world.

But still he lived on, while his friends fell all around him. On 7 October he wrote to Keate:

On opening your letter I was pleased to find that I had still one friend on this side of the grave. Of late I have lost so very many that I began to doubt it. Poor Dodsley! But why poor? Let us give him joy of his escape.

> None would live past years again,
> Yet all hope pleasure in what yet remain,
> And from the dregs of life hope to receive
> What the first sprightly runnings could not give.
> I'm tired of waiting for this chymic gold,
> Which fools us young and beggars us when old.   (Dryden)

When Mrs Gataker told me that Dodsley had his doubts as to Christianity, an argument for it occurred to me, which is not to be found, I think, in writers on that subject. As it is but short, and to me most convincing, I will tell you what it is: first, such is the nature of Christianity that the plan of it could not possibly have entered into the mind of man; secondly, if it had entered, it could not possibly have been received by mankind without a supernatural interposition in its favour.[37]

This was the same Young as he had always been; the defender of Christianity, thinking up new formulas to confound the doubters, as he had with Tindal at All Souls fifty years before; the moralist preaching that death is an escape to happiness, though personally grieved for his friend the publisher of the *Night Thoughts*; and the end of the letter showed him again as the champion of Shakespeare, whom he had praised in his first work, the *Epistle to Lord Lansdowne*, in 1713 and almost his last, the *Conjectures*, in 1759:

> As for Voltaire, I have not seen what you mention.[c] But as long as there is fear and pity in the heart of man, reading a page of Shakespeare will be a sufficient reply to what Voltaire can urge against him.[38]

Strangely, as 1765 began, rumour apparently reported the death not of the poet but his son. On 5 January the old man

---

[c] In 1764 Voltaire reprinted his *Appel à toutes les nations de l'Europe* as a treatise on English drama. This 'dissertation against the barbarous English', as he called it, was first published in 1761 as a reply to an article in the *Journal Encyclopédique*, comparing Shakespeare and Corneille to the latter's disadvantage, which Voltaire saw as a criticism of his own work. In 1776 Le Tourneur, the translator of Young, produced a translation of Shakespeare, which provoked an even more furious reaction from Voltaire in his *Lettre à l'Académie Française*.

appeared before a local Justice of the Peace to sign an affidavit in which he 'made oath that Mr Frederick Young, of Balliol College, Oxford, was living on the fifth day of January now last past'.[39] Such legal concern about Frederick's survival was presumably connected with his life annuity of £300, which he had perhaps failed to draw. But whatever the reason for it, the affidavit shows that his father knew where he was, and such other evidence as we have confirms that when Frederick finally walked out in August, 1762, he did not vanish from his father's ken. The corrector of Croft said he could 'well remember that during the misunderstanding with his own son, on being told of a lively remark made by him, the Doctor discovered both in words and manner the true pleasure of a father',[40] and Boswell's gossiping barber of Stevenage asserted that Frederick 'married the daughter of a clergyman in whose house he had lived and been supported during his father's displeasure'.[41] Actually Frederick married the daughter of a local squire, Giles Thornton Heysham, who was not only a neighbour and friend of his father but a trustee of the charity-school; so it is possible that, though the barber was mistaken about the profession of the father-in-law, the Heysham family did give him shelter. Mrs Hallows knew where to send for him to come to his father's deathbed, and it was certainly not far away.[f]

As the winter drew towards its end, Young had the pleasure of a visit from a surviving friend, Joseph Spence, who noted down some anecdotes with the date 'from Dr Young, Feb. 7–11, 1765'.[42] But while he enjoyed recounting his memories in company, he could not be bothered to put them on paper and he had pleaded ignorance or forgetfulness when, six months earlier, Thomas Percy had attempted to pump him for anecdotes for a new edition of the *Spectator*.[g] Even letters to his friends were an

[f] In 1816 a certain W. C. Dyer published an *Enquiry into the Moral Character of Dr Young* (G.M., LXXXVI, 511–14), in which he claimed to have known Frederick at this time, 'an unhappy wanderer, friendless and often I believe, almost penniless, but certainly *deficiente crumena*'. But Dyer's mistakes about Frederick's 'want of academical education', 'minor age' and so on, make the reliability of his memories somewhat suspect.

[g] Percy told Lord Hailes, 21 August, 1764: 'At present we are pumping the memory of Dr Young and other literati of the last age; but I am sorry to say that what is remembered bears but a small proportion to what is forgotten.' (*The Percy Letters*, Louisiana, 1954, 86.) Percy told Boswell, 26 March, 1772, 'he could not so much as say *Virgilium tantum vidi*, for that he had not seen him, but had one letter from him.'

effort nowadays, as is shown by one written to the Duchess on 19 February – the last surviving letter of his life:

> It is so long since I had the honour of writing to you that you may possibly look on this as a letter from the dead. But I am still above ground, though I can hardly venture to say that I am quite alive; the severe weather on Sunday night almost destroyed me. My being so long silent was not occasioned by disrespect, for I bear to your Grace the greatest, nor was it occasioned by want of power, for I bless God I am pretty well, nor was it occasioned by want of inclination, for I desire nothing more than to hear of your Grace's welfare. Whatever therefore was the cause of it, I beg your Grace to permit me now to enquire after your health and the health of all those who have the happiness of being related to, or of being esteemed by you . . . You was about to make a round of visits to several entitled to one or to both of the characters above. I hope you found and left them well, and brought home at your return an increase of health and satisfaction. Air and exercise are not greater friends to the former than the cheerful smiles of those we love are to the latter; and when is it more necessary to provide for our private satisfaction and peace than at a time when that of the public seems to be in some hazard of being impaired, if not lost? But what have I to do with the public affairs of this world? They are almost as foreign to me as to those who were born before the Flood. My world is dead; to the present world I am quite a stranger, so very much a stranger that I know but one person in it, and that is your Grace.[43]

Really, of course, he still had plenty of friends, new ones as well as old, and among them was the benevolent, pious and poetical physician of St Albans, Dr Nathaniel Cotton.[h] Dr Cotton ran a madhouse under the resounding title of the 'Collegium Insanorum', in which the poet William Cowper was at this time confined. Cowper, who had been there since 1763, was now well on the way to recovery and his treatment included religious conversation with his doctor. One of their subjects of conversation was the sage of Welwyn. On 12 July, 1765 Cowper told Lady Hesketh:

---

[h] Nathaniel Cotton (1705–88) settled at St Albans in 1740. The description of Young's last hours comes from a posthumous collection of *Various Pieces in Verse and Prose*, 1791.

Our mentioning Newton's *Treatise on the Prophecies*[i] brings
to my mind an anecdote of Dr Young . . . Dr Cotton, who
was intimate with him, paid him a visit about a fortnight
before he was seized with his last illness. The old man was
then in perfect health; the antiquity of his person, the
gravity of his utterance and the earnestness with which he
discoursed about religion gave him in the doctor's eye the
appearance of a prophet. They had been delivering their
sentiments upon this book of Newton, when Young closed
the conference thus: 'My friend, there are two considerations upon which my faith in Christ is built as upon a rock.
The fall of man, the redemption of man and the
resurrection of man, the three cardinal articles of our
religion, are such as human ingenuity could never have
invented, therefore they must be divine. The other
argument is this: if the prophecies have been fulfilled (of
which there is abundant demonstration), the Scripture
must be the word of God, and if the Scripture is the word of
God, Christianity must be true!'[44]

This meeting must have been early in March, for about 22
March Young was seized with the illness that at last conquered
his resistance. According to both Mrs Hallows and John Jones
his illness lasted about a fortnight and was extremely painful. Dr
Yate of Hertford was first called in, and three or four days later
Dr Cotton as well. Yet it was not for ten days that the old man
took to his bed and, if we may believe an unsupported anecdote,
his spirit and wit had not deserted him:

In his last illness, a friend mentioning the recent decease
of a person who had long been in a decline and observing
that he was quite worn down to a shell before he died, 'Very
likely,' replied the Doctor, 'but what is become of the
kernel?'[45]

Jones, who had been away in London, arrived back at Welwyn
on 1 April and wrote on the 2nd that Young 'took to his bed
yesterday about 11 in the forenoon and has not been up since'.[46]
It must have been at that stage that Mrs Hallows sent for
Frederick, who arrived on the morning of the 2nd. That day the

---

[i] This was the work of Thomas Newton (1704–82), Bishop of Bristol. The first
volume of his *Dissertation on the Prophecies*, showing how they had been or were
being fulfilled, came out in 1754, the second and third in 1758.

old man took a turn for the worse, while next day, Wednesday, the doctors gave up the case for lost. But the poet's constitution did not let him die for another two days. On Friday, 5 April, Good Friday 1765, the physicians took their leave at noon and Cotton went home to write a letter describing Young's last hours. That night, at some time between half past nine and eleven, the poet was at last granted a merciful release from his pains and escaped to the bliss that he had so often proclaimed.

Such are the bare bones of the sequence of events at Young's deathbed, of which we have four first-hand accounts, two written before the end and two after. The two former were the letters of Jones on 2 April and of Cotton on the 5th itself, and each adds some vivid details to the scene. First, John Jones:

> As soon as I got home I enquired after Dr Young and found that he had gone through very great pains since the time when I left him, and the pains return pretty frequently. Dr Cotton of St Albans and Dr Yate of Hertford meet at his house every day on consultation. But whatever they may think of his disorder and the probable consequences, little or nothing as yet transpires; only all that attend him constantly imagine there is little or no hope of his doing well again. For my own part I judged so from the beginning. I find that opiates are frequently administered to him, I suppose to render him the less sensible of his pain. His intellects, I am told, are still clear, though what effect the frequent use of opiates may by degrees have upon him I know not. I am pretty much of his son's sentiments as to this, viz. that those ingredients, if for some time longer continued, may have an ill effect upon the brain. Having mentioned this young gentleman, I would acquaint you next that he came hither this morning, having been sent for, as I am told, by the direction of Mrs Hallows. Indeed she intimated to me as much herself; and if this be so, I must say that it is one of the most prudent acts she ever did or could have done in such a case as this, as it may prove the means of preventing much confusion after the death of the Doctor. I have had some little discourse with the son; he seems much affected and I believe really is so. He earnestly wishes his father might be pleased to ask after him. For you must know he has not yet done this, nor is, in my opinion, like to do it. And it has been said farther that upon a late application made to him on the behalf of his son he desired

that no more might be said to him about it. How true this may be I cannot yet be certain. All I shall say is, it seems not improbable. Mrs Hallows has fitted up a suitable apartment in the house for Mr Young, where I suppose he will continue till some farther event. I heartily wish the ancient man's heart may grow tender towards his son; though, knowing him so well, I can scarce hope to hear such desirable news.[47]

Dr Cotton's description of the 'important scenes' that he had witnessed was written before he knew for certain of Young's death:

I was called to Welwyn. When I arrived there, I found Dr Yate waiting for me. It seems he had been sent for three or four days before my assistance was desired. Dr Young's disorder was attended with some obscurity. But on Tuesday matters wore a very discouraging aspect; and on Wednesday Yate and myself gave up the case as lost. From that period to the present Dr Young hath been dying. Whether the scene be closed this evening I cannot take upon me to say; but this day at noon the physicians took their leave. Dr Young, although in his eighty-sixth year, had disputed every inch of ground with death from the strength of his constitution, never impaired in early life by riot and debauchery. As I sat by his bedside, how earnestly did I wish the vital knot untied! . . . For long and painful agonizings of nature under her dissolution appear to me sufferings hardly inferior to some of the severest tortures of martyrdom . . . I was very fond of Dr Young's company and greatly venerated his mental abilities.[48]

The posthumous accounts were in letters from Mrs Hallows to George Keate, written about three weeks after, and from Jones again, the day after the funeral. Mrs Hallows's words do not add much to our knowledge but make her a more touching and sympathetic figure than was pictured by Kidgell and Jones. There is no doubt that she was genuinely devoted to her master, and he to her.

The particulars you desire [she wrote] will but add to your concern, as every recollection does to mine. But I comply in saying that the blessed gentleman passed a fortnight in some distressful circumstances and expired on Good Friday night half past nine without a groan – excuse me further, my tears prevent me.[49]

Jones's letter of 13 April is more important, for it authoritatively refutes the last traditional indictment of Young's character, the legend of his cruel and implacable treatment of his penitent son:

> The father on his deathbed, and since my return from London, was applied to in the tenderest manner by one of his physicians and by another person to admit the son into his presence to make submission, entreat forgiveness and obtain his blessing. As to an interview with his son he intimated that he chose to decline it, as his spirits were then low and his nerves weak. With regard to the next particular he said, 'I heartily forgive him'; and upon mention of the last he gently lifted up his hand and, letting it gently fall, pronounced these words, 'God bless him!'[50]

CHAPTER 21

Aftermath

One week after his death Edward Young was buried in the chancel of his church at Welwyn, by the side of his wife. The entry in the parish register is simple and, as to his age, inaccurate:

> Young Edward LL.D. Rector of this Parish was buried ye 12th day of April (He died Apr 5th in the 85th year of his age).[1]

He was actually in his 82nd year. But he had lived so long and won such fame that he had become a legend even during his lifetime – and after his death the legends grew till, with the usual reaction against too great contemporary reputation, some of them became libels. Young, as a celebrated moralist, boosted by his admirers as a prophet and saint as well as one of the world's great poets, was peculiarly vulnerable to this very human reaction. As the first obituaries went over the long-forgotten details of his early life, it was found that he was really as other men were and it began to be hinted that he must therefore be a hypocrite. This was somewhat unfair to Young, who had never pretended to a halo and had indeed himself provided much of the ammunition for his attackers. But the public image demanded saintly perfection and when he was found to be less than perfect, the blame was laid on him for deception rather than on the public for self-deception.

The hints that all was not well started even with his funeral. This was conducted by Jones, who wrote on 13 April:

> [He] was decently buried yesterday about six in the afternoon, in the chancel of this church, close by the remains of his lady under the communion table. The clergy, who are the trustees for his charity-school, and one or two more attending the funeral, the last office at interment being performed by me.[2]

But the correspondent of the *London Chronicle* in its issue of 13–16 April was not so satisfied with the last tribute to the poet:

Last Friday were interred the only mortal remains of the learned, pious and incomparable Dr Young . . . Though he lived celebrated, he was buried with the utmost obscurity . . . The common forms of interring the meanest person were not violated on this occasion, the bell did not ring till his corpse was brought out of his house, which is opposite the church; and though he was both Founder and endower of a charity school in his parish, neither the master nor the children attended his funeral. His pall was supported by the Rev. Dr Yarborough, the Rev. Mr Wynne and several other divines, who were Rectors or Vicars of the neighbouring parishes. The mourners were his son, his nephew, another near relation, his housekeeper, most of the bearers and the whole town of Welwyn.[3]

This report was copied by the monthly magazines and later by the *Biographia Britannica* – and by then the smallness and simplicity of the poet's funeral had become a matter of serious criticism, and somehow his fault. The *Biographia* glossed that he was little talked of at the end of his life and fell unwept by the Muses[a] – 'an instance that when any man resolves to forsake the world, the world is willing enough to leave him'.[4] The implication was that nobody carerd about Young's death; but for once Croft, to score off the *Biographia*, did justice to the poet by reminding readers: 'They who lament that these misfortunes happened to Young forget the praise he bestows upon Socrates, in the Preface to *Night Seven*, for resenting his friend's request about his funeral.'[5] The story of Socrates, in Young's words, was that 'his friend asking him, with such an affectionate concern as became a friend, "Where should he deposit his remains?", it was resented by Socrates as implying a dishonourable supposition that he could be so mean as to have a regard for anything, even in himself, that was not immortal."[6] Such an idea might well explain the privacy of Young's burial; just as he wanted no manuscripts preserved after his death, so he humbly desired burial with the minimum of pomp – no Dukes and Duchesses, no Westminster Abbey, just his family and friends.

After the funeral the poet's will was handed over to

---

[a] Actually two anonymous poems and an epigram to the memory of Young were published by *The London Chronicle* during April.

Frederick by Mrs Hallows and opened in her presence.[b] It was a normal, businesslike document, remembering his church and household, his parishioners and neighbours, a few surviving friends and relations and his old College, and leaving the residue to his son.[7] That this still, despite their estrangement, reflected the father's dying wishes is shown by the well-informed account in the *Gentleman's Magazine*, 1782, of the poet's last hours:

> I can only give one passage, which I had from a very good authority (for I was not present at this awful scene), that when his son arrived to pay the last duties, he sent to him his blessing and forgiveness with an assurance that he did not refuse to see him from any remains of resentment; but that his bodily pain was so exquisite that he was unable to bear so affecting a meeting; and that he would find by his last will that he had always considered him as his son and never meant to carry his displeasure to the grave.[8]

After Frederick the chief beneficiary was Mrs Hallows, whom the poet had 'never degraded by paying her wages';[9] she was left £800, which the codicil made up to £1000. Jones was next with £200; Young's nephew, Richard Harris £50: his four servants £10 each; All Souls £50 to buy books; and so on, while his silver and embroidered work for the altar, with the Speaker's Bible, went to the church with £100 to his successor for repairs. Lastly there were the usual mourning rings for his friends, and it is worth noting them in full, since this was another of the points on which Croft chose to moralize on mistaken premises:

> It may teach mankind the uncertainty of worldly friendships to know that Young, either by surviving those he loved or by outliving their affections, could only recollect the names of two *friends*, his housekeeper and a hatter, to mention in his will; and it may serve to repress that testamentary pride which too often seeks for sounding names and titles, to be informed that the author of the *Night Thoughts* did not blush to leave a legacy to his 'friend Henry Stevens, a hatter at the Temple Gate'.[10]

Actually Young recollected his neighbours Mrs Ward, Mrs Battell and Mr Shotbolt; his City friends Richardson, Alderman

---

[b] Mrs Hallows's deposition on this was made to the legal authorities on 25 April and attached to the will.

Gosling and Stevens the hatter; his relatives Walter Bigg, Richard Harris and 'two cousin Youngs'ᶜ of St Martin's Lane, as well as Jones and Mrs Hallows. Further, in the 1764 codicil, he added rings for the Duchess of Portland, Nancy Richardson and five neighbouring squires and clerics including George North, the antiquarian Vicar of Codicote. Croft was right enough that Young did not care a whit about 'sounding names and titles' – he can surely be acquitted of ambition in naming the Duchess with whom he had corresponded for twenty-five years. But certainly he did not blush to leave 20 guineas to the hatter of Temple Gate. It would not have occurred to him to do so; but equally certainly it was not because he could not think of any other friends, because he did in fact remember a lot more.

In his letter of 13 April to Birch John Jones reported with unusual mellowness:

> I know it will give you pleasure to be farther informed that he was pleased to make respectful mention of me in his will, expressing his satisfaction in my care of his parish, bequeathing to me a handsome legacy and appointing me to be one of his executors next after his sister's son (a clergyman of Hampshire), who this morning set out for London in order to prove the will at Doctor's Commons. So that, much according to my wishes, I shall have little or nothing to do in respect of executorship.¹¹

But Jones spoke too soon. Although Richard Harris took the will to London and got it proved in less than a fortnight, Jones's autobiography complained that 'that relation of his declining the trust,ᵈ the sole management of the executorship devolved upon me'.¹² Poor Jones – he always had a grievance, even when he had just been left what was for him the princely sum of £200; and by 17 December he was lamenting that 'a considerable part of the small fortune which I had honestly acquired is in danger

---

ᶜ See Pettit and Collins, *Genealogy of Edward Young*: 'One of the two 'cousin Youngs' of the will is almost certainly Mary Young, spinster, of Bloomsbury (d. 1788), a daughter of John Young (1651–1707) and granddaughter of Dean Young's brother John, of London (1627–1670). In her will she left a bequest to 'my Kinsman Frederick Young of Welwyn in the County of Hertford'. The second cousin referred to in the poet's will may have been Mary's brother Robert.

ᵈ According to the endorsement of the will Harris renounced on 30 April.

of being lost by the means of perfidy in a point of trust where I least expected it'.[13] But at least, as the testator had so earnestly desired in his codicil, there were no lawsuits over the will.

The same letter of Jones mentioned Frederick's inheritance with the comment that 'the young gentleman, who bears a fair character and behaves well as far as I can hear or see, will, I hope, soon enjoy and make a prudent use of a very handsome fortune'.[14] Frederick's fortune was indeed handsome; even after the payment of nearly £1500 in legacies the residue came to £12,500 in stocks, to add to his £300 a year life annuity. But Jones's pious hope that he would make prudent use of it was, alas, vain. Frederick's new bank account shows exactly the same characteristics as before, an unceasing overspending of his income relieved by the sale of large blocks of his capital twice a year, till the cornucopia finally ran out ten years later.

For the moment, however, Frederick was very well off and he settled down at Guessens to the life of a country gentleman. 'Squire Young', as he was known (though he was not, like his father, Lord of the Manor, which went with the Rectory), dutifully played the part, being elected a trustee of his father's charity school on 5 June, 1765[15] and sitting on committees and sessions with the High Sheriff of Hertfordshire and other local dignitaries.[16] On 5 October, 1765[17] he married Elizabeth, the eldest daughter of Giles Thornton Heysham, the squire of St Paul's Walden, who may have given him shelter after the final break with his father, and two years later, on 20 October, 1767,[18] their only child was baptized, a daughter named after her mother. All very respectable – yet by the end of the year he had managed to spend over £1100 and on 18 December[19] he was obliged to sell £1000 South Sea Stock.

In 1766 he erected a monumental marble on the north wall of the chancel of Welwyn Church with the simple but pointed inscription:

M.S./Optimi parentis/EDWARDI YOUNG LL.D./Hujus ecclesiae Rect./et/ELIZABETHAE/Foem. praenob./ Conjugis ejus amantissimae/Pio et gratissimo animo/Hoc marmor posuit/F.Y./Filius superstes/1766.[20]

'To the sacred memory of the best of parents . . . and his most loving wife, his surviving son set up this marble with dutiful and most grateful feelings' – Frederick was deliberately stressing the love that existed in his family between husband and wife, parent and child. It would have been easy enough for him to praise the poet and forget the father if he had harboured any resentment against him. Instead Frederick did his best in this public declaration of devotion to scotch the rumours of his father's ill-treatment of him. But a marble in a country church could hardly compete with the circulation of the *Biographia Britannica*, of which the supplement, containing his father's life, came out the same year.[21] This mentioned their quarrel and gave currency to the insinuation that Frederick was the model for the wicked Lorenzo of the *Night Thoughts*, a libel which seems to have been doubly unfair, being not only impossible, as a comparison of the relevant dates could prove, but also out of character, if we may judge by such comments as we have on Frederick. He was not the Lorenzo type at all; weakness, not wickedness, seems to have been the fatal flaw in his make-up. Jones said he bore 'a fair character and behaves well';[22] Hayley referred to 'the poet's very liberal and amiable son';[23] Croft wrote of his 'worth and sensibility'[24] and said he was 'born with genius and talents';[25] and W. C. Dyer asserted that 'he was possessed of superior talents and a well-cultivated understanding, enriched with a lively imagination and a vein of poetical fancy not inferior, time and circumstance considered, to that of his father'.[26] But all these good qualities could not save him from the consequences of his incorrigible extravagance.

The entries in his bank account give no clear clue as to the cause of his downfall. Those recipients that can be identified were mostly Welwyn tradesmen – carpenter, bricklayer, blacksmith, collar-maker, butcher, barber, innkeeper – but the sums paid to them seem excessive for normal services. Occasionally we find the names of local squires, including his father-in-law and brothers-in-law Giles and Edmund Heysham, which might indicate gambling debts. But who was John Wintle, who in the first five years was paid by Frederick a total of £443? Or Mr Jaques, who by 1775 had got altogether £776.8s. out of him? And why was Herbert Croft paid the substantial sum of 48 guineas on 28 February, 1774?[27]

Though we cannot explain the Croft entry, it is significant as showing that by the beginning of 1774 Frederick was acquainted with the future biographer of his father; and it was owing to this friendship and the desire to defend Frederick's reputation that Croft was inspired to undertake the poet's life. At that time Croft was only 22 years of age and he was studying for the Bar at Lincoln's Inn.[c] It is possible that he met Frederick through Thomas Maurice, the elder son of Young's friend, the headmaster of Christ's Hospital, Hertford, though Maurice was then only 19. The latter's *Memoirs* speak of 'our friend, Mr afterwards Sir Herbert Croft, the author of *Love and Madness*,[f] with whom and the son of Dr Young we almost daily dined at the White Hart Tavern in Holborn.'[28] But surely these 'many convivial hours in the taverns of London' with Frederick must have occurred later, when Maurice was a little older – perhaps after the death of Frederick's wife, who was buried at Welwyn on 16 October, 1775.[29]

By that time, in less than ten years, Frederick had managed to run through his entire fortune, having sold the last £500 of his £12,500 inheritance on 8 February 1775,[30] so that he was left with no income but his life annuity. But he still could not contain his expenditure within the limits of £300 a year and in 1776 he took the fatal step of selling one third of his annuity. Then for four desperate years he managed to hold out before selling a further third in 1780, but the last third followed quickly in 1781. The last payment into his account was £50 on 22 January; of this £35 was paid out again the same day, and the last £15 went a month later, on 23 February.[31] Frederick was penniless once more.

It is ironical that just at this time, when Frederick had once again contrived to ruin himself and justify his father, Croft's defence of his character should appear in Johnson's *Lives of the Poets*. Johnson's introduction to the *Life of Young*, published on 18 May, 1781, states that it was written 'at my request by a gentleman who had better information than I could easily have

---

[c] Croft was baptized 2 November, 1751; entered Winchester College 1765; matriculated at University College, Oxford, 1771, but changed to the study of law, qualifying as barrister-at-law at Lincoln's Inn in 1775.

[f] *Love and Madness*, 1780, was based on a *cause célèbre* of 1779, when James Hackman, newly ordained ex-Army officer, shot dead Martha Ray, mistress of Lord Sandwich, when she refused to marry him. Into this tale Croft interpolated the story of Chatterton, using original information partly supplied by Maurice from questioning Chatterton's landlady, Mrs Angel, sackmaker of Brook Street.

obtained';³² and it is clear that he lazily adopted Croft's version of Young's life, prejudice and all, merely crossing out some of the more libellous passages. What is puzzling is the reason for Croft's prejudice, why he felt it necessary, for his avowed object of vindicating Frederick against the *Biographia*, to put the worst interpretation on all Young's actions even before his son was born. Could it be that he picked up this tone from his source, that the son really felt a grudge against his father which he only confessed privately to his young admirer in the intimacy of a tavern? But Croft himself asserted the contrary: 'But the son of Young would almost sooner, I know, pass for a Lorenzo than see himself vindicated at the expense of his father's memory.'³³ And Frederick himself, far from saying that his mother was overlooked and despised (as alleged in the passage that Johnson struck out and D'Israeli revived), told Johnson personally that his father was never cheerful after her death.

Frederick's encounter with Dr Johnson took place on 2 June, 1781, just two weeks after the publication of the *Life of Young*, when the Doctor and Boswell were passing through Welwyn. Boswell was determined to bring his hero to the home of the poet he so much admired, but great adroitness was required in handling the meeting. His account in the *Life of Johnson* can be supplemented by the notes from his journal. The finished version reads:

> I hastened to Mr Young's, found he was at home, sent in word that a gentleman desired to wait upon him and was shown into a parlour, where he and a young lady, his daughter, were sitting. He appeared to be a plain, civil, country gentleman; and when I begged pardon for presuming to trouble him but that I wished much to see his place, if he would give me leave, he behaved very courteously and answered, 'By all means, sir. We are just going to drink tea; will you sit down?' I thanked him, but said that Dr Johnson had come with me from London and I must return to the inn and drink tea with him . . . 'Sir, (said he) I should think it a great honour to see Dr Johnson here. Will you allow me to send for him?' Availing myself of this opening, I said I would go myself and bring him when he had drunk tea; he knew nothing of my calling here. Having been thus successful, I hastened back to the inn and informed Dr Johnson that Mr Young, son of Dr Young, the

author of *Night Thoughts*, desired to have the honour of
seeing him at the house where his father lived. Dr Johnson
luckily made no enquiry how this invitation had arisen, but
agreed to go; and when we entered Mr Young's parlour, he
addressed him with a very polite bow, 'Sir, I had a curiosity
to come and see this place. I had the honour to know that
great man, your father.'[34]

The journal expands and modifies this critical moment.
Johnson was really very suspicious, asking, 'What is the
meaning of this? One does not like to accept, nor does one like
to refuse'; and muttering on the short walk from the Swan to
Guessens, 'If I had known there was to be such trouble, I
would not have come. I have a great mind to go back.'[35] Both
he and Frederick were embarrassed at the start. Young was
'bluntly silent' and Johnson, in a bad temper, thought him 'very
unknowing' and wondered 'how he got such uncouth manners'.
But things went more smoothly when they went out into the
garden and looked at the 'handsome Gothic arch' of Young's
lime-tree walk; Johnson called it 'a fine grove' and Boswell
beheld it with reverence. As they sat in the summer-house, they
discussed the poet:

> I said to Mr Young that I had been told his father was
> cheerful. 'Sir, (said he) he was too well-bred a man not to be
> cheerful in company; but he was gloomy when alone. He
> was never cheerful after my mother's death, and he had
> met with many disappointments.' Dr Johnson observed to
> me afterwards that this was no favourable account of Dr
> Young; 'for it is not becoming in a man to have so little
> acquiescence in the ways of Providence as to be gloomy
> because he has not obtained as much preferment as he
> expected; nor to continue gloomy for the loss of his wife.
> Grief has its time.' The last part of this censure was
> theoretically made. Practically, we know that grief for the
> loss of a wife may be continued very long, in proportion as
> affection has been sincere. No man knew this better than Dr
> Johnson.[36]

It is hardly surprising that Frederick was not at his best as a
host since by then he had nothing left but the house itself. And
soon afterwards another blow fell when his daughter, only
fourteen years old, ran off with the younger son of a local

maltster. It is said that it was a Gretna Green wedding;[g] but if so, the marriage was regularized on Boxing Day, 1781,[37] when 'Joseph Hankin, minor, and Elizabeth Young, minor, of Welwyn' were married at the bridegroom's home of Stansted Abbotts near Ware – with Herbert Croft as one of the witnesses. The couple's only child, the poet's great-granddaughter, was born in 1784, but she only lived one day;[38] and with her the Young line ended.[h] Meanwhile Frederick was obliged to sell his last asset, Guessens,[i] in 1783[39] and he dropped out of Welwyn life. The school trustees, who had rashly appointed him Treasurer, twice fixed meetings in 1782 at which he failed to appear, and on 21 July, 1783[40] they added a despairing note to the accounts that the balance of £2.13s.0½d. was in the hands of Frederick Young, Esqr. Thereafter his place on the board was taken over by the Rev. Mr Rowse, the new owner of Guessens, and the only record of Frederick is that he was buried at Welwyn on 28 May, 1788.[41]

The following December his friend Croft, on a visit to the Ladies of Llangollen, told them a story which Lady Eleanor Butler reported in her diary as follows:

> Young the poet a bad man, thought of nothing but his poetry and drinking, and entirely neglected the education of his children. In consequence of that neglect his son, born with genius and talents, died in jail; on an income of four hundred a year spent twenty thousand pounds.[42]

Though one would hardly call eight years at Winchester and seven at Oxford a neglected education, Croft's figures of Frederick's finances are not far out and he may have been right about him dying in gaol – a debtors' prison, presumably. His burial at Welwyn was perhaps arranged by his daughter to save the son of the poet from a pauper's grave.

[g] The Gretna Green story comes from *N&Q*, 11 S, III, 148, where the Rev. E. L. H. Tew of Upham stated that Elizabeth 'was married to a Mr Haine [*sic*] about December, 1781' but gave no authority for his statement.

[h] Elizabeth Hankin survived till 1794, when she was buried at Welwyn on 11 April, aged twenty-six.

[i] Frederick last paid Land Tax on Guessens in 1783; thereafter the Rev. Mr Rowse (sometimes Rouse) on 'late Mr Young's'.

CHAPTER 22

Decline and Fall

Meanwhile Croft's *Life of Young* had stirred up controversy in the press over the character of the poet. His sneers and smears, coming out with all the weight of Johnson's authority behind them, undoubtedly harmed the 'image' of the poet, setting the tone for the now traditional picture of the worldly moralist, the hypocritical preacher, the disappointed climber whose gloom was caused by thwarted ambition rather than bereaved affection. As yet there was not any suggestion that Young was anything but a great poet, but to accuse a moral poet of insincerity is to strike at the roots of his work. Croft by his treatment of Young's character and Johnson by his *imprimatur* for this version were undermining Young's reputation as a poet too. Many readers, of course, did not realize that the *Life of Young* was not Johnson's own work and Croft had done his best to imitate the magisterial severity of his master. On this point Boswell told a story:

> It has always appeared to me to have a considerable share of merit and to display a pretty successful imitation of Johnson's style. When I mentioned this to a very eminent literary character [Burke, according to a note by Malone] he opposed me vehemently, exclaiming, 'No, no, it is *not* a good imitation of Johnson; it has all his pomp without his force; it has all the nodosities of the oak without its strength.' This was an image so happy that one might have thought he would have been satisfied with it, but he was not. And setting his mind again to work, he added with exquisite felicity, 'It has all the contortions of the Sybil without the inspiration.'[1]

But whether inspired or not,[a] Croft's mud stuck and the

---

[a] Croft was bitterly attacked in the *Deformities of Dr Samuel Johnson*, Edinburgh, 1782: 'The life of Dr Young has been written by a lawyer, who conveys the meanest thoughts in the meanest language. His style is dry, stiff, grovelling and impure . . . He continues in the same fretful tone from the first line to the last. He is at once most contemptuous and contemptible . . . He is the bad imitator of a bad original; and an honest man will not peruse his libel without indignation . . . And yet this critical assassin, this literary jackal, is celebrated by the Doctor.'

authoritative but anonymous refutation of his mistakes in the *Gentleman's Magazine*[2] in 1782[b] only served to spread the rumours against Young. The writer was obviously personally acquainted with the poet and, like all the others who actually knew Young, he was strongly in his favour. The points on which his article defended the poet against the strictures of Croft were his flattering dedications, his association with Wharton, his soliciting of preferment, his quarrel with his son and the terms of his will; and these, despite the corrector's efforts, are still the accusations that are brought up against Young. The malicious legend of his un-Christian treatment of his son, reinforced by Isaac D'Israeli, hardened and by 1816 Mr W. C. Dyer was able to assert without contradiction that Frederick was banished just after leaving school and had to 'struggle under the frowns of adversity'[3] owing to his want of education. By then Young's neglect of his son had become an article of faith, as had the shamefulness of his association with the Duke of Wharton (despite the dates of this association) and with Mrs Howard (despite the example of Swift), the servility of his flattery (despite the equally fulsome compliments of Thomson and Fielding) and his insatiable preferment-hunting (despite the facts of the Duchess of Portland's campaign). All his conduct was perfectly acceptable in terms of the author of *The Revenge* or *The Universal Passion*; but the trouble was that he was also the author of the *Night Thoughts*. Those who knew him as he was, a fallible, lovable human being, remembered him with affectionate admiration; but they were gone, Johnson in 1784, the Duchess in 1785, Mrs Temple in 1789, Mrs Montagu in 1800. The public demanded an image of inhuman saintliness and were disillusioned when Croft and the rest showed him otherwise.

By the beginning of the nineteenth century, then, the reputation of Young as a man was, justly or not, beginning to get tarnished; but his reputation as a poet was at its height throughout Europe. In his native land the critics were more reserved than

[b] The article was provoked by the comment of one R.H. in the previous number of *GM*: 'When I assert, on undoubted authority, that his [i.e. Frederick's] father refused the most powerful solicitations of his friends to see him on his deathbed with this severe reply, "It cannot be, consistently with the happiness of either of us"; it would suggest no unfair suspicion that he treated him with a severity to which the worst excesses are hardly entitled on such occasions.' (*GM*, LII, 22.)

their continental colleagues, but as yet there was no question of Young's poetic stature, even among those who criticized his faults of art or character. Johnson's considered verdict in the *Life of Young* (for the Doctor did not leave to Croft the critical appreciation of the poet) was, 'With all his defects he was a man of genius and a poet';[4] though in argument with Mrs Thrale, who 'forced him one day, . . . to prefer Young's description of night to the so much admired ones of Dryden and Shakespeare, as more forcible, and more general', he was less complimentary. When she asserted that 'every reader is not either a lover or a tyrant, but every reader is interested when he hears that:

> Creation sleeps; 'tis as the general pulse
> Of life stood still, and nature made a pause;
> An awful pause – prophetic of its end.

"This," said he, "is true; but remember that, taking the compositions of Young in general, they are but like bright stepping-stones over a miry road. Young froths, and foams, and bubbles sometimes very vigorously; but we must not compare the noise made by your tea-kettle here with the roaring of the ocean." '[5]

It was the inequality of Young's works that puzzled his countrymen; like Goldsmith, who said in his *Beauties of English Poetry* (1767) that the *Night Thoughts*[c] were then 'spoken of differently, either with exaggerated applause or contempt, as the reader's disposition is either turned to mirth or melancholy';[6] or 'Courtney Melmoth'.[d] who in his *Observations on the Night Thoughts of Dr Young* (1776) admitted that he knew of no production 'more unequally written, nor is there probably in the world of letters a greater mixture of bad and of good';[7] or Isaac Reed,[e] who gave in

---

[c] Goldsmith also noted that Young's *Satires* 'were in higher reputation when published than they stand in at present', adding, 'He seems fonder of dazzling than pleasing; of raising our admiration for his wit than our dislike of the follies he ridicules.' (*Collected Works*, V, 328.)

[d] 'Courtney Melmoth' was the pseudonymn of Samuel Jackson Pratt. The *Observations* consist of fourteen epistles to a young friend named Archibald. Pratt compares Young's poetry to Johnson's prose as having 'a nerve in their writings which gives them in *strength* what they may be thought to require in *harmony*' and expresses his preference for their superior power over the smoothness of Pope and Addison. (*Observations*, 5.)

[e] Isaac Reed (1742–1807) had previously edited the sixth volume of *The Works of the Author of the Night Thoughts* (1778), consisting of the last uncollected scraps of Young's writings, dedications, naval lyrics, occasional verses, etc.

the *Biographia Dramatica* (1782) an account of the poet's character so hostile (not to mention inaccurate) as to make Croft seem positively fair, but summed up his works thus:

> In the poetical as well as prose compositions of Young there is much originality but little judgement. We scarcely recollect a single line or expression that he has borrowed from any other English writer. His defects and beauties are alike his own.[8]

The same uncertainty was shown by James Beattie, the poet of the insipid *Minstrel*, who remarked in 1779 in a letter to the Duchess of Gordon:

> When one begins to find pleasure in sighing over Young's *Night Thoughts* in a corner, it is time to shut the book and return to the company. I grant that, while the mind is in a certain state, those gloomy ideas give exquisite delight; but their effect resembles that of intoxication upon the body; they may produce a temporary fit of feverish exultation, but qualms and weakened nerves and depression of spirits are the consequence.[9]

And Johnson's 'unclubbable' friend, Sir John Hawkins, was equally unsettled in his opinion, when asked by his daughter Laetitia-Matilda to 'direct her judgement' on the *Nights*:

> I really hardly know what to say; and as I cannot decide for myself, I cannot fairly do it for you. The *Narcissa* has been commended by able men and there are parts of it very fine; but the whole is a favourite with the vulgar and you know that is not a recommendation with me.[10]

'A favourite with the vulgar' – that was indeed true, but it is no reproach. Melmoth's excuse for his commentary was that 'no composition can be more favourable to literary scrutiny nor any boast a greater number of readers'.[11] John Wesley, who had pirated the *Nights* in 1744, published a popular *Extract from Dr Young's Night Thoughts*[f] in 1770 for the benefit of his humble

---

[f] Wesley wrote in the preface: 'It is the observation of a late ingenious writer that "what is usually called a correct taste is very much offended with Dr Young's *Night Thoughts*". It is obvious that the poetry sometimes sinks into childish conceits or prosaic flatness; but oftener rises into the turgid or false sublime; and that it is often perplexed and obscure. Yet this work contains many strokes of the most sublime poetry and is full of those pathetic strokes of nature and passion which touch the heart in the most tender and affecting manner.' (*Extract*, iii.)

disciples, while his brother Charles not only transcribed the poem in 1754 (noting in his *Journal*, 'No writings but the inspired are more useful to me')[12] but in 1773 set his daughter to learn the fourth *Night* by heart. In 1777 one G. Wright produced a popular edition with a glossary to explain the hard words;[g] and with these and endless other cheap editions Young's works became familiar even to the poorest and inspired uneducated poets from the Ayrshire ploughman, Burns (who, Campbell said, 'was a great reader of Young, as the Scotch indeed universally are')[13] to the Bristol milkwoman, Ann Yearsley, whose discoverer, Hannah More, reported:

> I was curious to know what poetry she had read. With the *Night Thoughts* and Paradise Lost I found her well acquainted, but she was astonished to learn that Young and Milton had written anything else.[14]

Apart from these two she knew a few Shakespeare plays and the *Eloisa* of Pope and nothing else, not even the names of Spenser, Dryden or Thomson. Young was a popular poet in the most literal sense.[h]

His work also made a particular appeal to the ladies. Such literary lights as Mrs Thrale, Fanny Burney and Anna Seward, the 'Swan of Lichfield', were his enthusiastic admirers. 'What a nobleness of expression, when noble, has this poet!' rhapsodized the authoress of *Evelina*, as she listened to 'Mr Fairly' reading Young's poems,[i] 'What exquisite feeling! what forcible ideas! I forgot, while I listened, all my own little troubles and disturbances.'[15] Miss Seward's letters, written between 1784 and 1807, frequently treated of Young, on whom her verdict was:

---

[g] Wright's preface (p. xi) alleged that 'Dr Young was convinced of the impropriety of writing the *Night Thoughts* in a style so much above the understanding of common readers and said to a friend, a week or two before he died, that was he to publish such another treatise, . . . it should be in less elevated language and more suited to the capacities of all.'

[h] Blake was another enthusiast. He actually made 537 illustrations for R. Edwards's folio edition of the *Night Thoughts*, 1797. But only 43 were engraved for the first volume, *Nights I–IV*, after which the project was abandoned as too costly. A facsimile was published by Dover Publications, New York, in 1975.

[i] The reader, Col. Digby, was more temperate, saying that 'Young was an author not to be read on regularly, but to dip into in times of solitude and sadness'. (D'Arblay, *Diary*, IV, 262.)

> I sometimes long to lop and compress the *Night Thoughts*.
> If that could be judiciously done, a work might remain of
> unexcelled sublimity and poetic beauty in the sombre style;
> for the genius of their author was great and original.
> Judgement was his grand desideratum.[16]

Mrs Thrale noted in her diary that 'Miss Cooper, hearing that
she was to lose her sight, set about getting the *Night Thoughts* by
heart – so much did she delight in the poetry of Dr Young.'[17]
Samuel Rogers,[j] the banker–poet, recalled in his *Table-Talk* that
in his youth the *Nights* were 'a very favourite book, especially
with ladies. I knew more than one lady who had a copy of it in
which particular passages were marked for her by some popular
preacher.'[18] And William Lisle Bowles,[k] whose sonnets inspired
Coleridge, wrote in his *Days Departed*:

> This book, my mother, in the weary hours
> Of life – in every care, in every joy –
> Was thy companion.[19]

Such was the picture in Young's own country at the end of the
century, when Wordsworth and Coleridge proclaimed their
revolution. Young's fame was established; and though himself a
precursor of the Romantic revolution,[l] he could not hope to
escape the fate of the establishment. Too original and individual
to be imitable, he had had a personal success in English poetry,
but his influence had not been directly fruitful. The domination
of Pope was still too strong and Young's lead had weakened into
watery sentimentalism rather than growing into full-blooded
Romanticism. But that was only in England; on the Continent his
influence was very different.

---

[j] Samuel Rogers (1763–1855), though he collaborated with Byron and was
offered the Laureateship on the death of Wordsworth, was born before Young's
death and referred here to the late eighteenth century.

[k] W. L. Bowles (1762–1850), like Rogers, was born before Young's death and
outlived the great Romantics. He was one of the favourite pupils of Joseph
Warton at Winchester.

[l] James Sutherland's *Preface to Eighteenth Century Poetry* sums up: 'The *Night
Thoughts*, formless, egotistical, vague, unrestrained, ambitious and grandiose, . . .
are the antithesis of almost all that neo-classical poetry stands for; and yet they
were enormously popular. Young, with his bleeding heart, his secret or his
suggestion of a secret, his determined gloom, his conscious loneliness, is an early
romantic egoist, a Byron of the middle classes, whose woes, real or imaginary,
fell with an impressive sound on the ears of a listening Europe.' (*Preface*, 160.)

The tide of 'Youngism' in Europe flowed in two separate waves, the Germanic and the Gallic. The first had already reached its height at the time of the poet's death; the French wave rose later, but more abruptly, and spread wider because of the wider knowledge of the French tongue. Thus, while the conscientious Germans tried to render the *Nights* as faithfully as possible in their translations and were duly followed by the Danes, Swedes and Dutch, the French translator did not hesitate to civilize and re-arrange Young's nine chaotic books into the epic number of twenty-four, neat, coherent and emasculated, and it was this version that was passed on to the rest of Europe, in Italian, Portuguese, Spanish, Russian, Polish and eventually Magyar, Czech, Turkish, modern Greek and even Maltese. One way or another the name and spirit of Young reached the farthest confines of Europe, and in both forms it caused profound changes in the literary atmosphere of the various countries.

After the hyperboles of Ebert and Cramer, Klopstock and Lessing, a natural reaction began in Germany in the 1760s. By 1761 Nicolai was mocking the swarm of 'Nachtgedankenmacher' and at the end of the decade Michaelis too was satirizing the grave-loving 'Younglings', while Klotz condemned Young as the 'king of night-owls'[20] and a menace to German letters. Wieland, who had said that Young 'rises to the plane of the very angels',[21] became critical of his corrupting influence and Lessing, who had called the *Nights* 'this masterpiece of one of the sublimest poets',[22] also cooled as he grew older. But Herder remained a lifelong admirer of Young, as did Klopstock, while Ebert continued working on more and more elaborate translations in edition after edition right down to his death in 1795. But whatever their opinion, no writer in Germany could neglect the influence of Young on the literature of the time, not only through the *Night Thoughts* but also the *Conjectures on Original Composition*. This work, immediately translated into German, with its theory of the 'cult of genius' exactly fitted the demands of the nascent *Sturm und Drang* movement and fired critics like Hamann, who was already a worshipper of the *Nights*. Herder made extensive extracts from the *Conjectures* and, as Professor J. L. Kind put it in his exhaustive study of *Edward Young in Germany*:

Herder took up the ideas of originality in literature as preached by Young and corroborated by Hamann, and not only laid stress on the same principles but sought to exemplify them and apply them for the purpose of arousing national pride in German letters. Thus he helped to free Germany from the servility of imitation and. prepared the way for the literature that has made Germany famous.[23]

The 'Storm and Stress' movement owed a double debt to Young – and not least the greatest of these poets, Goethe, who in 1766[24] told his sister that he was learning English from Milton and Young and in his *Dichtung und Wahrheit* confessed Young's influence on himself while writing *Werther* and also in creating the spiritual conditions that caused that seminal drama to strike a responsive chord everywhere.

Young's contribution to the Romantic movement in Germany was thus direct and vital. The German movement had a strong effect on the leaders of our own Romantic Revival, and Coleridge commented in the *Biographia Literaria*:

> Three of the most popular books in the German language were the translations of Young's *Night Thoughts*, Hervey's *Meditations* and Richardson's *Clarissa Harlow*. Now we have only to combine the bloated style and peculiar rhythm of Hervey . . . with the strained thoughts, the figurative metaphysics and solemn epigrams of Young on the one hand; and with the loaded sensibility, the minute detail, . . . the self-involution and dreamlike continuity of Richardson on the other hand; and then to add the horrific incidents and mysterious villains . . . and the perpetual moonshine of a modern author . . . – and as the compound of these ingredients duly mixed you will recognize the so-called *German* drama . . . The so-called German drama therefore is *English* in its origin, English in its materials and English by re-adoption.[25]

Though hardly complimentary, this comment was at least an admission that Young was in fact among the pioneers of the Romantic movement and thus one of their literary ancestors, if only by re-adoption. His direct effect on English letters, by breaking down the classic tyranny and bringing back the personal note into poetry, was more distant and so perhaps harder to be seen, even by so acute a critic as Coleridge. The track was clearer by the German detour.

The French began to translate Young some ten years after the Germans. The first attempts actually appeared during the poet's lifetime, when the Comte de Bissy published prose translations of *Night I* in 1762 and *Night II* in 1764. The Count was as enthusiastic as the Germans:

> I will venture to say that in point of depth this poet is what Homer and Pindar are in point of grandeur. I should find it difficult to explain the effect produced upon me by my first perusal of this work. I might experience much the same impression in the heart of the desert on a dark and stormy night, when the surrounding blackness is pierced at intervals by flashes of lightning.[26]

Nevertheless he admitted the suppression of 'beaucoup de traits gigantesques, obscurs ou de mauvais goût'.[27] This typically French assumption of the monopoly of good taste was carried to far greater lengths by the next French translator, Pierre le Tourneur, who produced a complete version of the *Night Thoughts* in 1769. In his preliminary discourse the translator boldly asserted:

> The poem of the *Nights* or *Complaints* presents numerous faults which it is almost as easy to avoid as to perceive; but it is nevertheless the most sublime elegy on the miseries of the human condition . . . What seemed to me needed was a certain re-arrangement . . . My intention has been to extract from the English Young a French Young, who could please my nation . . . So I have regarded this first translation as an architect would treat a mass of materials for a building, cut and ready for placing but piled haphazard in eight or nine different places and mixed with rubbish. I have assembled and sorted as best I can under a common title all the fragments which corresponded and formed a sort of whole.[28]

So he chopped up the nine *Nights* and re-assembled them as twenty-four books with such titles as 'The Greatness of the Soul', 'The World', 'Pleasure and Suicide', banishing all the theological passages to notes and avoiding the unseemly 'enthusiasm' of the original. He even added ideas and images and refined the style

in accordance with the prevailing taste, modestly commenting
that 'If it should be true that I have embellished the original, this
would be a success for which I render all the credit to him. I
would owe it solely to the feelings with which he filled me.'[29]

Thus the *Night Thoughts* became known to the French-
speaking world in a much-altered form, a series of neat and
logical prose essays on moral topics, and this transformation was
highly approved by Le Tourneur's compatriots.[m] M. de la
Harpe commented in the *Mercure de France*, that 'When he [Le
Tourneur] takes the place of Young, he is at least his equal';[30]
and Voltaire wrote to the translator from Ferney on 7 June,
1769:

> You have done a great honour to my old friend Young; it
> seems to me that the translator has more taste than the
> author. You have put as much order as you could into this
> collection of commonplaces, tumid and obscure . . . I
> believe that all foreigners will prefer your prose to the
> poetry of this Englishman, half priest and half poet.[31]

Le Tourneur, in fact, successfully catered to the taste of his time
in France, where the classic ideas of elegance still prevailed. It
was a long time before a French critic could write, like Villemain
in his *Essai sur Young*, of the 'measured pomp and monotonous
elegance of the French version':

> For the irregularities of poetic imagination, the mixture
> of high and low, sublime and ridiculous, in sum for the
> shocks of the soul that the English poet feels and gives, he
> substitutes the doleful uniformity of his vulgar elegance.
> He never gives a vigorous and simple word; he is afraid of
> the natural. He is less bizarre, but much more affected,
> than his model.[32]

The success of Le Tourneur's version was instant and
sensational. Published in April, 1769,[n] a second edition was

---

[m] Some English critics also approved. The *Monthly Review*, Appendix to 1769,
wrote: 'What gives frequent disgust to every reader of taste in the *Night Thoughts*
is the turning and twisting of the same sentiment into a thousand different
shapes. The translator very judiciously has taken great liberty with his author in
this respect.'

[n] Besides the Paris editions there were editions printed at Amsterdam and
Lyon in 1769, and Basle in 1770. (Forster, *Book Collector*, Spring 1971, 48–9.)

called for by September, a third in 1770, followed the same year by a 'new edition'. In spite of the imposed elegance something of the spirit of the poem survived and appealed to the French public.° The new wave of feeling that had swept Germany was infiltrating the classic bastion of France and already in 1765 Baculard d'Arnaud had spoken, in connection with Young, of 'horreurs délicieuses'.[33] On 12 September, 1769 Mme Riccoboni wrote to Garrick, 'Young's *Night Thoughts* have had a great success here. It is an irrefutable proof of the change of the French spirit.'[34] Even the critics approved; the *Journal Encyclopédique* had a long article that summed up, 'Whatever place we light upon, we are sure of finding the true character of poetry',[35] while the *Année Littéraire* ended, 'In spite of his faults Young is one of the greatest poets that Nature has produced in recent times.'[36] The same craze for 'youngizing' as had overcome the Germans before, now hit France. The first imitation, *Nuits Parisiennes*, appeared the same year, and 1770 saw the *Nuits Anglaises* as well as versified versions of various of Le Tourneur's books by at least three poets. Grimm found 'too many bells, too many tombs, too many funeral chants and cries, too many ghosts'[37] in these, but was contradicted by Diderot; while an Abbé wrote a corrective entitled *Les Jours*, addressed to a French youth 'tormented by an excess of Youngism'.[38] And so it went on throughout the '70s, so that, according to the *Almanach des Muses* in 1775, one could see on the coquette's dressing table –

> Les crêpes d'Young se mêler
> Parmi les pompoms de toilette.[39]

The leaders of the French Revolution were devotees of Young too. Robespierre kept a copy of the poet's works under his pillow and Danton found consolation in them in prison. So did their opponents; Camille Desmoulins re-read the *Nights* on the eve of his execution. The name of Young was as famous in France as in Germany, and from France it soon spread throughout the other Latin and French-influenced countries.

° Mme du Deffand wrote to Horace Walpole, 26 April, 1769: 'I have begun reading what I am not sure that I shall continue; it is the translation of the *Nights* of Young. Nothing can be sadder, I have read only two books of it as yet. There is a lot of poetic fustian, but it has fire and strokes. I think I shall read it right through.'

The translations into Italian, Spanish, Portuguese and Polish were all based upon Le Tourneur, and most of the Russian ones too. In 1770 one Italian version was published in Marseilles by the Abbé Alberti and another in Pisa by Dr Bottoni; a freer attempt by L. A. Loschi, under the title of *Le Lamentazioni*, came out in Venice in 1774 and proved the most popular, being reprinted in Milan (1783), Naples (1795), Rome (1808), Padua (1819) and Turin as late as 1846. Italy was thus saturated with Youngism too and melancholy became the staple of poetry, such as Foscolo's *Le Rimembranze*, which refers to Young lamenting over the corpse of Narcissa. Next came the Russians with full-scale translations from 1778 onwards, the Portuguese in 1782 and the Poles in 1785. Last of the Latin countries came Spain with the *Obras Selectas* in 1789, owing to the greater strictness of the Inquisition towards a heretic. It is surprising that the strongly Protestant *Night Thoughts* were accepted so easily in the Catholic countries, but evidently the extraordinary prestige of the poem made it impossible to suppress. Le Tourneur's version, duly approved by the French Chancellor, omitted only one or two 'declarations of a Protestant against the Pope' and a couple of 'fanatical verses';[40] the episode of Narcissa's secret burial, far from being cut, was actually illustrated in the frontispiece to the second volume. Loschi was able to quote a Jesuit Abbé, who called Young 'a man well known for his sombre and severe enthusiasm, who, though separated from our sacred communion, is nevertheless Christian';[41] while the Spanish authorities licensed a translation 'purged of all errors' by Juan de Escoiquiz, who was not only a Canon of Saragossa Cathedral but tutor to the Prince of the Asturias, the heir to the throne. The preface explained:

> As Young had the misfortune to live . . . in a land where the freedom of thought, speech and writing knows no restraint, he has mixed among the most useful truths many propositions that do not conform to the sacred dogmas . . . I have suppressed all that I noted as worthy of censure . . . In giving the public this version exempt from error, the nation will not be deprived of a work of so great value and the clandestine introduction of other versions will be prevented.[42]

Even the Inquisition could not ban Young altogether.

At the turn of the century, then, Young's *Night Thoughts* were known throughout Europe, not to mention the newly independent United States of America,[p] where ten local editions have been noted between 1777 and 1800.[q] Nor was it only his greatest poem that was known. The indefatigable Ebert had translated the whole of Young's authorized *Works* except for the tragedies and odes, plus the *True Estimate* and, as soon as it appeared, *Resignation*; while several German versions of the tragedies by other translators were in circulation. Le Tourneur had included *The Last Day, Job* and the *Force of Religion* in his edition of the *Nuits*, and a further two volumes of *Oeuvres Diverses* added the *True Estimate, Centaur, Conjectures, Busiris* and *The Revenge*, and even an extract from the *Epistle to Lord Lansdowne* in which Young compared the English and French theatre. The satires had to wait for a French translator till 1787, while *The Brothers* was ignored, perhaps because it was taken from a French original. The satellites of German and French culture followed their leaders, with a Danish *Force of Religion* as the first of the lesser works in another tongue. Further editions, new translations and fresh imitations continued to pour from the presses of Europe for the first fifty or sixty years of the nineteenth century, but in diminishing volume. Though still popular with the common reader, Young had to pay the price of too great reputation and critical opinion turned against him about 1800 in Germany and France[r] as well as at home.

It is strange, however, that in his native country, where Young's work had never inspired such unhealthy excesses of imitation as abroad, the critics of the Romantic Revival should show such extreme antipathy to one of the pioneers of their movement.[s]

---

[p] *A Virginian Gentleman's Library, As proposed by Thomas Jefferson to Robert Skipwith in 1771* (Colonial Williamsburg, 1959), lists Young's *Works*, 4 vols, sixteenth among 148 titles. In 1733 Benjamin Franklin sent a copy back to America from England.
[q] Pettit's *Check-List of Young's 'Night Thoughts' in America*, 1948, with additions, 1950, lists altogether 126 editions of the *Nights* in U.S.A. before 1900.
[r] In the *Mercure de France* of March, 1801 Chateaubriand attacked Young with the significant charge that he showed 'in all his declamations on death only disappointed ambition'.
[s] Landor showed particular hostility to Young, but his remarks were too fantastical to make good criticism, e.g. 'He pins butterflies to the pulpit-cushion' (*Imaginary Conversations*); 'Young's cassock was flounced round with plaintive pun' (*A Satire on Satirists*); and in *Last Fruit*:
Thou dreariest droll of puffy short-breath'd writers!
All thy *night-thoughts* and day-thoughts hung on mitres.
(*Complete Works*, ed. S. Wheeler, 1936, . . .; XV, 176; XVI, 220.)

Jeffrey led the attack in the *Edinburgh Review* of August, 1811:

> Young exhibits, we think, a curious combination, or contrast rather, of the two styles [classic and romantic] . . . Though incapable either of tenderness or passion, he had a richness and activity of fancy that belonged rather to the days of James and Elizabeth than to those of George and Anne. But then, instead of indulging it, as the old writers would have done, in easy and playful inventions, in splendid descriptions or glowing illustrations, he was led by the restraints and established taste of his age to work it up into strained and fantastical epigrams or into cold and revolting hyperboles . . . and thinking it necessary to write like Pope, when the bent of his genius led him rather to copy what was best in Cowley and most fantastic in Shakespeare, he has produced something which excites wonder instead of admiration and is felt by everyone to be at once ingenious, incongruous and unnatural.[43]

Hazlitt in his *Lectures on the English Poets* (1818) characterized Young as a 'gloomy epigrammatist' who had 'abused great powers of thought and language'.[44] But six years later in the *Select British Poets* he was even severer than Jeffrey:

> Young is a poet who has been much overrated from the popularity of his subject and the glitter and lofty pretensions of his style. I wished to have made more extracts from the *Night Thoughts*, but was constantly repelled by the tinsel of expression, the false ornaments and laboured conceits. Of all writers who have gained a great name, he is the most meretricious and objectionable. His is false wit, false fancy, false sublimity and mock-tenderness.[45]

After this wholesale condemnation the remarks of the other anthologists of the time seem quite mild. 'No English poem,' said Southey, 'has ever been so popular on the Continent as the *Night Thoughts*; . . . for there is genius enough for the few and folly enough for the many';[46] and again, 'Young's manner is unique, a compound of wit and religious madness; but that madness is the madness of a man of genius.'[47] Thomas Campbell also allowed the poet some merit: 'The *Night Thoughts* certainly contain many splendid and happy conceptions, but their beauty is thickly marred by false wit and over-laboured antithesis . . . As a poet he was fond of exaggeration, but it was that of the fancy more than of the heart.'[48]

The tide of critical opinion was against him. Because he was witty, he was not allowed to have a heart, and because he was religious, he was not allowed to be witty. He must, in fact, be a hypocrite; and the denigration of his character, started by Croft, served to reinforce the Romantics' distate for his kind of poetry, enabling them to condemn the poet on moral as well as critical grounds. Thus Crabbe wrote in a letter of 1817:

> There is in Dr Young's life and character something not easily reconcilable with our respect and veneration. That excessive gloom, with that play of words and that false wit – the dreadful estimate of life, with the perpetual seeking after its emoluments – that strong aspiration after the future enjoyments of the soul, with that cheerful, not to say light, spirit which led him into common and frivolous society – all these have much of that incongruity which the children of infirmity possess, but from which we reasonably expect some to be in a great measure free.[49]

Even popular preachers caught the prevailing mood of disillusion and turned against him, like the Rev. Richard Cecil:[1]

> Young is, of all other men, one of the most striking examples of the disunion of piety from truth . . . It is a melancholy fact that he was hunting after preferment at eighty years old and felt and spoke like a disappointed man. The truth was pictured on his mind in the most vivid colours. He felt it while he was writing . . . Notwithstanding all this, the view did not reach his heart . . . He told a friend of mine, who went to him under religious fears, that he must *go more into the world!*[50]

Here is the groundwork of the fatal charge of worldliness that proved the *coup de grâce* for his reputation at the hands of George Eliot.

Yet the popularity of Young was by no means finished during the first half of the nineteenth century. Coleridge still believed that 'there were parts in him which must be immortal' and 'loved to read a page of Young and walk out to think of him',[51] while

---

[1] Richard Cecil (1748–1810) was the intellectual leader of the evangelical revival and a friend of John Newton.

Wordsworth actually expanded the bald words 'Doctor Young' of the 1805 text of the *Prelude* into the following lines in the 1850 edition:

> . ... and the Bard
> Whose genius spangled o'er a gloomy theme
> With fancies thick as his inspiring stars.[52]

Bulwer in his *New Phaedo* (1835) went so far against the new fashion as to praise the *Nights* as 'a poem entitled to rank immediately below the *Paradise Lost*'[53] and to defend the sincerity of the author's character. But in general it is the evidence of the editions that shows Young's continuing hold on the affections of the public despite the critics. Apart from the many popular duodecimos and collections like Bell's and Chalmers' Poets there were new critical editions in 1834 by the Rev. John Mitford in the Aldine series, in 1841 by H. F. Cary, the translator of Dante, in 1853 by George Gilfillan and in 1854 the *Complete Works* in two volumes, edited by James Nichols with a long new life by Dr John Doran.

At the middle of the nineteenth century, with over a hundred years of continuous popularity behind him, the position of Young among the immortals of English poetry must have seemed secure. Yet now, another hundred years on, his name is almost forgotten. What can have caused this eclipse? It would perhaps be an exaggeration to say his reputation was murdered by an article in the *Westminster Review*, as Keats was killed by the *Quarterly* – established fame is less susceptible than a sensitive youth. Yet the fact remains that from the time that George Eliot launched her full-scale attack on the sincerity of Young's character and works in 1857[u] under the title of *Worldliness and Other-Worldliness*, there have been no more new editions of the *Night Thoughts* and a steep falling-off and petering-out of reprints. If her article was not the cause, it must at least have coincided with and summed up the prevailing feeling of the reading public with such deadly finality that Young has never

[u] It is a melancholy coincidence that the same year also saw the demolition of a more tangible proof of the poet's benevolence, when on 30 April, 1857 the trustees of his charity-school agreed to let the Welwyn Vestry buy the site and pull down the building, the foundation being merged with the National School. (MS Welwyn, Vestry minutes.)

yet recovered. The aesthetic dissatisfaction of the Romantics
combined with the moral disapproval of the Victorians,
however unjustified in either case, made a millstone round his
neck that (as Sir Robert Birley put it in his Clark Lectures on
'Some Forgotten Masterpieces') sank him 'without trace'.

George Eliot brilliantly built up the case against the poet
from the case against the man, all the more vehemently
because of her disappointed passion for him. After a summary,
none too accurate, of the life of this 'sort of cross between a
sycophant and a psalmist' she went on:

> Young's biographers and critics have usually set out
> from the position that he was a great religious teacher and
> that his poetry is morally sublime . . . *We* set out from
> precisely the opposite conviction . . . Young's poetry was
> low and false, and . . . the *Night Thoughts* are the reflex
> of a mind in which the higher human sympathies were
> inactive.[54]

She admitted that this judgement was entirely opposed to her
youthful predilections and that early enjoyment still gave
extrinsic charm to 'passages of stilted rhetoric and false
sentiment'; but 'the sober and repeated reading of maturer
years has convinced us that it would hardly be possible to find a
more typical instance than Young's poetry of the mistake which
substitutes interested obedience for sympathetic emotion and
baptises egoism as religion.'[55] This was the line of attack, that
his life was false and his poetry was false, and there can hardly
be a more damaging one for a moral poet. Phrases like
'parasitic', 'inflated panegyric', 'ingenious humility', 'the most
servile of poets', 'clay compounded chiefly of the worldling and
the rhetorician', 'ambitious and greedy discontent', fill her
account of Young's life and make Croft's smears seem
indulgent by comparison; and when she passed on to the
works, though obliged to admit a 'real spark of Promethean
fire' in this 'unmistakable poet' and an 'outburst of genius' in
the first few *Nights*, she laboured the point of his insincerity.
'His Muse never stood face to face with a genuine, living
human being',[56] she asserted, calling him 'always at a telescopic
distance from mother Earth and simple human joys'; his

'radical insincerity as a poetic artist', his 'adherence to abstractions allied with want of genuine emotion', his 'negation of sympathy' led her to the conclusion:

> In Young we have the type of that deficient human sympathy, that impiety towards the present and the visible,· which flies for its motives, its sanctities and its religion to the remote, the vague and the unknown.[57]

We may agree with Birley's comment:

> I know of nowhere in all critical literature where the critic seems to be so totally removed from the work under consideration as George Eliot's essay on the *Night Thoughts* . . . 'Place him on a breezy common, where the furze is in its golden bloom, where children are playing and horses standing with fondling necks, and he would have nothing to say.' In the face of such heartiness Young would indeed be silent.[58]

Unfortunately one cannot deny the effectiveness, real or accidental, of this formidable mid-Victorian denunciation. The picture that George Eliot drew of the servile hypocrite is still the accepted image in the reference books and literary histories, while her indictment of Young's works as insincere and deficient in humanity is echoed by those who have never tried to read him. Those later critics who have taken the trouble to read the *Night Thoughts* and the *Love of Fame* and *The Revenge*, like Gosse and Saintsbury and Mackail – and more recently Sir Robert Birley, Isabel St John Bliss and Brian Hepworth – agree that his work is worth reading and should still be read. But the miasma of prejudice against the man – what Dr Bliss calls 'a kind of traditional denigration'[59] – still lingers and makes us reluctant to embark on poems of such length when their sincerity is in doubt.[v]

It has been my effort in this book to show that Edward Young was the opposite of his legend – a warm, good-hearted,

---

[v] As Sutherland puts it, 'So little was the eighteenth-century poet habituated to the free expression of spontaneous emotion that, when a writer like Edward Young attempts to "give a loose" to feeling in his *Night Thoughts*, we are apt today to doubt his sincerity and deplore his exhibitionism. We feel almost as if we had come unawares upon the poet in his underclothes.' (*Preface*, 71.)

lovable and sincere Christian whose main fault was a lack of common sense and whose great poem was the spontaneous product of genuine emotion. If this should persuade the modern reader to look without prejudice into these too long neglected works, I shall be well satisfied.

REFERENCES

Abbreviations

A MANUSCRIPT

MS *All Souls*	Archives of All Souls College, Oxford (Acta, minutes of meetings; Martin, C. Trice Martin, Catalogue of the Archives of All Souls College, Oxford, 1877)
MS *Army*	Army list, 1745, Public Record Office
MS *Ayot St Peter*	Parish register, Ayot St Peter, Herts
MS *Balliol*	Archives of Balliol College, Oxford (BB, Buttery Books; Battells, Bursar's Book of Battells; Register, Register of Admissions and Degrees)
MS *Chancery*	Chancery Proceedings, Public Record Office
MS *Chetwynd*	Warrants for Pensions 1715–30, Bodleian
MS *Chiddingfold*	Parish register, Chiddingfold, Surrey
MS *Close Rolls*	Close Rolls, Public Record Office
MS *Corpus*	Archives of Corpus Christi College, Oxford (BB, Buttery Books)
MS *Dillon*	Dillon papers, Oxfordshire County Record Office
MS *Egerton*	Egerton papers, British Library
MS *Ellis*	Ellis papers, British Library
MS *Forster*	Forster collection, Victoria & Albert Museum
MS *Gosling*	Gosling's Bank Ledgers, Barclay's Bank, 19 Fleet Street, London
MS *Jersey*	Jersey papers, British Library
MS *Jones*	Jones papers, Dr Williams' Library, 14 Gordon Square, London
MS *Liebert*	Temple MS, Liebert collection, Yale
MS *New Coll.*	Archives of New College, Oxford (*Registrum*, Register of Wardens, Fellows and Scholars)
MS *Palmerston*	Diaries of 1st Viscount Palmerston, Hampshire County Record Office, Winchester
MS *Portland*	Portland papers, Longleat, Wilts.
MS *Rawlinson*	Rawlinson papers, Bodleian Library, Oxford
MS *St Mary-le-Strand*	Parish register, St Mary-le-Strand, Westminster Public Library

MS *Sarum*	Chapter Act Books, Diocesan Record Office, Salisbury, Wilts.
MS *Somerset Ho.*	Copies of wills, Somerset House, London
MS *Stanstead Abbotts*	Parish Register, Stanstead Abbotts, Herts
MS *Tanner*	Tanner papers, Bodleian Library, Oxford
MS *Treasury*	Treasury warrants, money books, etc., Public Record Office
MS *Upham*	Parish register, Upham, Hants (Durleigh Rectory, Southampton)
MS *Walpole*	Walpole papers, Cambridge University Library
MS *Welwyn*	Parish records, Welwyn, Herts (*PR*, parish register; *Vestry*, minutes of vestry meetings; *School*, minutes of Charity School meetings; *Transcripts*, Bishop's annual transcripts of the parish register, Hertfordshire County Record Office)
MS *Win. Coll.*	Muniments of Winchester College, Hampshire (WCM, muniments; Long Rolls, yearly lists)
MS *Winton.*	Archives of Winchester Diocese, Diocesan Registry, Winchester

B   PRINTED BOOKS

Atkyns	*The English Reports*, XXVI, Chancery VI (containing Atkyns I–III), Edinburgh, 1903
Barbauld	A. L. Barbauld, ed. *The Correspondence of Samuel Richardson*, 6 vols, 1804
Biog. Brit.	*Biographia Britannica*, 6 vols & Supplement, 1760–66
Biog. Dram.	*Biographia Dramatica*, by D. E. Baker, continued by I. Reed and S. Jones, 3 vols, 1812
Birley	R. Birley, *Sunk without Trace*, 1962
Bliss	Isabel St John Bliss, *Edward Young*, New York, 1969
Branch Johnson	W. Branch Johnson, *Welwyn, By and Large*, Welwyn, 1967
Burrows	M. Burrows, *Worthies of All Souls*, 1874
Chalmers	A. Chalmers, *The Works of the English Poets, from Chaucer to Cowper*, 21 vols, 1810
Chambers	R. Chambers, *The Book of Days*, 2 vols,
Climenson	Emily J. Climenson, *Elizabeth Montagu, The Queen of the Blue-Stockings*, 2 vols, 1906
Clutterbuck	R. Clutterbuck, *The History and Antiquities of the County of Hertford*, 3 vols, 1821
Conjectures	E. D. Jones, ed. *English Critical Essays (XVI–XVIII Century)*, Oxford (World's Classics), 1930

Cook	A. K. Cook, *About Winchester College*, 1917
Croft	Sir J. Hawkins, ed. *The Works of Samuel Johnson, LL.D*, 11 vols, 1787
DNB	*Dictionary of National Biography*
D'Israeli	I. D'Israeli, *Miscellanies of Literature*, 1840
Doran	*The Complete Works, Poetry and Prose, of the Rev. Edward Young* [with] *a Life of the Author*, by John Doran, ed. James Nichols, 2 vols, 1854
Eliot	George Eliot, *Essays and Leaves from a Note-Book*, Edinburgh, 1884
Foster	J. Foster, *Alumni Oxonienses (1715–1886)*, 1888; ES (Early Series, 1500–1714), Oxford, 1891
Foxon	D. F. Foxon, *English Verse, 1701–1750, a Catalogue*, 2 vols, Cambridge, 1975
Gosse	E. Gosse, *A History of Eighteenth Century Literature*, 1896
Halsband	R. Halsband, ed. *The Complete Letters of Lady Mary Wortley Montagu*, 3 vols, Oxford, 1966
Hamwood	Mrs G. H. Bell, ed. *The Hamwood Papers of the Ladies of Llangollen*, 1930
Hawkins	Laetitia-Matilda Hawkins, *Memoirs, Anecdotes, Facts and Opinions*, 2 vols, 1824
Hayley	W. Hayley, *Plays of Three Acts*, 1784
Hearne	*Remarks and Collections of Thomas Hearne*, Oxford Historical Society, 10 vols, Oxford, 1885–1915
Hepworth	*Edward Young, selected poems*, Carcanet Press, 1975
Hill	G. Birkbeck Hill, ed. *The Lives of the English Poets*, by Samuel Johnson, Oxford, 1905
Hill-Powell	G. Birkbeck Hill, ed., revised by L. F. Powell, *Boswell's Life of Johnson, together with Boswell's Journal of a Tour to the Hebrides*, 6 vols, Oxford, 1934
HMC	Historical Manuscripts Commission, *Reports*, HMSO
Holgate	C. W. Holgate, *Winchester Long Rolls*, 2 vols, Winchester, 1899; 1904
Howe	P. P. Howe, ed. *The Complete Works of William Hazlitt*, 21 vols, 1934
Jacob	Giles Jacob, *The Poetical Register*, 2 vols, 1723
Jones (Sarum)	W. H. Jones, *Fasti Ecclesiae Sarisberiensis*, 1879
Jones, Mary	Mary Jones, *Miscellanies in Prose and Verse*, Oxford, 1750
Kidgell	John Kidgell, *The Card*, 2 vols, 1755
Kind	J. L. Kind, *Edward Young in Germany*, New York, 1906
Kirby	T. F. Kirby, *Annals of Winchester College*, Winchester, 1892; *Winchester Scholars*, 1888

Le Hardy	W. Le Hardy, *Hertfordshire County Records* (Sessions Books), Hertford, 1935
Le Tourneur	P. Le Tourneur, *Les Nuits d'Young*, 2 vols, Paris, 1769
Lewis	W. S. Lewis, ed. *Horace Walpole's Correspondence*, 39 vols, Yale, 1937–74
Lipscomb	G. Lipscomb, *The History and Antiquities of the County of Buckingham*, 4 vols, 1847
Little	D. M. Little & G. M. Kahrl, ed. *The Letters of David Garrick*, 3 vols, OUP, 1963
Llanover	Lady Llanover, ed. *The Autobiography and Correspondence of Mary Granville, Mrs Delany*, 6 vols, 1861–2
London Stage	*The London Stage, 1660–1800*, 5 parts, Illinois, 1960–8
Maurice	T. Maurice, *Memoirs of the Author of Indian Antiquities*, 2 vols, 1819
McKillop	A. D. McKillop, ed. *James Thomson 1700–1748: Letters and Documents*, Kansas, 1958
Manning	O. Manning & W. Bray, *The History and Antiquities of the County of Surrey*, 3 vols, 1804
Mitford	J. Mitford, ed. *The Poetical Works of Edward Young, with a Memoir*, 2 vols, Aldine, 1896
Montagu	Matthew Montagu, ed. *The Letters of Mrs Elizabeth Montagu*, 4 vols, 1809
Nichols	John Nichols, *Literary Anecdotes of the Eighteenth Century*, 6 vols, 1812
Osborn	J. M. Osborn, ed. *Joseph Spence, Observations, Anecdotes and Characters of Books and Men*, 2 vols, Oxford, 1966
Parry	C. H. Parry, *A Memoir of the Revd Joshua Parry*, ed. Sir J. E. Eardley-Wilmot, 1872
Peerage	G. E. C(okayne), *The Complete Peerage*, 13 vols, 1910–59
Pennington	M. Pennington, ed. *Letters from Mrs Elizabeth Carter to Mrs Montagu*, 3 vols, 1817; *A Series of Letters between Mrs Elizabeth Carter and Miss Catherine Talbot*, 2 vols, 1808
Pettit	H. Pettit, ed. *The Correspondence of Edward Young*, Oxford, 1971
Rothschild	*The Rothschild Library, a Catalogue*, 2 vols, Cambridge, 1954
Shelley	H. C. Shelley, *The Life and Letters of Edward Young*, 1914
Shenstone	Marjorie Williams, ed. *The Letters of William Shenstone*, Oxford, 1939
Sherburn	G. Sherburn, ed. *The Correspondence of Alexander Pope*, 5 vols, 1956

SP	*Calendar of State Papers*, HMSO
Stephen	L. Stephen, *English Literature and Society in the Eighteenth Century*, 1920
Stuffed Owl	D. B. Wyndham Lewis & C. Lee, ed. *The Stuffed Owl, an Anthology of Bad Verse* (enlarged), 1930
Sutherland	J. Sutherland, *A Preface to Eighteenth Century Poetry*, Oxford, 1962
TB	*Calendar of Treasury Books*, HMSO
Thomas	W. Thomas, *Le Poète Edward Young*, Paris, 1901
Tracy	C. Tracy, ed. *The Poetical Works of Richard Savage*, Cambridge, 1962
Victor	B. Victor, *Original Letters, Dramatic Pieces and Poems*, 3 vols, 1776
Warburton	R. Hurd, ed. *Letters from a Late Eminent Prelate to One of his Friends* (3rd ed.), 1809
Warton	Joseph Warton, *Essay on the Genius and Writings of Pope*, vol. I, 1756; vol. II, 1782
Williams	H. Williams, ed. *The Correspondence of Jonathan Swift*, 5 vols, Oxford, 1963–5; *The Journal to Stella*, 2 vols, Oxford, 1948
Wimsatt	W. K. Wimsatt & F. A. Pottle, *Boswell for the Defence*, 1960
Young, Dean	Edward Young (father), *Sermons on Several Occasions*, (2nd ed.), 2 vols, 1706

C NEWSPAPERS AND PERIODICALS

CR	*The Critical Review*
DC	*The Daily Courant*
DJ	*The Daily Journal*
DP	*The Daily Post*
Englishman	*The Englishman* (ed. R. Blanchard, Oxford, 1955)
EM	*The European Magazine*
EP	*The Evening Post*
GA	*The General Advertiser*
GIJ	*The Gray's Inn Journal* (2 vols, Vaillant, 1756)
GM	*The Gentleman's Magazine*
Guardian	*The Guardian* (2 vols, Tonson, 1751)
JE	*Journal Etranger*, Paris
LC	*The London Chronicle*
LDP	*The London Daily Post*
LEP	*The London Evening Post*
LJ	*The London Journal*
LM	*The London Magazine*

MM	*The Monthly Magazine*
MR	*The Monthly Review*
PA	*The Public Advertiser*
PB	*The Post Boy*
Plain Dealer	*The Plain Dealer* (2 vols, Richardson, 1730)
Spectator	*The Spectator* (5 vols, ed. D. F. Bond, Oxford, 1965)
Tatler	*The Tatler* (vol. V, 2nd ed., 1720)
WEP	*The Whitehall Evening Post*
WJ	*The Weekly Journal, or Saturday's Post*

D ARTICLES

Blackwood	*Blackwood's Magazine* (W. R. Hughes, 'Dr Young and his Curates', 1932)
BC	*The Book Collector* (H. Forster, 'Edward Young in Translation', 1970–1)
ELN	*English Language Notes* (H. Forster, 'The Ordination of Edward Young', 1963)
MLN	*Modern Language Notes* (Charlotte E. Crawford, 'Edward Young and Wycombe Election', 1945)
MP	*Modern Philology* (P. J. Crean, 'The Stage Licensing Act of 1737', 1938)
N&Q	*Notes and Queries* (various)
PAPS	*Proceedings of the American Philosophical Society* (H. Pettit, 'Edward Young and the Case of Lee vs. D'Aranda', 1963)
UCS	*University of Colorado Studies* (Series in Language and Literature), no. 5 (H. Pettit, 'A Bibliography of Young's Night Thoughts', 1954); no. 10 (H. Pettit and E. Collins, 'The Genealogy of Edward Young', 1966)

REFERENCES

Footnotes

CHAPTER 1

1. MS Upham (baptisms 1598–1734).
2. *UCS*, no. 10, 81.
3. Ibid.
4. Kirby, *Scholars*, 189.
5. *UCS*, no. 10, 82
6. MS Somerset Ho., PCC86 Pembroke 1.
7. Foster (ES), IV, 1703.
8. MS Winton, Visitations, 1686.
9. Young (Dean), *Sermons*, I, 1.
10. Shelley, 4.
11. MS Tanner, 39, f. 97.
12. MS New Coll., 1663.
13. Young (Dean), *Sermon . . . at Whitehall*, Birch, 1679.
14. Shelley, 5.
15. Shelley, 6.
16. MS New Coll., 1663.
17. MS Winton, Morley I, 86.
18. MS Tanner, 37, f. 249.
19. Jones (Sarum), 385.
20. Young (Dean), *Sermon . . . at Guildhall*, Kettilby, 1683.
21. Young (Dean), *Sermons*, I, 144.
22. Jacob, II, 241.
23. Doran, I, 260.
24. Mitford, I, ix, n. 2.
25. MS Tanner, 30, f. 89.
26. Atwood, *Christian Love*, t.p.
27. Hill, III, 368.
28. Young (Sarum), 377.
29. Young (Dean), *Sermons*, I, 182.
30. Young (Dean), *Sermons*, I, 217.
31. Young (Dean), *Sermon . . . at Whitehall*, Kettilby, 1693.
32. Young (Dean), *Two Sermons . . . at Whitehall*, Kettilby, 1694.
33. *DNB*, art. Ellis, John.
34. Shelley, 8–9 (N.B. dating).
35. Shelley, 7–8.
36. Pettit, 189.
37. Young (Dean), *Sermons*, II, 1; 40.
38. Young (Dean), *Sermons*, II (appx.).
39. Holgate, I, 78.
40. MS Win. Coll., WCM 21482[x].
41. Holgate, I, 79–98.
42. MS Win. Coll., WCM 21852.
43. Cook, 247.
44. Holgate, I, 98.
45. Shelley, 10–11.
46. *SP* (Domestic), 1700–2, 523; 532.
47. *SP* (Domestic), 1702–3, 359.
48. MS Sarum, XX (Frome), 1702.
49. MS Jersey, 28.890, ff. 198–9.
50. Jacob, II, 241.
51. Kirby, *Annals*, 523–6.
52. Kirby, *Annals*, 524.
53. Ibid.
54. Kirby, *Annals*, 525.
55. MS Win. Coll., WCM 556.
56. MS Win. Coll., WCM 556 reverse.
57. Holgate, I, 103.
58. Osborn, 849; 788.
59. Kidgell, I, 264.
60. Osborn, 836.
61. Osborn, 838–9.
62. Kirby, *Annals*, 533–4.

63. Pettit, 278.
64. Cook, 302.
65. Chalmers, XII, 440.
66. *Biog. Brit.*, V, 3353.
67. Mitford, II, 305.
68. C. Pitt, *Poetical Works*, Bell, 1782, (v).

CHAPTER 2

1. Foster (ES), IV, 1703.
2. MS Sarum, XX (Frome, 1702–3).
3. MS Win. Coll., WCM 556.
4. Shelley, 11.
5. MS Rawlinson, 92, f. 169.
6. MS Upham (marriages, 1622–1734).
7. Shelley, 11.
8. Foster (ES). IV, 1502.
9. MS Rawlinson, 92, f. 169.
10. MS Corpus, BB 1702–3.
11. MS Corpus, BB 1704–5.
12. Manning, I, 656.
13. Foster (ES), II, 657.
14. *Account.*
15. *Account.*
16. *Account.*
17. Kirby, *Scholars*, 14.
18. Foster (ES), II, 657.
19. MS Upham (as 6).
20. *Account.*
21. MS New Coll., 1731.
22. MS Rawlinson, 93, f. 216.
23. MS Corpus, BB 1704–5.
24. MS Rawlinson, 92, f. 216.
25. MS Sarum, XX (Frome), 1705.
26. Foster (ES), IV, 1703.
27. Hill, III, 363.
28. Nichols, I, 5–6.
29. Pettit, 1.
30. Thomas, 33.
31. MS Corpus, BB 1704–5.
32. Hearne, I, 266.
33. MS Corpus, BB 1705–6; 1706–7; 1707–8.
34. Pettit, 1–2.

35. MS All Souls, Martin, 320, no. 219.
36. MS Corpus, BB 1707–8; 1708–9.
37. MS All Souls, Martin, 413 (BB).
38. MS All Souls, *Registrum*, II.
39. Hill, III, 364.
40. Stubbes, *Laurel and Olive*, Sanger, 1710, iii.
41. Holgate, I, 105–9.
42. *Tatler*, V, 146.
43. *Tatler*, V, 147.
44. Foxon, Y72.
45. Foxon, Y109.
46. *Peerage*, VII, 435.
47. Foster (ES), II, 663.
48. Pettit, 88–9.
49. Hill, II, 306.
50. Chalmers, XI, 102.
51. Mitford, II, 294.
52. Mitford, II, 297–8.
53. Mitford, II, 298.
54. Mitford, II, 299.
55. Mitford, II, 304.
56. Mitford, II, 304, note.
57. Mitford, II, 305.
58. Osborn, 841.
59. Williams, *Stella*, 54.
60. Osborn, 843.
61. Williams, *Stella*, 619–20.
62. MS All Souls, Martin 413 (BB).
63. Mitford, II, 305–6.
64. Hearne, IV, 151.
65. Pettit, 54.
66. *Guardian*, I, 223; 225 (no. 51).
67. Foxon, Y109.
68. Mitford, II, 12.
69. Hill, III, 393.
70. Gosse, 209.
71. Doran, I, 287.
72. Ibid.
73. Mitford, II, 5.
74. Mitford, II, 6.
75. *Englishman*, 49–50.
76. Hill, III, 384.
77. Doran, I, 261.
78. *N&Q*, NS vol. X, no. 6, 219.
79. Ibid.

80. Ibid.
81. Hill, I, 314.
82. *N&Q* (as 78).
83. Ibid.
84. Young, *Epistle to Bolingbroke*, 1714, 2.
85. *Englishman*, 49–50.
86. MS All Souls, Martin 413 (BB).
87. *Guardian*, no. 92, advt.
88. Osborn, 818.
89. *DC*, 31 December, 1713.
90. MS All Souls, Martin 413 (BB).
91. MS Chiddingfold (baptisms).
92. Nichols, I, 6, note.
93. *DNB*, art. Young.
94. *PB*, 20–3 March, 1713/14.
95. Foxon, Y74.
96. Hill, III, 394.
97. Foxon, Y75.
98. *London Stage*, Pt. 2, 351–5.
99. Doran, I, 316.
100. Hill, III, 394.

CHAPTER 3

1. Foxon, Y99.
2. Mitford, II, 277.
3. Mitford, II, 278.
4. Mitford, II, 279.
5. Mitford, II, 283.
6. Osborn, 822; 820.
7. Osborn, 827.
8. Osborn, 844.
9. Osborn, 829.
10. Osborn, 832.
11. Manning, I, 653.
12. Sherburn, I, 223.
13. Pettit, 3.
14. Chalmers, XI, 116.
15. Pettit, 5–6.
16. Osborn, 163.
17. MS All Souls, Acta, 8 November, 1716.
18. Hearne, V, 240.
19. Hearne, VI, 12.
20. Pettit, 89.
21. Doran, II, 308.
22. MS Egerton, 2174, f. 310.
23. Pettit, 8–9.
24. Pettit, 15.
25. MS All Souls, Martin 413 (BB).
26. Mitford, II, 194.
27. *Spectator*, IV, 161 (no. 469).
28. MS Corpus, BB 1702–3.
29. *EP*, 29 August, 1717.
30. Pettit, 10.
31. Pettit, 11, n. 3.
32. Pettit, 12.
33. Pettit, 13.
34. Pettit, 14.
35. Pettit, 14–15, n. 2.
36. MS All Souls, Martin 413 (BB).
37. Ibid.
38. Foxon Y100.
39. Pettit, 14.
40. Hill, III, 399.
41. Mitford, II, 171, note.
42. Mitford, II, 170.
43. Hill, III, 395.
44. Pettit, 74–5.
45. Foxon, Y102.
46. Mitford, II, 178.
47. Mitford, II, 179.
48. Pettit, 17.
49. Pettit, 18.
50. Pettit, 517–18.
51. Pettit, 16.
52. *London Stage*, Pt. 2, 530.
53. *London Stage*, Pt. 2, 536.
54. 'Corinna', *Critical Remarks*, Bettenham, 1719, t.p.
55. *DC*, 8 April, 1719.
56. Doran, II, 159.
57. T. Rundle, *Letters*, ed. J. Dallaway, Gloucester, 1789, II, 8.
58. Ibid.
59. J. Dennis, *Critical Works*, ed. E. N. Hooker, Baltimore, 1939, II, 166.
60. 'Corinna' (as 54), 56–67.
61. Gosse, 209.
62. Doran, II, 159.
63. Doran, II, 172.
64. Doran, II, 179–80.
65. *Biog. Dram.*, II, 72.

66. MS All Souls, Acta, 16 March, 1718 (1719).
67. J. Mitchell, *Lugubres Cantus*, London & Edinburgh, 1719, A2v.
68. MS All Souls, Acta, 26 May, 1719.
69. *DNB*, art. Young.
70. MS All Souls, Martin 413 (BB).
71. *Conjectures*, 362.
72. Pettit, 521–2.
73. *Conjectures*, 359.
74. Mitford, II, 197.
75. Chalmers, XI, 122.
76. Pettit, 9.
77. Mitford, II, 197–8.

CHAPTER 4

1. Atkyns, 496.
2. Hill, III, 369.
3. Hill, III, 368.
4. Osborn, 836.
5. MS All Souls, Martin 413 (BB); Pettit, 7–15.
6. *WJ*, 25 January, 1718.
7. Pettit, 17, n. 1.
8. MS All Souls, Martin 413 (BB).
9. Pettit, 20.
10. Pettit, 18.
11. Pettit, 19.
12. Pettit, 20.
13. Atkyns, 496.
14. Pettit, 21.
15. Lipscomb, I, 572.
16. MS All Souls, Martin 413 (BB).
17. MS Chancery, C/11/1435/28 (8 June, 1723).
18. MS Chancery, C/11/1435/28 (5 March, 1722/3).
19. *Conjectures*, 342.
20. Williams, *Swift*, II, 285.
21. MS All Souls, Martin 413 (BB).
22. Pettit, 29, n. 1.
23. *WJ*, 30 July, 1720.
24. Burrows, 397.
25. MS All Souls, Martin 413 (BB).
26. Burrows, 397–8.
27. Burrows, 397.
28. HMC, Portland V, 601.
29. MS All Souls, Acta, 26 November, 1720.
30. Doran, II, 188.
31. Doran, II, 189.
32. Doran, II, 190.
33. Ibid.
34. *EP*, 27–9 April, 1721.
35. Hill, III, 364.
36. Ibid.
37. Osborn, 847.
38. Parry, 133.
39. Mitford, II, 296.
40. Doran, II, 189.
41. Chalmers, XII, 371.
42. Jacob, II, 241.
43. Chalmers, X, 99.
44. *London Stage*, Pt. 2, 624.
45. *Guardian*, I, 159–60 (no. 37).
46. *Biog. Dram.*, III, 203.
47. *Biog. Dram.*, III, 202–3.
48. Hill, III, 397.
49. Doran, II, 207.
50. Doran, II, 229.
51. *London Stage*, Pt. 3, 1129–60.
52. *London Stage*, Pt. 4, 321–2.
53. L. A. Marchand, *Byron*, New York, 1957, I, 96.
54. L. A. Marchand, *Byron*, New York, 1957, I, 96, n. 5.
55. Howe, V, 227–8; XVIII, 252–4; XVIII, 373.
56. Mitford, I, xxiv.
57. Warton, II, 471.
58. MS All Souls, Acta, 4 November, 1721.
59. HMC, Portland VII, 309.
60. Parry, 121–2.
61. Atkyns, 496.
62. MS All Souls, Acta, 11 December, 1723.
63. H. Walpole, *Royal and Noble Authors*, ed. T. Park, 1806, IV, 131.
64. Parry, 122.
65. Atkyns, 496.

66. MS Close Rolls, C54/5218.
67. Atkyns, 496.
68. MS Chancery, C/11/1435/28 (5 March, 1722/3).
69. MS Chancery, C/11/1435/28 (7 November, 1729).

CHAPTER 5

1. Chalmers, XII, 371.
2. Ibid.
3. R. Cumberland, *Memoirs*, Lackington, 1806, 147.
4. Pettit, 22.
5. Ibid.
6. Pettit, 23–4.
7. Pettit, 24.
8. Pettit, 23, n. 1.
9. Ibid.
10. Pettit, 25.
11. Pettit, 25, n. 4.
12. *DNB*, art. Tickell, Thomas.
13. Pettit, 26.
14. Pettit, 27.
15. Pettit, 28–9.
16. Pettit, 30.
17. Pettit, 32–3.
18. Pettit, 33–4.
19. Pettit, 35–6.
20. Pettit, 37.
21. Pettit, 38.
22. *ELN*, I, no. 1, 27.
23. Pettit, 39.
24. Pettit, 47.
25. Hill, III, 364.
26. Pettit, 28.
27. Pettit, 34.
28. Pettit, 36.
29. *DP*, 25 January, 1725.
30. *DC*, 2 April, 1725.
31. Young, *The Universal Passion*, Satire II, 1st ed., Roberts, 1725, 17.
32. *DC*, 26 April, 1725.
33. *DP*, 11 June, 1725.
34. *DP*, 17 January, 1726.
35. Mitford, II, 78.

36. *Spectator*, I, 311 (no. 73).
37. Mitford, II, 55.
38. Mitford, II, 54.
39. Mitford, II, 56.
40. Tracy, 68.
41. Warton, II, 203.
42. Ibid.
43. Mitford, II, 67.
44. Mitford, II, 89.
45. Mitford, II, 81.
46. Mitford, II, 135.
47. Mitford, II, 89.
48. Mitford, II, 71.
49. Mitford, II, 62.
50. Mitford, II, 67.
51. Mitford, II, 75.
52. Mitford, II, 136.
53. Mitford, II, 80.
54. *EM*, VI, 192–3.
55. *Plain Dealer*, II, 298.
56. *Plain Dealer*, II, 438.
57. Cooke, *Battle*, Roberts, 1725, 15.
58. Williams, *Swift*, IV, 153.
59. Chalmers, XI, 453.
60. Mitford, II, 134.
61. Mitford, II, 135.
62. Mitford, II, 57–8.
63. Mitford, II, 72.
64. Mitford, II, 77.
65. Pettit, 44.
66. Ibid.
67. *DP*, 17 January, 1726.
68. Pettit, 47–8.
69. MS Chetwynd, Add. D4, no. 96.
70. Pettit, 45.
71. *MLN*, LX, 459–61.
72. *LJ*, 16 July, 1726.
73. Hearne, IX, 166.
74. MS Chetwynd (as 69).
75. *DJ*, 5 July, 1726.
76. McKillop, 41.
77. *DP*, 22 July, 1726.
78. Shippen, *Remarks*, Moore, 1726, 4.
79. Ibid.
80. Shippen, *Remarks*, 13.

CHAPTER 6

1. Pettit, 47.
2. Pettit, 49.
3. Mitford, II, 104.
4. Pettit, 30.
5. Pettit, 40.
6. Pettit, 45.
7. Young, *Specimen*, Wilkins, 1726 (2).
8. Pettit, 49, n. 2.
9. *DP*, 8 February, 1727.
10. Pettit, 34.
11. A. Ramsay, *Works*, ed. G. Chalmers, Edinburgh, 1851, II, 278–9.
12. Williams, *Swift*, IV, 53.
13. Pettit, 53.
14. Pettit, 52–3.
15. Osborn, 940.
16. Chalmers, XII, 422.
17. Pettit, 54.
18. Pettit, 55–6.
19. Pettit, 57.
20. *DP*, 2 June, 1727; *WEP*, 3 June, 1727.
21. Thomas, 586.
22. Victor, I, 266; 268.
23. Pettit, 59–60 (N.B. dating).
24. Thomas, 582–3.
25. Doran, II, 326.
26. *DP*, 17 November, 1727.
27. Pettit, 58.
28. Hill, III, 379.
29. Doran, II, 321.
30. Pennington, *Talbot*, I, 74.
31. Hill, III, 379.
32. Pettit, 34.
33. Pettit, 62.
34. Pettit, 58.
35. Ibid.
36. Mitford, II, 375.
37. Hill, III, 376.
38. Warton, II, 204–5.
39. Voltaire, *Essay*, Jallasson, 1727, advt.
40. Osborn, 854.
41. Foxon, Y136.

42. Mitford, II, 96.
43. Mitford, II, 93.
44. Mitford, II, 106–7.
45. Mitford, II, 96.
46. *LC*, LXXIX, 291.
47. Pettit, 47.
48. Pettit, 54.
49. Pettit, 31–2.
50. Osborn, 798.
51. Rothschild, II, 709.
52. Mitford, II, 97.
53. Mitford, II, 103.
54. Mitford, II, 110.
55. Mitford, II, 116.
56. Mitford, II, 120.
57. Mitford, II, 100.
58. Mitford, II, 99–100.
59. Mitford, II, 117.
60. Mitford, II, 120.
61. *DC*, 18 March, 1728.
62. Pettit, 60–1.
63. Pettit, 59, n. 1.
64. *DJ*, 13 December, 1728.
65. Osborn, 507.
66. Tracy, 106.
67. Pettit, 65.
68. Ibid.
69. Mitford, II, 108.
70. Pettit, 64.

CHAPTER 7

1. Mitford, II, 132.
2. Pettit, 63–4.
3. *Biog. Brit.*, VI, Pt. 2, Supplement.
4. *ELN*, I, no. 1, 27.
5. Ibid.
6. Foxon Y94.
7. Mitford, II, 141.
8. Mitford, II, 147–8.
9. Mitford, II, 151.
10. Mitford, II, 156.
11. Mitford, II, 152–3.
12. Mitford, II, 153.
13. Mitford, II, 166–7.
14. Mitford, II, 168.

15. Doran, II, 379.
16. Doran, II, 380.
17. *LEP*, 25–7 March, 1729.
18. Mitford, I, xxx–xxxi.
19. Hill, III, 370.
20. *Biog. Brit.*, VI, Pt. 2, Suppt., 259, note (F).
21. Victor, III, iv.
22. McKillop, 63.
23. Chalmers, XII, 294.
24. Chalmers, XII, 318.
25. Foxon, Y117.
26. Mitford, II, 92.
27. Mitford, II, 307–8.
28. Mitford, II, 320.
29. Mitford, II, 321.
30. Mitford, II, 322.
31. Welsted, *One Epistle*, Roberts, n.d., 22, note.
32. *DNB*, art. Wharton, Philip.
33. MS Chancery, C/11/1435/28 (7 November, 1729).
34. Pettit, 66–7, n. 4.
35. MS All Souls, Martin 413 (BB).
36. Ibid.
37. Ibid.
38. Mitford, II, 335.
39. *DP*, 6 April, 1730.
40. Mitford, II, 337.
41. Mitford, II, 357.
42. Mitford, II, 372.
43. Mitford, II, 343.
44. Mitford, II, 373.
45. Mitford, II, 336.
46. Pettit, 68–9.
47. Pettit, 565.
48. W. Clark Russell, *The Book of Authors* (1871), 176.
49. *Lord Orford's Reminiscences*, 1818, 80.
50. Chalmers, XII, 282.
51. Williams, *Swift*, III, 423.
52. MS Rawlinson, J. 40, i, 116.
53. *GM*, I, 72.
54. MS All Souls, Acta, 20 July, 1730.
55. Elwin, X, 261, n. 2.
56. Sherburn, I, 380.

CHAPTER 8

1. Foster (ES), III, 1085.
2. MS All Souls, Martin 413 (BB).
3. Ibid.
4. Clutterbuck, II, 499.
5. Pettit, 67, n. 2.
6. Llanover, I, 253–4.
7. *DP*, 27 March, 1730.
8. MS Walpole, 80, 293.
9. Llanover, I, 192.
10. *Biog. Brit.*, VI, Pt. 2, Suppt., 257–8.
11. MS Dillon, DIL/XXI/4.
12. *LC*, LXXXIV, 356.
13. MS Chetwynd, Add. D4, no. 118.
14. MS All Souls, Martin 413 (BB).
15. MS Welwyn, Vestry, 14 January, 1730 (Poor Rate).
16. *DP*, 3 April, 1730.
17. MS Treasury, XXX, 345 (T52/37).
18. *UCS*, no. 10, 157.
19. Atkyns, 496.
20. MS Welwyn, Transcripts, 1730/1.
21. *GM*, LII, 72.
22. MS Welwyn, Transcripts, 1734.
23. Pettit, 85.
24. *LC*, XVII, 368.
25. Hill-Powell, IV, 120.
26. Doran, II, 446.
27. Clutterbuck, II, 310, note.
28. Clutterbuck, II, 325.
29. Clutterbuck, II, 227.
30. Clutterbuck, II, 265.
31. Clutterbuck, III, 36.
32. Clutterbuck, II, 157.
33. Clutterbuck, II, 323.
34. Clutterbuck, II, 400.
35. Clutterbuck, I, 515.
36. Clutterbuck, II, 158.
37. Clutterbuck, II, 320.
38. MS St Mary-le-Strand, vol. 4 (births).
39. Ibid. (christenings).
40. *Biog. Brit.* (as 10), 258.

41. Hill, III, 390.
42. Foster (ES), II, 657.
43. Foster, II, 614.
44. R. F. Bigg-Wither, *History of the Wither Family*, Winchester, 1907, 45–6.
45. *DNB*, art. Lee, Fitzroy.
46. MS Dillon, DIL/XXI/21.
47. *Peerage*, VII, 647.
48. Williams, *Swift*, IV, 153.
49. *GM*, V, 731.
50. *DJ*, 5 February, 1735.
51. Mitford, II, 393.
52. MS Welwyn, PR, 24 June, 1735.
53. *Peerage*, X, 294.
54. *GM*, LII, 72.
55. Mitford, I, 32.
56. Chambers, 503.
57. Ibid.
58. MS Palmerston (October, 1736).
59. F. G. Lee, *History of the Prebendal Church of Thame*, 1883, 643.
60. Croft, IV, 250.
61. *Biog. Brit.*, VI, Pt. 2, Suppt., 258, note (D).
62. Le Tourneur, I, 60.
63. Mitford, I, 40–1.
64. Chambers, 502.
65. Gardenstone, *Travelling Memorandums*, Edinburgh, 1791, I, 187.
66. Young, *Works*, 3 vols, 1802, I, ix–x, note.
67. Chambers, 502.
68. Smollett, *Travels*, World's Classics, 1907, 91.
69. Croft, IV, 250.
70. *GM*, LII, 70.
71. Pettit, 73.
72. MS Liebert.
73. Pettit, 562.
74. MS Welwyn, Transcripts, 1736/7.
75. Pettit, 359, n. 1.
76. Pettit, 467.
77. MS Welwyn, Vestry, 5 January, 1737/8.
78. MS Palmerston, 10 March, 1738.
79. *Peerage*, X, 294.
80. MS Somerset Ho., PCC 220 Brodripp.
81. *DP*, 27 October, 1737.
82. *MP*, XXXV, 239–55.
83. Pettit, 71.
84. Pettit, 74–5.
85. Pettit, 76.
86. Mitford, I, 111–12.
87. *LDP*, 30 January, 1739/40.

CHAPTER 9

1. Mitford, I, 109.
2. Chalmers, X, 243.
3. Pettit, 77.
4. Pettit, 78–9.
5. Pettit, 80.
6. Atkyns, 496.
7. Pettit, 82.
8. Pettit, 83.
9. Pettit, 84.
10. Pettit, 85.
11. Pettit, 86.
12. Pettit, 87.
13. Pettit, 88.
14. Pettit, 88–9.
15. Mitford, I, 16.
16. Pettit, 89.
17. Pettit, 90.
18. Ibid.
19. Pettit, 92.
20. Pettit, 93.
21. Pettit, 95.
22. Climenson, I, 60.
23. Montagu, II, 57–8.
24. Climenson, I, 61.
25. Montagu, II, 62–3.
26. Montagu, II, 65.
27. Pettit, 99.
28. Pettit, 102.
29. Pettit, 100.
30. Pettit, 101.
31. Pettit, 103–4.
32. Pettit, 102.
33. MS Army, IND/5437.
34. Pettit, 102.

35. Pettit, 110.
36. Pettit, 116.
37. Pettit, 117.
38. Pettit, 80, n. 1.
39. Pettit, 106.
40. Atkyns, 496.
41. Pettit, 107.
42. Pettit, 113.
43. Pettit, 114.
44. Pettit, 109 (N.B. dating).
45. Atkyns, 496–7.
46. Atkyns, 497.
47. Ibid.
48. Pettit, 111 (N.B. dating).
49. Pettit, 112.
50. MS Welwyn, Transcripts, 1740/1.
51. Pettit, 120.
52. Mitford, I, 85.
53. Pettit, 74–5, n. 3.
54. Pettit, 74; 76; 88.
55. Pettit, 74–5, n. 3.
56. Ibid.

CHAPTER 10

1. *GM*, LII, 72.
2. Thomas, Appx I, 600.
3. Osborn, 860.
4. Pettit, 122.
5. Climenson, I, 85.
6. Pettit, 126.
7. Pettit, 125.
8. Pettit, 129.
9. Montagu, II, 60–1.
10. Climenson, I, 91.
11. Pettit, 130–1.
12. Pettit, 139–40.
13. Foxon, Y24.
14. *UCS*, no. 5, 6.
15. Foxon, Y25.
16. Victor, I, 75–6.
17. Victor, I, 74.
18. Mitford, I, 1–2.
19. Stephen, 52.
20. Gosse, 212.
21. Pettit, 142.

22. Pettit, 144.
23. Pettit, 145.
24. Pettit, 97.
25. Pettit, 138.
26. MS Win. Coll., WCM 21727.
27. MS Win. Coll., WCM 21482^x.
28. Pettit, 147.
29. Pettit, 150.
30. Foxon, Y32.
31. *UCS*, no. 5, 21.
32. Pettit, 149.
33. Wharton, II, 204, note.
34. Doran, I, 46.
35. P. Doddridge, *Correspondence*, ed. J. D. Humphreys, 1830, IV, 198.
36. Shenstone, 59.
37. Mary Jones, 253.
38. Foxon, Y43.
39. Doran, I, 46.
40. *DP*, 6 June, 1743.
41. Warton, II, 205, note.
42. Mitford, I, 5.
43. Mitford, I, 7.
44. Mitford, I, 6–7.
45. Mitford, I, 5.
46. Mitford, I, 13–14.
47. Mitford, I, 20.
48. Mitford, I, 24.
49. Mitford, I, 18–19.
50. Mitford, I, 29.
51. Mitford, I, 29–30.
52. Gosse, 213.
53. Pettit, 359, n. 1.
54. Pettit, 562.
55. Mitford, I, 7–8.
56. Mitford, I, 32.
57. Mitford, I, 28.
58. Mitford, I, 74.
59. Ibid.
60. Mitford, I, 52–3.
61. Mitford, I, 72.
62. Foxon, Y43.
63. *Peerage*, VII, 646.
64. Pettit, 157.

CHAPTER 11

1. Pettit, 152.
2. Mitford, I, 52.
3. Pettit, 154.
4. Pettit, 154–5.
5. Pettit, 159 (N.B. dating).
6. Pettit, 156.
7. MS Win. Coll., WCM 21482ˣ.
8. Pettit, 165–6.
9. *UCS*, no. 10, 158.
10. *UCS*, no. 10, 145, n. 6.
11. Pettit, 167–8.
12. Pettit, 171.
13. *UCS*, no. 10, 145.
14. *UCS*, no. 10, 145–6, n. 6.
15. Pettit, 172.
16. Pettit, 173.
17. Pettit, 181 (N.B. dating).
18. Pettit, 174.
19. Pettit, 175.
20. *UCS*, no. 10, 156.
21. Llanover, II, 295.
22. Pettit, 176–7.
23. Foxon, Y49.
24. Foxon, Y47, note.
25. Foxon, Y47.
26. Pennington, *Talbot*, I, 74.
27. Shenstone, 80.
28. Llanover, II, 243.
29. Foxon, Y50.
30. Pettit, 180.
31. Pettit, 182.
32. Pettit, 182–3.
33. Pettit, 182.
34. Pennington, *Talbot*, I, 68.
35. Pennington, *Talbot*, I, 74.
36. Barbauld, I, 102.
37. Pettit, 186.
38. Ibid.
39. Ibid.
40. Pettit, 187.
41. Pettit, 188.
42. Pettit, 190.
43. Pettit, 191–2.
44. Pettit, 192.
45. Pettit, 193–4.
46. Foxon, Y52.
47. Mary Jones, 267.
48. Mary Jones, 268.
49. Pettit, 198.
50. Ibid.
51. Pettit, 200.
52. Pettit, 201.
53. Pettit, 206.
54. Montagu, III, 9–11.
55. Montagu, III, 12–13.
56. Pettit, 208–9.
57. Montagu, III, 17–24.
58. Pettit, 208.
59. Pettit, 211.
60. Mitford, II, 211–12.
61. Pettit, 215.
62. Pettit, 216.
63. Pettit, 216–17.
64. Pettit, 218–19.
65. Pettit, 220.
66. *GA*, 29 January, 1745/6.
67. Foxon, Y58; 59.
68. Foxon, Y61.
69. Foxon, Y60; 61.
70. Foxon, Y64.
71. Hill-Powell, IV, 61.
72. Mitford, I, 219–20.
73. Mitford, I, 228.
74. Hill, III, 396, n. 2.
75. Hill, III, 399, n. 6.

CHAPTER 12

1. *GA*, 29 January, 1745/6.
2. Pettit, 222.
3. Pettit, 225.
4. Pettit, 226.
5. Pettit, 228.
6. Pettit, 224, n. 4.
7. Pettit, 228.
8. Pettit, 229.
9. Pettit, 230.
10. Pettit, 234.
11. Ibid.
12. MS Welwyn, Vestry, 17 July, 1746.
13. Pettit, 247.
14. Pettit, 246.

15. Pettit, 236.
16. Pettit, 238.
17. Pettit, 243–4.
18. Pettit, 249.
19. Pettit, 252–3.
20. Lew Lewes, *Memoirs*, 1805, I, 10.
21. Pettit, 235.
22. Pettit, 247.
23. Pettit, 255.
24. Pettit, 267.
25. *UCS*, no. 10, 146.
26. *UCS*, no. 10, 155.
27. *UCS*, no. 10, 158–9.
28. Pettit, 246.
29. Pettit, 261.
30. Pettit, 278.
31. Pettit, 279.
32. Pettit, 208.
33. Pettit, 273.
34. Ibid.
35. Pettit, 283.
36. Pettit, 284.
37. Ibid.
38. Pettit, 287.
39. Pettit, 289.
40. Pettit, 290.
41. Pettit, 294.
42. Pettit, 296.
43. Foxon, Y61.
44. Pettit, 289–90.
45. Pettit, 291.
46. Ibid.
47. Pettit, 295–6.
48. Pettit, 298, n. 1.
49. Pettit, 299–300.
50. *UCS*, no. 10, 147.
51. MS Welwyn, Transcripts, 1748/9.
52. *GM*, XXXIX, New Series, 1853, 157.
53. Pettit, 303.
54. Pettit, 303–4.
55. Pettit, 327.
56. Pettit, 305.
57. Pettit, 310.
58. Pettit, 307.
59. Pettit, 308.
60. Pettit, 311.

61. Pettit, 311–12.
62. Pettit, 300.
63. Pettit, 313–14.
64. Pettit, 317.
65. Pettit, 319, n. 1.
66. Pettit, 320.
67. Pettit, 323.
68. Pettit, 326.
69. Pettit, 329–30.
70. Pettit, 330.
71. Pettit, 332–3.
72. Pettit, 335.
73. Pettit, 336.
74. Pettit, 333.
75. Pettit, 338, n. 1.
76. Llanover, II, 524.
77. Pettit, 339.
78. Pettit, 340.
79. Pettit, 314.

CHAPTER 13

1. Mitford, I, 54–5.
2. Mitford, I, 55.
3. Pettit, 158–9 (N.B. dating).
4. Pettit, 157.
5. Pettit, 162.
6. Pettit, 165–6.
7. Pettit, 171.
8. Pettit, 173.
9. Pettit, 137 (N.B. dating).
10. Pettit, 175–6.
11. Mitford, I, 138.
12. Mitford, I, 28.
13. *London Stage*, Pt. 3, 1129.
14. *London Stage*, Pt. 3, 1129–60.
15. Pettit, 200.
16. Pettit, 201.
17. Pettit, 202.
18. Pettit, 204.
19. Pettit, 206.
20. Pettit, 205.
21. MS Portland, V. 15 (Index).
22. Mitford, I, 225.
23. Mitford, II, 199.
24. Ibid.
25. Mitford, II, 216.

26. Pettit, 221.
27. Pettit, 231.
28. Pettit, 232.
29. Pettit, 233–4.
30. Pettit, 265.
31. Pettit, 262.
32. Pettit, 265.
33. Pettit, 263.
34. Pettit, 266–7.
35. Pettit, 269.
36. Pettit, 270.
37. Pettit, 270–1.
38. Pettit, 278.
39. *London Stage*, Pt. 3, 1263; 1257.
40. Pettit, 248, n. 1.
41. Pettit, 279.
42. Kind, 136.
43. *GM*, XVII, 444.
44. Pettit, 288.
45. Pettit, 292.
46. Pettit, 301.
47. *Stuffed Owl*, 64.
48. Gosse, 210.
49. Victor, I, 267.
50. Hill, III, 390.

CHAPTER 14

1. MS Welwyn, Vestry, 1 June, 1747.
2. MS Welwyn, Vestry, 7 October, 1747.
3. Defoe, *Tour*, 5th ed., 1753, 185.
4. Branch Johnson, 17.
5. Pettit, 323.
6. Defoe, *Tour* (as 3).
7. Pettit, 377.
8. Pettit, 381.
9. Branch Johnson, 18.
10. MS Welwyn, Vestry, 29 December, 1748.
11. MS Jones, 39 B.19, I.
12. MS Welwyn, Vestry, 2 April, 1752.
13. MS Welwyn, Vestry, 3 April, 1755.
14. Pettit, 310.

15. Pettit, 306.
16. *GM*, LII, 71.
17. Pettit, 327.
18. Pettit, 333.
19. Pettit, 337.
20. Pettit, 341, n. 1.
21. Pettit, 339.
22. *GA*, 22 January, 1749/50.
23. Pettit, 336–7.
24. Pettit, 326.
25. Pettit, 346.
26. Pettit, 341.
27. Pettit, 345–6, n. 3.
28. Hill-Powell, I, 214–15.
29. Barbauld, I, 169.
30. Holgate, II, 64–71.
31. Pettit, 349.
32. Pettit, 345.
33. Pettit, 348.
34. *Conjectures*, 316.
35. Pettit, 351.
36. Pettit, 354.
37. Kind, 136.
38. Pettit, 359.
39. Thomas, 599.
40. *MM*, XLI, Pt. 1, 390–1.
41. Ibid.
42. *Blackwood*, MCCCXCIX, 629.
43. Mitford, II, 193.
44. Wimsatt, 33–4.
45. Wimsatt, 34.
46. Wimsatt, 66.
47. Hill-Powell, V, 271.
48. HMC Bath, I, 340.
49. Kidgell, I, 67.

CHAPTER 15

1. Pettit, 363–4.
2. MS Gosling, ledger N9, f. 410.
3. Pettit, 523.
4. Pettit, 366.
5. Pettit, 366–7.
6. Pettit, 367–8.
7. Pettit, 370.
8. MS Welwyn, Vestry, 17 October, 1751.

9. Pettit, 372.
10. Pettit, 375.
11. Pettit, 376.
12. Pettit, 376–7.
13. Pettit, 378.
14. Ibid.
15. Pettit, 279.
16. Pettit, 317 (N.B. dating).
17. Pettit, 318 (N.B. dating).
18. Rothschild, II, 709.
19. Pettit, 344.
20. Pettit, 380.
21. Pettit, 383.
22. Pettit, 385.
23. Pettit, 387.
24. Pettit, 382, n. 1.
25. Pettit, 381.
26. Pettit, 382–3.
27. *London Stage*, Pt. 4, 56.
28. *London Stage*, Pt. 4, 120.
29. *London Stage*, Pt. 4, 265–97.
30. Little, I, 182.
31. Little, I, 172 (N.B. dating).
32. Little, I, 186.
33. Pettit, 388.
34. *London Stage*, Pt. 4, 321.
35. *London Stage*, Pt. 4, 322.
36. Bellamy, *Apology*, 3rd ed., 1785, II, 130–6.
37. *London Stage*, Pt. 4, 355.
38. *London Stage*, Pt. 4, 358.
39. Chalmers, XIV, 12–13.
40. Doran, II, 303.
41. *Biog. Dram.*, II, 70.
42. Ibid.
43. *GIJ*, I, 148 (no. 22).
44. *London Stage*, Pt. 4, 356.
45. R. Straus, *Robert Dodsley*, 1910, 347.
46. Pettit, 382, n. 3.
47. Barbauld, VI, 246–7.
48. Barbauld, VI, 246.
49. *GIJ*, I, 144 (no. 22).
50. Shenstone, 355.
51. Shenstone, 357.
52. *MR*, VIII, 239.
53. Davies, *Garrick*, I, 178–9.
54. Maurice, 10.

55. Maurice, 19.
56. Ibid.
57. Pennington, *Talbot*, I, 68, note.
58. Hawkins, I, 170, note.
59. Maurice, 20.
60. Hill-Powell, IV, 59–60.
61. Pettit, 392.
62. Pettit, 393.
63. Pettit, 396–7.
64. Pettit, 400–1.
65. MS Gosling, Ledger N10, f. 345.
66. Holgate, II, 68–73.
67. Pettit, 372, n. 1.
68. Foster, IV, 1629.
69. MS Balliol, BB 1752/3; 1753/4.
70. MS Balliol, BB 1753/4.
71. Barbauld, IV, 89–90.
72. Pettit, 404.
73. MS Forster, XIV (3), f. 131.
74. Pettit, 406–7.
75. Pettit, 407.
76. Pettit, 410.
77. Pettit, 409.
78. Pettit, 411.
79. Pettit, 412.
80. Clutterbuck, I, 466.
81. Pettit, 412.
82. Barbauld, V, 142–3.
83. *GM*, LXXXVII, Pt. 2, 210.
84. Ibid.
85. Pettit, 415.
86. Doran, II, 535.
87. Pettit, 416–17.
88. Pettit, 418.
89. *LEP*, 1–4 March, 1755.
90. Doran, II, 417.
91. *LEP*, 15–17 April, 1755.
92. *PA*, 17 November, 1755.
93. *Scots Magazine*, Edinburgh, 1755, XVII, 163.
94. *MR*, XII, 385 (May, 1755).
95. Pennington, *Talbot*, II, 201.
96. HMC, 9th Report, II, 241.
97. Barbauld, V, 70–1.
98. Doran, II, 422.
99. Doran, II, 477.
100. Doran, II, 457.

101. Doran, II, 455.
102. Pettit, 478, n. 1.
103. *Annual Register for 1765*, 5th ed., 1793, Pt. 2, 36.
104. *Biog. Brit.*, VI, Pt. 2, Suppt, 259.
105. Hill, III, 382.
106. D'Israeli, 505.
107. Pettit, 177.
108. Pettit, 230.
109. Pettit, 301.
110. Hill-Powell, V, 270–1.
111. MS Balliol, BB 1754/55.
112. MS Balliol, Register, 8 October, 1755.

CHAPTER 16

1. *London Stage*, Pt. 4, 463; 511; 561.
2. *London Stage*, Pt. 4, 533.
3. *GIJ*, 8 June, 1754 (no. 86).
4. *Blackwood*, MCCCXCIX, 623.
5. H. Jones, *The Relief*, 1754, 4.
6. MS Ayot St Peter, 16 April, 1752.
7. Kidgell, I, 9–10.
8. Kidgell, I, 190.
9. Kidgell, I, 264.
10. Kidgell, I, 67–8.
11. Kidgell, I, 142.
12. Pettit, 424.
13. Pettit, 432.
14. Llanover, III, 353.
15. Pettit, 423.
16. Hill-Powell, IV, 59.
17. Pettit, 424, n. 1.
18. Pettit, 426.
19. Ibid.
20. *LEP*, 30 September–2 October, 1755.
21. *PA*, 26 November, 1755.
22. Mitford, II, 377.
23. *Peerage*, X, 268.
24. Pettit, 430.
25. Pettit, 431.
26. Ibid.

27. Pettit, 433.
28. Pettit, 435.
29. Branch Johnson, 24.
30. Pettit, 438.
31. Pettit, 439.
32. Pettit, 442.
33. Pettit, 444.
34. Pettit, 451.
35. Pettit, 442.
36. Barbauld, IV, 112.
37. Pettit, 452.
38. Young, *Works*, 4 vols, 1757 (A2).
39. *UCS*, no. 5, 43.
40. Hill, III, 365.
41. Hill, III, 373.
42. Hill, III, 376.
43. Sotheby & Co., *Catalogue of Books for Sale*, 27 March, 1961, lot 1295.

CHAPTER 17

1. Pettit, 440.
2. Pettit, 441.
3. *Conjectures*, 316.
4. Pettit, 428–9, n. 2.
5. Elwin, I, 9.
6. Pettit, 428.
7. Warton, I, iii–vi.
8. Hill, III, 383.
9. Pettit, 445–51.
10. Pettit, 452–3.
11. Pettit, 452.
12. Hill-Powell, V, 269–70.
13. Pettit, 453.
14. Pettit, 454.
15. Pettit, 455.
16. Pettit, 458.
17. Pettit, 460.
18. Pettit, 461.
19. Pettit, 456.
20. Pettit, 457.
21. Pettit, 458.
22. Pettit, 459.
23. Pettit, 462.
24. Pettit, 463.

25. MS Welwyn, PR (marriages), 11 January, 1757.
26. MS Jones, 39.B.101.
27. Ibid.
28. MS Jones, 39.B.17(3).
29. Pettit, 463.
30. Ibid.
31. Pettit, 462, n. 2.
32. Pettit, 464.
33. Barbauld, III, 139.
34. Barbauld, III, 143.
35. Pettit, 466.
36. Pettit, 467.
37. Pettit, 468.
38. Pettit, 469.
39. Pettit, 470–1.
40. Pettit, 472.
41. Pettit, 473.
42. Doran, II, 540.
43. Doran, II, 538.
44. Pettit, 475.
45. Barbauld, III, 152.
46. Pettit, 474.
47. Pettit, 476–7.
48. Pettit, 478.
49. MS Gosling, ledger N12, f. 286.
50. MS Balliol, BB 1758/9.
51. Barbauld, IV, 118.
52. Pettit, 479.
53. Pettit, 479–80.
54. Pettit, 480.
55. Pettit, 497.
56. Pettit, 481.
57. Pettit, 483.
58. Pettit, 482.
59. Pettit, 484.
60. Pettit, 484–7.
61. *Conjectures*, 315.
62. Pettit, 485.
63. Pettit, 487.
64. Pettit, 488.
65. Pettit, 488–92.
66. Pettit, 493.
67. Pettit, 495.
68. Pettit, 495, n. 1.
69. Pettit, 498–9.
70. Pettit, 502.
71. Pettit, 503.

72. Warburton, 285.
73. Shenstone, 513.
74. *MR*, XX, 501.
75. *CR*, VII, 483–5.
76. *Conjectures*, 340.
77. *Conjectures*, 362.
78. *Conjectures*, 337.
79. Llanover, III, 558.
80. *Conjectures*, 320.
81. *Conjectures*, 324.
82. *Conjectures*, 326.
83. *Conjectures*, 332.
84. *Conjectures*, 333–4.
85. *Conjectures*, 335.
86. *Conjectures*, 336.
87. *Conjectures*, 339–40; 342–4.
88. *Conjectures*, 341–2.
89. *Conjectures*, 352–4; 357–8.
90. *Conjectures*, 356–7.

CHAPTER 18

1. *PA*, 18 June, 1759.
2. *Conjectures*, 364.
3. Pettit, 506, n. 1.
4. MS Jones, 39.B.19.
5. Pettit, 507.
6. MS Jones, 39.B.19.
7. Pettit, 513, n. 2.
8. Pettit, 520 and n. 1.
9. Clutterbuck, II, 503.
10. Pettit, 601.
11. Pettit, 510.
12. Pettit, 511.
13. Manning, III, 73.
14. MS Somerset Ho., PCC Lynch 16.
15. Pettit, 511, n. 2.
16. Pettit, 601–2.
17. Pettit, 601.
18. Pettit, 512.
19. Pettit, 511.
20. MS Balliol, BB 1758/9.
21. MS Gosling, ledger N13, f. 405.
22. MS Balliol, BB 1760/1.
23. Pettit, 499.
24. Pettit, 492–3.

25. Pettit, 515.
26. Pettit, 518.
27. Pettit, 519.
28. MS Forster, XI, f. 271.
29. Hayley, 95.
30. HMC Fortescue, I, 141.
31. Pettit, 526, n. 1.
32. *GM*, LII, 71–2.
33. *GM*, LII, 72.
34. Pettit, 521.
35. Pettit, 523.
36. Pettit, 523, n. 1.
37. Pettit, 524.
38. Pettit, 525.
39. Barbauld, V, 145–6.
40. *GM*, New Series, XXXIX, 157 (1853).
41. Pettit, 526.
42. Pennington, *Montagu*, I, 111.
43. MS Gosling, ledger N14, f. 303.
44. MS Balliol, BB 1760/1.
45. MS Balliol, Battells 1760/1 (1st Quarter).
46. MS Balliol, BB 1760/1.
47. MS Gosling, ledger N15, f. 267.
48. Nichols, I, 620.

CHAPTER 19

1. Pettit, 529.
2. Pettit, 530.
3. Pettit, 540.
4. Pettit, 541–2.
5. Young, *Resignation, &c. In Five Parts*, London, 1761, 10.
6. Mitford, II, 228.
7. Pettit, 543.
8. Climenson, II, 257.
9. Pettit, 545.
10. Pettit, 546.
11. Pettit, 533.
12. *BC*, XIX, no. 4 (Winter 1970), 491.
13. Pettit, 531.
14. Pettit, 532.
15. Pettit, 534.
16. Pettit, 535.

17. Pettit, 536.
18. Ibid.
19. Pettit, 539.
20. Pettit, 528–9.
21. Pettit, 539.
22. Kind, 66.
23. Kind, 106.
24. Kind, 106.
25. Pettit, 544.
26. MS Jones, 39.B.17(3).
27. Ibid.
28. MS Welwyn, Vestry, 9 July, 1761.
29. Pettit, 547.
30. Pettit, 550–1.
31. Pettit, 565–6.
32. Pettit, 551.
33. Pettit, 549.
34. Pettit, 552.
35. Pettit, 553.
36. *PA*, 25 May, 1762.
37. *MR*, XXVI, 462.
38. Hill, III, 396.
39. Mitford, II, 221.
40. Mitford, II, 228.
41. Mitford, II, 229.
42. Mitford, II, 242.
43. Mitford, II, 247–9.
44. Mitford, II, 271.
45. MS Jones, 39.B.17(3).
46. Pettit, 555.
47. Nichols, I, 617.
48. Nichols, I, 618.
49. Nichols, I, 620.
50. Ibid.
51. MS Jones, 39.B.17(3).
52. Ibid.
53. Ibid.
54. Ibid.
55. Ibid.
56. Ibid.
57. Ibid.
58. Ibid.
59. Ibid.
60. Ibid.
61. Ibid.
62. Nichols, I, 585–637.
63. Nichols, I, 620–1.

64. MS Jones, 39.B.18.
65. Nichols, I, 622.
66. Nichols, I, 623.

CHAPTER 20

1. Pettit, 563–4.
2. Pettit, 565.
3. Nichols, I, 631.
4. Pettit, 559.
5. Pettit, 560.
6. Pettit, 564–5.
7. Pettit, 567.
8. Pettit, 558.
9. Pettit, 569.
10. Pettit, 571.
11. Ibid.
12. Keate, *The Alps*, 1763 (vii).
13. Pettit, 571.
14. Pettit, 573.
15. Pettit, 574.
16. Pettit, 573–4.
17. Pettit, 577.
18. Ibid.
19. Pettit, 578.
20. Ibid.
21. Nichols, I, 626.
22. Nichols, I, 627.
23. MS Welwyn, PR (marriages 1754–81).
24. Nichols, I, 627.
25. Nichols, I, 627–9.
26. Nichols, I, 638.
27. Pettit, 580–1.
28. Pettit, 583.
29. Pettit, 584.
30. Pettit, 585.
31. Pettit, 581.
32. Pettit, 586.
33. Ibid.
34. Pettit, 587.
35. Ibid.
36. Pettit, 602.
37. Pettit, 588–9.
38. Pettit, 589.
39. Pettit, 591, n. 3.
40. *GM*, LII, 70.

41. Wimsatt, 33.
42. A. Wright, *Joseph Spence*, Illinois, 1950, 166.
43. Pettit, 590.
44. Pettit, 596.
45. Young, *Works*, 3 vols, 1802, I, xiii–xiv.
46. Pettit, 592.
47. Pettit, 591–2.
48. Pettit, 593.
49. Pettit, 595.
50. Pettit, 594.

CHAPTER 21

1. MS Welwyn, PR (burials).
2. Nichols, I, 634.
3. *LC*, XVII, 368 (13–16 April, 1765).
4. *Biog. Brit.*, VI, Pt. 2, Suppt, 259.
5. Hill, III, 390.
6. Mitford, I, 137.
7. Pettit, 601–2.
8. *GM*, LII, 72.
9. *GM*, LII, 71.
10. Hill, III, 389.
11. Nichols, I, 633–4.
12. MS Jones, 39.B.101.
13. Nichols, I, 636.
14. Pettit, 594.
15. MS Welwyn, School, 1765.
16. Le Hardy, VIII, 152; 203; 298.
17. Thomas, 211.
18. MS Welwyn, PR, 28 November, 1767.
19. MS Gosling, ledger N16, f. 51.
20. Hill, III, 392.
21. *Biog. Brit.*, VI, Pt. 2, 1766.
22. Pettit, 594.
23. Hayley, 95.
24. Hill, III, 379.
25. Hamwood, 160.
26. *GM*, LXXXVI, Pt. 2, 513.
27. MS Gosling, ledger S3, f. 415.
28. Maurice, Pt. 2, 156.
29. MS Welwyn, PR (burials).
30. MS Gosling, ledger S3, f. 416.

31. MS Gosling, ledger S6, f. 441.
32. Hill, III, 361.
33. Hill, III, 382.
34. Hill-Powell, IV, 119–20.
35. Hill-Powell, IV, 493, note.
36. Hill-Powell, IV, 120–1.
37. MS Stanstead Abbotts, PR (marriages).
38. MS Stanstead Abbotts, PR (baptisms; burials).
39. MS Welwyn, Vestry (Land Tax).
40. MS Welwyn, School, 1782–3.
41. MS Welwyn, PR (burials).
42. Hamwood, 160.

CHAPTER 22

1. Hill-Powell, IV, 59.
2. *GM*, LII, 70–2.
3. *GM*, LXXXVI, Pt. 2, 513.
4. Hill, III, 399.
5. *Johnsoniana*, Murray, 1836, 17.
6. Goldsmith, *Collected Works*, ed. A. Friedman, 1966, V, 328.
7. Melmoth, *Observations*, 1776, 3.
8. *Biog. Dram.*, I, 768.
9. Sir W. Forbes, *Life of Beattie*, Edinburgh, 2nd ed., 1807, II, 178.
10. Hawkins, I, 169.
11. Melmoth, *Observations*, 3.
12. T. Jackson, *Journal of the Rev. Charles Wesley*, 1849, II, 106; 275.
13. Hill, III, 395, n. 4.
14. Lewis, XXXI, 218.
15. Mme D'Arblay, *Diary and Letters*, ed. C. Barratt, 1905, IV, 262.
16. Anna Seward, *Letters*, Edinburgh, IV, 36.
17. *Thraliana*, ed. K. C. Balderston, Oxford, 2nd ed., 1951, 362.
18. S. Rogers, *Reminiscences and Table-Talk*, ed. G. H. Powell, 1903, 16.
19. W. L. Bowles, *Poetical Works*, ed. G. Gilfillan, 1855, II, 22.
20. Kind, 69.

21. Kind, 106.
22. Kind, 106.
23. Kind, 57.
24. Kind, 109.
25. Coleridge, *Biographia Literaria*, Everyman, 1930, 305–6.
26. *JE*, February, 1762, 143.
27. Thomas, 523.
28. Le Tourneur, I, vi; lii; lvi.
29. Le Tourneur, I, lix.
30. Thomas, 533.
31. Voltaire, *Oeuvres Complètes*, Paris, 1831, LXXXIX, 62.
32. Thomas, 532, n. 1.
33. Thomas, 524.
34. Thomas, 534.
35. Ibid.
36. Ibid.
37. Thomas, 535.
38. Ibid.
39. Thomas, 536, n. 2.
40. Thomas, 527.
41. Thomas, 555.
42. Thomas, 570.
43. F. Jeffrey, *Contributions to the Edinburgh Review*, 2nd ed., 1846.
44. Howe, V, 114.
45. Howe, IX, 241.
46. Hill, III, 395, n. 4.
47. Hill, III, 393, n. 1.
48. T. Campbell, *Specimens of the British Poets*, 1841, 466.
49. G. Crabbe, *Poetical Works . . . and Life*, 1834, VI, 9, note.
50. R. Cecil, *Remains*, ed. J. Pratt, 8th ed., 1825, 289–90.
51. Hill, III, 399, n. 6.
52. *Wordsworth's Prelude*, ed. E. de Selincourt & H. Darbishire, 2nd ed., 1959, 252–3.
53. E. L. Bulwer, *The Student*, Paris, 1835, 226.
54. Eliot, 36–7.
55. Eliot, 37.
56. Eliot, 21.
57. Eliot, 78.
58. Birley, 108.
59. Bliss, (7).

INDEX OF NAMES